CW01394391

HUMAN RIGHTS IN THE MARKET PLACE

Markets and the Law

Series Editor:
Geraint Howells
Lancaster University, UK

Series Advisory Board:
Stefan Grundmann – Humboldt University of Berlin, Germany
Hans Micklitz – Bamberg Univeristy, Germany
James P. Nehf – Indiana University , USA
Iain Ramsay – York University, Canada
Charles Rickett – University of Queensland, Australia
Reiner Schulze – Münster University, Germany
Jules Stuyck – Katholieke Universiteit Leuven, Belgium
Stephen Weatherill –University of Oxford, UK
Thomas Wilhelmsson – University of Helsinki, Finland

Markets and the Law is concerned with the way the law interacts with the market through regulation, self-regulation and the impact of private law regimes. It looks at the impact of regional and international organizations (e.g. EC and WTO) and many of the works adopt a comparative approach and/or appeal to an international audience. Examples of subjects covered include trade laws, intellectual property, sales law, insurance, consumer law, banking, financial markets, labour law, environmental law and social regulation affecting the market as well as competition law. The series includes texts covering a broad area, monographs on focused issues, and collections of essays dealing with particular themes.

Other titles in the series

Global Perspectives on E-Commerce Taxation Law
Subhajit Basu
ISBN 978 0 7546 4731 7

The Yearbook of Consumer Law 2008
Edited by Christian Twigg-Flesner, Deborah Parry,
Geraint Howells, and Annette Nordhausen
ISBN 978 0 7546 7152 7

International Insolvency Law
Themes and Perspectives
Edited by Paul J. Omar
ISBN 978 0 7546 2427 1

For more information on this series, visit www.ashgate.com

Human Rights in the Market Place

The Exploitation of Rights Protection by Economic Actors

CHRISTOPHER HARDING

UTA KOHL

and

NAOMI SALMON

Aberystwyth University

ASHGATE

© Christopher Harding, Uta Kohl and Naomi Salmon 2008

All rights reserved. No part of this publication may be reproduced, stored in a retrieval system or transmitted in any form or by any means, electronic, mechanical, photocopying, recording or otherwise without the prior permission of the publisher.

Christopher Harding, Uta Kohl and Naomi Salmon have asserted their moral right under the Copyright, Designs and Patents Act, 1988, to be identified as the authors of this work.

Published by
Ashgate Publishing Limited
Gower House
Croft Road
Aldershot
Hampshire GU11 3HR
England

Ashgate Publishing Company
Suite 420
101 Cherry Street
Burlington, VT 05401-4405
USA

www.ashgate.com

British Library Cataloguing in Publication Data
Harding, Christopher
   Human rights in the market place : the exploitation of
   rights protection by economic actors. - (Markets and the
   law)
   1. Human rights - Economic aspects 2. Consumer protection
   3. Competition, Unfair 4. Social responsibility of business
   5. Anti-globalization movement
   I. Title II. Kohl, Uta III. Salmon, Naomi
   341.4'8

Library of Congress Cataloging-in-Publication Data
Harding, Christopher.
 Human rights in the market place : the exploitation of rights protection by economic actors /
by Christopher Harding, Uta Kohl, and Naomi Salmon.
   p. cm. -- (Markets and the law)
 Includes bibliographical references and index.
 ISBN 978-0-7546-4694-5
 1. Human rights--Economic aspects--Europe. I. Kohl, Uta. II. Salmon, Naomi. III. Title.

KJC5132.H37 2008
341.4'8--dc22

2008016615

ISBN: 978 0 7546 4694 5

Mixed Sources
Product group from well-managed forests and other controlled sources
www.fsc.org Cert no. SGS-COC-2482
© 1996 Forest Stewardship Council
FSC

Printed and bound in Great Britain by
TJ International Ltd, Padstow, Cornwall

Contents

List of Figures

List of Tables

Preface

At first glance, it might appear surprising that three researchers whose recent work had dealt respectively with the subjects of criminal responsibility, jurisdiction in relation to the internet, and the regulation of biotechnology should come together to analyse the use of basic rights argument. But we were not such strange bedfellows. We shared a common interest in the nature and exercise of corporate power and the relationship between individual and organisational actors in the transnational (or, as some would like to style it now, 'globalised') context. And this is essentially a book about the exercise of power, and more specifically legal power – by large corporations, by national and intergovernmental officials, by civil society organisations, and also by human individuals acting as human individuals – in that inescapable contemporary arena that we conveniently refer to as the 'market'. More specifically the work here is a response to and comment on an intriguing phenomenon – the deployment of argument about basic (human) rights as part of the interplay of competing economic and political interests in the early twenty-first century market place: companies asserting the equivalent of fundamental human rights, and consumers claiming a high order of legal entitlement in relation to their acts of consumption. Does it make sense? What does it achieve in legal and political terms? What is the impact of such argument and strategies on the sophisticated contemporary national and international systems of market regulation? Such were the basis questions which prompted this study.

We should provide at the outset a brief note of advice on how the book should be approached and read. The discussion falls broadly into two main parts. The first part is a theoretical exploration of underlying argument: how to locate and define the principal market actors within a spectrum of supply and consumption; the case for both corporate and consumer claims for some kind of overriding legal entitlement; and the strategic and practical value of asserting higher order rights. Each of the first four chapters constitutes an essay in its own right, but a reading of all four is advisable for purposes of fully appreciating the remaining part of the discussion in Part II. The second section comprises an application of the theoretical discussion to four areas of contemporary significance: supplier claims in the EU context; consumer arguments in the EU context; both of these in the global context; and the legal position of both suppliers and consumers in relation to freedom of speech in the market place. The intention in this latter section of the book is to examine and assess both the manner and outcome of the deployment of basic rights argument in this context, and again each chapter may be read individually, but with more benefit as a whole. Finally, we group together some summary and conclusions in Chapter 9. Another feature of the presentation should also be noted at the outset here. To provide the reader with some sense of the economic, political and social relevance of the legal discussion, each of the eight central chapters has been prefaced with a narrative account of specific supplier and consumer action – stories of crises and events which are intended to inform the reader's appreciation of where the legal discussion and argument is located in the global scale of things.

The book as it has finally emerged was conceived first as a smaller-scale project and has typically evolved with the feeling that there is always so much more to say – and that there remains at this 'final' point a good deal more to say. We have some conclusions, but these will not prove to be last words by any means. The work for the book took longer than planned and was carried out in more places than planned. We would like to express our appreciation for the support and interest of a number of colleagues, family and friends, to the Department of Law and Criminology at Aberystwyth University and the Arts and Humanities Research Council for enabling research leave to be taken, and in a less tangible way for the inspiration gained from our sojourn in the Ceredigion and Bordeaux regions of Europe.

Christopher Harding, Uta Kohl and Naomi Salmon
Aberystwyth

Introduction:
Rights Talk in the Domain
of Supply and Demand

The purpose of this study is to examine the way in which different economic actors employ argument relating to basic legal rights to protect their interests. The ideology of human rights protection has gained considerable momentum during the second half of the twentieth century at both national and international levels. As both a legal and a political strategy, framing argument as a matter of basic human rights protection increasingly appears as an effective lever for effecting legal change. This is especially evident in a context such as that of penal reform – for instance, in relation to the removal or stricter control of capital punishment through the use of such argument. But it is also a strategy which may be employed in other contexts, such as those involving environmental or commercial policy. Thus economic or commercial actors may invoke basic rights argument as a means of 'trumping' opposing interests and claims. In this way, the language and logic of fundamental human rights has infiltrated the economic and commercial sphere, so making this a study of how the 'public law' discourse of basic rights protection has been transported and used in the 'commercial law' context of economic policy, business activity and corporate behaviour.

Inevitably, the discussion of this subject tends to centre upon two significant different and largely opposing interests: those of the suppliers and consumers of economic commodities. The present intention is to compare the deployment of argument in these two main interests, not only in order to identify the range of basic legal rights which are exploited by these principal economic actors, but also to investigate their respective success in using such legal argument, at different levels of the legal system and across jurisdictions. In this way, the discussion may be seen as an analysis of the 'rights talk' which is now emerging in the economic domain of supply and demand.

This subject-matter is naturally informed by some main underlying themes. One such theme arises from the market context, and concerns the way in which economic policy and market developments may drive and condition legal development and the deployment of legal argument. At the beginning of the twenty-first century, a major issue of this kind is the global movement towards market liberalisation and the impact of the goal of market freedom within the legal domain. Especially with the emergence of the EU and WTO regimes, it is pertinent to consider the extent to which dominating single and global market objectives are the motor of legal programmes such as free movement and consumer or environmental protection. Another crucial, though different, theme is the increasing global commitment to protecting rights, enunciated through the growing international human rights protection systems, which are in turn linked to the broadening commitment to democratic governance. How does this relate to economic themes and to what extent do the two tendencies have an impact upon each other?

The resort to rights-argument by economic actors, whether large corporate producers or individual consumers, is a fertile site for exploring these themes. The coincidence of economic motive and the political force of rights-based argument has resulted in an instructive dynamic of legal development. This has manifested itself in both the appearance of complex and sophisticated regulatory systems[1] and the development of new channels of litigation and legal representation. At the same time, economic actors – corporate, collective and individual – have thereby acquired new or fuller legal identities as right-holders, in turn influencing the character of legal systems and legal process.

At this stage a number of preliminary points should be made about the scope and organisation of this discussion.

First of all, the approach taken is *comparative* in terms of the *jurisdictions* which are covered in the study, although inevitably some jurisdictions invite more comment than others, given the subject-matter. Much of the legal development referred to here has taken place in international and transnational contexts, particularly those of the EC/EU regime over the last forty years and that of the WTO more recently, as sites within which different and competing economic interests have been balanced through the formation of policy and law. None the less, some national legal orders remain significant, in so far as they contribute through their own example and heritage to the process of law development at the international level, or play a role in the subsequent implementation and enforcement of international norms. Moreover, new issues and novel dimensions of the subject may well make their first appearance at the national level, so that national courts and legislatures may be the initial venue for new conflicts. Although therefore a comparison between EU and WTO approaches provides a useful focus for much of the discussion, it is still necessary and useful to refer to developments at the national level: the subject is by its nature multi-layered.

Secondly, much of the following is a discussion of the exploitation of basic rights – of how such argument may feed into the law-making process, or be employed in dispute resolution and litigation. For that purpose, it is necessary to explore the *framework* of rights discourse and the legal strategies employed by the main actors, and this requires some consideration of the theoretical underpinning of economic rights. Inevitably, some thought must be given to how the relevant rights are defined and classified in order to understand how rights are then used in political and legal process. It will be evident, for instance, that the discussion will cover both substantive 'economic' rights (such as the right to carry out a trading activity, or to exercise choice as a consumer) and 'civil' and 'political' rights (such as rights of defence in the context of regulatory enforcement procedures). It is customary in much writing

---

1 Producers of goods and services have increasingly been subject to legal regulation, through the development of such regimes as those comprising 'competition law' and 'consumer law'. For a useful overview of the development of this area of law, see Colin Scott and Julia Black (2000), *Cranston's Consumer and the Law* (London: Butterworths, 3rd edn), Ch. 1.

on basic rights to categorise such entitlement as programmatic economic rights, requiring some public authority intervention, on the one hand, and reactive political rights, triggered spontaneously as a matter of legal process, on the other hand. But some reflection of the interplay of interests as between economic suppliers and economic consumers suggests rather that the process of rights deployment is circular and continuous in nature. Rights discourse is generated within a cycle of market problems, generating legal argument through processes such as lobbying or litigation, which then contributes to policy and law making, the new law then entering into the market place and supplying the content of new issue and problems (see Figure I.1 below). It is useful therefore to explore the resort to rights-argument and its dynamic within this *circular* framework of political and legal processes, rather than to view the matter within a more abstract scheme of rights classification.

Third, and following on from that point, it may be helpful to identify the *main arenas* within which economic actors deploy argument relating to basic rights. There would appear to be two main sites for this legal activity. First, attempts may be made to influence the formation of the increasing amount of policy and law concerning the regulation of industry and commerce. Thus a range of actors may present their arguments, often competitively, to policy makers and law makers at different levels and in different jurisdictions, through lobbying, taking advantage of consultation processes and by exploiting a variety of media. Secondly, and in a more characteristically legal form, the conflict of economic interest is likely to give rise to more specific disputes and argument which may then be taken forward to litigation of some kind for its resolution. This provides the opportunity in particular for courts to translate the conflict of interests into a conflict of rights which may then be amenable to legal resolution. Courts of law provide the classic venue for rights-argument and so inevitably have a high profile in the working-out of legal solutions.

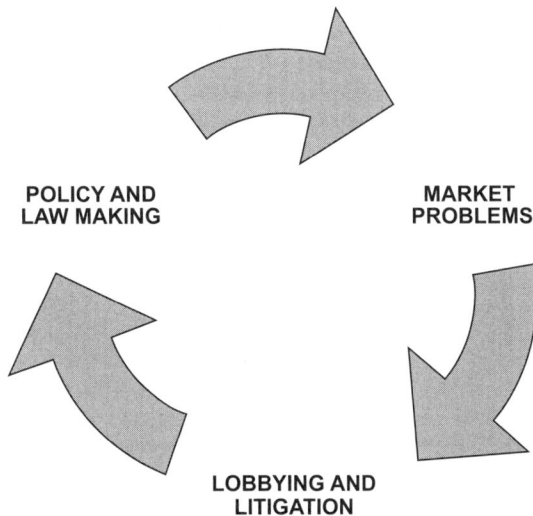

POLICY AND
LAW MAKING

MARKET
PROBLEMS

LOBBYING AND
LITIGATION

Figure I.1   Rights discourse within the cycle of political and legal processes

Fourth, it is of course also necessary to identify the *main types of actor* occupying the economic, political and legal stage which is the subject of discussion here. In the first place, there are the main protagonists asserting a range of rights, and these actors may perhaps be most usefully viewed along an economic continuum of supply and demand, ranging through stages of supply and consumption of economic commodities, from the producer to the ultimate end-consumer. This continuum includes the more obvious players on the stage of supply and demand (such as manufacturers, wholesalers, retailers and end-purchasers), but also some market participants who may fit less neatly within that spectrum (such as lenders, shareholders and other investors). Alongside these principal protagonists, there are other types of actor who may in some sense be seen as secondary, although their role is increasingly significant. In particular, reference should be made to interest groups who may be used by collectively by producers, retailers or consumers, to represent more collectively their respective interests, and to the public (or wider) interest regulators who are entrusted with the implementation or enforcement of broader economic policy, at both the national and international levels (for instance, competition and fair trading authorities). Both of these latter types of actor may be regarded as playing a representative role in relation to the primary interests of the main economic actors, but this representative and managing function has of itself acquired increasing significance and, it may be argued, some autonomy within the economic and legal orders.

This leads finally to some consideration of the role and process of legal regulation of economic activity and more specifically the identity and role of those agencies entrusted with the enforcement of such regulation. The activity of such regulators symbolises the 'public' intervention in the market place and as such these enforcement agents provide the most evident presence of a broader public interest in the commercial field. But it is important to pose more probing questions about the interests actually represented by this kind of agency – more precisely, what is this broader 'public' interest? It may be asked, for example, in relation to EC competition policy whether it serves ultimately the interests of consumers or small traders as economic actors, or a more diffuse interest encapsulated in the dominating idea of the 'single market'. Or, if it serves both, in what proportions, and how do the two kinds of interest relate to each other in the process of regulation? Finally, it is interesting to speculate on the increasingly *protective* role of such regulators – especially in the context of rights-argument – as these agencies acquire more initiative in the management of policy and law enforcement. Arguably, this is a development which reprises the historically earlier process by which the State took over the control and management of criminal proceedings, becoming eventually the predominant legal actor within that field.

PART I
Theoretical Issues

Chapter 1

A Fracas in the Cosmetics Market: Competing Rights and the Spectrum of Economic Actors

Markt Intern before the Court of Human Rights

Late in 1975, Markt Intern, a German publishing firm based in Dusseldorf, published an information bulletin for chemists and retailers of cosmetics which described an incident involving a British mail order company, Cosmetic Club International. The incident concerned a failure to reimburse a dissatisfied customer and the bulletin went on to ask retailers whether any of them had had a similar experience with Cosmetic Club. Markt Intern was described in the later judgment of the European Court of Human Rights in the following way:

> [The firm] which was founded and is run by journalists, seeks to defend the interests of small and medium-sized retail businesses against the competition of large-scale distribution companies, such as supermarkets and mail-order firms. It provides the less powerful members of the retail trade with financial assistance in test cases, lobbies public authorities, political parties and trade associations on their behalf and has, on occasion, made proposals for legislation to the legislature. However, its principal activity in their support is the publication of a number of bulletins aimed at specialised commercial sectors such as that of chemists and beauty product retailers … These are weekly news-sheets which provide information on developments in the market and in particular on the commercial practices of large-scale firms and their suppliers … Markt Intern claims to be independent. Its income is derived exclusively from subscriptions.[1]

In December 1975, Cosmetic Club sought and obtained an injunction in the Hamburg *Landgericht*, prohibiting Markt Intern from repeating the statements published in the bulletin; the Court held that in its bulletin Markt Intern had generalised its criticism and ought to have made further enquiries, but not by soliciting information from retailers. Although this ruling was overturned on appeal by the Hanseatic *Oberlandesgericht*, it was later confirmed by the *Bundesgerichtshof* (Federal Supreme Court).[2] The latter considered that the injunction was justified on the basis

---

1 *Markt Intern and Beermann* v. *Germany,* Judgment of 20 November 1989, Series A, No. 164; Application No. 10572/83; 12 (1990) *European Human Rights Reports (EHRR)* 161, at 163. See also the discussion in Chapter 8 below.

2 Ibid., at 167–9.

of Section 1 of the 1909 Unfair Competition Act,[3] in order to restrain action contrary to honest business practices. Although there was not a competitive relationship between Markt Intern and Cosmetic Club, the 1909 legislation was, in the Court's view, applicable to this situation since the conduct was objectively advantageous to an undertaking, to the detriment of a competitor; Markt Intern had not merely provided information as an organ of the press but was representing the interests of the specialised chemists' trade and had attacked the Club's commercial practices in order to promote those interests. A final appeal in 1982 by Markt Intern, claiming a violation of its freedom of expression under Article 5(1) of the German Constitution, to the *Bundesverfassungsgericht* (Federal Constitutional Court) was not admitted by the latter Court, since:

> ... the requirements which must be satisfied in order for freedom of expression and of the press to override other legal interests protected under statutes of general application are not fulfilled where an item published in the press is intended to promote, in the context of commercial competition, certain economic interests to the detriment of others.[4]

Following this setback, Markt Intern finally in 1983 made a claim against the German State under the European Convention on Human Rights, alleging a violation of its right to freedom of expression under Article 10 of the Convention.

The Commission on Human Rights found in favour of the company,[5] then prompting the German Government in 1988 to engage in the last phase of this litigation, before the Court of Human Rights. In the Government's view (following the opinion of the Constitutional Court), the relevant issue was not one of freedom of expression, but of economic competition since Markt Intern, in representing the interests of smaller traders, was effectively a competitor of Cosmetic Club. However, the Court considered that the protection of Article 10 of the Convention was not limited to certain kinds of information, ideas, or forms of expression, and therefore the company had undoubtedly suffered from an interference by a public authority in the exercise of the right of free expression. The relevant issue for the Court was whether this was an acceptable infringement according to the terms of Article 10(2), as an act prescribed by law and 'necessary in a democratic society'. The majority view in the Court was that States enjoyed a margin of appreciation in determining such necessity and in this particular case the balancing of competing interests – of reputation on the one hand and of freedom of information on the other hand – was within that margin of appreciation, with which the Human Rights Court should not interfere. The crux of this majority judgment was the following:

---

3 'Any person who in the course of business commits, for purposes of competition, acts contrary to honest practice may be enjoined from further engaging in those acts and held liable in damages.'

4 1990 *EHRR,* at 169–70. Note that this is a 'field constitution' argument. This aspect of the argument will be discussed further below. The Constitutional Court viewed the matter primarily as a dispute between competitors, and therefore outside the scope of Article 5. Compare the view of the Human Rights Court on this point, discussed below.

5 Report of 18 December 1987, 11 (1989) *EHRR* 212.

In a market economy an undertaking which seeks to set up a business inevitably exposes itself to close scrutiny of its practices by its competitors. Its commercial strategy and the manner in which it honours its commitments may give rise to criticism on the part of consumers and the specialised press. In order to carry out this task, the specialised press must be able to disclose facts which could be of interest to its readers and thereby contribute to the openness of business activities. However, even the publication of items which are true and describe real events may under certain circumstances be prohibited: the obligation to respect the privacy of others or the duty to respect the confidentiality of certain commercial information are examples. In addition, a correct statement can be and often is qualified by additional remarks, by value judgments, by suppositions or even insinuations. It must also be recognised that an isolated incident may deserve closer scrutiny before being made public; otherwise an accurate description of one such incident can give the false impression that the incident is evidence of a general practice. All these factors can legitimately contribute to the assessment of statements made in a commercial context, and it is primarily for the national courts to decide which statements are permissible and which are not.[6]

This reasoning indicates clearly the conflict of legally protected interests in the context of this case. On the one hand, there is the interest in market transparency, invoked in this case by a body set up to represent the interests of specialised small traders, but this is also an interest of end-consumers, and is embodied in the freedom of expression under Article 10 of the Convention. On the other hand, there is the interest of larger traders, in broad terms a freedom of trading, but more specifically in this case materialising as a right to protect commercial reputation. The balancing of these interests, as the Court recognised, may not be a matter of easy agreement. The market circumstances may be interpreted differently, as was pointed out in the joint dissenting opinion in the Court of Human Rights: 'Consumers, who are exposed to highly effective distribution techniques and to advertising which is frequently less than objective, deserve, for their part too, to be protected, as indeed do retailers.'[7]

The context in which such a balancing of interests takes place is stressed equally in the dissenting opinion of Judge Martens:

... it is necessary to ask whether it was established convincingly ... that the private interests of the Club were more important than the general interest, in accordance with which not only the specialised reader but also the public as a whole should have been able to acquaint themselves with facts having a certain importance in the context of the struggle of small and medium-sized retail undertakings against the large-scale distribution companies.[8]

The extent of the entitlement – of the degree of protection afforded to particular complainants – may therefore depend upon an analysis of their relative position of power or vulnerability on the market. And such an assessment may be contestable.

Two main points emerge from the review of the *Markt Intern* litigation. The first concerns the resolution of such arguments as a process of balancing competing

---

6 (1990) *EHRR,* at 174–5 (para. 35 of the judgment).

7 Ibid., at 177.

8 Ibid., at 181–2.

claims to rights. The second point relates to an appreciation of the role and position of particular economic actors within this process.

In the economic field in particular, the assertion of rights is commonly grounded in a clear conflict of interests, both of which may appear equally compelling, giving rise to difficulty in balancing such claims in any process of adjudication. In *Markt Intern*, for example, the claim to a right to publish provoked a responding claim, that to a right to reputation. These were grounded respectively in an interest in market transparency, and an interest in restraining critical comment. In many other cases, as will become evident in our later discussion, the opposition is typically that between a freedom of trading and economic disposition, and consumers' rights to choice, safety and health standards. In more immediate legal terms, this follows clearly from the qualification of many guaranteed basic rights in favour of other interests (often expressed as more general or 'public' interests). This was true, for instance, of both Article 5 of the German Constitution and Article 10 of the Human Rights Convention, mentioned above. It is also a characteristic of human rights claims which has led some commentators, such as Martii Koskenniemi, to describe such adjudication of fundamental rights as a bureaucratic allocation of resources.[9]

This may explain some of the reluctance of the majority of the judges in the Human Rights Court in *Markt Intern* to become involved in the actual adjudication of competing claims, seeing the matter in some respects as a policy choice (in human rights parlance, a 'margin of appreciation') which could just as well be decided at the national level. For present purposes, the important point to draw from this example is the rather finely balanced oppositional nature of rights claims in the market context. This is then connected with the second main point made above: that any attempt to balance such competing claims may well be informed by some perception of the position of the particular actors in the market. For instance, a common perception – and one which provides an important theme for much of the discussion in this book – is that producers are relatively strong and consumers are relatively weak. This perception clearly influenced the dissenting opinions in the Court of Human Rights in *Markt Intern* towards taking a more interventionist stance, providing more support for the position of Markt Intern as the representative of the perceived weaker parties in the market.

It would be helpful at this stage of the discussion to reflect further on this common perception of market relationships, in particular to understand how it arises as a widely subscribed view. But, while this fundamental opposition of interests as between supplier and consumer is an inescapable characteristic of any market, there are dangers in working from an unrefined model of such opposition. Just as the economic concepts of supply and demand may be subtle, so too any characterisation of economic actors as 'supplier' or 'consumer' should avoid monolithic description. There are different kinds of both supplier and consumer and indeed it may be more useful to regard the two categories, not as watertight separate classifications, but as descriptions which merge into each other along a continuum. The retailer, for

---

9 Martti Koskenniemi (1999), 'The Effect of Rights on Political Culture', Chapter 3 in Philip Alston (ed.), *The EU and Human Rights* (Oxford: Oxford University Press), at 110. Koskenniemi refers to the 'judicial everyday' as a 'banal exercise'.

instance, is both a purchaser and a supplier, and in *Markt Intern* there was some attempt to place small 'specialist' retailers in the same camp as end-consumers.

The following sections of discussion in this chapter will therefore explore, first, the paradigmatic view of the 'powerful supplier' and 'weak consumer', and then go on to place the range of main economic actors on a continuum of activity and roles within the market.

Probing The 'Supplier-Consumer' Paradigm: The Rise of 'Consumer Protection'

Let us explore further this idea that, in economic markets, producers of commodities are typically powerful and consumers are typically vulnerable. Although some of the following observations may appear at first sight rather obvious, they may none the less prove helpful in constructing a socio-legal profile of these two paradigmatic market place entities.

First, we could begin with some commonplace observations regarding the main characteristics of producers, in their principal economic role of supplying goods and services. In many markets, such producers are now commonly large economic actors, virtually always corporate in character, and increasingly transnational in their location and scope of activity.[10] As such, they clearly possess considerable economic and political power. One manifestation of this is the comparison of the economic producer as a global actor with the traditional main form of global actor, the sovereign State. For instance, a report for the Institute of Policy Studies in 2000 analysed the leading economies in the world, finding that of the largest one hundred, fifty-one were corporations and forty-nine were countries; at the same time, the top two hundred corporations' sales were growing at a faster rate than overall global economic activity.[11] A natural consequence of this relatively powerful position and concomitant resources is a high level of access to both governmental and intergovernmental policy making process[12] and legal support in the event of disputes and litigation.[13] Thus, once we begin to consider the role of the typical

---

10 For a useful account of the development of multinational companies and a profile of such corporate actors, see J. Dunning (1993), *Multinational Enterprises in a Global Economy* (Reading, MA: Addison-Wesley). Dunning identifies a number of 'true global industries', dominated by large corporations operating in all the world's largest economies (at 40).

11 Sarah Anderson and John Cavanagh (2000), *Top 200: The Rise of Corporate Global Power* (Institute of Policy Studies, 2nd version). The Report reflects upon the implications of this growth in corporate power: 'The main beneficiaries of the market-opening policies of the major multilateral institutions over the past decade and a half are these large corporations, especially the top 200. This growing private power has enormous economic consequences ... however, the greatest impact may be political, as corporations transform economic clout into political power' (at 7).

12 See Justin Greenwood (2003), *Interest Representation in the European Union* (Basingstoke: Palgrave Macmillan); Belén Balanyá et al. (2003), *Europe Inc.: Regional and Global Restructuring and the Rise of Corporate Power* (London: Pluto Press).

13 On how the legal profession may serve the interests of powerful 'private' clients, to the detriment of regulatory effort, see D. McBarnet (2002), 'Transnational transactions:

producer-actor in the legal arena, it is clear that such actors command a relatively highly advantageous position.

The role and position of the typical consumer appears very different in this respect. In the first place, and fairly obviously, this typical consumer (and here we are referring for the moment to 'end-consumers',[14] rather than, for instance, intermediate buyers) is a 'small' person, frequently, for many products and services, an individual human being.[15] Individually, the economic power of each consumer is very small compared to that of typical producers, and additionally is dispersed. This relatively vulnerable economic position of most consumers explains of course a vocabulary of 'consumer protection', which now appears almost axiomatic. One natural response to this potential vulnerability is to use the strategy of combination, forming representative consumer groupings[16] which collectively could exercise greater political and economic leverage. None the less, as a strategy, this still requires positive action and a degree of determination and organisation in order to prove effective. Moreover, in the legal arena, the balance of advantage may still lie with producers as corporate actors, in that the latter possess a definite legal personality, providing immediate access to most forms of legal process. The legal identity of consumer groups as representative organisations is less securely established and in particular their representative role and standing for purposes of litigation may be open to question. As Douglas-Scott has argued:

> Multinationals and monopolies which are more able to show individuation are strengthened at the expense of small companies and individuals, who are deprived of the mutual support needed to win complex court cases.[17]

---

legal work, cross-border commerce and global regulation', Ch. 5 in Michael Likosky (ed.), *Transnational Legal Processes: Globalisation and Power Disparities* (London: Butterworths). McBarnet comments: 'the driving force of clients' interests means legal work is not concerned to promote effective control but all too often is concerned to undermine it ... Efforts at global control of business may be set up at macro level, only to be destroyed by stealth through routine private legal work' (at 112).

14 In German terminology, the *Endverbraucher*. Compare the definition of 'consumer' in the 1973 UK Fair Trading Act as a person who does not contract in the course of a business but deals with someone who does.

15 There is a good deal of discussion and writing on the concept of the consumer. In particular, there is an interesting and important debate on 'consumer sovereignty' and on the construction of consumer identity, for instance, the important earlier work by J.K. Galbraith (1984), *The Affluent Society* (London: André Deutsch, 4th edn). Note also the concept of the 'confident' consumer, used in the 1999 UK Government White Paper, *Modern Markets: Confident Consumers* (Cmd 4410). See further the discussion of consumer identity in Chapter 3 below.

16 For an overview of consumer groups, see Colin Scott and Julia Black (2000), *Cranston's Consumer and the Law* (London: Butterworths, 3rd edn), at 12–22.

17 Sionaidh Douglas-Scott (2002), *Constitutional Law of the European Union* (Harlow: Pearson), at 364. Douglas-Scott discusses the disadvantaged position of representative groups in European-level litigation, at 363–6.

Thus the consumer, even in a collective manifestation, is likely to be at a disadvantage in terms of both resources and legal identity.[18] There is also one further aspect of the consumer's economic vulnerability *vis-à-vis* producers and suppliers. In so far as power is based on knowledge, the typical consumer is at a relative disadvantage in terms of knowledge regarding the product or service being consumed. Put simply, how easily may a consumer know that he or she is being economically exploited or materially damaged by the producer? Theoretically, consumers possess considerable market power in that their consumption is necessary and producer power is therefore moderated by the possibility that consumers will reject what is offered. But this market power is dependent on the will to reject, and also presupposes an awareness of the defects of what is being offered in the first place. In that respect, producers usually hold the trump card and it may be necessary to employ legal intervention rather than a reliance on market forces to ensure that crucial information is passed from producer to consumer (for instance, through labelling requirements).[19] Sure enough, consumers can vote with their feet, but only if they are aware that there is reason to do so.

We turn next to consider more specifically the kind of legal argument and rights typically invoked respectively by producers and consumers in the legal arena. Since the producer's role is active (the supply of goods or services), in legal terms one of the main outcomes is likely to be the need to deal with any injury to others arising from that supply. That in turn is likely to cast the producer in a defensive role, so leading to an assertion of producer rights as defence rights. Another major context in which producer rights may be asserted is also defensive, in the case of any restrictive regulation of the producer's economic activity as a matter of economic and trading policy. There are significant examples of both these types of 'defensive' rights claim at the European legal level. The first situation is well illustrated by legal action taken against producers for causing anti-competitive harm (often to the interests of consumers). As the subject of such enforcement procedure (investigation, hearing, imposition of sanctions), producers may well assert civil and political rights of defence, and this area of the subject will be considered further below. The second situation is also widely evident in the context of European market regulation, which frequently entails restrictions on the conditions of production (for example, quotas) and trading (for example, licences). Here again, the response of producers may well be defensive, but this time invoking a different category of rights, clustering around the concept of freedom of economic activity.[20] Suffice it to say for present purposes that in both these areas there has been a vigorous producer response to such regulation, involving legal challenge and a resulting case law and development

---

18 Scott and Black, note 16 above, at 19–22.

19 The principle of disclosure of information to consumers is now a well-established plank of consumer protection law: see the White Paper, *Modern Markets: Confident Consumers*, note 15 above, Ch 3. For a detailed account of legally required disclosure of information, see Scott and Black, note 16 above, Ch. 9.

20 Some of the 'pioneering' basic rights judgments of the European Court of Justice related to claims to freedom of trading, and rights to property and economic self-determination. See in particular: Case 11/70, *Internationale Handelsgesellschaft* v. *EVSt* (1970) ECR 1125; Case 4/73, *Nold* v. *Commission* (1974) ECR 491.

of legal doctrine. In short, corporate rights of defence in relation to competition proceedings and rights associated with the freedom to trade are both well-developed areas of European law.

Conversely, the consumer's role is passive, in the sense of being the recipient of goods and services. As such, the likely kind of legal problem, from the consumer's perspective, relates to damage of a material or economic kind, such as injury arising from consumption, restriction of choice, or economic exploitation (typically through having to pay unduly high prices). Legally, therefore, the consumer may well be cast in a kind of 'victim' role and as such would wish to claim 'protective' rights. Such rights would comprise not only reactive, *ex post facto* legal claims to compensation, but also a proactive entitlement to protection, in the sense of pre-empting such injury. The latter type of protection – now a familiar aspect of 'consumer law' – necessarily relies upon intervention within the framework of an expert and resourced regulatory infrastructure, imposing and enforcing standards of production and trading as a means of preventing and minimising injury to consumers. Burgeoning areas of regulation – for instance, in relation to competition, the imposition of standards in relation to trading and health and safety, and environmental protection – exemplify the growing extent and significance of such legal control.

It should be noted that this reactive role of the consumer may potentially be played out on a number of stages. In its most basic form, it is an economic role undertaken simply as the consumer acting *qua* consumer in the market place, in deciding whether or not to consume. As already noted, however, if this choice is to be genuinely autonomous and critical (as a 'confident' consumer), it must be appropriately informed. A second platform for reaction is more of a political stage, whereby the consumer engages with the process of policy and rule formation in the development of protective standards. To be effective, this will almost certainly require consumer views to be mediated through representative groups, via standing committees ('comitology') and lobbying. The third platform is that of litigation after the event, seeking compensation or other appropriate remedies, but this may well raise questions concerning resources, expertise and representation in such proceedings. Finally, but significantly in practice, the matter may be handled by a regulatory agency on behalf of the consumer. This may comprise a proactive form of control – for instance, by monitoring standards – or occur *ex post facto* – for instance, acting upon complaints.

These platforms for the assertion of consumer claims are summarised in Table 1.1.

Some of the consumer rights arising within this whole scenario will be of a civil or political character – notably rights relating to participation in law and policy making directed towards the formulation of standards, and those related to access to litigation and procedures for complaint. The substantive rights of consumer protection are economic and social rights. But whatever their categorisation, their exercise may require some legal support and so give them a dependent character, and in this respect the consumer may often be in a distinctive position as a rights holder. To some extent, the development of supportive regulatory structures has been a response to the problem of consumer vulnerability referred to above. Regulatory intervention has taken over the task of protecting the consumer, transferring the

Table 1.1   Platforms of consumer claim

Platform for the assertion of consumer interests	Characteristic method
Consumer acting in the market place	Direct economic choice
Lobbying policy makers and legislators	Use of representative bodies
Litigation	Response to damage
Imposition of regulatory standards	Indirect and proactive monitoring

initiative in taking direct legal action to an expert monitoring body and rendering the consumer more an object than a subject of protection. While relieving the consumer of much of the burden of ensuring producer accountability, it also reduces the role of the individual consumer to that of a minor player.[21] As regulators develop a stronger sense of their own professional role and mission, this may reinforce the dependent position of the consumer, both in the context of policy and rule formation (deciding on the appropriate standards of consumer protection) and in the context of enforcement. Again, this is well exemplified in the context of competition law and policy, in which the role of the regulator has become increasingly significant. In a European context, accountability for anti-competitive damage has become very much a public law activity (administrative or even criminal law control exercised by competition authorities)[22] rather than a matter of private law, depending on the initiative of the injured party (civil claims against the anti-competitive actor).[23]

In this way, some significant areas of consumer protection now comprise the enforcement of rights which have an indirect and programmatic – or perhaps it may be said, 'unowned' – character. Consumer interests which are protected in this way by the action of public agencies are dependent not only on the choice and initiative of the latter, but also on the level of resources and expertise within the regulatory system. Thus, whatever consumer rights might comprise more specifically, a system of regulatory protection does not naturally encourage a direct and 'own' assertion of such rights, even when the latter may be practically feasible.

---

21 There is an analogy with the role of the victim of crime in criminal procedure. In modern criminal law, the State has typically taken over the role of enforcement, so that the majority of prosecutions are undertaken by an official agency, sometimes irrespective of the wishes of the victim of the offence in question, thus marginalising one of the major actors in the actual criminal event.

22 This also involves some autonomy on the part of the competition authority, *vis-à-vis* the injured trader or consumer, in deciding on what action to take: see for instance, Case T-24/90. *Automec* v. *Commission* (1992) ECR II-2223.

23 Equally, civil claims, certainly in a European, but not in an American context, have been rare on account of uncertainty of legal outcome and economic disincentives.

The Spectrum of Economic Actors: Interests and Identities

A mapping of legal argument on to the basic economic landscape of supply and demand inevitably leads to a main categorisation of market actors as either suppliers or consumers. In this way, legal discussion (as in the previous section) has to a large extent been based upon a dichotomy between suppliers' (or traders') and consumers' rights. However, this broadly dualistic and oppositional depiction of the legal landscape may obscure what is in reality a more complex range of economic and legal interests and identities within the market place. As suggested above, it may be more accurate to think in terms of a continuum between the extreme points of economic supply and demand. Even then, the picture may still be over-simplified, since there are significant actors within the market who are more indirectly located in relation to the line of supply and demand – for instance, investors, funders, or the labour force.

In the first place, it may be helpful simply to provide a descriptive account of how this line of supply and demand is populated. If this line is regarded as a continuum, with the principal producer or supplier of services at one end, and the end-consumer at the other, some main types of economic actor may be listed. But alongside these it would be useful to add some indirect contributors to the process of supply, and also, on the other side, a range of actors who provide some kind of critical assessment of the process. These various actors are listed in Table 1.2.

An appreciation of the range and diverse identity of these actors is important in any discussion of legal claims, since any convincing argument regarding their entitlement should proceed from an understanding of their economic position and interests. This general point may be easily illustrated with reference to the idea both of the company as a supplier of commodities and of the end-consumer of such commodities.

Table 1.2   Economic actors along the line of supply and demand

>	Line of supply and demand	<
	Large-scale producers and suppliers of services, for example, transnational corporations	
Funders, lenders of capital, for example, banks	Small- and medium-sized suppliers	Representative organisations
Suppliers of technology, for example, intellectual property holders and licensors	Wholesalers	Public regulatory bodies
Investors, for example, company shareholders	Large-scale retailers, for example, supermarkets, mail order firms	Independent press
Labour force	Specialist retailers	Government policy
	End-consumers	

First, a moment's reflection should make it clear that, whatever the similarity in legal form, there may be a world of difference in economic and political terms between a transnational corporation (TNC)[24] and a small company comprising a few people, supplying a local market and with a relatively small turnover. There is now a large literature on the role of the former type of corporate actor: the archetypical 'corporation' in popular language, an international actor operating on a global market, whose power and influence may be compared with that of sovereign States. Equally, it is now common to find references to 'small and medium-sized enterprises' (SMEs) as a distinct category of (usually corporate) actor. The well-recognised difference in the economic and political positions of these respective types of corporate person inevitably has an impact on their legal regulation, and legal analysis should take on board these significant differences.

The background to the legal regulation of the activities of TNCs is summarised in the following way by O'Brien and Williams:

> The shift towards transnationalization by many enterprises has also changed traditional state-firm relations, with policies of cooperation essential to the economic planning of both actors. The large amounts of capital owned and controlled by TNCs combined with their participation in virtually every national economy in the world has given them a great deal of strategic power in the global political economy and their role in influencing international trade negotiations and other international agreements is an important issue in the contemporary global economy.[25]

Such observations have implications for the legal identity of TNCs. The legal identity of the large and powerful modern firm was presciently outlined by Berle and Means in their classic analysis of corporate structures first published in 1932:

> The rise of the modern corporation has brought a concentration of economic power which can compete on equal terms with the modern state – economic power versus political power, each strong in its own field. The state seeks in some aspects to regulate the corporation, while the corporation, steadily becoming more powerful, makes every effort to avoid such regulation. Where its own interests are concerned, it even attempts to dominate the state. The future may see the economic organism, now typified by the corporation, not only on an equal plane with the state, but possibly even superseding it as the dominant form of social organization. The law of corporations, accordingly, might well be considered as a potential constitutional law for the new economic state, while business practice is increasingly assuming the aspect of economic statesmanship.[26]

---

24 A number of terms are used to describe such large corporate actors with an international economic role, in particular 'multinational', 'transnational' and 'global'. Following O'Brien and Williams, the term 'transnational' may be preferred as connoting more precisely what is usually being referred to: they argue that 'transnational' more accurately 'reflects the fact that these firms are usually owned and controlled by the nationals of one country and enter into direct productive activities abroad.' (Robert O'Brien and Marc Williams (2004), *Global Political Economy: Evolution and Dynamics* (Basingstoke: Palgrave Macmillan), at 170.)

25 Ibid., at 197.

26 Adolf A. Berle and Gardiner C. Means (1932), *The Modern Corporation and Private Property* (Ardsley, NY: Transnational Publishers, 7th edn 2005), at 313.

In turn, such perceptions of the role and position of the large-scale modern trading company then affect the discussion of that actor's legal entitlement. This argument will be explored further in Chapter 2 below: for instance, it may be asked whether – if a TNC is viewed in some respects as the equivalent of a State – it should then be entitled to the kind of legal (human rights) protection designed for individual human beings. Certainly, it should be considered whether the TNC and the SME should be treated alike in terms of such entitlement. This indeed was part of the background to the *Markt Intern* litigation, since an important *raison d'être* of Markt Intern itself was the representation and protection of the interests of small, specialist retailers, particularly in relation to larger-scale suppliers, such as supermarkets and mail order firms.

Equally, the term 'consumer' may encompass a variety of actors in terms of their market role and interests. Even confining attention to the 'end-consumer', there may be different kinds of interest involved. For example, the consumer of beer may on the one hand be a regular but unreflective and undiscriminating drinker, or on the other hand a member of the Campaign for Real Ale, with a serious concern for how the product is manufactured and marketed, so that consuming the beer is a matter of considering its specific origin, method of dispense, branding, and the context of its production and marketing (such as the situation of the workforce at the brewery, of licensees of public houses). The latter category of consumer, having different (higher) expectations as a consumer is also thereby likely to assert different and stronger rights of consumption. Again, the idea of the consumer is more fully explored later in the discussion, in Chapter 3.

Rights claims, and decisions on entitlement, may therefore be coloured by the more specific position and interests of economic actors. But reductive legal categorisation (for instance, as a company, or as a natural person) and also that of standard economic analysis (for instance, as a producer, retailer, or consumer) may obscure the way in which legal determinations involving a balance of interests are arrived at. What is at issue here is an often complex underlying *interplay* of interests which is barely revealed by the main legal forms or by purely economic market analysis. This point is made, for instance, in the dissenting opinion of Judge Pettiti in the *Markt Intern* judgment:

> The problem is all the more serious because often the States which seek to restrict the freedom [of expression] use the pretext of economic infringements or breaches of economic legislation such as anti-competition or anti-trust provisions to institute proceedings for political motives or to protect 'mixed' interests (State-industrial) in order to erect a barrier to the freedom of expression … The economic pressure which groups or laboratories can exert should not be underestimated. In certain cases this pressure has been such that it has delayed the establishment of the truth and therefore put back the prohibition of a medicine or substance dangerous for the public health.[27]

This quoted argument concisely refers to a potentially powerful range and combination of interests – the manufacturer of medicine, the developer of technology used in its production, and the State in managing and promoting a particular economic sector.

---

27 (1990) *EHRR*, at 178–9. See also the narrative of the BSE saga in Chapter 3 below.

All are stakeholders in the process of supply and will therefore be interested in legal argument concerning the freedom to supply.

The importance of this kind of analysis of the identity and interests of various economic actors for argument concerning legal entitlement and, more specifically, claims to basic rights may be appreciated with reference to one or two particular examples. One thought-provoking illustration arises from the examination of the typical large corporation as a supplier of commodities and services. When such a company invokes, for instance, a basic right to property – in the form of the freedom to dispose of its assets as it wishes – it may be asked more precisely whose property interests underlie such a claim. In their analysis of the internal organisation of the corporation in modern (early twentieth-century) society, Berle and Means emphasised the way in which two aspects of ownership – the risking of collective wealth in a profit-seeking enterprise, and the ultimate management of responsibility for that enterprise – had become divorced. Writing later on in the preface to the revised edition of the work in 1967, Berle commented that in the first edition of their book they had raised certain questions:

> Must we not, therefore, recognise that we are no longer dealing with property in the old sense? Does the traditional logic of property still apply? Because an owner who also exercises control over his wealth is protected in the full receipt of the advantages derived from it, must it *necessarily* follow that an owner who has surrendered control of his wealth should likewise be protected to the full? May not this surrender have so changed his relation to his wealth as to have changed the logic applicable to his interest in that wealth? An answer to this question cannot be found in the law itself. It must be sought in the economic and social background of law.[28]

And he goes on to point out that these questions had been based on:

> the growing dominance of the corporate form, the increasing decision-making power of corporate management, the increasingly passive position of shareholders, and the increasing inapplicability of the ethical and economic justification given (rightly enough at the time) by classic economists.[29]

This question of 'whose property interest?' in relation to the corporation, whether it is that of the investing shareholders, or that of the management, or the public, would appear to be increasingly relevant to the example of TNCs and other large companies who now energetically invoke such fundamental rights. Are the rights and interests of management and shareholders the same in such a context? And if not, as Berle and Means suggested, it would then seem to be necessary to identify distinct rights to property, a narrower right of the corporation (associated with the interests of its management) and a background right of investment, associated with the shareholders.[30] After all, it may be said that shareholders may be more

---

28 Berle and Means, note 26 above, at xx.

29 Ibid.

30 Note, for example, the distinction drawn by the European Court of Human Rights as between shareholder and company interests in *Agrotexim* v. *Greece* (1995) *EHRR* 250, discussed in Chapter 2 below.

interested in their shareholding, which for them is a disposable asset in itself, than in the company as such. Moreover, such investors may well be substantial corporate (or 'institutional') actors in their own right, typically banks and pension funds, so possessing a strongly distinctive identity as economic actors of another kind.

A further illustration arises again from the *Markt Intern* case, and relates to the Markt Intern itself as an organisation. What was the identity of this organisation? On the one hand, it had been established and was operated by journalists. Its business was the publication of news sheets and bulletins, lobbying, providing support in test cases; generally, therefore it could be described as an information-providing and campaigning organisation, working in the cause of market transparency. Such a description suggests something in the nature of a political and economic NGO, broadly concerned with the interests of small traders and consumers. On the other hand, it worked within particular commercial sectors, those of chemists and beauty product retailers. Its specific representative role in this respect led the Federal Constitutional Court and the German Government to characterise the organisation as a market participant, a kind of agent of the specialised retailers, and so in effect a competitor of the mail order company Cosmetic Club. For the German Government, Markt Intern's role was not to influence or mobilise public opinion, but 'to promote the economic interests of a given group of undertakings'. As such, its activities could be seen as deserving one kind of legal protection (that is, within the scope of the freedom to conduct business and engage in competition), but not another kind (that is, within the scope of the freedom of expression). The Government argued that Markt Intern's bulletin:

> did not contribute to a debate of interest to the general public, but was part of an unlawful competitive strategy aimed at ridding the beauty products market of an awkward competitor for specialist retailers.[31]

This kind of argument is an example of what might be described as 'field constitution' – what Koskenniemi describes as a process of 'structuring the normative field in focus'[32]. Another way of describing this process would be to refer to the choice of a frame of reference for argument. Such field constitution may be decisive for the outcome of legal argument, simply by determining the relevant rights which may be invoked in support of that argument. In *Markt Intern*, the issue of field constitution was a choice between the applicability of the freedom of expression regime or of the competition regime: was it a matter of human rights law or unfair competition law? The answer depended upon the identity of the key actor, Markt Intern: was it an organ of the press, or a commercial organisation competing in the cosmetics market? The majority opinion in the Court of Human Rights implied treatment of the organisation as an organ of the press, confirming its entitlement to freedom of expression, although then limiting that entitlement with reference to the qualification of the freedom under Article 10(2) of the Human Rights Convention. The dissenting opinion of Judge Martens was more categorical in its depiction of Markt Intern as an organ of the press, referring to the organisation as part of the 'socio-economic press'.

---

31 (1990) *EHRR*, at 173.
32 Koskenniemi, note 9 above, at 106.

His opinion is also explicit regarding the different consequences of constituting the relevant field as one of 'unfair competition' or 'freedom of expression'. He argues that on the one hand:

> The law on unfair competition governs the relationships between competitors on the market. It is based on the assumption that in engaging in competition the competitors seek only to serve their own interests, while attempting to harm those of others ... It is permissible for a competitor to criticise another publicly only if he has sufficient reasons for so doing and if the nature and scope of his criticism remain within the limits required by the situation. In this field the prohibition on publishing criticism is therefore the norm and it falls to the person who takes the risk of publishing such criticism to show that there were sufficient grounds for his criticism and that it remains within the strictest limits. In considering whether this proof has been furnished, the court weighs up only the interests of the two competitors.

Whereas, on the other hand:

> In the field of freedom of expression the converse is true. In this field the basic assumption is that this right is used to serve the general interest, in particular as far as the press is concerned, and that is why in this context the freedom to criticise is the norm. Thus in this field it falls to the person who alleges that the criticism is not acceptable to prove that his claim is well-founded. In determining whether he has done so, the court must weigh up the general interest, on the one hand, and the individual interests of the party who claims to have been injured, on the other.[33]

According to this kind of analysis, the identity of the actor (in this case, as competitor, or organ of the press) is crucial for constitution of the legal field, and so then for the relevant kind of rights entitlement. In this way, interests, identity and the working-out of claims to basic rights are closely connected.

Fundamental Rights Claims and Legal Identity

Using basic rights argument in the context of markets and economic activity is not simply a matter of transferring existing legal, ethical and political argument and concepts from the traditional domain of such legal protection to that of industrial and commercial activity. Traders, consumers and other participants in markets are, whatever their legal form, economic actors. As such, they have distinctive interests and motivation, and such identity as economic actors necessarily provides the basis for and will inform the nature of their legal entitlement. This is particularly so in relation to any entitlement which is described in the language and currency of fundamental rights. Any examination and evaluation of what has happened in practice in allocating a high order of legal protection to economic actors needs to take on board this perspective and bear in mind not only the specific context of economic and commercial activity but also the identity of the actors who may be bearing these rights. There are challenging questions, for instance, regarding the

---

33 (1990) *EHRR,* at 180–81. See further, on the question of freedom of expression in the commercial context, the discussion in Chapters 4 and 8.

basis for awarding fundamental 'human' rights to corporate actors, or regarding the role of the human individual as an economic consumer, which have often hitherto not been very fully considered in the practice of legal development.

Before proceeding to a substantive examination of the resort to human rights argument in the economic domain, it will therefore be useful to explore more fully some underlying issues: the basis and justification for the allocation of fundamental 'human' rights to both corporate actors and consumers, and the nature and force of fundamental rights argumentation in itself. These questions will now be considered in greater depth in the next three chapters.

Chapter 2

The Sun, Liverpudlians and 'The Truth': A Corporate Right to Human Rights?

The Sun, Liverpudlians and 'The Truth'

In 1989, *The Sun* newspaper ran a story on the Hillsborough Stadium football disaster in which ninety-six spectators died.[1] The story, entitled 'THE TRUTH', made false claims about Liverpudlians behaving monstrously in the wake of the disaster. Liverpudlians took offence and even after fifteen years many refuse to buy the newspaper. The hatred of Liverpudlians has never been directed at the then editor, Kelvin MacKenzie, who has long left the newspaper. The dislike attaches directly to *The Sun* – that is, the newspaper, the company. So attempts by new editors to appease Liverpudlians, most recently an apology in 2004, were bound to have and in fact had little effect. Moreover, any apology is perceptively treated with scepticism as its motive is seen as none other than to win back a lucrative market of readers.

This saga reveals much about contemporary society and the role of commercial actors within it. It provides a comment on the use and abuse of power by companies, on their morality or lack of it, on the identity they project to consumers and how they are in fact perceived, as well as on the power of consumers flexing their economic muscle. It also highlights that popular discourse is not necessarily rationally defensible. If *The Sun* itself, as opposed to its staff, can be blamed for its conduct, should it not also be capable of showing remorse? On the other hand, if remorse by a commercial enterprise can never be genuine because of its ultimate concern for profits, can the act itself – which is no more than a classic act of a profit-motivated institution – be reprehensible?

For the purposes of this chapter, this episode is insightful because the reaction by the Liverpudlians is clearly predicated upon the humanised company – the company who ('which' or 'who'?) has a personality, who cannot just act but also feel, be dishonest and untrustworthy, who has the potential of being reformed, the company who can be a friend or an enemy. It is based on a view of the company as a fully fledged moral agent who can think, make decisions and know about right and wrong. This is the popular view which companies themselves encourage through branding. Humanisation is profitable: 'The smart corporations understand that people make comparisons in human terms … because that's the way people think.'[2] Sometimes, as *The Sun* now knows, it can backfire, leaving the demonised company in an intractable

---

1 The disaster occurred on 15 April 1989 in a football stadium in Sheffield.

2 Joel Bakan (2004), *The Corporation* (London: Constable), 26 (internal marks omitted, quoting Chris Komisarjevsky). For a recent critique on the notion of corporate 'humanity', see

position. Humanisation has also proved rather advantageous to companies in the legal field, as, for example, it has allowed them to use human rights to further their agenda. Companies can deploy many human rights arguments just like their natural antagonists. This chapter explores whether companies should, both as a matter of principle and practicality, be able to do so. Should the legal fiction of treating the company as a legal person be extended to treating it like a human and what are the problems with such extension in the human rights context?

While the discussion below is mainly confined to one aspect of companies' involvement in the human rights agenda, as beneficiaries of human rights, they have assumed other roles in this context. This chapter is written with the large publicly traded companies, generally transnational corporations (TNCs), in mind and these companies have been players at both ends of the human rights spectrum, most prominently and well documented, as abusers of human rights,[3] but also, as they like us to believe, as protectors and even promoters of these rights.[4] These other roles are examined only to the extent to which they help to shed light on the main question as to the human rights entitlement of companies.

The discussion here provides one of the conceptual pillars for the later chapters which focus on particular human or basic rights arguments actually used by and against companies and which implicitly comment on the merits of letting companies ride the human rights bandwagon. A wider issue opened up for discussion is whether the human condition may be improved if companies were legally treated for what they are factually in society: the new power brokers who often supplant the State and whose unbridled power calls for a watchful eye.

Finally, it is worth reminding ourselves that the discourse here is not concerned with whether companies should have rights *per se* and, if so, what these rights are or should be. Most people would accept that companies make invaluable contributions to our societies and thus should be encouraged through a mix of facilitative and

---

Anna Grear (2007), 'Challenging Corporate "Humanity": Legal Disembodiment, Embodiment and Human Rights', *Human Rights Law Review* 7: 511.

3 There is ample literature on this topic and so the following is no more than a small selection: Bakan ibid.; Janet Dine (2005), *Companies, International Trade and Human Rights* (Cambridge: Cambridge University Press); Sarah Joseph (2004), *Corporations and Transnational Human Rights Litigation* (Oxford: Hart); James Gobert and Maurice Punch (2003), *Rethinking Corporate Crime* (Oxford: Butterworths); Stephen Bottomley and David Kinley (eds) (2002), *Commercial Law and Human Rights* (Aldershot: Ashgate); Jedrzej George Frynas and Scott Pegg (eds) (2003), *Transnational Corporations and Human Rights* (London: Palgrave); International Council on Human Rights (2002), *Beyond Voluntarism: Human Rights and the Developing International Legal Obligations of Companies* (February), at <http://www.ichrp.org>; David P. Forsythe (2000), *Human Rights in International Relations* (Cambridge: Cambridge University Press) part Ch. 8 ('Transnational corporations and human rights'); Sally Wheeler (2002), *Corporations and the Third Way* (Oxford: Hart); Daniel Aguirre (2004), 'Multinational Corporations and the Realisation of Economic, Social and Cultural Rights' *California Western International Law Journal* 35: 53.

4 On Corporate Responsibility Reporting see Kate Nicholas (2005), 'Keeping up Appearances' in *The Independent* (13 June) 12; more generally, Stephen Bottomley 'Corporations and Human Rights' in Bottomley and Kinley, note 3 above, 47.

restrictive regulation, varying depending on the State's relative priorities. The question here is whether any rights companies enjoy or could enjoy deserve the 'basic human rights' label, a label designed to protect the most fundamental and inalienable rights of man and woman.

The Legal Status Quo

Before delving into the justification for corporate human rights, it is useful to explore whether companies have in fact been entitled to human rights protection. As a way of illustrating quite how fundamentally split the camps are in this respect, the selected examples are based upon the approaches taken under the International Covenant on Civil and Political Rights (ICCPR)[5] and the European Convention for the Protection of Human Rights and Fundamental Freedoms (ECHR).[6]

At the international level, the ICCPR excludes companies from its protective regime. Under Article 2(1) the contracting parties undertake to ensure the Covenant rights of all 'individuals'. This has been found to encompass the collective right of peoples to self-determination,[7] but otherwise precludes collective bodies, whether groups of people or legal persons such as companies, from being beneficiaries under the Covenant. This position is consolidated by Article 1 of the First Optional Protocol[8] which makes only communications by individuals about alleged violations admissible in the complaints process. Thus the Human Rights Committee took a restrictive approach in the case of *A Newspaper Publishing Company* v. *Trinidad and Tobago*[9] where it simply stated that 'only individuals may submit a communication … A company incorporated under the laws of a State party to the Optional Protocol, as such, has no standing … regardless of whether its allegations appear to raise issues under the UN Covenant.'[10]

---

5 In force since 1976.

6 For an in-depth discussion of corporate human rights under the ECHR, see Marius Emberland (2006), *The Human Rights of Companies* (Oxford: Oxford University Press). Examples could also have been drawn from various national instruments, for example, the US Constitution: *New York Times Co.* v. *Sullivan* 376 US 254 (1964), or the Canadian Charter of Human Rights and Fundamental Freedoms: *Irwin Toy Ltd* v. *Quebec* (AG) [1989] 1 SCR 927.

7 David Harris (1995), 'The International Covenant on Civil and Political Rights and the United Kingdom: An Introduction' in David Harris and Sarah Joseph (eds), *The International Covenant on Civil and Political Rights and United Kingdom Law* (Oxford: Clarendon Press), 1, 3.

8 In force since 1976.

9 (360/1989). For the position of NGOs, see *Group of Handicapped Person* v. *Italy (163/1984)*.

10 *A Newspaper Publishing Company* v. *Trinidad and Tobago* (360/1989) para. 3.2. In the same paragraph, it also states that the communication had not 'indicated whether and to what extent … individuals rights under the Covenant have been violated by the events referred to in the communication' which suggests that the Committee thought that the case might well involve a violation of an individual right. See also *A Publishing and Printing Company* v. *Trinidad and Tobago* (361/1989) para. 3.2.

In contrast, the European Court of Human Rights[11] has allowed companies to benefit from the ECHR. This has happened without much ado; indeed the 'Court has never engaged in a technical legal sense with the question of whether the artificiality of the corporation imposes limitations on its ability to be the victim of a rights violation.'[12] Admittedly, Article 34 of the European Convention is more conducive to such an approach, as it allows for complaints by a '*person*, non-governmental organisation or a group of individuals'.[13] In relation to the protection of property, Article 1 of the First Protocol to the Convention[14] specifically confers the right on 'every natural or legal person'. Thus, perhaps not surprisingly in *Yarrow* v. *United Kingdom*,[15] the Commission on Human Rights held that the application by the company, but not the claims by its minority shareholders, was admissible where an interference with the company's property rights was alleged. In contrast, professional and non-governmental associations and trade unions can only allege human rights violations[16] if they can show that one of their members has directly been affected by the violation.[17] Similarly, in the more recent case of *Agrotexim and Others* v. *Greece*,[18] the European Court of Human Rights did not allow the claim by the applicant companies, not because of their artificial nature, but rather because they had suffered their loss only indirectly as majority shareholders in another company (whose right to peaceful enjoyment of its possession was alleged to have been violated). The Court was of the view that the complaint should have been made by the 'violated' company and not its shareholders, particularly as at

---

11 Or in the earlier cases, the Human Rights Commission.

12 Alan J. Dignam and David Allen (2000), *Company Law and the Human Rights Act 1998* (London: Butterworths), 173. Emberland, note 6 above, 37: 'It is not in the Court's nature to philosophize ... .'

13 Emphasis added. This is incorporated into UK law by virtue of Section 7 of the Human Rights Act 1998 which allows a person who is a 'victim of an unlawful act' by a public authority to bring proceedings against the authority relying on the European Convention rights. Section 7(7) specifically provides: 'For the purposes of this section, a person is a victim of an unlawful act only if he would be a victim for the purposes of Article 34 of the Convention if proceedings were brought in the European Court of Human Rights in respect of that act.'

14 Protocol to the Convention for the Protection of Human Rights and Fundamental Freedoms (Paris, 20.III.195).

15 (1983) 30 DR 155. Here the applicants complained that inadequate compensation was paid on the nationalisation of Yarrow Shipbuilders and invoked Article 1 of the Protocol No. 1 to the Convention alone and in conjunction with Article 14 of the Convention, and Articles 6 and 13 of the Convention.

16 *Klass* v. *Germany* (1978) 2 EHRR 214; *Confederation des Syndicats Medicaux Francais* v. *France* (1986) 47 DR 255; *Council of Civil Service Unions* v. *UK* (1987) 50 DR 228; cf. *Christians Against Racism and Fascism* v. *UK* (1980) 21 DR 138; discussed in Dignam and Allen, note 12 above, 31ff and 127.

17 In addition, it must be shown that the organisation had the authority to act for the member: *Confederation des Syndicats Medicaux Français* v. *France* (1986) 47 DR 255. So when these organisations have been entitled to bring a human rights claim, it is on behalf of their members only. The assumption is that the organisation as such cannot suffer a human rights violation as it is in fact no more than the aggregate of its members.

18 (1996) 21 *ECHR* 250.

the time of the shareholders' application, the company 'had not ceased to exist as a legal person'.[19] So the Commission and the Court clearly equated the company's legal capacity with a capacity to be a human rights victim and indeed goes further by making the company's claim superior to that of its ultimately natural investors.[20] Given the explicit reference to 'legal persons' in respect of the right to property, it seems justified also to interpret 'person' in Article 34 broadly, as otherwise companies would have a right but not a remedy (in terms of making a complaint). But perhaps such broad interpretation should have been limited to the right to the protection of property. Yet, this has not been the case.

Companies also have been beneficiaries of the right to freedom of speech,[21] to privacy[22] and a fair trial[23] – all of which are conferred on 'everyone'. So, for example, in *Autronic AG* v. *Switzerland*,[24] the Court held that 'neither Autronic AG's legal status as a limited company nor the fact that its activities were commercial nor the intrinsic nature of freedom of expression'[25] would deprive the company of free speech protection. It stressed that Article 10 is worded as being applicable to 'everyone' and thus, according to the Court, to any 'natural or legal person'.[26] What is surprising about the non-property rights is not so much that companies have been

---

19 (1996) 21 *ECHR* 250, para. 69.

20 Here the investors were also companies but ultimately every investment can of course be traced back to natural investors. Judge Walsh in his dissenting opinion picks up on the oddity that the corporate claim should be stronger than the claim by the human participants: 'While it is true to say that such a body corporate has neither a soul to be damned nor a body to be beaten nonetheless the shareholders have and the existence of the corporate entity gives no protection to the shareholders as individuals against the loss in value of their shares or against criminal or civil liability for their individual activities in the commercial advancement of the companies' (1996) 21 ECHR 250, para. 2.

21 See discussion below. See also Emberland, note 6 above, 117ff; Dignam and Allen, note 12 above, Ch. 11.

22 See discussion below. See also Emberland, ibid., 132, 172ff; Dignam and Allen, ibid., Ch. 10.

23 Article 6, applied in, for example, *Editions Périscope* v. *France*, 234 *Eur. Ct. H.R.* (ser. A) 56, 67 (1992) (holding that France had violated the right of a French company to a hearing within a reasonable time). Note in *Saunders* v. *UK* (1996) 23 *EHRR* 313, para. 62, 74 (concerning the criminal conviction of the former CEO of Guinness plc) the European Court of Human Rights rejected the submission by the UK government that the privilege against self-incrimination should be treated with less strictness in corporate and financial fraud cases because of their complexity. See also Dignam and Allen, Ch. 9. But the 'European Court of Human Rights may not grant the same scope of protection under the privilege against self-incrimination to legal persons in proceedings ... to the extent that these proceedings will lead only to the imposition of fines on legal persons.' L. Garzaniti, Jason Gudofsky and Jane Moffat, 'Dawn of a New Era? Powers of Investigation and Enforcement under Regulation 1/2003' *Antitrust Law Journal* 72 (2004): 159.

24 *Sunday Times* v. *UK* (1979) 2 EHRR 245; *Market Intern Verlag Gmbh and Beerman* v. *Germany* (1990) 12 *EHRR* 161; *Groppera Radio AG* v. *Switzerland* (28 March 1990) Series A, No. 173 followed in *Autronic AG* v. *Switzerland* (1990) 12 *EHRR* 485.

25 Ibid., para 47.

26 Ibid.

able to benefit from them, but the ease with which such status was granted – with the same ease with which the victim status was withheld from companies under the UN Covenant. To argue that the wording 'everyone' clearly encompasses companies is hardly persuasive even taking a legalistic approach. First, as in respect of the right to the protection of property 'legal persons' are specifically mentioned as being beneficiaries, it suggests that where no such wording is used, companies were not intended to benefit. Secondly, other rights, such as the right to life or the right to liberty and security, are also conferred on 'everyone', yet are generally presumed not to apply to companies. So the term 'everyone' as far as companies are concerned is at the very best inconclusive. Furthermore, following a less legalistic tune, by, for example, taking into account the nature of human rights, there could be equally plausible interpretations of 'everyone' which would exclude companies, an argument explored in more depth below.

Despite companies' prima facie entitlement to human rights protection under the European Convention, their artificial nature has, as one would expect, imposed some limitations. Companies cannot enjoy the right to life, to freedom from torture, or the right to marry. Yet, these boundaries are being pushed constantly. In the 2002 case of *Société Colas Est* v. *France*,[27] publicly traded companies successfully relied on 'the right to respect for private and family life' under Article 8 of the Convention, and specifically the right to respect for their 'home'. The right was invoked in respect of the raiding of the companies' premises in the context of investigations of anti-competitive practices, which subsequently led to their conviction. One might ponder how these companies could have possibly managed to carry off that argument. But the Court did not see anything strange in the notion of the 'private and family life' of a company:

> The Court reiterates that the Convention is a living instrument which should be interpreted in the light of present-day conditions … Building on its dynamic interpretation of the Convention, the Court considers that the time has come to hold that in certain circumstances the rights guaranteed by Article 8 of the Convention may be construed as including the right to respect for a company's registered office, branches or other business premises.[28]

It remains a mystery what exactly these 'present-day conditions' might be and why a 'dynamic interpretation of the Convention' favours greater protection of companies, as opposed to the same or even less protection. More than anything, this case shows how the initial human right has been stretched beyond recognition. Can the right to a 'private and family life' fairly be said to accommodate the right of a commercial and artificial player to have its offices protected from governmental interference?[29]

---

27 (2004) 39 EHRR 17. For a critique of the case and related cases, see 'Roquette Frères, ECJ Case C-94/00' (2003), *Columbia Journal of European Law* 10: 137. See also Emberland, note 6 above, 132ff, 140ff. For a discussion of the parallel jurisprudence of the European Court of Justice, see Chapter 5 below.

28 *Societe Colas Est* v. *France* (2004) 39 *EHRR* 1, para. 41. See also Emberland, ibid., 152f.

29 A similar approach has been taken by the European Court of Justice when analogous claims have been presented under European Community law. Such an approach there can

From the brief perusal of the legal *status quo* of the corporate right to human rights, the following propositions emerge:

1. there is no general consensus on the corporate right to human rights;
2. positions at either end of the spectrum are taken with the confidence attached to obvious unarguable facts (which can partly be attributed to the wording of the instruments in question);
3. where, as in Europe, companies have been granted the victim status in respect of some human rights, the basis for that protection appears to have been the status of the company as a legal person;[30]
4. the company's most explicit entitlement is to the right to the protection of property, and
5. the artificial nature of the corporate person has even in Europe meant that companies cannot take advantage of all human rights.

The opposing views taken on the corporate right to human rights perfectly crystallise the main issue under consideration: should companies have a right to human rights? This question may be approached through alternative routes: first, via a principled inquiry into the essential nature of human rights and the compatibility of corporate human rights with that nature, and, secondly, via a more utilitarian inquiry into the consequences of granting human rights to companies. These two approaches are explored below.

Arguments For and Against Corporate Human Rights

Human Rights For Legal Persons?

Explicitly, companies have been allowed to claim human rights protection on the basis of their status as legal persons.[31] This raises the questions, what exactly is meant by the notion of a 'legal person' and does it provide a valid basis for human rights protection?

In ordinary discourse, the term 'person' is used to refer to human beings. In law, it means 'a subject of rights and duties'. Upon incorporation, the company is born as such a person in law. It acquires legal capacity in its own right, distinct from the rights and duties enjoyed by, or imposed on, the individuals who make up the company. The creation of a legal person is designed to enable a group of individuals

---

draw textual support from the reference in the original Article 173 (now Article 230) of the EC Treaty, providing for judicial review, to both 'natural and legal persons', so clearly providing the right to corporate persons to present claims.

30 This phenomenon is by no means limited to Europe; see Jens David Ohlin (2005), 'Is the Concept of the Person Necessary for Human Rights?' *Columbia Law Review* 105: 209, 226ff.

31 See Grear, note 2 above, 516: 'Arguably, by invoking the concept of 'human' rights, corporations extend their rights-claims by invoking something approaching a form of legal humanity.'

to become collectively a player in the legal world, to make it a subject of legal rights and legal duties, as opposed to moral rights and duties. These rights and duties are found in the company legislation of its place of incorporation or seat of management, and in the general laws (such as contract, tort, taxation, labour, environmental and competition law) in the places of its domicile or activities. Many of these rights and duties are the same as those enjoyed by, or imposed on, individuals. So is 'human rights protection' a natural extension of the company's status as a legal person?

Is legal capacity a necessary or sufficient condition for human rights entitlement? There seems to be some correlation between human rights entitlement and legal capacity. Under national legal systems, legal capacity has generally been reserved to individuals and not, for example, animals, plants, or inanimate objects,[32] and it is also individuals who are the prime beneficiaries of human rights protection.[33] On a practical level, legal capacity also seems a prerequisite for human rights enjoyment in so far as enforcing rights requires legal capacity. Does this mean that legal capacity is one of the bases for human rights entitlement? The answer is negative. First, legal capacity cannot be a prerequisite for human rights entitlement as it itself is a recognised human right. Article 6 of the Universal Declaration of Human Rights (1948) states that 'Everyone has the right to recognition as a person before the law', mirrored by Article 16 of the ICCPR.[34] If legal capacity is a human right granted, it means that even those who do not in fact enjoy it, still come under the human rights umbrella. Secondly, a significant minority of individuals have under national legal systems only limited or no legal capacity at all, but – far from depriving them of human rights protection – this has made them the particular focus of the human rights movement. In the past and to a lesser extent today, these would have been slaves, women and other discriminated-against minorities.[35] Also children or mentally handicapped people always have very limited or no legal capacity under national law,[36] but are very much intended beneficiaries of human rights.

Some have argued, under the choice or will theory of rights, that rights are not rights properly-so-called[37] if the rights bearer does not have the right to enforce or waive them, that is, does not have legal capacity. Yet, first, it would seem perverse to deny the human rights entitlement of women or slaves because they lacked or lack

---

32 For example, an office, such as the Crown, may have legal capacity.

33 For example, the Universal Declaration of Human Rights (1948) states in its preamble: 'Whereas the peoples of the United Nations have in the Charter reaffirmed their faith in fundamental human rights, in the dignity and worth of the *human* person ...' (emphasis added).

34 Article 16: 'Everyone shall have the right to recognition everywhere as a person before the law.'

35 On the national and later international abolition of slavery see Paul Sieghard (1985), *The Lawful Rights of Mankind* (Oxford: Oxford University Press) 33ff, 126ff.

36 For example, The Age of Legal Capacity (Scotland) Act 1991 provides that persons under the age of 16 shall have no legal capacity. On lack of capacity see also Hans Kelsen (1945), *General Theory of Law and State* (New York: Russell & Russell) 90ff.

37 For example HLA Hart: 'talk of the rights of animals or babies ... makes an idle use of the expression "right"', discussed in Alex Gourevitch, 'Are Human Rights Liberal?' (2004) at <http://www.columbia.edu/cu/polisci/pdf-files/gourevitch.pdf> 16.

legal capacity under some legal systems. If human rights do not depend on actual legal capacity, it would seem possible to argue that legal capacity and human rights enjoy the same foundations. Under the will theory, this foundation would be the autonomous, rational moral agent. The real question is whether the company is such an agent, and that is addressed below. Secondly, adopting the interest theory of rights, the power to enforce or waive rights is an ancillary remedial legal power which – although of practical importance – cannot be the basis of substantive rights.[38] Rights are needs, interests, or desires protected in certain ways by the imposition of legal or moral normative constraints on the acts and activities of others.[39] In short, whatever theory one may adopt, legal capacity per se is never a prerequisite for, and much less so the foundation of human rights enjoyment, but rather its consequence.[40]

Some general comments about legal capacity may elucidate its link with human rights protection. Legal capacity is inextricably linked to the legal order from which it is derived. Different legal orders give legal capacity to different persons, organisations and institutions. National legal orders tend to give capacity to most individuals and companies; some also give capacity to temples[41] or funds.[42] In the international legal order, capacity is first and foremost enjoyed by States and only for very specific purposes by individuals, companies,[43] or NGOs. In other words, there is no such thing as legal capacity *per se*, disconnected from a particular legal order.[44]

---

38 Neil MacCormick (1982), 'Children Rights: A Test-Case for Theories of Rights' in *Legal Right and Social Democracy: Essays in Legal and Political Philosophy* (Oxford: Clarendon Press) 154, 157.

39 Ibid., 160. See also Kenneth Campbell, 'Legal Rights' in *Stanford Encyclopaedia of Philosophy* at <http://plato.stanford.edu/entries/legal-rights> section 2, where the author notes: 'The question is whether the duty, etc, grounds the right, or the right the duty. Most older writers (e.g., Bentham, Austin, Hohfield, Kelsen) appear to have adhered to the first view, whilst more recent writers (e.g., MacCormick, Raz, Wellman) take the second, The second view has the implication that the force of a right is not necessarily exhausted by any existing set of duties … [and] seems to accord better at least with the way that constitutional legal rights work.'

40 See the argument made by Ohlin, at note 45 below.

41 *Bumper Development Corporation Ltd* v. *Metropolitan Police Commissioner* [1991] 4 All ER 638.

42 *Arab Monetary Fund* v. *Hashim* (No. 3) [1991] 1 WLR 1362.

43 *Presbyterian Church of Sudan et al.* v. *Talisman Energy Inc* (13 June 2005) US DC for the Southern District of New York, holding that customary international law prohibiting violations of *ius cogens* norms such as genocide applies to private actors in addition to state actors. The Court held that the Supreme Court in *Sosa* v. *Alvarez-Machain* 124 S Ct 2739 (2004) explicitly contemplated the existence of corporate liability under customary international law.

44 This is most clearly reflected in Kelsen's account of legal capacity/personhood (Kelsen, note 36 above, 93): 'The concept of the legal person – who, by definition, is the subject of legal duties and legal rights – answers the need of imagining a bearer of the rights and duties … In reality, however, the legal person is not a separate entity besides '"its" duties and rights, but only their personified unity or – since duties and rights are legal norms – the personified unity of a set of legal norms.' In short, absent legal rights and duties there is no legal person: the creation of rights and duties creates and is the legal person.

Consequently, legal capacity cannot be transferred from one legal order to another, but may or may not be newly created in another order. By the same token, absence of legal capacity in one legal system does not mean a lack of capacity in another. Or, as a variation of this point, legal capacity for one purpose does not entail legal capacity for another: children cannot enter into contracts but have the capacity to be the bearers of human rights.

What does this entail for the corporate right to human rights? It simply means that the company's legal capacity under national legal orders (which itself is restricted) does not by itself entail an entitlement to human rights in the national, European, or international legal order. If, as in Europe, the decision is made to grant companies human rights, this confers legal capacity on companies, the legal capacity to be the beneficiaries of the rights in question: 'We do not ascribe human rights because an entity is a [legal] person – it is a person because we ascribe human rights to it.'[45] When the European Court of Human Rights asserts that a company enjoys a particular right *because* it is a legal person, it disguises the fact that its very decision to give a company certain human rights recognises the company as a legal person for human rights purposes; it makes it the subject capable of enjoying the right.[46] Which simply begs the question: why?

Human Rights for the Humanised Corporate Actor?

It is tempting to argue that human rights have been called *human* rights, as opposed to basic or fundamental rights, precisely because they were peculiarly designed for humans, to protect their specific needs and aspirations. Companies have simply taken what was not for them to take and, if anyone, it is the individuals behind the company who can be human rights victims. Yet, even if historically the term 'human rights' was chosen so as to preclude other persons or entities from enjoying them, it still leaves open the question as to whether, as a matter of principle, such exclusion is justified. If companies share certain characteristics which make human individuals worthy of human rights, then consistency demands extending them to companies.

The Historical Emergence of the 'Human' Cornerstone of Human Rights   From a historical perspective,[47] it is clear that corporations (and for that matter any other institution or collective) were not amongst the intended beneficiaries of modern human rights. Indeed, the ultimate triumph of the international human rights movement after the Second World War lies in the endorsement of the universality of human rights – a concept which makes the human being (and its needs and

---

45 Ohlin, note 30 above, 237, also: 'We do not determine that an entity is a [legal] person first and then chart the moral and legal consequences of that ascription later ... .'

46 So it is not inconceivable that human rights could be enjoyed by partnerships and associations which do not in their own right enjoy legal capacity under national law, although such entitlement would then require national law to give these groups of people the legal capacity to challenge any alleged breaches.

47 For a useful discussion, see Mordecai Roshwald (1959), 'The Concept of Human Rights', *Philosophy and Phenomenological Research* 19: 354.

aspirations) the very cornerstone or essence of human rights.[48] No matter who you are and where and when you live, there are certain minimum rights all individuals possess, or ought to possess, by virtue of being human: 'The only place where the universal makes a royal appearance is in the discourse of human rights.'[49] While the concept of universality has had challenges from various quarters,[50] the Universal Declaration of Human Rights (1948) has been approved by virtually all States[51] and many human rights norms are today considered part of customary international law and even *ius cogens*.[52] Even the challengers of universality are hard pushed to deny the moral force in the idea of the inherent worth or dignity of every individual:[53]

> ... none of them is now prepared to submerge the individual completely. Utilitarians will not sanction slavery, or torture, even 'for the greatest good.' Communitarians increasingly recognize that a legitimate community can be maintained only with respect for individual human rights. Socialism recognizes that socialism is acceptable and viable only if it has a human face.[54]

Indeed, opposition to the current human rights regime seems rarely, if ever, based, on a rejection of the inherent worth and dignity of every individual, but rather on the belief that human rights may not the best means to protect it.[55]

The necessary link between the universality of human rights and their human beneficiaries is also apparent from earlier conceptions of basic rights which were not based on universality and thus neither extended to all humans nor limited to

---

48 Emberland, note 6 above, 37ff where the author comments on the 'inherent dignity' of the human being as a prominent value underlying the ECHR. By the same token, on the 'responsibility' front, the Nuremberg Tribunal in 1945 stressed that war crimes were committed by men, not abstract entities.

49 Costas Douzinas (1996), 'Justice and Human Rights in Postmodernity' in Conor Gearty and Adam Tomkins (eds), *Understanding Human Rights* (London: Mansell) 115, 118. But not all agree, see, for example, Dine, note 3 above, 42: 'moral universalism was not generally accepted, i.e. the equal moral status of all human beings was not established.'

50 Classically, universalism is juxtapositioned to cultural relativism. For a description and rejection of cultural relativism, see Jerome J. Shestack (1998), 'The Philosophic Foundations of Human Rights' *Human Rights Quarterly* 20: 201, 228ff. For a critique on the abstract version of universalism or equality of current human rights from a feminist perspective, see Catherine A MacKinnon (1993), 'Crimes of War, Crimes of Peace' in Stephen Shute and Susan Hurley (eds), *On Human Rights* (The Oxford Amnesty Lectures) (New York: Basic Books) 83.

51 Similarly, almost all States have incorporated these human rights into their national constitutions: Louis Henkin (1989), 'The Universality of the Concept of Human Rights' *Annals of the American Academy of Political and Social Science* 506: 10, 13.

52 Para. 701 of the *Restatement (Third) of the Foreign Relations Law* (US, 1987), note 4.

53 There are a number of human rights theorists who sought to construct the entire catalogue of human rights on the basis of human dignity. See Shestack, note 50 above, 224ff. See also Emberland, note 6 above, 37ff, noting that human dignity is one of the fundamental values underlying the ECHR.

54 Henkin, note 51 above, 14.

55 R. Jayakumuur Nayar (1996), 'Not Another Theory of Human Rights!' in Conor Gearty and Adam Tomkins (eds), *Understanding Human Rights* (London: Mansell) 170, 186ff.

them. For example, the English Magna Carta of 1215, often cited as one significant predecessor of modern human rights, granted basic rights to *freemen*, thus excluding 'a great proportion of the population ... from the enjoyment of certain rights and liberties'.[56] Also as rights were not granted to man *qua* human being, but – consistent with feudal conception of society – on the basis of class, early 'corporate' rights were unproblematic. Article 1 of the Magna Carta provides: 'The English Church shall be free and shall have her rights entire and her liberties inviolate.'[57] This is a right 'belonging to a corporate body – an approach typical of the political and legal conceptions of feudalism'.[58]

The decisive step towards the humanisation of basic rights occurred with the rise of secular 'natural law' theories in the seventeenth century,[59] most prominently by John Locke,[60] who reconceived rights as being based on the 'law of nature'. Thus individuals – 'who are by nature all free, equal, and independent' – enjoy rights on the basis of their human nature.[61] And as these rights are a gift of nature, individuals cannot divest themselves of them; they are inalienable and it is the function of the government to protect them.[62] Although Locke's ideas shine through all modern human rights documents, they also formed the philosophical basis for their predecessors, the French Declaration of the Rights of Man and Citizens (1789) and the US Declaration of Independence (1776). Yet, neither instrument accorded rights universally. One commentator notes in respect of the latter document: 'It is sobering to note ... that while we amended the Constitution to include the Bill of Rights and continued the Declaration of Independence, we maintained slavery for another eighty years, maintained racial discrimination for a hundred years more, and limited suffrage until recently.'[63]

So despite the rhetoric about 'the natural, unalienable, and sacred rights of man',[64] clearly not all *men* were man-enough for human rights. Human rights were still tied to the 'achievement of status and the attainment of qualities that would admit one to political society, to civil society, and, indeed, full humanity.'[65] They were (at times

---

56 Roshwald, note 47 above, 363ff.

57 Ibid., 363.

58 Ibid.

59 The origins of natural law are generally traced back to antiquity by the Greek Stoics and then the Romans, followed later by St Thomas Aquinas, who understood natural law as part of divine law. See, for example, Shestack, note 50 above.

60 John Locke (1690), *Two Treatises of Government*.

61 Roshwald, note 47 above, 364ff.

62 Christian Tomuschat (2003), *Human Right – Between Idealism and Realism* (Oxford: Oxford University Press), 11.

63 Henkin, note 51 above, 12.

64 Preamble to the French Declaration of the Rights of Man and Citizens.

65 Gershon Shafir (2004), 'Citizenship and Human Rights in an Era of Globalization' in Alison Brysk and Gershon Shafir (eds), *People Out of Place* (London: Routledge), 11, 16.

expressly so[66]) the prerogative of citizens,[67] those who had the 'maturity, however defined, to share in political power … [and as] personhood was yoked to property, human rights hinged on property ownership.'[68] Companies who often try to portray themselves as good citizens, are generally not recognised as citizens in law. For example, in the US, it was held that a citizen can only be a natural person, a member of the body politic, owing allegiance to the state, and not artificial persons created by the legislature, possessing only the attributes which the legislature has prescribed.[69] So the corporate person was regarded as lacking certain essential attributes, such as a possible allegiance to the State, which makes it unworthy of citizenship.[70] But lack of citizenship did not prevent companies from enjoying certain rights of man. This is not surprising given the underlying focus of the rights of man on property ownership. The right to a fair trial, adopted with freed slaves in mind, was soon more successfully deployed by companies than its intended beneficiaries.[71]

But times have changed: citizenship (whether or not racist or sexist) and property ownership no longer provide the entry ticket to human rights: '… with the "emancipation" of human rights from reliance on citizenship did their universal character come to assume its proper place.'[72] Basing human rights simply on the humanity of its beneficiaries makes them all inclusive as far as humans are concerned, but equally excludes all non-human beneficiaries, whether animals, churches, or companies. Thus, bar making out a compelling case for an exception, corporate human rights are as much an anachronism as basing human rights on citizenship or property ownership.

---

66 See, for example, Articles 6, 7, 11, 12, 13 and 14 of the French Declaration of the Rights of Man and Citizens. See also the US case of *Fire Department of City of New York* v. *Stanton* 51 NYS 242(1898).

67 See *Scott* v. *Sandford* 60 US (19 How.) 393 (1857), where the Court held that US citizenship is enjoyed by white persons born in the US as descendents of 'persons, who were at the time of the adoption of the Constitution recognized as citizens in the several States' and those migrants who had been naturalized.

68 Shafir, note 65 above (internal marks omitted).

69 *Paul* v. *Virginia* 8 Wall 168 (1868); see also *Fire Department of City of New York* v. *Stanton* 51 NYS 242 (1898) where the Court said: 'Corporations may be "persons" within the fourteenth amendment to the constitution of the United States, and as such within the provision that no state shall deprive any person of life, liberty, or property without due process of law, or deny to any person within its jurisdiction the equal protection of the law. They are not, however, "citizens" within the meaning of this or any other clause in the constitution.' But note in Ireland, corporations have been able to enjoy constitutional rights *qua* citizens since *Irish Rail and Bernard Patrick Dowling* v. *AG* (HC, 28 April 1995, Keane J). Generally, see M. Bovens (1998), 'The Corporate Republic: Complex Organisations and Citizenship' in E Christodoulidis (ed.), *Communitarianism and Citizenship* (Aldershot: Ashgate).

70 As citizenship and human rights have often run parallel, interacted, or overlapped, it would be interesting, but beyond this discussion, to compare the treatment of corporate persons with respect to both concepts; raised as an issue in Bottomley, note 4 above, 62.

71 Bakan, note 2 above, 16.

72 Shafir, note 65 above, 16ff.

Companies as Derivative Right-holders   What may appear to be the most persuasive argument in favour of corporate human rights is to see the company as a derivative right-holder: corporate human rights are held by companies for the benefit of its natural protagonists, its shareholders but also its directors and employees.[73] Companies, unlike individuals, have no intrinsic worth:

> Rather, their worth is extrinsic and stems from the benefits flowing to the natural individuals involved ... the death of a corporation is cause for concern only for its effects on individuals ... By contrast, the death of an individual may be cause for concern regardless of its consequences, because the life of an individual has an intrinsic moral worth.[74]

Letting the company enforce these rights ensures that they are enforced efficiently and fairly.[75] One practical problem with this argument is that 'we should be wary of assuming that all people within a corporation are equally placed. In granting human rights protection to a corporation we may simply be enhancing the interests or power of corporate managers or majority shareholders at the expense of minority shareholders or employees.'[76]

Holding that companies are derivative rights-holders is also problematic simply because the law does not treat them as such. Often there is no infringement of the relevant right of the natural protagonist. For example, in the above-mentioned case *Société Colas Est* v. *France*, where the company's privacy was held to have been infringed by searches of corporate offices, it would be impossible to argue that the act violated in any way the shareholders' right to privacy. Their investment may have suffered as a result of the search and subsequent conviction, and thus their property rights may indirectly have been interfered with, but not their right to privacy. Given the legal separation of corporate property from shareholder property, a search of corporate premises is not a search of shareholder premises and thus cannot amount to a violation of the shareholders' right to privacy. If companies were simply derivative holders of the human rights of its shareholders (and perhaps directors and employees), the human rights enforceable by companies would have to reflect the interest of the stakeholder in the company. In the case of shareholders, this would be limited to the interests of the shareholder flowing from their shares, that is, financial and association rights, and this in turn would no doubt limit the number of actions and appropriate rights significantly. The legal reality is that companies have always been treated as having rights in their own right and not merely as derivative right-

---

73 The derivative argument is also addressed by Grear, note 2 above , 517ff.

74 Ohlin, note 30 above, 227.

75 Generally, this is one of the rationales for not allowing minority or even majority shareholders to bring actions for acts directed against the company. See Dignam and Allen, note 12 above, 178ff. Under ECHR, the shareholders have to show that it is 'impossible for the company to apply to the Convention Institutions through the organs set up under its articles of incorporation' *Agrotexim* v. *Greece* (1995) 21 EHRR 250, paras 65–6. Applied by the Commission in *JW* v. *Poland* 00027917/95 (1997), *Penton* v. *Turkey* 24463/94 (1994) and *Credit and Industrial Bank and Moravec* v. *Czeck Republic* 00029010/95 (1998).

76 Bottomley, note 4 above, 64.

holders. Unlike unincorporated organisations, they never had to show that a member has been affected by the act in question.[77] The question is whether companies can persuasively be held to enjoy human rights in their own right.

Companies as Right-holders in their Own Right   An argument in favour of corporate human rights could be that human beings enjoy human rights not simply 'because they are human – a contention which is overtly speciesist and … [unacceptable] on moral and intellectual grounds',[78] but on the basis of values or attributes inherent in all humans. If others, such as animals, trees, or companies, share these qualifying attributes they should also benefit from human rights.[79] While this argument seems relatively straightforward, it raises difficult questions within the deep and murky waters of human rights jurisprudence.

What makes humans worthy of rights, and more specifically human rights, has been disputed for centuries: [80]

> Is it the faculty of reason, or perhaps, the faculty of discourse? But a full-grown horse or dog is beyond comparison a more rational, as well as a more conversable animal, than an infant of a day, or a week, or even a month old. But suppose the case were otherwise, what would it avail? The question is not, Can they reason?, nor, Can they talk? But Can they suffer?[81]

More pervasive than the capacity to suffer, to experience pleasure and pain,[82] as a basis of rights has been the notion of moral agency and the rational, self-willing agent:

> the idea of rights is based on a view of the human individual as essentially a thinking agent, endowed with an ability to deliberate morally, to see things from others' point of view, and to transcend a preoccupation with his or her own particular or sectional interests.[83]

The will or choice theories of rights have been crowded into the background by interests theories of rights which focus on the 'needy [embodied] individual whose

---

77 Note 16 above. Grear, note 2 above, 518, arguing that even if the corporate right was treated as type of group right, it would still not be a right of its *human* protagonists, given that the focus of a group right is 'the subject' rather than the 'object' of the right which in the corporate case is the non-human corporation: 'A corporation holds its rights as a unitary entity, rather than a collective.'

78 Mike Radford (1996), 'Can Rights Extend to Animals?' in Conor Gearty and Adam Tomkins (eds), *Understanding Human Rights* (London: Mansell) 403, 417.

79 Other organisational actors such as partnerships may shares these attributes quite regardless of whether or not the law recognises them as distinct entities for other purposes.

80 Particularly in respect of borderline cases, such as intelligent animals on the one hand and on the other hand the very young, the very old and the mentally defective' Radford, note 78 above, 417. See also Ohlin, note 30 above.

81 Bentham discussed in Radford, note 78 above, 408.

82 Radford, note 78 above, 407.

83 Jeremy Waldron cited in Gourevitch, note 37 above, 2. See also, Shestack, note 50 above, 216.

vital interests need protection'[84] and according to which the dignity of the individual is preserved by protecting his welfare, rather than his liberty. And finally, there are also those who dispute the value of any search for the foundation of human rights.[85] For the purposes of this discussion, it is unnecessary to decide on the most persuasive basis, if any, of human rights, because, it is argued, companies do not satisfy any of them. Even if it is accepted that companies have a capacity to make autonomous decisions[86] (which itself is not uncontroversial) or have worthy interests and needs, these things are not in any meaningful way comparable to the *human* capacities, interests or needs and thus do not justify treating companies en par with humans for human rights purposes.

(a) The company – an autonomous moral agent   There is a widespread school of thought which doubts whether the company can have a capacity to reason or make any autonomous choices. According to the 'legal fiction' theorists, the company has no existence or reality other than in law; it is merely the sum total of the relevant legal rules:

> [The company] has neither body, parts, nor passions. It cannot wear weapons or serve in wars. It can be neither loyal, nor disloyal. It cannot compass treason. It can be neither friend nor enemy. Apart from its corporators it can have neither thoughts, wishes, nor intentions, for it has no mind other than the minds of the corporators.[87]

---

84 Gourevitch, note 37 above, 1 and 18ff. Other proponents, for example, Nayar, note 55 above; Grear, note 2 above, 520, insisting on 'human embodiment and vulnerability as the ethical foundation of human rights'.

85 Richard Rorty (1993), 'Human Rights, Rationality, and Sentimentality' in Stephen Shute and Susan Hurley (eds), *On Human Rights* (New York: Basic Books), 111, 114ff (also on the decline of interest in our essential human nature as a prerequisite for human righrs). See also John Rawls, 'The Law of Peoples' in Shute and Hurley (eds), ibid., 41, 68; Rawls denies that human rights 'depend on any particular comprehensive moral doctrine or philosophical conception of human nature, such as, for example, that human beings are moral persons and have equal worth, or that they have certain particular moral or intellectual powers that entitle them to these rights.' He continues: 'This would require a quite deep philosophical theory that many if not most hierarchical societies might reject as liberal or democratic, or in some way distinctive of the Western political tradition and prejudicial to other cultures. We therefore take a different tack and say that basic human rights express a minimum standard of well-ordered political institutions for all peoples who belong ... to a just political society of peoples.'

86 For such an argument, see Christopher Harding (2007), *Criminal Enterprise: Individuals, Organisations and CriminalResponsibility* (Collumpton, UK: Willan Publishing), Ch. 3.

87 *Continental Tyre and Rubber Co* v. *Daimler* (1915) 1 QB 893, 916 (Buckley LJ, dissenting). More recently, *Meridian Global Funds Management Asia Ltd* v. *Securities Commission* (1995) 2 AC 500, 506f (Lord Hoffman): 'There is in fact no such thing as the company as such, no ding an sich, only the applicable rules.'

If the company is viewed as no more than a legal 'thought bubble',[88] there is no person which could have the attributes necessary for human rights enjoyment. The only reasons, intentions, feelings the company has are those of its human participants which are imputed by law or otherwise to the company: 'The concept of the legal person – who, by definition, is the subject of legal duties and legal rights – answers the need of imagining a bearer of the rights and duties ... In reality, however, the legal person is not a separate entity besides "its" duties and rights, but only their personified unity.'[89] The view of companies as a mere artificial construct is just one of the theories about the nature of companies – theories which have been triggered by changing corporate landscapes over the last two centuries. Two developments significantly contributed to the view of the company as a real entity in its own right which is essential if it is to be the bearer of attributes such as rationality or sentiency.

Initially, companies were conceived of as much as a vehicle of, and for, the State as its investors. The chartered company, the forerunner of the modern registered company, was essentially 'a "franchise" (Norman-French "privilege"): i.e., the very existence of the corporation was conditioned upon a grant from the state'.[90] This grant entailed privileges, such as a monopoly over public utilities,[91] in which the State had a significant interest, and the charters were individually negotiated with the State, culminating in tightly State-controlled agreements.[92] So not surprisingly, these companies were seen as instruments created by and for the State – a notion which is reflected in the 'concession theory' of companies.[93] The introduction of the modern registered company, in Britain in 1844,[94] undermined that notion.[95] It made incorporation a matter of administrative procedure, granting equal access rather than being limited to worthy individuals and subjecting the new companies to standardised legal requirements.[96] Despite residues of the initial concession theory

---

88 See the discussion in Harding, note 86 above, Ch. 4. Note this view is a reductionist argument from below: whenever there are facts at different levels, it is always the lowest-level facts which matter. This has led some to deny the existence of 'upper-level facts' such as social facts.

89 Kelsen, note 36 above, p. 93. He also states: 'The law, sharing the tendency to abstract and universalize, turns concrete people into generalized legal subjects. But the legal subject is a fiction and the natural (legal) subject is infinitely more fictitious than the corporate. The legal subject is a *persona*, a mask or blindfold put on real people who, unlike the abstractions of moral philosophy, suffer pain.'

90 A.A. Berle and G.C. Means (1932), *The Modern Corporation and Private Property* (London: Transaction Publishers), 120.

91 William W. Bratton (1981), 'The New Economic Theory of the Firm: Critical Perspectives from History' *Stanford Law Review* 41: 1471, 1484.

92 Berle and Means, note 90 above, 122.

93 Bratton, note 91 above, 1475, 1483ff.

94 Companies Registration and Regulation Act 1944.

95 Eilis Feran (1999), *Company Law and Corporate Finance* (Oxford: Oxford University Press), 8ff.

96 Yet, the new legislation on both sides of the Atlantic was still spurned by the State's desire to facilitate large-scale undertakings requiring large investments such as the building of railways. The overnight success of companies and their ingenuity in circumventing the rigid State-imposed restrictions quickly paved the way for more relaxed, privately ordered

in modern company law,[97] today access to the company seems hardly a 'product of sovereign grace'.[98]

Not only did the corporate person cut its conceptual tie from the State, but it also separated itself from its investors. The emergence and rapid economic dominance of large companies in the late nineteenth century[99] was accompanied by a shift of shareholders from active participants into passive, constantly fluctuating investors,[100] whose investment was managed by salaried expert managers.[101] The surge of this new management company made it conceptually less sound to see the company as a mere device of its shareholders or the personification of their collective will.[102] Indeed, the result was that the company was increasingly viewed as an institution or creature in its own right.[103]

An explanation for this rather curious phenomenon was proffered by Walther Rathenau:

> The depersonalisation of ownership simultaneously implies the objectification of the thing owned. The claims to ownership are subdivided in such a fashion, and are so mobile, that the enterprise assumes an independent life, as if it belonged to no one, such as in earlier day was embodied only in state and church … .[104]

Like a child cutting the cord to both its parents, the company grew up into a person in its own right, making itself heard across the industrial world, standing on its own feet, with its own reality and personality. Indeed, given the economic, social and political reality of companies today, it seems fictitious to hold that the company is a fiction which 'exists only in the contemplation of law'.[105] The company itself is more than real to the employee who has just been made redundant, the manager taking home his end-of-year bonuses, the consumer pleased to have made a bargain at the sales, the 12-year-old worker in the Indonesian factory, the tennis player having landed a sponsorship deal, or the NGO investigating corporate practices.

---

company law regimes. For a concise historical overview see Paul L. Davies (1997), *Gower's Principles of Modern Company Law* (London: Sweet & Maxwell, 6th edn), Chs 2, 3.

97 Remnants of the concession idea were, and are to some extent, still apparent in various forms and guises. For example, in the UK companies were until recently restricted by the notion of limited capacity (that is, they could not act beyond their stated objects) consistent with the notion of the company as a statutory, state-controlled fictional device created for a limited purpose.

98 Bratton, note 91 above, 1486.

99 For possible reasons see Bratton, note 91 above, 1488f.

100 Excellently described in Berle and Means, note 90 above, 64ff.

101 The first classic account of the separation of ownership and control and its consequences, Berle and Means, note 90 above.

102 Particularly as the managers' (legitimate and illegitimate) interests are often divergent from those of the shareholders. See Bratton, note 91 above, 1496.

103 Janet Dine (2000), *The Governance of Corporate Groups* (Cambridge: Cambridge University Press), 34ff.

104 Berle and Means, note 90 above, 309.

105 *Continental Tyre and Rubber Co* v. *Daimler* (1915) 1 QB 893, 916 (Buckley LJ, dissenting).

The understanding of companies as "real" social facts, as 'a real thing having an existence, like a spiritual being',[106] is captured by the realist theory which dates back to the German theorists in the nineteenth century and was later recycled in the political theory.[107] Bakan describes companies in such realist terms: 'Now viewed as an entity, not imaginary or fictitious, but real, not artificial but natural ... the corporation had been reconceived as a free and independent being ... The logic was that, conceived as natural entities analogous to human beings, corporation should be created as free individual.'[108]

Even judges who, true to their profession, tend to support the legal fiction theory, have on occasion slipped onto realist territory. Companies have been held to be capable of having the attributes of an enemy, a conscience and 'feelings ... [and] feeling aggrieved'.[109]

The realist theory often provokes the humanisation of the company but this is neither necessary nor justified. According to the realists, companies are organisational actors which are as real as human actors, which is not to say that they are *like* humans. Humanisation simply allows us to be mentally lazy and not to make the 'effort of imagination which conceptualises rationality and action in a non-human form'.[110] Some may defend the anthropomorphic corporate view on the basis that corporate actions and rationality are necessarily the result of those *human* actors behind the company. Yet, there is ample evidence that the individual morality or rationality often transforms in the group setting: 'The decision-making capacity of certain groups melds the individual intentions into a corporate intention that is often different from the intentions of any of the members of the group ... [The corporate] acts are not understandable unless they are conceptualised as part of a larger process.'[111]

Within this collective entity, the individual is subordinated – he or she, in his or her peculiarity, becomes irrelevant and replaceable.[112] The tune to which everybody in the group dances is played by the entity itself through its corporate or collective ethos, which often prompts individuals to act in ways they would not otherwise do.[113] In large companies, '[m]ultiple layers of control and ownership insulate individuals from a sense of responsibility'[114] and 'dilute individual moral ... responsibility among groups of business people'. Examples of such double-

---

106 Bratton, note 91 above, 1475.

107 Most notably Otto von Gierke. For a succinct summary of the various theories, see Ferran, note 95 above, 8ff. On the realist theory: David Foxton (2002), 'Corporate Personality in the Great War' *Law Quarterly Review* 118: 428.

108 Bakan, note 2 above, 16 (internal marks omitted).

109 Respectively, *Daimler Co Ltd* v. *Continental Tyre and Rubber Co (Great Brtiain) Ltd* [1916] 2 AC 307; *Winkworth* v. *Edwards Baron Development Co Ltd* [1987] 1 All ER 114, 118; *Re Lindsay Bowman Ltd* [1969] 3 ALL ER 601, 604.

110 Harding, note 86 above, 10.

111 Larry May and Stacey Hoffman (eds) (1991), *Collective Responsibility: Five Decades of Debate in Theoretical and Applied Ethics* (Rowman & Littlefied), 3 (Introduction).

112 Harding, note 86 above, 11.

113 Ibid., 12.

114 Beth Stephens (2002), 'The Amorality of Profit: Transnational Corporations and Human Rights' *Berkeley Journal of International Law* 20: 45, 46.

lives, with one determined by the group or corporate culture, abound, ranging from the extreme to the inconspicuous. In Nazi Germany, SS officers would spend their working hours in concentration camps killing hundreds including children without a second thought, only to return home to be caring fathers and mothers. The corporate ethos of NHS hospitals in Britain dictates that lateness, no matter how unreasonable, is not apologised for; so even doctors with otherwise good manners shed all skins of etiquette when entering their workplace. The important point to note is that just because an organisation is formed by, and made up of, individuals does not entail that it is humanised. Indeed, at times the reverse appears to happen: the organisation dehumanises its human participants – not in the sense of making them evil, but in terms of stripping them of their 'normal' rationality, morality and autonomy, making them interlocking wheels in the corporate clock.[115] As an aside, it should be stressed that just because individuals often shed their moral responsibilities when entering organisations,[116] does not mean this is morally right and should be legally condoned.

So what makes the company tick? If the company does not inherit the humanity of its actors, what is its personality and is this personality deserving of human rights protection? The ethos or cultures of companies vary, just as the personalities of humans vary. But as all humans share common qualities,[117] so it is with companies. One such trait is that companies can often outperform individuals in realising the mission for which they are created; they are 'remarkably efficient economic entities [and] formidably effective and swift machines'.[118] Perhaps this is simply because they can pursue it more single-mindedly, unhampered by human mortality and morality. In the case of trading companies, the single mission is profit maximisation.[119] Indeed, the law allows their controllers no other final aim.[120] Moral concern is permitted to the extent to which it increases profits – a contradiction in terms. From the point of view of the economist, companies are the perfect rational actor: 'the lack of emotions and feelings promote rather than hinder considered rational choice.'[121] Everything is reducible to a price, allowing for a clear cost-benefit analysis. Rational from an economist's point of view companies may be, but moral they are not:

---

115 Bratton, note 91 above, 1486.

116 See also Gobert and Punch, note 3 above, Ch. 1 on the roots of corporate criminality and the behaviour of individuals within the corporation.

117 This is in fact an overgeneralization; see, for example, Ohlin, note 30 above, on the difficulty, even impossibility, of isolating the relevant attribute that all humans or human rights beneficiaries share.

118 Stephens, note 114 above, 56 (internal marks omitted).

119 Bakan, note 2 above, 35: 'Corporations are not institutions that are set up to be moral entities ... they are institutions which have really only one mission, that is to increase shareholder value.'

120 *Hutton* v. *West Cork Railway Company* (1883) 23 Ch D 654 where the judge famously stated: 'The law does not say that there are to be no cakes and ale, but there are to be no cakes and ale except such as are required for the benefit of the company.'

121 Brent Fisse and John Braithwaite (1993), *Corporations, Crime and Accountability* (Cambridge: Cambridge University Press) 30ff.

the pursuit of profit is, by definition, an amoral goal – not necessarily immoral, but rather morally neutral. An individual or business will achieve the highest level of profit by weighing all decisions according to a self-serving economic scale.[122]

There is ample evidence – both past and present – that companies lack genuine moral concern. IBM supplied the Nazis with a data management system which was instrumental in the extermination program, but:

> IBM's motivation for working with the Nazis … was never about Nazism … it was always about profit, which is consistent with the corporation's amoral nature. Corporations have no capacity to value political systems, fascist or democratic, for reasons of principle or ideology. The only legitimate question for a corporation is whether a political system serves or impedes its self-interested purposes.[123]

IBM was not the only company which benefited from the Second World War and neither is this period a historic aberration. Today it is environmental destruction, support of dictatorships, suppression of democratic protest, corrupting governments and violating labour and children's rights on a grand scale in developing countries which is written on the corporate slate: 'These and a thousand other points of darkness, from Bhopal and the *Exxon Valdez* to epidemic levels of worker injury and death and chronic destruction of the environment, are the price we all pay for the corporation's flawed character.'[124] Good deeds of companies are done to gain a competitive advantage via the media and when corners can be cut quietly this will be done and this could not be otherwise. The character of the company has remained fundamentally unchanged.

The problem for human rights purposes is not that the company's character is morally flawed. The human character is hardly angelic: self-interest and the desire for personal profit are the very human motives upon which capitalism is based. The problem is that the company is monorail: it enshrines and institutionally legitimises self-interest and profit. The company has the capacity to understand, and reason with, one thing: profit.[125] The company's rationality is simple and predictable: it is limited to processing information for profit purposes. There is no moral understanding or reasoning; beauty, art or suffering are incomprehensible to the corporate amoral mind. There is only a soulless machine.[126] As such, the company is a far cry from the autonomous self-willing moral agent who provides the core and *raison d'être* of human rights under the liberal tradition.

(b) Corporate interests and needs? Corporate human rights are *prima facie* perhaps less difficult to accommodate under the interest theory of rights. According

---

122 Stephens, note 114 above, 47. See also Bakan, note 2 above, 79, citing Frank H. Easterbrook, and Daniel R. Fischel: '… the corporation feels no moral obligation to obey the law. Only people have moral obligations … Corporations can no more be said to have moral obligations than does a building, an organization chard, or a contract.'

123 Bakan, note 2 above, 88 (internal marks omitted).

124 Ibid., 73.

125 This is of course not so in the case of charitable and other not-for-profit companies.

126 Descartes' view of animals, see Radford, note 78 above, 405.

to this theory, rights are interests or needs that ought to be protected by law through restraints imposed on the acts of others. As under this theory, rights 'derive not from the liberty of the individual, but from the moral philosopher's conception of the good',[127] it has always been capable of accommodating more rights, such as social, economic and cultural rights, and more subjects, such as children and mentally handicapped people, than could the will theory.

Having said that, MacCormick argues, it makes no sense to speak of (pre-legal) rights in relation to treatment which is justifiable only by reference to some greater utility: 'such arguments are necessarily inept in justifying the ascription to them of a right to that treatment. Consider the oddity of saying that turkeys have a right to be well fed in order to be fat for the Christmas table, or of saying that children have a right to care and nurture lest they become a charge on the taxpayer.'[128] In other words, the right must relate to a treatment which, if withheld, would be wrong in itself. This certainly would foreclose pre-legal corporate rights as any treatment of the corporation could never be justified by reference to the well-being of the corporation itself.[129]

One profound objection to the interest theory of rights is that it cannot easily justify why rights are needed at all. Interests and needs may be protected through duties and powers, with rights being not obviously necessary.[130] When interest-theory advocates respond by saying that rights language is 'useful because it carries with it a certain peremptory force appropriate for weighty issues',[131] they piggy-back on the moral force derived from the will-based theory of rights.[132] So, even the interest-theory of rights ultimately depends on a certain sacredness of rights as a necessary aspect of rights. And this need then significantly narrows the initial proposition that a right is any interest that ought to be protected by law through some constraint on the activity of others. It creates the need to distinguish between different interests and isolate the worthiest. In the human rights context, the parameter for this selection process has been 'human nature'. It has led to an examination of the pre-political 'human nature' in order to identify the basic human needs the fulfilment of which is necessary for a dignified life. Grear, for example, argues:

> The ethical appeal of human embodiment as a foundation for human rights is directly linked to the fact that our embodiment is the source of our vulnerability … Embodied vulnerability also has the virtue of lying close to the heart of the founding impulse of the UDHR as a response to the starkly material suffering imposed during the Nazi holocaust.[133]

---

127 Gourevitch, note 37 above, 19.

128 MacCormick, note 38 above, 159.

129 Clearly, as the whole point of the company is to create a subject of rights and obligations, the company ought to enjoy some rights, for example, the right to sue and be sued in its own name, hold property, and so on, as otherwise its object is defeated.

130 Gourevitch, note 37 above, 20ff.

131 Ibid., 21.

132 Ibid., 21.

133 Grear, note 2 above, 539. See also, Nayar, note 55 above.

Without further elaboration, it is beyond argument that the company falls outside these parameters; corporate needs and interests bear no resemblance to basic human needs and interests such as life, absence of pain, food, shelter, and so on, which provide the common foundations of human rights.

Ultimately, the above arguments confirm the obvious, namely that human rights are exactly that: rights for humans. They are rights which are – depending on which theory one favours – designed to protect the human either as an autonomous moral agent or his or her peculiar human needs and interests. In either case, allowing companies to enter the picture is to seriously distort what is meant by moral agency or human welfare. Jurisprudentially corporate human rights violate the parameters of the human rights framework.

So why have companies actually been given human rights? Psychologically, they may simply have benefited from the lucky combination of a lack of physicality on the one hand and the legal rhetoric of personhood on the other hand. The latter creates the mental pictures of individuality and humanity and the former means there is no physical reminder as to how non-human they in fact are. Politically, the company is the vehicle for, and embodiment of, capitalism; giving it human rights strongly protects trade, profit and property and thus reinforces the market economy – often at the expense of other interests, such as those of workers, consumer interests and civil society.[134] Whatever may be the actual reasons behind corporate human rights, jurisprudentially it is difficult to justify them.

Corporate Human Rights Benefit Society

A pragmatic jurist may discard any theoretical difficulties and indeed the usefulness of such foundational inquiries: 'There is a growing willingness to neglect the question "What is our nature?" and to substitute the question "What can we make of ourselves?"'[135] And perhaps with corporate human rights we can make more of ourselves than without them. Rabossi argues that 'philosophers should think of this [human rights] culture as a new, welcome fact of the post-Holocaust world. They should stop trying to get behind or beneath this fact.'[136]

... by promoting a healthy market economy and democracy? A pragmatist could, for example, assert that when a company exercises its right to freedom of commercial expression through advertising,[137] shareholders, managers and employees may benefit from increased sales. Consumers may also benefit from a more competitive, information-rich market place which allows the best product to succeed. Employment

---

134 Grear, note 2 above, 534: 'Human rights, and their precursors natural rights, emerge as deeply enmeshed with liberal capitalism. This aspect of human rights discourse emerges as a fully identifiable conception intimately linked to the elevation of property and corporate sovereignty … global corporations take advantage of a legal discourse that is structurally and ideologically well suited to them.'

135 Rorty, note 85 above, 115.

136 Discussed in ibid.

137 See Chapter 8 below.

is efficiently channelled into these products and all this makes for a healthy market economy beneficial to civil society as a whole. Corporate human rights may also have positive democratic repercussions. When a media company exercises its right to freedom of expression through critical news reporting, it acts as a watchdog over government and thereby strengthens governmental accountability and democracy.[138] How convincing are these consequentialist arguments?

Just because an activity, such as advertising, contributes to a well-functioning market economy does not entail that it should to be protected by human rights.[139] There are many activities upon which a market economy depends which are not, need not and should not be protected by human rights. Shopping springs to mind. It is not rights-protected because it is neither considered profound enough nor likely to be illegitimately interfered with. If usefulness of an activity would be decisive, the list of would-be rights would be very long indeed. Yet, increasing the number of human rights is not unproblematic since, first, it creates a greater diffusion of priorities and more conflicts between competing rights and, secondly, as noted above, it inflates the currency of human rights and undermines the perception of sacredness upon which the effectiveness of human rights strongly depends.[140]

Appealing to the wider economic benefits of corporate human rights seems like an attempt to resurrect Adam Smith's idea that free trade, competition and choice can by itself create a happy world. Corporate human rights go hand in hand with Smith's *laissez-faire* philosophy in that they are invariably used as a shield against democratically legitimised State regulation – which is exactly what is necessary to overcome the short-comings of *laissez-faire*, including human rights violations. For example, it is public service broadcasting requirements which counteract the tendency of private media companies to dumb down, trivialise, scandalise, and effectively limit free expression and access to a wide variety of information. It is governmental interference and content requirements which ensure the quality of programming, rather than the absence of such restrictions. Similarly, the era of globalisation has given rise to a growing unease about multinational corporations: far from requiring human rights protection, multinational corporations are a threat to them, largely because they can evade or trade out of governmental regulation simply through their economic power and manipulation of jurisdictions. Granting them human rights worsens the situation rather than alleviates it: it is like taking the sling and stone from David and giving it to Goliath.

Democracy-based arguments are perhaps less easily swept aside, although of course most corporate activity does not directly fall within the public realm of

---

138 Raised as an argument in Bottomley, note 4 above, 62.

139 As happens at present in the EU and the US. See the discussion in Chapter 8 below.

140 For critical accounts of the usefulness of human rights, see Phillip Alston and Mary Robinson (eds) (2005), *Human Rights and Development – Towards Mutual Reinforcement* (Oxford: Oxford University Press); and see the discussion in Chapter 4 below. Assessing the effect of rights is notoriously difficult, see Phillip Alston (1984), 'Conjuring up New Human Rights: A Proposal for Quality Control' *American Journal of International Law* 78: 607. On the dangers of expanding the list of human rights beyond the traditional civil and political rights, see also Gourevitch , note 37 above, 27.

democratic governance.[141] One argument that may be advanced is that, for example, freedom of speech could often be enforced effectively through individual claims, for example, journalists or editors, without the need to resort to corporate free speech.[142] Having said that, publication or broadcasting decisions are generally corporate decisions with individual responsibility lurking only in the background. The article 'THE TRUTH' in *The Sun* was precisely what one may expect from that company regardless of the editor. It may be rather artificial to restrict the right to freedom of speech to the journalist rather than the real decision-maker: the company. Similarly governmental interferences with free speech through structural measures, such as licensing requirements, are first and foremost directed at companies and thus it would make sense to allow the corporation rather than the individual to assert the right.

… by strengthening the rule of law?   It can also be argued that corporate human rights, particularly procedural rights – flowing from the rule of law (that is, the notion of the *Rechtsstaat*) – provide a wider public good by ensuring that the State upholds the rule of law generally.[143] By allowing companies to insist, for example, on defence rights, such the right to a fair trial, judicial impartiality, the presumption of innocence, or equality of treatment and foreseeability of legal obligations, these standards are strengthened for the benefit of all.

This argument has also been advanced to explain why even individuals whose abhorrent activities seem to disentitle them from human rights protection should still benefit from them.[144] There it is used to bolster the claim of those who appear to have forgone their prima facie entitlement to human rights protection; it is a secondary argument to resurrect a primary claim in certain limited circumstances by appealing to the wider benefits of providing protection. Yet, in respect of companies, that primary entitlement is precisely what is under consideration, and so this secondary argument seems much less appropriate. To make the above argument a primary argument for corporate human rights also creates circularity: the question (and not the answer) is whether not giving companies certain human rights, such as privacy, would reinforce the rule of law and the notion of the *Rechtsstaat*. The question too is whether denying companies, for example, the right to a fair trial would violate the requirements of the rule of law; so again this cannot be the answer. Put it another way: should rabbits and kangaroos also have the right to a fair trial on the basis that it would strengthen compliance with rule of law requirements? Exactly.

We are not morally offended by arbitrary governmental inference against companies *per se*, but the direct or indirect interference with the interests of those associated with the company. Take, for example, the recent case of Yukos, Russia's

---

141 See Emberland, note 6 above, 39ff, discussing 'democracy' as one of the fundamental values underlying the ECHR, as well as the relationship between private enterprise and liberal democracy, and 120f noting the mismatch between the democracy justification of the right to free speech and 'commercial speech'.

142 On the uncertainty as to who enjoys the freedom of expression see Eric Barendt (2005), *Freedom of Speech* (Oxford, Oxford University Press, 2nd edn), 418, 441ff.

143 See Emberland, note 6 above, 44ff; Steve Foster (2003), *Human Rights and Civil Liberties* (London: Pearson), 12ff.

144 Foster, ibid.

biggest oil company, which was seized by Russian authorities and sold at undervalue to a state-owned company.[145] The international outcry against the action of the Russian State was directed at the trial and conviction (to nine years' imprisonment) of Mikhail Khordorkovsky, the CEO and largest shareholder of Yukos. Khordorkovsky's conviction was ostensibly based on the legitimate grounds of tax evasion and fraud, but in fact was designed to counteract the Kremlin's fear of the company's charismatic pro-democracy leader and politically motivated the trial. This and the illegitimate expropriation of Khordorkovsky are objectionable, but does it really matter what happens to the company *per se* – provided the *human* protagonists, such as shareholders and directors, are adequately compensated and not otherwise subjected to arbitrary state action? It is unlikely that a legal treatment of companies which was more robust than that tolerable for individuals (for example, reducing the criminal burden of proof for companies) would tarnish a State's commitment to the rule of law or be perceived as such.

... by strengthening the claims for corporate duties?   Last but not least, it has been argued that by granting companies human rights, it will be easier to impose duties on them: 'one potential benefit from granting human rights protections to corporations is that we might sharpen the claim that corporations owe human rights responsibilities to others.'[146] This proposition seems defensible in so far as responsibilities depend on rational agency – just as, according to some, rights do. So at times the granting of rights has 'spurred a corresponding movement to subject corporations to the same criminal liability as regular citizens'.[147] But does the logic behind no-rights-without-responsibilities really apply to the human rights framework?

Human rights are 'designed to reconcile the effectiveness of state power with the protection against that same state power'.[148] The State is given the power to protect the public good, which it may misuse. Human rights are to guard against abuses in the form either of arbitrary public power or the tyranny of the majority:

> The progression of human rights law has been in the direction of according protection to individuals against their States, with the "anti-State" stance flowing from the assumption

---

145 Christina Koningisor (2005), 'Supply and Demand on the Volga – A Tale of Russia's Martha Stewart' (21 April), *The College Hill Independent*, at <http://www.theindy.com>, commenting on the wider cost of such State actions: '... while Putin may have eliminated potential opposition, such political rivals were not the only casualties of the president's attempt to consolidate power; when Khodorkovsky's oil company was later sold at a fraction of its value to a state-owned company. Foreign investors who feared the return of nationalization began to flee. Confidence in the stability of the market, so crucial to foreign investment, was the price of Khodorkovsky's arrest. According to *The Washington Post*, capital flight from Russia last year was $9.5 billion, five times what it had been in the prior year.'

146 Bottomley, note 4 above, 62. Convincingly rejected by Grear, note 2 above, 519f.

147 Ohlin, note 30 above, 227.

148 Tomuschat, note 62 above, 7.

that individual persons must be protected from the abuse of power of parliaments, governments and public authorities.'[149]

So it is the State which – by virtue of its exceptional power over individuals – is subjected to the restraints on this power in form of human rights obligations. Given this rational, the State and its institutions are subject to human rights responsibilities without enjoying any corresponding human rights. Indeed, such a proposition would be absurd. So the human rights responsibilities flow from the power of the State over individuals – rather than from the State enjoying human rights.

Within the classic human rights framework, companies owe human rights obligation only if they are State-owned or controlled or discharge a public function[150] and if that is the case they can also not benefit from human rights.[151] Yet, this situation is rather exceptional; most trading companies are private persons and thus subject to human rights duties, only indirectly, where the State is required to ensure protection against 'horizontal' violations by private actors.[152] Even in these cases ultimately the human rights obligation rests with the State and private violators cannot, in the absence of appropriate domestic legislation, be held accountable for their actions.[153] As in developing countries, such domestic legislation or the will or capacity to enforce it, is frequently absent, TNCs have been able to carry on their operations in these countries paying little or no respect to the human rights of the local people. This, perhaps more than any other development, has given rise to the call that companies, especially TNCs, should owe human rights obligations comparable to the traditional position of the State and its institutions – consistent with an understanding of human rights 'as concepts of resistance to forms of power that oppress human beings'.[154] If this argument was to be accepted and TNCs were treated like quasi-public institutions, this would appear to weaken rather than strengthen the case for corporate human rights. In other words, precisely because they are considered so powerful as to require a restraint of power in the form of human rights obligations, giving them human rights would be paradoxical. On a practical level, it would also be questionable whether they were indeed in need of such rights, as they would generally not be vulnerable to oppression.

---

149 Javaid Rehman (2003), *International Human Rights Law – A Practical Approach* (London: Pearson), 8 (internal marks omitted).

150 Section 6(1) and 6(3)(b) of the Human Rights Act; for an in-depth discussion see Dignam and Allen, note 12 above, 153–64. This distinction between 'public' and 'private' entities gives naturally sometimes rise to difficulties, especially in the context of privatised or self-regulatory bodies.

151 *Ayuntamiento de M* v. *Spain* (1990) 68 DR 209; discussed in Dignam and Allen, note 12 above, 31 ff, 160ff.

152 See Dignam and Allen, note 12 above, 36ff. The effect of this is that human rights duties are also often owed indirectly between private parties, but a breach can ultimately only ever be alleged against the State for failing to prevent them, as enshrined in Article 34 of the European Convention.

153 Bar a few exceptions, as discussed below.

154 Grear, note 2 above, 521.

The question to what extent TNCs are comparable to States and should thus be treated like quasi-public institutions has been subject to some debate and cannot and need not be explored fully here. Suffice to say, the power balance between TNCs and the State has fundamentally changed, so much so that it is now often States (and not just in the developing world) which are at the mercy of TNCs:

> Corporations have become sufficiently powerful to pose a threat to governments ... and that is particularly the case with respect to multinational corporations, who will have much less dependence upon the positions of particular governments ... corporations and their leaders have displaced politics and politicians as ... the new high priests and reigning oligarchs of our system.[155]

The economic and thus quasi-political power of TNCs is well-documented:[156] 'General Motors, for example, is larger than the national economies of all but seven countries. The largest fifteen corporations have revenues greater than all but thirteen nations.'[157] States wooing for their investment are keen to oblige with regulatory favours.[158] So the very actors charged with keeping a regulatory grip on companies are often compromised by their need to accommodate them. And companies cannot be relied upon to voluntarily respect human rights: 'the profit motive will inevitably exert pressure against responsibility, creating incentives to cut corners, and to commit abuses.'[159] Clearly there is room for arguing that large publicly traded companies have assumed a position of power in all spheres of life comparable to the power traditionally exercised by States, simply through being less amenable to that State power. Thus on balance, in view of the relative *de facto* power of companies, it would seem more appropriate to treat them like a State rather than like an individual within the human rights framework, that is, give them obligations but no rights.

Finally, it is worthwhile to briefly examine to what extent these calls for corporate human rights duties have been answered by legal developments, as it would suggest the need for parallel reverse developments in respect of corporate human rights. Although the traditional structure of human rights is still firmly in place, there are some significant cracks in the classic anti-state lens of human rights duties. Most significantly, TNCs have recently had to defend claims under the US Alien Tort Claims Act which allows for 'any civil action by an alien for a tort only, committed in violation of the law of nations'. These claims have brought the issue of corporate human rights obligations under international law to the forefront.[160] While there is no

---

155 Bakan, note 2 above, 25.

156 Wielded both individually and collectively through, for example, the WTO; see the literature cited in note 2 above.

157 Stephens, note 114 above, 57.

158 While this trend is hardly new, it has gained renewed impetus recently: Stephens, note 114 above, 58. Note the early insightful comments by Berle and Means, note 90 above, 220: 'for years ... general corporations laws have multiplied powers and made them increasingly absolute ... charters have to an increasing extent included immunity clauses and waivers of "rights." It seems not to have occurred to draftsmen that, through the very nature of the corporate entity, responsibility goes with power.'

159 Stephens, note 114 above, 63.

160 Discussed in depth, for example, in Joseph, note 3 above.

need or space here to examine these actions in any depth, significant for the present discussion is the recognition that under customary international law, private actors, including companies, can be directly guilty of human rights abuses – either when acting in concert with the State, or, in respect of a few particularly serious human rights violations even on their own. The former instance is closely modelled on the traditional State-focused position of human rights law.[161] The latter instance, on the other hand, departs from the classic anti-State focus of the human rights framework: it imposes human rights obligations directly on individuals or legal persons regardless of State involvement. Although these latter claims are currently confined to particular serious abuses (such as genocide, certain war crimes, piracy, slavery, forced labour and aircraft hijacking), this is a highly 'dynamic area of international law … [and] it is likely that the recognised customary duties of corporations and other private entities will increase in the near future'.[162] It is time that these developments are matched by, at the very least, a re-evaluation of the appropriateness of corporate human rights.

And this call for a re-examination of corporate human rights is not weakened by the fact that the above argument about the power of companies *vis-à-vis* the State is not applicable to all companies but only to large ones. The difficulty of drawing a line between large multinationals and smaller domestic companies was used by the court in the 'McLibel' saga as one reason for upholding the right of any company to bring a defamation action.[163] This all-or-nothing position could equally have been used to support the opposite conclusion. Here the argument about the power of *some* companies *vis-à-vis* the State is simply one of a number of arguments against the desirability and rationality of the right of *any* companies to claim human rights.

Conclusion: Fundamental Corporate Rights

Academic, popular and corporate literature is besieged with talk of corporate (social) responsibilities, flowing from a growing recognition of the extensive power that large multinationals enjoy in respect of all spheres of life, set against the truism that 'unlimited power is itself a bad and dangerous thing.'[164] Meanwhile, much more quietly, a different story has unfolded in Europe (following in American footsteps) in which companies resist State intervention by reliance on human rights. This chapter has tried to show that a corporate right to human rights cannot be supported, either – as it is currently – by simply relying on the legal personality of the company or reference to the rationality of the corporate agent, or more promisingly but ultimately

---

161 This does not mean that the State is necessarily the main violator and the company in any way the inferior actor. Indeed, the concepts of 'joint action' and 'partnership' to determine the liability of the TNC reflect that there is often equality in the relationship, and in some cases the company appears to have been main instigator of the violation.

162 Joseph, note 3 above, 48.

163 *Steel* v. *McDonald's Corp. & Anor* [1999] EWCA Civ. 1144, 16; see further discussion in Chapter 9, note 121 and accompanying text, and more generally in Chapter 4 below.

164 Alexis De Tocqueville (1835), *Democracy in America* (translated from French by Henry Reeve), Vol. 1, Ch. 15.

still unsuccessfully by reference to the wider benefits of corporate rights. Most importantly, such enjoyment is not only difficult to accommodate within the human rights framework but it is also harmful: it devalues human rights and hinders States' legitimate and necessary efforts to regulate companies, efforts which are already severely compromised by the economic dependence of States on TNCs, but without which the real human rights of millions of individuals are threatened.

But this is not quite the end of the story. While it is not desirable to squeeze companies into the established human rights regime, there may be an argument for the creation of a charter of basic corporate rights. Keeping corporate rights separate from human rights would encourage a more conscious regard to the distinct characteristics and vulnerabilities, if any, of the company and its intended and actual impact in our society. It would also raise a greater awareness of the relative leverage of, and interaction between, corporate rights and human rights and, hopefully, a more considered resolution of any conflicts between them. A discussion of what rights such a charter should include is beyond this chapter's scope, but some such rights may very well mirror some existing corporate human rights, such as the right to freedom of expression and the right to property, and more generally economic self-determination rights, such as the right to trade, as well as procedural defence rights, as discussed in Chapters 5 and 7.

Chapter 3

Profit in the Beef Industry and Human Health: Consumer Rights as Basic Human Rights

Profit, Risk and Health: The BSE/vCJD Saga

A few days before Christmas 1984, Mr Stent, a Sussex farmer, summoned a vet to attend a sick cow. Over the course of the next few months, more of the farm's herd fell ill, displaying what the vet described as 'unusual symptoms' including weight loss, head tremors, fearfulness and a lack of coordination. By the end of April 1985, Cow 133 (the first animal to fall ill) and five other cows from the herd had died from the condition that had, by then, earned the name 'Stent Farm Syndrome'.[1] Later in the summer, Cow 142 began to display symptoms that had become recognisable as 'typical' of the new syndrome. This animal was delivered live to the Central Veterinary Laboratory of the Ministry of Agriculture, Fisheries and Food (MAFF) for euthanasia and post-mortem. A finding of spongiform encephalopathy in the brain tissue was recorded, and it was concluded that the condition was attributable to some sort of poisoning.[2]

Meanwhile, on a dairy farm in Kent a similar tale was unfolding, and over the course of 1985 several cattle at that farm developed symptoms similar to those displayed by Mr Stent's cows – typically changes in character and behaviour, aggression, and a progressive failure of coordination so that eventually they were rendered incapable of getting to their feet unaided.[3] A senior pathologist from MAFF's Central Veterinary Laboratory (CVL) examined brain tissue from the Kent casualties and recorded a finding of 'multifocal spongy transformation of the brain parancyma and a degeneration of neurons, principally large neurons, in the brain

---

1 The term 'Stent Farm Syndrome' was coined by the vet in attendance and Mr Watkin-Jones a veterinarian at the Winchester VIC whom the former had consulted in connection with the outbreak at Pitsham Farm (The Philips Committee (2000), *The BSE Inquiry Report*, Vol. 3, at 4–5). The BSE Inquiry Report was published in sixteen volumes, and can be accessed in its entirety via the BSE Inquiry Homepage at <http://www.bseinquiry.gov.uk/pdf/index. htm>. For an informed and interesting analysis of the BSE/vCJD crisis (and other major food scares), see generally, H. Pennington (2003), *When Food Kills: BSE, E.Coli and Disaster Science* (Oxford: Oxford University Press).

2 See *BSE Inquiry Report*, Vol. 3, at 6–9 for a review of case of Cow 142 and the committee's consideration of the conflicting evidence surrounding the diagnosis of toxicity/ bovine scrapie. This was the earliest confirmed case of BSE, see ibid., at p. 4, para 1.7.

3 Ibid., Vol. 3, at 8, para 1.34.

stem'. His overall conclusion was that 'compared with most other animal disorders the changes [were] most closely related to scrapie, but there were subtle differences.'[4] The BSE saga had begun.[5] These earliest cases were rapidly followed by numerous others in an epidemic that would not peak until 1992, when a total of 37,280 cases were notified over the course of a single year.[6]

From the beginning, the political and economic repercussions of this new zoonosis caused significant concern in official circles – as is clearly evidenced in the initial (confidential) communication from the pathology department at CVL notifying key staff about the new disease in December 1986. Here, departmental chief Ray Bradley issued the warning that 'if the disease turned out to be bovine scrapie it would have severe repercussions for the export trade and possibly also for humans if for example it was discovered that humans with spongiform encephalopathies had close contact with cattle.'[7]

Despite the fact that there were arguably, by this point, very good reasons for actively raising awareness of the new disease within veterinary and farming circles, the dissemination of information about the emergent disease was initially tightly restricted. Early attempts to publish information about BSE in the professional press were suppressed, and it was not until October 1987 that a paper by Gerald Wells, the senior pathologist at CVL was finally published (following a notable delay) in *Veterinary Record*.[8] By then, twenty-nine cases of the new transmissible spongiform

---

4   Ibid., Vol.3 at 10, para 1.35.

5   There is some evidence that the first cases of BSE may have occurred prior to 1984–85. The Philips Committee was presented with evidence relating to a Wiltshire farm that had had cases of animals falling ill with classical symptoms of BSE as early as 1983. In 1987, a histological examination of a cow from this farm was confirmed the presence of BSE in the brain tissue. See ibid., Vol. 3, at 12, paras 1.41–1.42. Ultimately, the Philips Committee concluded that 'it is likely that the first cases of BSE pre-dated by some years – possibly as many as ten or more – the first case of BSE to be diagnosed as such', see ibid., Vol. 3, at 13, para 1.46.

6   Figure taken from a table originally produced by L'Office International des Epizooties <http://www.oie.int/eng/info/en_esb.htm>. This table is reproduced in T. Josling, D. Roberts and D. Orden (2003), *Food Regulation and Trade* (Washington, DC: Institute for International Economics), at 93.

7   *BSE Inquiry Report*, note 1 above, Vol. 3 at 10, para. 37. Hugh Pennington has expressed the view that Ray Bradley's comment here 'reveals aspects of the mindset at CVL that was to contribute negatively to the handling of the BSE crises'. He has also contrasted this attitude with that of the medical profession, commenting that one would not anticipate such an open concern for economic consequences from the head of a hospital or university medical school pathology department upon the probable discovery of a new disease. See Pennington, note 1 above, at 145.

8   The first half of Wells's paper provided a description of the new disease and the latter half drew comparisons with known TSEs, including the sheep disease, scrapie. Initially, publication of the full unedited paper was not sanctioned by the CVO for 'veterinary political reasons.' Moreover, there was some debate about whether or not the term 'scrapie' should appear in the article. See Pennington, *ibid.* at 144–7. See also, the definitive statement from Philips on the climate of secrecy that prevailed during the earliest years of the outbreak: 'Gathering of data about the extent of the spread of BSE was impeded in the first half of 1987

encephalopathy (TSE) had been confirmed and there were another 120 suspected cases.[9]

The emerging crisis required action on two fronts: first, preventive measures to contain the epidemic and protect animal health, and secondly, precautionary measures to address the possibility that the disease could be transmitted to humans. Consumer interests and trade interests were thrown into a state of conflict. In the face of continued uncertainty surrounding the potential scale and seriousness of the emergent epidemic, official responses (rather predictably) erred on the side of political and economic (pre)caution.

Animal Health

By December 1987, the practice of feeding meat and bone meal (MBM) to cattle – that is, feeding rendered sheep remains and other animal by-products to ruminants – had been implicated in the search for the root cause of the new TSE.[10] Six months later, in July 1988 (three years after the death of Cow 142) action was taken to remove what was by then considered to be the key source of infection; a UK-wide ban on the use of MBM in cattle feed was introduced. Although the ban represented decisive action on the part of the authorities, its effectiveness in halting the spread of the disease was limited by certain misconceptions about the scale of the infection and the quantity of infective material needed to transmit the disease. Being unaware of the fact that by now, infection rates had increased to thousands per week, the government allowed the animal feed industry a five-week 'period of grace' during which they could legally continue to sell (potentially contaminated) feed. This concession sent the wrong message to the feed and farming industries: as the Philips Inquiry Report comments, the period of grace was fully exploited by some industry players who 'being given an inch, felt free to take a yard', and consequently continued to clear feed stocks even *after* the ban came into force.[11] Moreover, as the damage limitation exercise gained momentum in the face of the growing furore over BSE, the government, struggling to balance the uncertainties surrounding infectivity against the more predictable trade implications of the disease, also failed to give what Philips described as 'rigorous consideration to the amount of infective material' capable of transmitting the disease. This particular failure gave rise to the (mistaken) assumption that any cross-contamination of cattle feed with pig or poultry feed – which could still legally contain MBM – 'would be on too small a scale to matter'.[12] In fact, experiments later revealed that a cow could become infected after consuming a tiny quantity of infectious tissue – a morsel as small as a peppercorn.[13] It seems

---

by an embargo within the SVS on making information about the new disease public. This should not have occurred', *BSE Inquiry Report*. note 1 above, Vol. 1, at xix.

9   Pennington, ibid., at 147.

10   Transmissible Spongiform Encephalopathy.

11   See, for example, the *BSE Inquiry Report*, note 1 above, Vol. 1, at xix–xxii, 38–42 and 252–3.

12   See, for example, ibid.

13   Ibid.

that so far as animal health was concerned, cautiously industry-friendly regulatory interventions, or at the very least a certain regulatory reticence, combined with fairly predictable industry practices, served to exacerbate the crisis.

Human Health

Scientific uncertainty about the scale of risks will sometimes provide a trigger for action. Alternatively, uncertainty may simply serve to legitimise inaction. In the case of BSE, initially at least, the absence of unequivocal evidence that this TSE could cross the species barrier to the human population enabled MAFF to effectively ignore the economically and politically devastating possibility that BSE might present a notable risk to consumers. Although public health concerns had been raised in the earliest years of the epidemic, attempts by experts within MAFF and CVL to publicise this possibility via journals such as the *British Medical Journal* or *The Lancet* were stifled on the basis that publicity 'would over emphasise the possible link to human spongiform encephalopathies'.[14] Eventually, of course, the silence was broken and warnings about the potential transmissibility of the disease were published in the medical press. One early article, co-written by a doctor and a dietician, and published in the *British Medical Journal* in June 1988, provided the following assessment of the potential threat to human health:

> It has generally been accepted that the slaughter of animals showing characteristic signs of infection – such as behaviour changes – as well as the usual processes of sterilisation and pasteurisation, are enough to remove any risk to the consumer. Unfortunately, this is a view that is naïve, uninformed, and potentially disastrous.

After drawing some comparisons between BSE, CJD, scrapie and Kuru, the authors went on to consider the manner in which infective material from cattle might enter the human food chain, before issuing a final warning and a call for government action to improve the level of protection provided for consumers:

> This is a disease for which there is no serological marker, and the incubation period is probably long. There is no way of telling which cattle are infected until features develop, and if transmission has already occurred to man it might be years before affected individuals succumb. It is possible, but unproved, that many asymptomatic cattle are nevertheless as infective as those symptomatic animals which are immediately destroyed for public health reasons. So should not the use of brains in British foods be either abolished outright or more clearly defined? Then in the absence of more compelling evidence those of us who wish to exclude it from our diets at least have that choice.[15]

Around the same time as the first expert commentaries were beginning to appear in the media and the professional press, the government established the Southwood Working Party to investigate and advise on the risks presented by BSE and the

---

14   Ibid., Vol. 3, at 122.

15   Tim Holt and Julie Phillips (1988) 'Bovine Spongiform Encephalopathy', *British Medical Journal,* 296:1581–2, at 1581.

precautionary measures necessary to counter those risks.[16] Reflecting the limited state of (scientific) knowledge about the new TSE at that time, whilst the tone of the Southwood Report was generally seen to be reassuring on the question of possible transmissibility of BSE to humans, it was also cautious in its conclusions. The Working Party took care to qualify its finding that 'it was most unlikely that BSE would have any implications for human health', by commenting that 'much further research was necessary.'[17] In his oral evidence to the Philips Inquiry ten years later, Sir Richard Southwood reiterated that:

> ... we were very particular about the wording of paragraphs; and that we did not want it to be too reassuring. We wanted to point out that there were enormous uncertainties. And that if these uncertainties turned out to be more likely than we had judged there could be catastrophic and very profound consequences.[18]

The scientific uncertainty surrounding BSE was, and indeed continues to be, problematic. If scientific evidence of a significant risk to human or animal health from BSE had been firmly established in the 1980s, determining the appropriate course of action would have been rather more straightforward. Expensive or politically divisive action to reduce risks is more easily justifiable where those risks are quantifiable. In fact, in such cases, action may well prove to be obligatory. The implementation of *precautionary* measures, however, tends to be a significantly trickier exercise – both politically and economically, particularly where potential risks are widely distributed; as Southwood recognised at the time, the whole of the UK herd was potentially implicated in any public health risk.[19]

The Southwood Report's qualified conclusion, that 'from the present evidence, it is likely that cattle prove to be a "dead-end host" for the disease and most unlikely that BSE will have any implications for human health',[20] was strategically and energetically employed to counter mounting public concern and inflammatory media assertions regarding the integrity of the food chain and the safety of UK beef and dairy products – but without any of the important qualifications.[21] Crucially, the Committee's express warning that 'if our assessments of these likelihoods are incorrect, the implications would be extremely serious',[22] failed to register in the

---

16   Sir Richard Southwood was keen to see the Working Party's terms of reference set as widely as possible. These were agreed to be '[t]o advise on the implications of Bovine Spongiform Encephalopathy and matters related thereto', *Report of the Working Party on Bovine Spongiform Encephalopathy* (The Southwood Report), February 1989, 3.

17   Ibid., quoted in *BSE Inquiry Report*, note 1 above, Vol. 4, at 1.

18   Ibid., vol.4, at 1. See also, The Southwood Report, February 1989.

19   As Sir Richard Southwood later commented 'enormous uncertainties' surrounding BSE made it extremely difficult for the Working Party to 'steer the proper course between causing excessive alarm and undue complacency' (extract from a letter written by Southwood to Dr Helen Grant in March 1989, and submitted as evidence to the Philips Committee: see *BSE Inquiry Report*, Vol. 4, at 55–56.

20   Ibid., 36.

21   For examples of press coverage in the late 1980s and early 1990s, see ibid., Vol. 6, 160–63.

22   See note 18 above.

official consciousness and was thus effectively ignored. In the face of uncertainty, the government persisted in treating the absence of evidence of risk as evidence of safety.

Then, in the spring of 1990, Max, a Siamese cat, died after contracting a 'scrapie-like' disease. This death did not trigger a review of policy but instead prompted the Chief Medical Officer to issue a press release reiterating the official line that there was 'no scientific justification for not eating British beef' and asserting that he had 'no hesitation in saying that beef can be eaten safely by everyone, both adults and children, including patients in hospital'.[23] Meanwhile, Minister of Agriculture John Gummer sought to reassure consumers by publicly tucking into a beefburger with his 4-year-old daughter at a boat show in the immediate aftermath of the unfortunate cat's demise.[24]

Unfortunately, the Minister's faith in British beef proved to be somewhat misplaced. Max was not to be the only non-bovine casualty, for not only did the number of cattle developing BSE continue to rise, but by September 1994 a varied selection of exotic animals and fifty-seven cats had been fallen victim to BSE.[25] Contrary to the earlier assumptions, BSE was clearly 'very good at jumping the species barrier'.[26] None the less, the government stuck stoically to its guns: any risk to human health was 'remote'.[27] By now though, official reassurances were sounding increasingly hollow in the face of mounting evidence that the risk to consumers might not be as 'remote' as everyone had been encouraged to believe.

Finally, in March 1996, the Health Minister Stephen Dorrell was forced to admit that BSE had probably jumped the species barrier to infect ten young human victims.[28] The public felt that they had been 'betrayed'[29] and confidence in the safety of the British food chain and the government's ability to protect consumers plummeted to an all-time low. Since these first cases of new variant CJD were confirmed, more people have contracted the disease. According to the CJD Surveillance Unit, by September 2007, the number of confirmed and probable human fatalities stood at 161.[30] There is no way to determine with any certainty the epidemiological significance of these human casualties. The number of cases of BSE being notified has declined steadily

---

23   Press release by Sir Donald Acheson, May 1990, quoted by Pennington, note 1 above, at 165.

24   The press photographed John Gummer and his daughter eating beef burgers at a boat show on 6 May 1990.

25   Other animals that contracted the disease included nyala, gemsbok, Arabian oryx, puma and cheetah. The condition had also been artificially transmitted to the marmoset in experiments, so by now, the ability of the disease to cross the species barrier was very clear indeed. See *BSE Inquiry Report*, note 1 above, Vol. 1, at 139.

26   Pennington, note 1 above, at 165.

27   As per the selectively quoted Southwood Report: Pennington, ibid., at 165. See also, *BSE Inquiry Report,* note 1 above.

28   Between 1970 and 1989, no one under the age of 30 contracted CJD in the UK: *BSE Inquiry Report*, note 1 above, Vol. 1, at 154.

29   Ibid., Vol. 1, at xviii.

30   CJC Surveillance Unit, *CJD Statistics* (1990–2007), available at <http://www.cjd. ed.ac.uk/figures.htm>.

over recent years, indicating that perhaps the animal disease has been brought under control. Unfortunately, the same cannot be said of vCJD. Whilst some experts are hopeful that 'high numbers of future deaths in the UK from the human form of mad cow disease are unlikely',[31] others are less optimistic, asserting that 'any belief that vCJD incidence has peaked and that we are now through the worst of this sinister disease must now be treated with extreme scepticism.'[32] Worryingly, researchers have suggested that the incubation period for the disease could be as long as fifty years,[33] and that secondary transmission (from person to person) may prove to be 'far easier' than infection across the species barrier from cattle to consumer.[34] Overall, it seems that it could be quite some time before the full scale of the epidemic finally becomes clear.

Although the Philips Inquiry ultimately concluded that the Ministry of Agriculture, Fisheries and Food had not *expressly* prioritised the interests of agricultural producers over those of the consumer in its handling of BSE, the manner in which government responded to the crisis as it unfolded was subject to a certain degree of criticism. In particular, Philips found that at times, officials showed a lack of rigour in considering how policy should be put into practice, to the detriment of the efficacy of the measures taken; at times, bureaucratic processes resulted in unacceptable delay in giving effect to policy; the Government introduced measures to guard against the risk that BSE might be a matter of life and death not merely for cattle but also for humans, but the possibility of a risk to humans was not communicated to the public or to those whose job it was to implement and enforce the precautionary measures.[35] Notwithstanding Lord Philip's conclusion regarding governmental priorities, these various shortcomings identified by the Inquiry are certainly indicative of a failure to *conscientiously prioritise* the end-consumer's right to safety in the balancing of political and economic risks and costs.

It is, perhaps, important to consider where the roots of this ongoing crisis really lie. The very fact that this BSE ever emerged at all says something extremely distasteful about the character and objectives of the agricultural and feed industries. As a basic matter of animal husbandry, the recycling of animal remains into cattle feed – effectively turning herbivores into carnivores – to increase protein intake and

---

31   Author unknown, 'vCJD Timebomb Fears Discounted', *BBC News*, 1 December 2005. This article reports the findings of research conducted by a team from Imperial College, London. Researchers tested 12,674 appendix and tonsil samples for infection, and found that around 3,800 people could ultimately be affected by the disease. Article available at <http://news.bbc.co.uk/go/pr/fr/-/1/hi/health/4162749.stm>.

32   Author unknown, 'vCJD May Develop Over 50 Years', *BBC News*, 22 June 2006. This article reports on research findings of a study conducted by a team of researchers from University College, London into kuru (a prion disease similar to vCJD). Report available at <http://news.bbc.co.uk/1/hu/health/5106808.stm>.

33   Ibid.

34   J. Meikle (2006), 'Fears increase on transmitting human form of BSE', *The Guardian*, 19 May.

35   *BSE Inquiry Report*, note 1 above, at xviii.

thus productivity is unnatural and highly questionable.[36] The recycling of animal waste increased profits for the rendering industry and animal feed companies and also increased the productivity of dairy cattle into the bargain. Economic expediency prevailed over common sense. As the broadcaster John Humphries concluded:

> There was one reason and one reason only for feeding ruminants on the ground up brains and spines and bones of other animals. It was profit. The left over bits of slaughtered animals cost the manufacturers relatively little and contained lots of protein … The manufacturers made more money and the farmers sold more milk and the price of food kept falling. So everyone was happy.[37]

In the end, it is impossible to argue against the conclusion of the Philips Inquiry that 'BSE developed into an epidemic as a consequence of an intensive farming practice – the recycling of animal protein in ruminant feed. This practice, unchallenged over decades, proved a recipe for disaster.'[38]

This cautionary tale of risk to profit versus risk to health (animal, then human) may prompt a number of reflections on the character and priorities of the food industry, the efficacy of governance in this field, and the need for effective consumer protection mechanisms. The discussion in this chapter explores the evolution of this area of legal protection, tracing the development of the thesis that the end-consumer, as a necessary but inherently vulnerable actor in the twenty-first-century market place, should in some circumstances be an active rights-bearer rather than just a passive object of protective regulation. Building upon an analysis of the end-consumer's role in the contemporary globalised market place, the argument will be tested that certain consumer rights should be invested with the higher valuation of basic human rights. Such investment could serve to focus regulatory attention more forcefully on protecting the interests of this inherently vulnerable stakeholder.

If such an argument may be accepted in principle, some important specific legal questions remain to be addressed. First, where and how may the boundary be drawn

------

36   In 1979, the Royal Commission on Environmental Pollution warned that 'The major problem encountered in this recycling process is the risk of transmitting disease-bearing pathogens to stock and thence to humans', *Royal Commission on Environmental Pollution*, 1979, quoted by O. Bowcott et al. (1996), 'Ministers Warned on Cattle Feed in 1980', *The Guardian*, London, 23 March, at 5. The recycling of sheep remains into animal feed began in the 1920s. Since 1980, important changes have been implemented in order to, as Pennington puts it, 'achieve the economics of scale'. Over time, practice shifted from batch cooking to continuous rendering, which in turn was thought to lead to processing at lower temperatures than previously. Also, as there has been a significant increase in the numbers of sheep being farmed – and consequently slaughtered – in the UK, the quantity of sheep remains being recycled in this way has also increased significantly. By the time BSE emerged, 'More heads were being rendered and more casualty and condemned animals were being processed because knackers were going out of business. The numbers of [sheep] scrapie cases had gone up, and the numbers of renderers had fallen from 200 to 58 meaning that the pools of processed material were larger', Pennington, note 1 above, at 148.

37   J. Humphries (2001), *The Great Food Gamble* (London: Coronet Books, Hodder and Stoughton) at 232.

38   *BSE Inquiry Report*, note 1 above, Vol. 1, at xvii.

between 'ordinary' and 'basic' or 'fundamental' (consumer) human rights? Then, if certain fundamental consumer rights can be identified, against whom and by what kind of legal process may they be asserted? Finally, to what extent should such a higher-order entitlement also be coupled with obligation? Bearing in mind that the market place is constructed from, and is dependent upon, a complex web of interdependent and co-dependent producer, supplier and consumer relationships, ought the consumer's protection (and especially that of the affluent, reflective and selective Western consumer) be ethically and legally counterbalanced by an obligation to protect other vulnerabilities, such as exploited labour or a degraded environment? In short, should the availability of the 'trump card' of fundamental consumer rights entitlement be additionally counterbalanced and moderated by a requirement that the deserving citizen-consumer should act also as a responsible consumer?

The Consumer's Place in the Market: Twenty-first-Century Realities

Although references to production and marketing 'chains' are commonplace, such linear descriptions inadequately convey the reality of today's highly complex and globalised[39] market arena. The various stages of production, distribution and marketing of many consumer goods, particularly manufactured or processed goods, cannot be easily disentangled from each other. Similarly, the roles of producer, supplier and consumer cannot be seen as entirely distinct. As argued in Chapter 1, the labels 'producer', 'supplier' and 'consumer' must be viewed as descriptions which merge into each other along a continuum. Thus, although the concept of 'the consumer' is now a familiar one, there is no entirely discrete class of economic actor playing out the role of consumer to the exclusion of all other roles.[40] In the light of the many and varied manifestations of 'the consumer' along the production and distribution chain, both human and non-human (man, woman, child, corporate entity, State), and the varying degrees of competence, strength and vulnerability

---

39   Definitions of globalisation abound, but this offering from Stiglitz provides a useful and concise representation of the process. He has described globalisation as the term denoting 'the closer integration of the countries and peoples of the world which has been brought about by the enormous reduction of costs of transportation and communication, and the breaking down of artificial barriers to the flows of goods, services, capital, knowledge, and (to a lesser extent) people across borders', J. Stiglitz (2002), *Globalization and its Discontents* (London: Penguin Books), at 9.

40   The sociologist Claus Offe found that consumers did not form a 'clearly delimitable and organizable complex of individuals. Rather they do constitute an abstract category which defines certain aspects of the social actions of almost all individuals. Everyone and at the same time no one is a "consumer"', C. Offe (1984), *Contradictions of the Welfare State* (Cambridge, MA: MIT Press), at 228, quoted by F. Trentmann (2006), in 'The Modern Evolution of the Consumer: Meanings, Knowledge, and Identities Before the Age of Affluence', Chapter 1 in J. Brewer and F. Trentman (eds), *Consuming Cultures, Global Perspectives: Historical Trajectories, Transnational Exchange* (Oxford: Berg Publishers), at 1.

with which these consumers engage with the market,[41] it is useful at this juncture to emphasise that the rights analysis offered in this chapter is concerned with the interests, rights and responsibilities of a specific subset of this eclectic class of actor: the 'end-consumer'. More specifically, it is the relatively affluent and sophisticated 'Western' consumer as the final purchaser of the products of the twenty-first-century market place who provides the main focus for this discussion.

Although individually, we may have other roles to play – that qualify us as producer, supplier, worker, or whatever – there is no escaping one fundamental reality of the modern world. Whatever else we might do in our daily lives, we, the citizens of thriving free market economies have no option but to engage with 'the market' and consume its products on a daily basis. We are all participants in, and dependents of, the complex tapestry of the global market place. We are all 'end-consumers'. Our lives, and indeed our identities are to a significant extent dependent upon, and defined by, the way we play out our roles as consumers and the consumption decisions we make. Moreover, as will be discussed later in this chapter, our moral selves and moral duties – and perhaps, even our legal duties – are, to some degree at least, derived from and defined by our daily engagement in the market place.

Traditionally, human needs – now construed as *consumer* needs – were satisfied primarily within the boundaries of small-scale, culturally embedded communities and localised economies. For example, as recently as 150 years ago, around 95 per cent of a family's food would have been produced 'within sight of the church steeple'.[42] Over the course of the last two hundred years, however, and particularly over the course of the last sixty years, the process of globalisation has steadily gathered pace, dramatically changing the shape and dynamics of the market place. Since the end of the Second World War, international trade in all manner of goods, from natural resources and consumer goods to military hardware, has grown twelve-fold, so that imports and exports now account for around $5.5 trillion annually.[43] The EU food and drink sector is now worth in excess of €799 billion; the meat processing industry alone, generates an annual turnover of €161 billion, of which €31 billion is profit.[44] In fact, locally produced food has come to be viewed as something of a novelty and

---

41   The categories identified here are very loose. Each of these general categories could be broken down further. In the case of corporations, for example, size and market share will be relevant criteria. In the case of human consumers, it is important to acknowledge that even within an apparently discrete subset, individual experiences of the market vary widely, being influenced by factors such as educational and socio-economic status, the character of the product and its market.

42   M. Schneider (1997), 'Tempo Diet', *Time and Society*, 6(1):85–95, quoted by B. Adam (1999), 'Industrial Food For Thought: Timescapes of Risk', *Environmental Values*, 8:219–38, at 227.

43   H. Nordberg-Hodge, T. Merrifield, and S. Gorlick (2002), *Bringing the Food Economy Home: Local Alternatives to Global Agribusiness* (London: Zed Books), at 12–13.

44   See C. Macmaoláin (2007), *EU Food Law: Protecting Consumers and Health in a Common Market* (Oxford: Hart Publishing), at 5–6. For an interesting and informative overview of EU food law, see generally, Macmaoláin, ibid.

as a consequence, despite the shorter route to market, local produce may command a notable premium.[45]

Clearly, the environment within which the roles of producer, supplier and consumer are played out today bears little resemblance to that which was in place a generation or so ago: the familiarity of small-scale, locally contained production and distribution chains has all but been replaced by the unbounded anonymity of the liberalised market place that characterises the twenty-first-century 'global village'. Although the fundamental connection between production and consumption remains as strong as ever, relationships within the increasingly complex tapestry of production and distribution have certainly become more tenuous as the *real* distance between human participants has increased. Many products upon which today's Western consumer has come to depend, from basic foodstuffs to luxury items, will routinely pass through many production/distribution stages and will travel thousands of miles before they reach their final destination.

This distance that modernity has created between the market's human players, producers and consumers, in both a physical and metaphorical sense,[46] is in part an inevitable result of technological advances and improved transportation and communication links.[47] However, this space has to some extent been created by, and has most certainly been expanded and filled by, the 'middle men' of globalised production and distribution: the powerful transnational corporate entities that now dominate the market landscape.

The modern commercial corporation now dominates production and distribution across all market sectors. As their influence has grown, the transnational corporations – the Goliaths of free trade – have pushed weaker competitors out of the game in their relentless search for a greater market share and increased profitability.[48] The family

---

45 Interestingly, there is currently a strong interest in, and drive for, the rejuvenation of localised food markets in the UK, Europe and the US. Thus, local production and marketing systems – for example, farmers' markets – are being enthusiastically supported by increasing numbers of consumers. On the subject of localised food economies generally, see for example, Norberg-Hodge, Merrifield and Gorelick, note 43 above.

46 The concept of the consumer is not a concept that sits comfortably against perceived realities of life outside of the complex post-industrial society. The label 'consumer', as the citizens of the wealthier parts of the world understand it, is a rather narrow concept that only has any real significance for a small proportion of the global human community. Figures published by the UNDP in 1998 illustrate the relative scale of consumption between North and South: 86 per cent of (global) private expenditure is accounted for by just 20 per cent of the world's population; the poorest 20 per cent account for 1.3 per cent! The richest 20 per cent of consumers consume 45 per cent of all the meat and fish produced worldwide, whilst the poorest people consume less that 4 per cent: UNDP (1998), *Human Development Report: 1998* (New York: UNDP).

47 Also, consumers now routinely demand more from their market place: there is an expectation that neither seasonal nor geographical barriers should defeat consumers' desires.

48 This occurs across all stages of the production and supply chain – from field to plate. At 'ground level', the industrialisation of agriculture and farming has led to the virtual demise of the traditional smaller-scale (and thus, economically 'inefficient') family farm, as the economies of scale force farming families from their land. The UK, for example, lost over half its 450,000 farms between the 1950s and the 1990s. T. Lang and M. Heasman (2004),

farms and small-to-medium-scale manufacturing enterprises, retail businesses that sat at the forefront of the domestic market until relatively recently, are no longer central features of economic landscape. In fact, despite the wide variety of goods displayed on the shelves, the wide-ranging needs of today's consumers are, to a great extent, served by a relatively small pool of extremely powerful corporate players. For example, although there may be as many as forty or fifty varieties of breakfast cereal and a similar number of different types of bread available in European supermarkets, the world grain market is now controlled by just a handful of major transnational corporations. According to Corporate Watch, just three companies – Cargill, Archer Daniels and Bunge – control almost 90 per cent of the global grain market.[49]

It is commonly the case that major transnational corporations will have interests that extend across several key market sectors and stages of the production and distribution process, and Cargill is fairly typical in this respect. In addition to its major share in the world grain market, it is also involved in a wide range of other activities from beef and poultry production to phosphate mining and fertiliser production in various countries across the world from the UK to Thailand.[50] Moreover, further along the supply chain, many of the cosy images associated with key food products – such as the traditional bakery conjured up in Hovis advertisements, or the image of the contented 'Anchor Butter' cows – are fictitious misrepresentations of contemporary production. Branding and clever advertising strategies are marketing tools designed to perpetuate a myth of familiarity in an attempt to attract consumers and encourage product loyalty. In many cases, publicising the reality of the production process could seriously jeopardise profitability![51]

Food Wars: The Global Battle for Mouths, Minds and Markets (London: Earthscan), at 149. At the other end of the supply chain, the destructive influence of big business has transformed the food retail sector so that now, just four supermarkets control over 75 per cent of the UK's food retail market – Tesco, Asda, Sainsbury's and Morrisons: Corporate Watch (2004), *What's Wrong With Supermarkets?* (London: Corporate Watch), available at <http://www. corporatewatch.org.uk> at 2.

49   A Netto (2007), 'Global: "MNCs Gaining Total Control Over Farming"', *Corporate Watch Briefing*, 7 December 2007 <http://www.corpwatch.org/article.php?id=14836&prints afe=1>. For a revealing and comprehensive insight into the corporate takeover of the food chain focusing on Cargill, see B. Kneen (2002), *Invisible Giant: Cargill and Its Transnational Strategies* (London: Pluto Press, 2nd edn).

50   See, for example, H. Nordberg-Hodge et al., note 43 above, at 90–91. See also, Joel Dyer's informative tale of an American farmer that illustrates very nicely the reach and range of Cargill's business interests: J. Dyer (1998), *Harvest of Rage*. (Boulder, CO: Westview Press), at 110. This tale is also reproduced by Nordberg-Hodge et al., at 9.

51   A more honest depiction of production processes – for example, industrial-scale breadmaking processes, or beef or poultry production – would probably encourage a lot of consumers to bake their own bread and resort to vegetarianism. On the disturbing realities of modern food production, see, for example, the following: G. Tansey and J. D'Silva (1999), *The Meat Business: Devouring a Hungry Planet* (London: Earthscan Publications); F. Lawrence (2004), *Not On The Label: What Really Goes Into The Food On Your Plate.* (London: Penguin Books); V. Hurd, (2000), *Perfectly Safe to Eat? The Facts on Food* (London: The Women's Press); A. Rowell (2003), *Don't Worry [It's Perfectly Safe to Eat]* (London: Earthscan Publications); Pennington, note 1 above.

Yet while the landscape may have shifted, the centrality of the end-consumer remains constant: without the consumer – without the *end*-consumer – there can be no market. Thus, whilst the citizens of thriving free market economies are dependent upon global trade to satisfy their daily needs, so too are the market's other key players dependent upon them. The consumer is central to the game; the lynchpin of both the domestic and the global markets. Despite the obvious power imbalances that exist between the individual consumer and the corporate actor, at base, the relationship between these key players is essentially one of co-dependency. This being the case, in theory, providing consumer satisfaction constitutes an important prerequisite for the successful achievement of corporate objectives, that is, profit maximisation and the protection of shareholder interests. Such economic producer-consumer co-dependency has underpinned much of the free trade ideology of the later twentieth century.

At the same time, there is an inevitable tension within this relationship. By definition, producers and consumers cannot exist without each other, but their natural interests differ and may not always be balanced by the forces of market competition. In particular, the inhuman and amoral character of the modern corporation may serve to disturb the market equilibrium in this respect. As Korten explains:

> Behind its carefully crafted public-relations image and the many fine and ethical people it may employ, the body of a corporation is its corporate charter, a legal document, and money is its blood. It is at its core an alien entity with one goal: to reproduce money to nourish and replicate itself. Individuals are dispensable. It owes only one true allegiance: to the financial markets, which are more totally creatures of money than even the corporation itself.[52]

When conflicts of interests become manifest, the natural inclination of the corporation will be to prioritise the interests, needs and rights of the consumer *only in so far as is absolutely necessary* to achieve primary corporate objectives. In the more extreme cases of conflict, the consumer may even come to be viewed with a certain degree of animosity – that is, as an 'enemy' rather than an essential ally of the corporate enterprise.[53] Where there is some mismatch of interests in the market, or where unscrupulous traders or corporate actors are at work, the end-consumer, as an individual human dependent on the market place will inevitably occupy a position of particular vulnerability.[54]

Hence, in order to ensure fair play, regulatory supervision of the market place has long been accepted as a necessary corollary of the 'free' market. English law, for example, has proactively mediated the relationship between market and consumer

---

52   D. Korten, (2005), *When Corporations Rule the World* (London: Earthscan Publications), at 67. See also the discussion in Chapter 2, above.

53   See C. Harding (2003), *Regulating Cartels in Europe: a Study of Legal Control of Corporate Delinquency* (Oxford: Oxford University Press), at 34–6.

54   The individual worker may well occupy a similarly vulnerable position, of course. This issue is addressed in the latter part of this chapter when the responsibilities of the consumer are explored.

for several centuries,[55] and since its inception, the European Community has necessarily been concerned to ensure that consumer interests are afforded adequate protection.[56] The ongoing process of globalisation has had a significant impact on the character and extent of the law's interventions in the market, so that now, this arena is governed by a complex system of national and supra-national regulatory structures and relationships. Contemporary market environments have been created out of, and have given rise to, these new systems of governance. As a major stakeholder in the market place, the State, both independently and via the various regional and international bodies created for the purpose, bears responsibility for the policing the market place. With its key interest in, and responsibility for, economic growth and security, there are very good reasons for this actor to have due regard to the interests and needs, and so promoting *the rights* of the consumer.[57]

Although national governments have a clear interest in the well-being (and political support of) their citizen-consumers, it is also important to acknowledge the extent to which the State has been transformed in recent times. The creep of the market has eroded and blurred the traditional boundaries between public and private spheres of activity. As Reich comments, the twentieth century was characterised not just by the rise of the welfare state but also by the trend towards sharing of 'sovereign power ... with large private interests'.[58] Many would argue that the process of globalisation, supported by the Holy Grail of free trade and alongside this, the merging, or 'marbelising' of the public and private spheres, has subverted the traditional role of the regulator giving birth to the proactively business-friendly

---

55   Early UK statutes dealing with food-related issues include the Bread Acts 1822 and 1836. The first general food law introduced in the UK was the Adulteration of Food or Drink Act 1860. For an informative and readable historical review and evaluation of the UK food law, see M. French and J. Phillips (2000), *Cheated Not Poisoned? Food Regulation in the United Kingdom 1875–1938.* (Manchester: Manchester University Press). This book provides an insightful historical perspective on the evolution of national food safety law and the enduring challenges facing legislators striving to protect both consumer and commercial interests.

56   For a review of community law in this field, see generally, Macmaoláin, note 44 above. See also Chapter 6, below.

57   The most cursory perusal of the official websites of bodies such as European Commission's DG for Consumer Health and Protection or those maintained by major corporate stakeholders serves to illustrate the consumer's central position within the market place. See, for example, the website of the European Commission's Directorate General for Health and Consumer Protection (DG Sanco) <http://ec.europa.eu/index_en.htm>.

58   C. Reich (1964), 'The New Property', *Yale Law Journal*, 73, at 764, quoted by M. Likosky, in 'Globalizing Rights? Response to George', in M.J. Gibney (ed) (2003), *Globalizing Rights* (Oxford: Oxford University Press), at 36–9. Though this process has certainly accelerated in recent years, it is not an entirely new phenomenon: more than forty years ago, in 1963, the American writer Michael Reagan commented that 'although discussions of the relationship between the state and private sectors in the second half of the twentieth century generally focus on the rise of the welfare state, an equally important synergetic phenomenon has characterised the period – the oligarchizing of the state by politicians and private commercial actors': M. Reagan (1963), *The Managed Economy* (New York: Greenwood Press), at 190, quoted by Likosky, ibid., at 36–7.

'oligarchic' Corporate State. Economic power begets political power. Hence the global trend towards privatisation of public services and the infamous 'revolving door' between regulatory institutions and major corporate interests, a phenomenon that has attracted significant attention (and criticism) in recent years. In fact, it is indisputably the case that the major transnational corporations dominating today's world trade wield immense economic *and political* power.

Corporations have emerged as the dominant governance institutions on the planet, with the largest among them reaching into virtually every country of the world and exceeding most governments in size and power. Increasingly, it is corporate interest more than human interest that defines the policy agendas of states and international bodies, although this reality and its implications have gone largely unnoticed and unaddressed.[59]

The Deployment of Basic Rights Argument in Favour of the Consumer: Establishing the Level Playing Field

What, then, is the case for recognising certain 'basic', higher-order consumer rights? The main argument may be derived from a summary of the foregoing discussion: that it is a basic human condition to be a consumer of some kind; that this condition is now experienced in a globalised market place dominated by large corporate actors, who in turn need to exploit consumers for their own profit; that this interdependent relationship of supply and demand is none the less characterised by an imbalance of power, which has been increasingly refereed by 'public' State and intergovernmental regulators, but this process has itself in turn been infected by a national and supranational interest in promoting a 'liberalised' market place. Or, to put the matter as concisely as possible – consumption is a vital activity which requires some regulatory protection, but how effective and balanced is the latter within the globalised economy of the twenty-first century?

As will be seen from some of the subsequent discussion (see in particular that in Chapters 5, 6 and 7), within the usual contemporary market place context the respective positions of suppliers and consumers tend naturally to be regulated in different ways. Partly this follows from the imbalance of power noted above. Suppliers tend to be fewer in number and as legal actors wield individually greater economic and political power. Consumers are individually larger in number but correspondingly, through their wide dispersal, much weaker than most suppliers.[60] In so far as there has been a 'public' intervention to regulate the supplier-consumer relationship through consumer protection and competition policy, this has naturally

---

59   Korten, note 52 above, at 54.

60   See Chapter 1, section 2 above. As Scott and Black comment: 'Everyone is a consumer, and since the consumer interest is so diffuse and widely shared it should not be surprising that people have difficulty in agreeing what the consumer interest entails … a business affected by a particular measure can afford to bring pressure to bear, but consumers with many other interests will have no overriding concern impelling them to act': C. Scott and J. Black (2000), *Cranston's Consumers and the Law* (London: Butterworths, 3rd edn), at 13–14.

enough tended to be restrictive of suppliers and protective of consumers. In turn, this has resulted in a *reactive* legal stance on the part of the former (regarding their economic freedom and the mode of their regulation), but a different situation of legal *reliance* on the part of consumers, who look to public authorities to defend their position. It is not surprising therefore that suppliers have seized upon basic rights argument (despite their corporate rather than human character[61]) to protect their interests,[62] whilst the active individual assertion of consumer interests has remained weak, in effect being transferred to third-party protective agencies. In one sense, therefore, the case for consumer rights as basic human rights is not so obvious, until the point is reached at which the level of robustness of the public system of consumer protection comes seriously into doubt. It is the possibility that this latter system of protection may be (perhaps in some subtle ways) compromised that requires further consideration.

An important point in this respect, and this will be explored in more detail in some of the later chapters of this book, concerns the balancing act carried out by a range of public regulators between 'public' consumer interests ('public' because widely dispersed among the consuming public) and 'private' supplier interests.[63] Regulatory bodies serve as guardians of the public consumer interest in relation to such issues as physical health, fair economic treatment, individual self-determination and a safe and sustainable environment. But also – and increasingly since the middle part of the twentieth century – public regulators have become as well the guardians of another kind of interest; that of the open, free and liberalised market, which is seen to benefit both traders and consumers, and in a wider sense, general economic development. In this way, a public authority such as the European Commission has found itself with an evolving role which must take into account the needs of both the Single Market and consumer protection, and so in balancing the competing economic claims of suppliers and consumers, moderate the exercise by reference to the abstract needs of the Single Market.[64] As will be shown later in a number of other specific contexts, trade liberalisation policies provide an important backdrop to any exercise in consumer protection and supplier regulation, and such concerns necessarily

---

61   See the discussion of this point in Chapter 2 above.

62   See the more detailed account in Chapter 5 below.

63   Care needs to be taken in using this nomenclature. It is reasonable to talk of a widely dispersed interest as 'public' and this conveys well the rationale of many derogation clauses in human rights instruments. 'Private', as used in relation to supplier companies, needs to be understood as 'individual' as in the sense of 'private claim'. There is some, but not a complete, congruence with the 'public/private' law dichotomy.

64   Thus in terms of policy, different departments of the Commission may have different objectives and priorities according to the different policy areas for which they are responsible. At the judicial level, the dominant role of the Single Market context may be seen in the classic statement by the European Court of Justice regarding the character of basic rights protection under EC law in Case 11/70, *Internationale Handelsgesellschaft v EVSt* (1970) ECR 1125: '... respect for fundamental rights forms an inmtegral part of the general principles of law protected by the Court of Justice. The protection of such rights, whilst inspired by the constitutional traditions common to the Member States, must be ensured within the framework of the structure and objectives of the Community', at 1134.

inform to some extent the outcome in particular cases and disputes. It is in so far as consumers may regard the role of protective regulators as being compromised by market liberalisation imperatives (or, as in the case of BSE, market *preservation* imperatives), that the case for a more autonomous assertion of consumer interests and rights becomes a relevant argument.

In exploring the need for a more autonomous role for the consumer in asserting interests and rights, two main questions are posed. The first is substantive: more specifically what kind of right or rights should be considered for promotion to the higher order so as to address the perceived compromise in regulatory protection? The second is procedural, and relates to the necessary strategy for enabling an effective independent assertion of rights by individual consumers. This second question, which is essentially one of process, will be considered further in the next section of this chapter; more immediately, the prior substantive issue will be considered.

A point to be made first of all concerns the nature of the consumer interests which merit a high level of protection. In a number of respects, these important interests already benefit from human rights protection if they are viewed more widely outside the context of consumer activity. For example, interests in human health and physical integrity, which indeed feed into the right to life, are already well-established in the canon of protection, and their projection as consumer rights is then a matter of context. To a lesser extent perhaps, the same could be said about economic self-determination[65] and environmental protection:[66] they are not 'first-generation' rights but they do appear prominently now in the general scheme of basic human rights protection (see, for instance, the EU Charter of Fundamental Rights). Thus it may become clear that the issue here is really one of consumer context: to what extent is it necessary to take that context – that is, to identify the relevant actor as the human-citizen-consumer – and elevate that in itself as a matter of more basic, entrenched protection? In other words, to engage in the language of basic consumer rights is to talk about claims for protection made *by consumers as consumers*. It is a matter of consumer identity and consumer interest, rather than the material interest (such as health, or wealth) underlying the claim.

---

65 Economic self-determination is less well and less consistently defined than political or personal self-determination. The formulation in Article 2(1) of the German Constitution ('everyone shall have the right to the free development of his personality') is very general. Article 1 of the International Covenant on Economic, Social and Cultural Rights refers to the right of self-determination of peoples rather than individuals, by which they may freely pursue their economic development and freely dispose of their natural wealth and resources, envisaging a more collective entitlement. The more recent EU Charter of Fundamental Rights moves towards a more fragmented presentation of economic self-determination, comprising choice of occupation (Article 15), freedom to conduct a business (Article 16), right to property (Article 17), and a high level of consumer protection (Article 38), although in the light of the present discussion it might be doubted whether the latter constitutes 'self-determination'.

66 Under the EU Charter, environmental protection (Article 37) may perhaps be better described as an 'integrated entitlement' rather than as a direct right: environmental protection and improvement of the environment shall be integrated into policy and into the principle of sustainable development.

In this way, we may appreciate that the crucial issue is consumer participation and representation, and the ability of human individuals, either individually or collectively, to achieve an effective legal platform for asserting their consumer identity. The underlying argument is that whilst concerns about physical health and safety are important (as in the case of BSE/vCJD), what is also important in a second sense is the *projection* of consumer identity. This is important in itself since the role of consumption is an inescapable fact of life. Thus, for example, accurate food labelling – that is, listing ingredients or identifying the country of origin – provides an essential tool for the vegetarian or the politically aware consumer who wishes to boycott products from certain countries or those that have been transported thousands of miles. Basic consumer rights – if that term is to be employed in a meaningful and convincing sense – are therefore rights associated with consumer status and the protection and enablement of that status. Put more bluntly, it is a matter of ensuring that the consumer's voice is effectively heard *and responded to* on a playing field which may not be level in a number of ways.

Any project of enabling consumers to speak for themselves – with a strong sense of entitlement – that is embodied in a basic right or rights, will face a number of psychological and practical hurdles. The psychological challenge resides in the embedded idea of the consumer as a dependent party, a passive subject of protective and perhaps paternalistic regulatory regimes. This is a rather subtle point of emancipation of the consumer from the status of a dependant and victim. On the one hand, consumers may be adopted as the convenient political playthings of governments in their fight against, for instance, monopoly power or inflation. On the other hand, consumer representative groups have faced a certain degree of legal discrimination, for instance, in comparison to the more privileged position of trade unions in representing worker interests.[67] Consumer rights will only move from the rhetorical to the practical domain when consumers themselves have the confidence, will and know-how to assert their entitlement independently and such enfranchisement is a psychological as much as a practical matter. Effective legal claims need to reside in a culture as much as being embedded in process.

But consumers' own identity, and the awareness on which it must be based, is still a phenomenon of some uncertainty, and its vigour may be variable, geographically, in terms of markets, and according to social factors.[68] As the discussion elsewhere in this work demonstrates, much may depend also on the historical accident of crises and politics, whereby certain issues achieve a high political and legal profile (such as the BSE problem described above), while others lay dormant. While the implications and risks of genetic engineering are now well established in public consciousness, there are other technologies whose applications have yet to become a subject of such consumer awareness. A contemporary example is nanotechnology, consisting of the atomic or molecular processing, separation, consolidation and deformation of

---

67   See generally, Scott and Black, note 60 above, Chapter 1. With such a history, it may be difficult to persuade many consumers of the reality of their economic and legal power, and strive to move beyond the protective public pale.

68   For a discussion of consumer protection in developing countries, see ibid. at 11–12.

materials, which is now being applied in the production of a range of commodities such as cosmetics, disinfectants, paint and varnish, and food packaging.[69]

At the same time, regulatory regimes are now well established and have acquired their own dynamic, professional self-interest and identity and may indeed wish to guard their established roles and sense of expertise. While much attention has been given to the possibility of 'regulatory capture' – the process by which regulatory systems may become closer to the interests of large firms which are subject to regulation[70] – the phenomenon of regulation as an enterprise or even 'industry' with its own self-interest also merits some consideration. In recent years, there has been a significant burgeoning of competition authorities, consumer protection offices and like agencies, and a concomitant establishment of professional identity and expertise, naturally generating its own self-interest. Empowerment of the consumer (as a kind of 'privatisation' of consumer protection) may then encounter some resistance and argument on the part of those hitherto supplying (public) legal protection and exercising judgment over the extent of that protection, especially in so far as the site of significant decision making may shift from that of regulatory standard setting to that of a judicial determination on rights. Autonomous right-bearing on the part of consumers may therefore be a matter of convincing both consumers themselves and regulators of consumer (and judicial) ability in this regard.

But that last issue is also a matter of practicalities. Consumer ownership of their legal interests is crucially dependent on information and resources, and both relate to the imbalance in the supplier-consumer relationship, already referred to. In particular, and as may be evident in the above narrative of the BSE crisis, both the perception and actuality of risks associated with consumption are based upon the availability of information and the ability to use such information. The problem here is compounded by the complexity and contestability of technical information and its interpretation (see in particular the discussion in Chapter 7 below regarding the standard-setting work of the Codex Alimentarius Commission and the way in which it uses scientific evidence). The handling of this kind of information in 'expert' regulatory and administrative processes is already a matter of some controversy; the challenge for the individual consumer will be so much greater. In the first place, there is the issue of supporting legal and administrative infrastructure. Effective collection and interpretation of often technical data presupposes a set of legal powers and rights of access, which may then need further implementation in more specific legal

---

69   A technology identified earlier by Richard Feynman in his seminal Caltech lecture for the American Physical Society, 'There's Plenty of Room at the Bottom', 29 December 1959. The term 'nanotechnology' was first used by Japanese physicist Norio Taniguchi. For a readable critical discussion, see E.E. Drexler (1990), *Engines of Creation: The Coming Era of Nanotechnology* (Oxford: Oxford University Press). For an inventory of applications in relation to consumer products, see the Woodrow Wilson Center for International Scholars, *Project on Emerging Nanotechnologies*.

70   Regulatory capture theory is also bound up with what is referred to as the 'revolving door' phenomenon – regulators seeking (better paid) jobs with the firms they previously regulated. For a critical discussion of 'capture' theory, see T. Makkai and J. Braithwaite (1995), 'In and Out of the Revolving Door: Making Sense of Regulatory Capture', *Journal of Public Policy*, 1:61.

requirements for technical approval and labelling[71] of products. Even with a shift towards more independent consumer-initiated claims, it will be difficult to divorce such a process too far from associated administrative procedures: for instance, the right to information via labelling presupposes some prior administrative course of action to enable information to be supplied in that way. Secondly, there is the issue of resources. The cost of legal process and the difficulty of access to evidence were of course reasons for the emergence of regulatory regimes in the first place, based upon some public funding of such legal protection. Finally, underlying this discussion of consumer emancipation, there is also a new problematic: the relationship, in legal and political terms, between any new consumer-centred rights-oriented scheme of protection and the continuing regulatory regime. A cogent legal development would require some sense of complementarity between the two types of process, based upon a recognition that the regulator's role is moving from the protective towards the (rights) supportive.

All of the foregoing suggests that a convincing focus for the idea of basic consumer rights should centre first of all on the issue of participation in critical debate on threats to consumer interests, along with the associated issue of effective representation in such debate, and then the consequential need for access to information and procedural standing for purposes of effective engagement in a judicial forum. In legal terms, such a catalogue of basic rights would include:

- direct participation in policy-making and critical discussion,
- legal standing and effective representation for purposes of direct legal challenge,
- access to information, and
- transparency,

each of which is exercisable on the basis of consumer status.

The Exercise of Consumer Basic Rights: By Whom and Against Whom?

Human rights protection regimes have developed largely on the assumption that the responsibility for violation of such rights lies with States, governments and public authorities within governmental structures. More recently, this assumption of a 'vertical' legal relationship as the essential nexus in such rights claims has been challenged by the argument that some significant violations are more appropriately attributable to non-State actors, and, in particular, powerful transnational corporations (TNCs).[72] In the market place context, this kind of argument relating to a 'horizontal'

---

71   For a concise overview of the development of labelling requirements, see Scott and Black, note 60 above, at 354–8.

72   The horizontal application of responsibility for human rights violations is sometimes referred to by the term *Drittwirkung* – the idea that principles of constitutional law may be directly applicable as between individuals or non-State actors, or in a private law setting. See S. McInerney (1999), 'The European Convention on Human Rights and Fundamental Freedoms and the Evolution of Fundamental Rights in the Private Domain', Ch. 10 in C.

violation of significant interests and rights (for instance, traders violating the rights of other traders or consumers, as 'private' actors at the same level) is especially relevant. As Kamminga has argued:

> In view of the increasing strength of MNCs and the concomitant risk of abuses, it no longer makes sense that international law addresses obligations to respect human dignity to States and to individuals but not to corporations. At the domestic level, this anomaly has been corrected in most States by acknowledging that companies may be criminally liable and subject to constitutional standards. It is now time to take this step also at the international level.[73]

In so far as consumer interests and rights suffer injury, this may be most directly as a result of the action of other economic actors, such as suppliers, and of course there may be a number of opportunities for 'horizontal' legal redress, even in the absence of responsibility for human rights obligations, most obviously via claims in contract or tort. But the practical difficulties associated with such routes of redress, in particular, lack of necessary resources, have provided one of the main reasons for the development of protective regulatory regimes, whereby protection of the interests of more vulnerable market actors (typically small consumers) has been entrusted to specialist administrative agencies, who may then intervene legally, acting on behalf of what is then identified as a wider public interest – whether this be the wider public interest in consumer protection, or a more general (and arguably, more trade-focused) public interest in the promotion of consumer confidence in the market. Moreover, it may be questioned whether courts are very well equipped to deal with the longer-term issues underlying private consumer claims. As Scott and Black remark:

> Perhaps the fundamental problem of private law, at least as a means of influencing the behaviour of businesses, is that its impact is interstitial rather than comprehensive. Courts are primarily concerned with settling concrete disputes on a case by case basis rather than with the long-term social implications of their decisions. Judicial decision-making is incremental, and an overall policy must be derived inductively from a succession of separate decisions, each based on its own facts. The nature of a seminal case can influence the entire trend of the law, but in many cases the courts will not be aware of the drift of legal change.[74]

Competition law provides a clear model for 'public' legal intervention in an area which could be left to private claims, effectively often dealing with consumer

---

Harding and C.L. Lim (1999), *Renegotiating Westphalia: Essays and Commentary on the European and Conceptual Foundations of Modern International Law* (Dordrecht: Martinus Nijhoff); A. Clapham (1993), *Human Rights in the Private Sphere* (London: Clarendon Press), reworked as A. Clapham (2006), *Human Rights Obligations of Non-State Actors* (Oxford: Oxford University Press).

73   M.T. Kamminga, 'Holding Multinational Corporations Accountable for Human Rights Abuses: A Challenge for the EC', Ch. 17, in Philip Alston (ed.) (1999), *The EU and Human Rights* (Oxford: Oxford University Press) at 568.

74   Scott and Black, note 60 above, at 517.

interests, although formally acting to ensure an appropriate level of competition in a market. Beyond North America, 'private' competition claims remain rare and problematical, and globally the predominant model of competition regulation remains that of 'administrative' intervention by a public authority.[75] In relation to human rights claims in the market place context, an important question is whether such legal action on the part of consumers should be located on the vertical axis, by reference to the role of the State or public authorities in the business of market regulation, or whether there should be an effort to develop such redress at the horizontal level.

If, following the argument of the previous section, one major focus for the consumer's basic rights argument would be the issue of participation in the formulation of policy and standards so as to ensure equality of arms in the market place, then the vertical axis would seem most appropriate. The discussion in Chapters 6 and 7 below will show that administrative control is likely to remain a central aspect of systems of market regulation, whether at the national, EU, or WTO level.[76] Much of the business of mediating the conflicting claims of different market actors is a matter of balancing trading freedom against injury to a range of interests, and this is largely achieved by reference to standards which inevitably need to be worked out by expert administrative bodies. Many contemporary consumer concerns relate to the way in which policy and standards are worked out by such agencies, and the basic rights argument identified above is in essence one of access to that process of policy determination (for instance, that the views and interests of consumers should bear equal weight to that of other market or governmental actors). One of the concerns to emerge in the later discussion in this work is that both the arguments of large corporate actors and the trade liberalisation imperative may be privileged in policy-making and administrative determinations, in terms of both formal status and practical hearing, as compared with the representation of consumer interests. To elevate the status of consumer participation rights would then serve to redress any such imbalance, by allowing consumers or their representative groups to play a potentially powerful trump card in relation to the course of policy formation and the determination of relevant standards that inform the resolution of disputes or conflict of interest between different market actors. Again, BSE provides a useful illustrative reference point: a more rights-oriented approach to risk management, particularly in the earlier stages of the crisis, could have both encouraged *and legitimised* a more overtly precautionary and consumer-centric accommodation of scientific uncertainty and thus, perhaps, a more effective containment of the epidemic.

This idea of the autonomous consumer, empowered through access to policy formation, dovetails with recent ideology of the 'strong' consumer. Within the

---

75   The European Commission's recent attempts to promote private competition claims (Commission Green Paper, *Damages Actions for Breach of the EC Antitrust Rules*, COM (2005) 672 final) have resulted in a lively and to some extent sceptical debate: see, for example, the papers contained in K.D. Ehlermann and I. Atanasiu (eds) (2007), *European Competition Law Annual 2006: Enforcement of Prohibition of Cartels* (Oxford: Hart Publishing), at 423–85.

76   Especially in relation to the need for expert analysis and decision making, for instance, regarding risk assessment.

UK, the 1999 Government White Paper *Modern Markets, Confident Consumers*[77] proclaimed its underlying aim of reinforcing the 'virtuous cycle of strong consumers and strong business', drawing upon the argument that demanding consumers in a home market would make business more competitive internationally, so gaining competitive advantage in a globalised economy.[78] The New Labour agenda embodied in *Modern Markets, Confident Consumers* talks in terms of both empowering and protecting consumers. This approach also draws upon the perception that consumer protection policy – unlike, for example, labour protection – has evolved in a top-down fashion, frequently hitched to the strategies of more powerful governmental or business interests that have constructed the identity of the consumer and consumer interests according to their own agenda.[79] Such policy shifts indicate the historically incidental and manipulated character of consumer identity and the need to place the actual consumer in a more genuinely independent and centre-stage position.

It should not be forgotten that consumers do possess a number of legal and non-legal options for the purposes of advocating their own interests and securing their position, from political lobbying, through to private claims against those parties who directly injure their interests, and public law remedies of judicial review; moreover, the latter type of judicial process may already employ the basic rights argument, which could be raised in a more general (that is, non-consumer specific) context. Thus a consumer could, for example, argue in principle that basic citizen rights to health, fair economic treatment, or environmental protection (in so far as guaranteed by the legal order in question) have been violated by allowing a certain trading practice to take place. But the success of the latter kind of claim will depend on an assessment of the State's management and regulation of economic activity, and the extent of its responsibility in that regard. Many of these avenues of claim or redress on the part of consumers are both unpredictable in their outcome and inevitably raise a number of practical hurdles. The advantage of a direct claim, based upon basic rights of participation, is that it relates clearly to what for practical purposes remains the core issue of consumer protection: an ability to engage fully and fairly in the formulation of proactive and protective policy. If informed consumer representations have been fully heard and considered, then the application of standards worked out in that way will be less open to legal question later in the day. In this way, the imbalance between consumer and other interests is clearly and relevantly addressed, by locating a strong legal entitlement at a timely point in the policy and law-making process.

In sum, what is contained in this particular prospectus for legal development is the identification of a higher-order 'basic' consumer right, which may be invoked against relevant public authorities responsible for managing the development and formulation of policies and standards relevant to significant consumer interests. Such an entitlement relates more broadly speaking to fair and effective participation in such processes, but would necessarily involve a cluster of subsidiary rights concerned

---

77 Department of Trade and Industry, Cmd 4410 (1999).

78 Argued in particular by M. Porter (1990) in *The Competitive Advantage of Nations* (New York: The Free Press).

79 M. Hilton (2003), *Consumerism in Twentieth-Century Britain* (Cambridge: Cambridge University Press).

with information, transparency[80] and representation, all of which are prerequisites of effective participation. The point of representation merits some emphasis, since this again relates to a significant practical impediment for individual end-consumers, who may frequently lack the resources for undertaking legal action as individuals. Consumer affairs is an area in which representative organisations have emerged as significant actors,[81] and their legal role in this context should be recognised as a matter of both practical necessity and fair opportunity to engage in legal process.

The Responsible Citizen-Consumer

In this discussion of consumer identity and legal entitlement, we may return finally to a certain characterisation of the end-consumer, as a relatively sophisticated and affluent actor, and what may follow from that view of consumer identity in both ethical and legal terms. The underlying argument here is that the contemporary use of the term 'consumer', if it is to bear some distinctive and relevant meaning, should imply that the consuming party possesses a certain level of sophistication as an economic actor. Thus, 'consumer' should not bear a purely literal meaning and extend to any kind of consumption in any circumstances. Admittedly, an impoverished person consuming basic food in a situation of near-starvation can be regarded as a significant category of consumer (since the consumption in question may be a matter of life and death),[82] but not in an economic, market place sense, that is, as an active and autonomous participant in the line of supply and demand. Indigence is a matter for rescue and protection rather than of active economic involvement. The term 'consumer' is being used here, therefore, to denote an actor of some economic significance and active legal capacity, and in actual and historical terms corresponds more with relatively affluent, choice-bearing, 'Western' market place consumer, as an active participant in the capitalist economic system.

'Consumer' in the present context is thus a person of some strength: most contemporary designations of consumer status would concede some kinds of power, or at least the potential to exercise power. Such autonomous, discerning consumers typically are able to exercise critical reflection, which may lead to the making of choice or critical comment; furthermore, the minimal impact of individual consumer decision-making may be organised into more powerful collective action. As noted above, by definition suppliers need consumers, and for that reason may ultimately

---

80   For an overview of the legal development of the provision of information and greater transparency to consumers, see S. Weatherill (2005), *EU Consumer Law and Policy* (Cheltenham: Edward Elgar), Ch. 4.

81   For a useful brief summary of the development and present character of consumer representation and advocacy, see I. Ramsay (2007), *Consumer Law and Policy: Text and Materials on Regulating Consumer Markets* (Oxford: Hart Publishing), at 25–31; and Scott and Black, note 60 above, at 12–22.

82   And as such, the party facing starvation may have significant human rights claims, but as a *human being* invoking the right to life, health, or a minimum standard of subsistence for purposes of survival. In such a context, the designation 'consumer' may appear as ironic, insulting, or even trivialising.

fear consumers. As one price-fixing executive said to another from a separate firm, referring to customers: 'They are not your friend. They are not my friend. And we gotta have 'em. Thank God we gotta have 'em, but they are not my friends. You're my friend. I wanna be closer to you than I am to any customer.'[83]

The consumer in this sense therefore has the power of rejection, and that is the supplier's nightmare. It is of course a conditional power, and in market reality, very much so, dependent most obviously on information, the availability of alternative sources of supply, and on the energy and will to exercise choice, which in turn may depend upon a number of personal, social and economic variables. That is the reason for protective intervention and regulation, such as competition law, and then perhaps also the need for according higher-status basic rights to consumers for certain purposes, as discussed above. None the less, the underlying consumer identity is that of an autonomous, rational actor, capable of exercising choice based on preference in order to accommodate self-interest, and such an identity is legally bolstered. Building upon that view of the consumer, it may be appropriate to consider some linkage between the model of the autonomous, self-serving and legally reinforced market participant-consumer, and that of the critically reflective citizen-consumer, who may be expected to exercise choice in a responsible or maybe even altruistic manner. There may be two main bases for legally developing the idea of the responsible citizen-consumer; the first follows from an ethical position; the second is based on the cogency of a basic rights protection system.

In the first place, it should be noted that the concept of consumer identity and legal entitlement being put forward here implies active economic and political engagement, based upon a reflective response to market opportunities and an interest in the political shaping of market regulation. The argument which urges the award of higher-order rights for purposes of participating in the process of policy formation in effect transforms the market participant-consumer into the citizen-consumer, converting the consumer from an economic into a political actor. Involvement in a process which is political as much as economic implies an active and reflective engagement with a range of other interests which intersect with those of the consumer. An elevated right on the part of consumers to project their own interests within a policy discourse implies also an obligation to hear about other relevant interests, some of which may compete with those of the consumer. Effective political engagement thus presupposes an obligation to consider other viewpoints and take into account the needs and interests of other parties. Any basic right of a consumer to participate in the formulation of policy and law is not simply a crude right to make a loud noise and expect that to prevail in the cacophony of debate. It is a right to engage in responsible discourse, and in turn the responsibility associated with that role will logically feed back into the core consumer role of exercising choice and making decisions in the market place. If the essential concern here is to ensure that the consumer is able to act autonomously and rationally and be treated fairly in the market, then that is a matter of responsibility as well as entitlement.

There are a number of aspects to such responsible consumer engagement. For instance, it may be argued that relatively affluent contemporary consumers should

---

83   Department of Justice transcript: Cartel meeting, Atlanta, GA, 18 January 1995.

have some awareness of consumer 'pathologies' which may have an impact on society in a general and long-term manner. It is easy enough, for example, to point to problems such as over-indebtedness and obesity as an outcome of the myopic and self-indulgent pursuit of short-term interests, which may then have adverse consequences in relation to healthcare and social and economic policy.[84] Also, many consumers may reasonably be expected to inform themselves and act upon an awareness of issues of environmental degradation or economic exploitation which may be linked to their exercise of consumer choice. Thus the Department of Trade and Industry paper *A Fair Deal for All: Extending Competitive Markets: Empowered Consumers, Successful Business*[85] urges that consumers should act reflectively, considering the impact of their consumption decisions on the environment. The Fair Trade Foundation has stated:

> The Fair Trade Foundation, Oxfam and Traidcraft have agreed the following common definition of fair trade:
>
> Fair Trade is an alternative approach to conventional international trade. It is a trading partnership which aims at sustainable development for excluded and disadvantaged producers. It seeks to do this by providing better trading conditions, by awareness raising and by campaigning.[86]
>
> Clearly, any kind of fair trade policy in this sense is dependent on, firstly, consumer education and awareness, but secondly also the inculcation of a sense of own responsibility for exercising economic choices on the part of consumers.[87]

But also the overall logic of any *system* of rights protection requires that the legal protection of the range of rights should be organised, in relation to each other, in a sensible and cogent way. Obviously, particular rights cannot be sensibly protected without reference to other claims. That is the reason why most basic rights are qualified by exceptions in favour of other interests, the latter often expressed in the form of a general or 'public' interest, broadly encapsulating a range of countervailing interests. In a similar way, it would be ethically and politically difficult to argue that any consumer rights should have an absolute character, beyond some exceptional life-threatening circumstances which would in any case fall within the scope of an absolute 'right to life' protection. Consumers acting as such therefore need to be aware of the possible consequences of their own market choices and preferences, and how the latter may have an impact on other significant interests which may be or should be in turn the subject of their own legal protection. This may become obvious in situations in which a conflict of interests emerges as a legal battle – for instance, when the rights of economic actors, such as suppliers or consumers, may be judicially balanced against interests of environmental protection (in the European

---

84   A. Offer (2006), *The Challenge of Affluence: Self-Control and Well-Being in the United States and Britain Since 1950* (Oxford: Oxford University Press).

85   London, TSO, 2005.

86   <www.fairtrade.org.uk/about_partnership.htm>.

87   Generally on the subject of sustainable consumption, and ethical and fair trade, see Ramsay, note 81 above, at 101–106.

context, for example, balancing the Single Market imperative against environmental claims). But it is also something which logically should be part of individual or collective consumer decision making within the market itself. So we arrive at the idea of the 'ethical' or 'responsible' consumer who considers the choice of a product or service by reference to such issues as the exploitation of cheap labour in certain countries, or the risk of environmental degradation, or damage to a competitive economy, or the risk to general human health or animal welfare. This kind of 'responsible' consumer reflection may result in expensive or inconvenient decisions for consumers themselves, at least in the shorter term: 'fair trade', shopping locally, buying 'organic' produce, becoming vegetarian, rejecting the use of plastic bags or 'fast food', and the like, may involve some extra cost. But it is relevant to consider to what extent and in what ways the concept of the responsible consumer is logically linked to the idea of the autonomous consumer, and whether therefore respect for other, sometimes competing, interests and rights ought to be incorporated formally or informally into the legal process of rights protection.

The Case for Basic Consumer Rights

The above line of argument, which explores the justification for a higher level of legal entitlement for purposes of protecting the interests of economic consumers, may be summarised in the following way.

The opening question is, necessarily, what is so distinctive about the consumer role that requires a higher level of protection and entitlement? The answer to this question resides first of all in the ubiquity of consumption as a necessary part of human existence and survival – there is no escaping the role of consumer, for any of us. Consumption, therefore, is also a matter of life protection and enhancement. But putting the matter in those terms also serves to remind us that such fundamental interests are already a matter of substantive legal protection, for instance, through the right to life, the right to health, the right to enjoy a sustainable environment, or the bundle of rights relating to economic self-determination. The distinctive problem for the individual consumer resides rather in their relatively vulnerable position in actual political or economic terms, especially compared to that of parties with naturally opposing or competing rights or interests – typically, large corporate suppliers. Thus, however the legal position of the consumer may be defined on paper, the actual possibility of effectively asserting that entitlement may be limited, for instance, through difficulty of access to significant information, or by limited resources and know-how for purposes of political lobbying or undertaking litigation. Importantly, then, there is not a level legal playing-field between supplier and consumer, although they may appear as equals in the catalogue of substantive rights. Legal nomenclature (which, for instance, accords a similar legal 'personality' to large corporate actors and individual human beings, and refers to both as 'private parties' in a 'horizontal' legal relationship) suggest an equality which is contestable upon further reflection.

In such an analysis, the consumer then begins to appear as a vulnerable category of person. In the context of human rights argument, there is an analogy then with such groups as children, women, indigenous persons, disabled persons, or the elderly, who merit identification as politically, economically, socially, or culturally vulnerable categories who have been awarded a special degree of legal protection based upon that perception. In the case of the consumer (as in some of those other categories), such vulnerability has already been addressed via regulatory intervention. But the latter comprises a *third party* (State or intergovernmental organisation) protective measure, which constructs its own (arguably 'captured') view of consumer interests and preferences; a view which may be moderated by broader policy objectives, and in particular, trade considerations as noted above, and as reflected in the UK Government's (mis)handling of the BSE epidemic.

Regulatory protection, therefore, is by definition and in practice not based upon an autonomous or self-determined expression of interest. The value of a project which provides for a higher-level and autonomous legal entitlement in relation to consumer interests is twofold. First, it enhances consumer confidence, through a process of political and ethical rhetoric. Secondly, it enhances the consumer's procedural role and *locus standi* so as to redress the imbalance between the respective positions of supplier and consumer, especially in relation to access to information, lobbying, and litigation opportunities. Effective lobbying and litigation may in turn require some recognition of the need to mobilise collective representation through organisations which can feasibly match the will and resources of large corporate actors. The gist of the case for basic consumer rights arises then from this market place reality: that the individual consumer is a vulnerable actor and also one in need of an autonomous expression of their own interests and preferences. Essentially, the promotion of the rights-led view of market governance outlined in this chapter could lead to a repositioning and strengthening of citizen-consumer's claim to adequate protection in his/her daily engagement within the market place.

Chapter 4

Taking the WTO to Task in Seattle: Basic Rights Protection as a Legal Strategy and the Political and Legal Leverage of Rights Argument

Sleepless in Seattle: Dramatising the Discourse of Conflict

I was there in the square, shouting my mouth off about saving some fish.
Now could that be construed as some radical view, or some liberal's wish?[1]

At the end of November 1999, a major World Trade Organisation (WTO) conference convened in Seattle in order to establish an agenda for the next round of global trade discussions. As 6,000 WTO delegates converged on Seattle, a large number of protesters – estimated at between 50,000 and 100,000 – arrived to participate in public demonstrations against WTO policies.[2] The protesters had diverse origins and affiliations, coming from both developed and developing countries, and comprising representatives of human rights, environmental protection and religious groups, along with students and labour rights activists. Also participating were some right-wing protectionist groups objecting against free trade policies for rather different reasons. As the protests took place, a minority of demonstrators engaged in some violence and looting, which prompted the police and National Guard to declare a state of emergency. This in turn led to the declaration of curfews, arrests and the use of tear gas, pepper spraying and firing of rubber bullets against the crowds. As these events outside the conference centre commanded the main media attention, the conference itself struggled with an unrealistic agenda and growing rifts between developed and developing States represented at the meeting. By the end of the week, thirty-six hours of continuous discussion by trade ministers resulted in an adjournment. This led to some euphoric claims by leaders of the protesters: 'We won – we really disrupted it. We certainly created an atmosphere to make it difficult for them to work.'[3] Certainly the 'riots' and the attempts to control the demonstrations

---

1   Bob Geldof, 'Someone's Always Looking At You' (1980).

2   There had been, in very recent history, some smaller-scale 'rehearsals' of this kind of public protest – for instance, demonstrations in Vancouver in November 1997, at the fifth annual APEC (Asian Pacific Economic Cooperation) leaders' meeting, at the University of British Columbia.

3   Tracy Katelman, 'Alliance for Sustainable Jobs and the Environment', CNN report, 4 December 1999.

resulted in media and public attention for an event which might not otherwise have engaged wide popular interest. Most significantly, it dramatised an ongoing debate about the nature of the international trading system and its impact on a range of matters: the power and influence of large transnational companies, environmental damage, economic deprivation, working conditions in developing countries, levels of health and safety, and the realisation of a number of human rights.

It is difficult to assess exactly the political and historical impact of an event such as the Seattle protests. Much depends on context. There may be a different significance according to whether the incident is viewed in the context of American history and politics or that of the international trading system. But, for purposes of the present discussion, the Seattle confrontation may be seen as possessing another kind of significance, in demonstrating a tactic or strategy in political, moral and legal debate and in relation to the way argument is conducted more generally.

There are two senses in which this strategic significance of the Seattle incident may be understood: one of expressing the substance of argument, and one of tactically deploying argument, but both have a *dramatic* force.

In the first place, the public demonstrations against the WTO ministerial meeting was a dramatic presentation of the argument about the management of international trade. In its simplest form, this is a dialogue between proponents of free trading at the international level, putting it forward as something economically and socially beneficial in itself, and those who are concerned that such global free trade should not compromise particular interests and values, relating to consumer choice, health and safety, environmental protection and, more broadly, economic and social justice. In short, in the context of international trade, this is the tension between the global liberalisation of markets and national protectionism used to protect these other types of interest. Underlying this dialogue are complex economic, political and ethical arguments which cannot easily be resolved, but the Seattle confrontation translated these arguments into a more dramatic, simplified, yet accessible form. Thus on one side, the Director-General of the WTO stated, 'Trade is the ally of working people, not the enemy … as living standards improve, so too does education, health, the environment and labor standards',[4] while the UK Trade and Industry minister argued that 'Free trade and open commerce are a bringer of opportunity and not a threat.'[5] On the other side of the argument, the WTO's policies and procedures, aimed at market liberalisation, were the subject of strong criticism: 'The WTO aims to eliminate what they are calling non-tariff trade barriers, and a lot of those trade barriers are actually hard-won environmental and food safety protections',[6] and, in relation to the WTO's dispute settlement process, 'People deciding the disputes are trade experts, and the focus is on facilitating trade, and that means when there's another concern, like the environment and human health, trade trumps.'[7] Such statements in themselves, and their presentation in the context of dramatic confrontation between civil society protesters and high-level official representatives, serve to transform the character

---

4   Mike Moore, WTO Director-General, CNN report, 29 November 1999.
5   Stephen Byers, UK Trade and Industry Secretary, CNN report, 4 December 1999.
6   Daniel Seligman, Sierra Club, CNN report, 29 November 1999.
7   Martin Wagner, EarthJustice Legal Defense Fund, CNN report.

of previously academic and scientific debate in a way that is likely to have political impact.

This point may be linked with the second, more tactical sense of dramatisation. In some ways, this may be described as a choice of forum. If people wish to challenge the conventional intergovernmental wisdom regarding the virtues of a free international market, there are of course a number of ways in which this may be done: by writing academic and scientific papers, by presenting arguments in national parliamentary debates, by lobbying relevant political actors, by mounting legal challenge to policies and rules, by campaigning through the distribution of literature and setting-up of websites. Attempts may be made to measure the relative effectiveness of such methods, and they may be chosen, singly or jointly, according to the more precise interest whose protection is sought and the main targets of criticism. But these various methods of challenge may be placed on a sliding scale in terms of how public or discreet they may appear, and in terms of political impact, that may also be an element in their choice. Would it be more effective to quietly 'bend the ear' of an influential person, or shout the message from the rooftops in front of television cameras while smashing windows? Thus it is not only the substance of the argument which may be dramatised, but also its method of delivery. Courtroom drama is another familiar example: the sense that there may be greater impact through having 'a day in court', using spoken rhetoric addressed to a public audience in a setting of ritual confrontation, compared to employing argument on paper or having a discussion in a private office.

Undoubtedly, the events in Seattle in 1999 served to dramatise and raise the level of media and public attention to a subject that might otherwise be seen as a remote matter of policy. But there is also a perception that it served as a 'defining' historical moment which may have brought about some shift in the history of the subject. Thus, in the words of one academic commentary:

> For some developed country governments, the street demonstrations were seen as a reflection of the strong links that existed between trade on one hand and the environment, workers' rights and child welfare on the other. Many in the public saw it as the beginning of a new era of 'people over profits', or 'globalization with a human face'. Whatever the perception, Seattle left the WTO bruised and polarized.[8]

This kind of impact may be described in various ways, so as to bring out the political force of such dramatising tactics. It might be presented, for instance, as a desirable 'shock to the system' or 'wake-up call', or more abstractly as a kind of energising event. What the example of the Seattle confrontation serves to convey is the tactical gain which may result from such dramatising methods. Furthermore, there may be lessons from this kind of example which may be employed in the more specifically legal context.

8　Bernard M Hoekman and Michel M Kostecki (2001), *The Political Economy of the World Trading System* (Oxford: Oxford University Press, 2nd edn), at 107.

Raising the Legal Stakes: Human Rights as the Trump Card

*Like any dealer he was watching for the card that is so high and wild he'll never need to
deal another.*[9]

The main subject of discussion in this work is the deployment of a particular kind
of legal argument, invoking entitlement to a special category of 'fundamental'
rights, in order to promote or defend certain interests. The resort to such basic
rights argumentation became increasingly widespread during the second half of
the twentieth century as the ideology of basic rights protection itself became more
entrenched as a feature of global legal culture. The particular interest here is the way
in which this type of argument has been used in the context of economic relations
within the market place by a range of actors, most of whom may be not be seen
as the typical or expected beneficiaries of fundamental human rights protection.
The question of the extension of this kind of protection to such actors as trading
companies and economic consumers has been considered in Chapters 2 and 3. Now
the method of argumentation will be probed.

The first point of inquiry concerns the political and legal force of transforming
(or, it may be said, dramatising) the debate, from a process of legal balancing of
competing interests and policies to one of arguing about fundamental entitlements.
The resort to basic rights argument may be seen to transform both the content and
the tone of the legal discourse. In short, if an interest is converted into a fundamental
right, it achieves a higher currency. In legal terms, a right is worth more than an
interest, and a fundamental right is worth more than an ordinary right. In the language
of rights discourse, possession of the fundamental right is equivalent to possession
of the winning hand in a card game – it is the trump. In Dworkin's well-known
argument, such a fundamental legal entitlement 'trumps' any opposing, utilitarian
interest or policy.[10]

In such a legal culture, therefore, securing entitlement to such rights provides an
improved chance of winning in the legal arena. This of course renders the resort to
legal argument more politically attractive, and in economic terms more profitable.
But also, in the uncertain and rather murky environment of economic and political
argument and debate about markets, the social effects of economic policy, and the
feasibility of managing international trade, it provides an alluring simplicity and
clarity of solution. Forget the everlasting contradictions of 'experts' on both sides
of the debate, for once a player has a fundamental right, that person has the political
and ethical power to 'trump' all else, and there is the quick and unarguable solution.
For lawyers, at least, it is a nice outcome, although it is likely to leave economists,
business experts, politicians and sociologists muttering outside the court.

In legal terms, the trump is the product of raising the stakes through a kind of
dramatisation of the argument and confrontation of interests, in a way which may
be seen as analogous to the Seattle demonstrations. Casting a legal breach or injury
to interests as a human rights violation elevates the matter to the highest level of

---

9   Leonard Cohen, 'The Stranger Song'.
10   Ronald Dworkin (1977), *Taking Rights Seriously* (London: Duckworth).

legal drama. This sense of the fundamental human rights claim as a dramatic and performative process is expressed revealingly by Klaus Günther in the following terms:

> By referring to a human right, a person *articulates* his or her suffering from an offence or a harm, and he or she claims that everybody is obliged *to listen* to the individual report of this experience. The declaration of a human right represents this experience, rejects it, and gives a conceptual framework to the interpretation of new experiences of injustice and fear … in the future.[11]

In this way, Günther argues, fundamental rights 'open political culture to experiences of injustice and fear, and provide a voice through which the pain … can be articulated and listened to.' This depiction of fundamental rights argument, as a kind of ethical and political dramatic performance, is telling. It enables us to appreciate the value and currency of such legal argument as a *dramatic raising of the stakes*. In the same way as a large public demonstration against high-ranking officials converts critical discourse into a dramatic confrontation, human rights argumentation serves to both dramatise and elevate legal discourse.

In the same way as some commentators saw the Seattle events as a key historical reference point, even defining the start of a 'new era', the resolution of a human rights claim, or even the use of human rights argumentation in itself, may have a political impact which goes beyond that of 'normal' legal process. To say that the invocation of core fundamental values and an imperative of legal protection transforms the nature of the legal process is to state the obvious. But what is important, and perhaps less readily appreciated, are the consequences and ramifications of such a transformation and dramatisation of legal process. It needs to be understood as a device for converting the mundane into the sensational. To give a brief example (and one that has been and will be examined further at a later point), it is a process which allows a business office to be re-presented as something similar to the sanctuary of the personal home in order to benefit from a fundamental entitlement to 'privacy'. This example raises important questions about both context (business premises as distinct from the private home) and personality and identity (the powerful corporate actor as distinct from the individual human person). In other words, revaluing the legal currency, or supplying the pack with a trump card, is to provide something powerful and requires care and consideration, in the same way that organising a public and aggressive confrontation is a strategy which should be considered advisedly.

The following sections of discussion will explore in more detail the political and ethical impact of human rights argumentation, first at a legislative and broader political level, and secondly at the judicial level of human rights litigation, before moving finally to examine what may be regarded as some of the systemic costs of employing human rights argument.

---

11   Klaus Günther (1999), 'The Legacies of Injustice and Fear: A European Approach to Human Rights and their Effects on Political Culture', Ch. 4 in Philip Alston (ed), *The EU and Human Rights* (Oxford: Oxford University Press), at 127.

The Impact of Human Rights Argument at the Legislative Level: Recasting the Normative Landscape

The 'trumping' thesis in relation to fundamental human rights argument implies that the recognition of such a legal entitlement, of being seen as the holder of such fundamental rights, produces a considerable legal advantage, if not the winning hand, in a legal dispute. Again, this may appear at first to be a statement of the obvious. By their nature, fundamental rights cannot be overridden, so that the possessor of that kind of right should prevail in a legal contest. But this 'obvious' assertion has been subject to some sceptical scrutiny. Koskenniemi, for example, has argued:

> ... rights-rhetoric is not as powerful as it claims to be. It does not hold a coherent set of normative demands that could be resorted to in the administration of society. To the contrary, despite its claim for value-neutrality, rights-rhetoric is constantly reduced to conflicting and contested arguments about the political good. The identification, meaning and applicability of rights are dependent on contextual assessments of 'proportionality' or administrative 'balancing' through which priorities are set among conflicting conceptions of political value and scarce resources are distributed between contending social groups.[12]

This kind of sceptical argument may be used as a test of the actual impact (whether measured in legal, ethical, or political terms) of the resort to fundamental rights argument. The assessment of such impact is in itself a complex matter and it may be useful to distinguish two levels of impact, since different conclusions may be drawn according to whether reference is being made to a more global political ('meta-level') impact or a more specific legal impact. Another way in which to express this difference is to talk about 'legislative' and 'judicial'-level impacts. Let us first consider the impact of human rights argument in the context of broader policy and legislation: what is the effect on the conduct of governments and legislatures?

There would appear to be mounting evidence of governmental and intergovernmental responsiveness to this kind of legal argumentation. This is no doubt an element of the increasing entrenchment of the protection of human rights in global legal culture. More and more, governments do not wish to be seen as rights-violators, and this is then a matter of not only legal but also political currency. It is not just a matter of being legally in the wrong or ethically on a weaker footing, but it may be politically and economically damaging. This would be most manifestly the case if human rights delinquency results in the loss of significant political, military or economic support, as the latter become increasingly subject to 'conditionality' (for instance, arms or economic aid will not be supplied, or membership of an organisation such as the EU will be denied, if there is a bad record on human rights protection).[13] Much of course depends on circumstances in this respect, since some

---

12   Martii Koskenniemi, 'The Effect of Rights on Political Culture', Ch. 3 in Alston (ed.), note 11 above, at 99.

13   There is a substantial literature on various aspects of such conditionality, at both the intergovernmental and national governmental levels. For instance on EU conditionality, see: P.J. Kuijper (1993), 'Trade Sanctions, Security and Human Rights and Commercial Policy',

States and governments are sufficiently powerful to withstand such losses, while others may be especially vulnerable. But, particularly in the context of an ascending global rhetoric of commitment to democratic governance, there is no doubt that overall the protection of human rights now has a strong political currency, for both State and non-State actors.[14] At the very least, there is widespread subscription to the rhetoric, even if actual performance may be less convincing.

It is instructive to take a few examples of situations in which resort to human rights argument may be seen as achieving considerable impact at this 'meta' level. Three cases will be considered here: human rights argument as an instrument of penal reform, as a means of converting the EC to serious human rights protection, and as a means of bringing corporate power to heel.

Penal Reform

This is the context in which meta-level resort to human rights argument has perhaps produced some of the most dramatic outcomes. Here, the impact of 'rational' and 'scientific' reformative argument may be instructively compared with that of ethical, more intuitive human rights-based reformative argument. Discussion of the effectiveness of penal measures is commonly based on research findings, relating for instance to the deterrent or corrective efficacy of such measures. Yet, even when such evidence may be convincing in academic and intellectual terms, entrenched public (and consequently, in democratic systems, official) opinion is often 'irrationally' or emotively committed to a retributive policy, which is resistant to the reform of strongly punitive measures. One of the clearest examples is provided by strong public support for the death penalty, in the face of convincing research evidence concerning its lack of deterrent effect. On the other hand, there have been some examples of legal reform of penal measures which has followed from ethical objection based on violation of human rights. Although such arguments may have an indirect character – for example, alleging rights violations in relation to 'death row' conditions, or discrimination in the application of a mandatory sentencing policy – the outcome

---

in M Maresceau (ed.), *The European Community's Commercial Policy After 1992: The Legal Dimension* (The Hague: Martinus Nijhoff), at 420; D. Napoli, 'The European Union's Foreign Policy and Human Rights' (1995), in N.A. Neuwahl and A. Rosas (eds), *The European Union and Human Rights* (The Hague: Martinus Nijhoff), at 306; B. Brandtner and A. Rosas, 'Human Rights in the External Policy of the European Community', *European Journal of International Law*, 9, and the contributions to Alston (ed), note 11 above, Chs 18–22. On respect for human rights as a condition for accession to the EU, see the Copenhagen 'political criteria' laid down by the European Council in June 1993, *Bull EC*, 6-1993. On the inclusion of human rights protection in the policies of international financial institutions, see: N.H. Moller (1997), 'The World Bank: Human Rights, Democracy and Governance', *Netherlands Quarterly of Human Rights* 15(21); N.D. Bradlow (1996), 'The World Bank, the IMF and Human Rights', *Transnational Law and Contemporary Problems* 6(47).

14   Many large corporations have now enthusiastically embraced the concept of 'corporate responsibility', issuing 'CR reports' as evidence of their socially and environmentally responsible policies. See further critical discussion of this in the Corporate Watch Report (2006), *What's Wrong with Corporate Social Responsibility?* (Oxford: Corporate Watch).

may none the less be practical non-implementation or legislative abandonment of the measure itself. In this way, using the trump card of human rights violation may achieve something that rational, research-based argument has failed to do.

There is clear evidence that in many jurisdictions the abandonment or non-activation of the death penalty is based on an overriding human rights objection. Schabas summarises legal developments in this area in the following way:

> Those [countries] that still retain [the death penalty] find themselves increasingly subject to international pressure in favour of abolition, sometimes quite direct, for example, in the refusal to grant extradition where a fugitive will be exposed to a capital sentence. Abolition of the death penalty is generally considered to be an important element in democratic development for States breaking with a past characterised by terror, injustice and repression. In some cases abolition is effected by explicit references in constitutional instruments to the international treaties prohibiting the death penalty. In others, it has been the contribution of the judiciary of judges applying constitutions that make no specific mention of the death penalty but that enshrine the right to life and that prohibiting cruel, inhuman and degrading treatment or punishment.[15]

There is a growing case law, across jurisdictions and within international tribunals and other bodies of using different kinds of human rights argumentation to prevent the use of capital punishment, for instance, by declaring the measure unconstitutional,[16] by ruling against extradition to a jurisdiction where the penalty is still used,[17] or declaring 'death row' detention a violation of basic rights.[18]

The way in which this kind of argument acts as a trump, in relation to the policy and other law supporting the use of capital punishment, is clearly expressed in the judgment of Justice Chaskalson, the president of the South African Constitutional Court, in the seminal ruling on the question, *State* v. *Makwanyane*, in that jurisdiction:

---

15   William A. Schabas (2002), *The Abolition of the Death Penalty in International Law* (Cambridge: Cambridge University Press, 3rd edn), at 2–3. Examples of Constitutional Courts resorting to human rights provisions in 'abolitionist' judgments include those in Hungary (1991), South Africa (1995), Ukraine (1999) and Albania (1995). Roger Hood comments, in relation to the linkage between abolition of the death penalty and human rights argument: 'There is good evidence to support the view that the abolition of capital punishment is linked to the development of political rights which emphasize 'human rights'': Roger Hood (2002), *The Death Penalty: A Worldwide Perspective* (Oxford: Oxford University Press, 3rd edn), at 22.

16   See, for example, the South African Constitutional Court in *State* v. *Makwanyane* (1995) 1 LRC 269; (1995) *Human Rights Law Journal* 16:154.

17   See, for example, the European Court of Human Rights in *Soering* v. *UK*, 11 (1989) *European Human Rights Reports (EHRR)*, 439.

18   See, for example, the 1993 ruling of the Privy Council in *Pratt* v. *Attorney General for Jamaica* (1994) 2 AC 1 (finding that the length of imprisonment on death row was inhuman and degrading punishment). Generally, for a good selection of legal source material on human rights and capital punishment, see Henry J. Steiner and Philip Alston (2000), *International Human Rights in Context: Law Politics Morals* (Oxford: Oxford University Press, 2nd edn), at 18–55.

If public opinion were to be decisive there would be no need for constitutional adjudication. The protection of rights could then be left to Parliament, which has a mandate from the public, and is answerable to the public for the ways its mandate is exercised, but this would be a return to parliamentary sovereignty and a retreat from the new legal order established by the 1993 Constitution ... By committing ourselves to a society founded on the recognition of human rights we are required to value these two rights [life and dignity] above all others. And this must be demonstrated by the State in everything that it does, including the way it punishes criminals.[19]

The judgment as a whole provides an informative review of the way in which human rights argument has been used in a number of jurisdictions to secure legal abolition of the death penalty, demonstrating how the outlawing of the penalty as 'cruel, inhuman and degrading punishment' has been based on the violation of basic legal entitlements – to human dignity, the unqualified right to life, the more specific content of the latter and protection against arbitrary and irrevocable treatment. Calling upon these rights is seen to trump the appeal on the other side of the debate to the need for deterrence and a strong sense of retribution in crime-ridden and violent societies. The dramatising effect of this trumping human rights argument is conveyed in the title of another book by Schabas: *The Death Penalty as Cruel Treatment and Torture: Capital Punishment Challenged in the World's Courts.*[20] In this linguistic shift, the term 'death penalty', suggestive of a legally valid measure is visibly translated into 'cruel treatment and torture', conveying the graphic image and vocabulary of an unqualified outlaw activity, on the high-profile stage of the global court system.

Other penal measures have been challenged through the use of human rights argument with some success. A recent example is to be found in the way in which mandatory sentencing provisions in Australia have come under legal and political pressure in this way.[21] So-called 'three strikes' legislation (an automatic prison sentence following three convictions for certain offences) in the Northern Territory and Western Australia has been criticised as violating rights to equal treatment, in that such measures target aboriginal and juvenile offenders disproportionately compared to other groups. Criticism on such grounds has been put forward by both Australian authorities (such as the Law Council of Australia and the Australian Law Reform Commission) and bodies outside Australia (such as Amnesty International and UN Committee on the Rights of the Child).[22] In 1997, the Committee on the Rights of the Child expressed particular concern regarding 'the enactment of new legislation in two States, where a high proportion of Aboriginal people live, which

---

19   *Makwanyane*, note 16 above, paras 88 and 144 of the judgment.

20   By William A. Schabas (1996) *The Death Penalty as Cruel Treatment and Torture: Capital Punishment Challenged in the World's Courts* (Boston, MA: Northeastern University Press).

21   See generally, Chris Cunneen (2002), 'Mandatory Sentencing and Human Rights', *Current Issues in Criminal Justice* 13:322; Neil Morgan (1999), 'Capturing Crime or Capturing Votes? The Aims and Effects of Mandatories', *University of New South Wales Law Journal* 22:267.

22   See the report prepared by ATSIC (Aboriginal and Torres Straits Islander Commission) by Chris Cunneen (1999), *Law and Justice: Mandatory Sentencing*, Conclusions and Executive Summary, 13.1–13.3 <www.atsic.gov.au/issues/law_and_justice/mandatory_sentencing>.

provides for mandatory detention and punitive measures for juveniles, thus resulting in a high representation of Aboriginal juveniles in detention'.[23]

This led to arguments that the Australian federal government would be in breach of its international obligations under the International Covenant on Civil and Political Rights, the Convention on the Rights of the Child, and the Convention for the Elimination of All Forms of Racial Discrimination. This criticism was seen as a significant factor in the decision of the government of the Northern Territory to repeal its mandatory sentencing regime in October 2001,[24] while a critical report from the Senate Legal and Constitutional References Committee in March 2002[25] placed pressure on the Government of Western Australia to consider its mandatory sentencing law.

Taking Rights Seriously in the EC Legal Order

The second example of the impact of human right argument concerns a now well-known story in the history of European law: the 'Damascene' conversion of the European Court of Justice to the cause of protecting fundamental rights as a matter of EC law. In the early 1970s, the Court of Justice was prompted, mainly by argument emanating from German courts, to confirm that fundamental rights were guaranteed under EC law to an extent commensurate with the constitutional protection provided under Member State law.[26] Detailed accounts of this legal episode are available elsewhere,[27] and what is important for the purposes of the present argument is to note how concern about a perceived European (Community) disregard of fundamental rights which were guaranteed at the national level was dramatised in the form of

---

23   Committee on the Rights of the Child (1997), *Concluding observations on Australia's first report under the Convention on the Rights of the Child*, 10 October.

24   In August 2001, a new Labour government was elected to office in the Northern Territory. The mandatory minimum regime for property offences was abandoned in the reform and replaced by a scheme which still limited judicial discretion to some extent, but was much more flexible.

25   Senate Legal and Constitutional References Committee (2002), *Inquiry into the Human Rights (Mandatory Sentencing of Property Offences) Bill 2000* (Parliament of Australia, March 2002). The Bill would have had the effect of overriding Western Australia's mandatory sentencing legislation on the ground of conflicting with Australia's international legal obligations. The Committee, although very critical of Western Australia's legislation, thought that the Bill should not proceed but that instead the Government of Western Australia should address 'the deleterious effect of mandatory sentencing on indigenous youth'.

26   For an overview of these legal developments, see: Sionaidh Douglas-Scott (2002), *Constitutional Law of the European Union* (Harlow: Longman), at 255–9, and 266–74; Paul Craig and Gráinne de Búrca (2007), *EU Law: Text, Cases and Materials* (Oxford: Oxford University Press, 4th edn), at 379 ff.

27   For critical discussion, see some of the studies referred to by both Douglas-Scott, and Craig and de Búrca, note 26 above. It is useful to view this earlier episode in the longer-term context of the ongoing dialogue between Community and national courts on this question; there is some interesting discussion published during the 1990s and more recently, which relates the earlier case law to more recent, post-Maastricht Treaty constitutional argument, among those references.

a high-level legal challenge, rather like a judicial throwing-down of the gauntlet. When this came to a head in the early 1970s,[28] both the *Verwaltungsgericht* (Administrative Court) of Frankfurt and the *Bundesverfassungsgericht* (German Federal Constitutional Court) invoked a trump card comprising both fundamental rights protection and also of basic principles concerning the foundation of the EC, its constitutional structure and the relationship between the Member States and the Community. Moreover, it should be remembered that the trigger for this seminal constitutional debate in the *Internationale Handelsgesellschaft* litigation was the mundane issue of a security payment in relation to an export licence.[29] In short, what was underlying these 1970s 'fundamental rights cases' was a willingness on the part of certain national courts (mainly in Germany and Italy[30]) to raise the stakes in a judicial confrontation with the European Court of Justice and the Community as a whole, in order to condition the way in which Community law was being made and applied. And in one sense and at one level, it was a tactic that succeeded, in that it converted an apparent indifference to the issue of fundamental rights at the EC level to a strong rhetoric of legal protection which subsequently became well embedded in the EU order as a whole.[31]

It would be useful to illustrate briefly the process of legal dramatisation and trumping within this episode. The earlier rights-unsympathetic attitude of the Court of Justice was evident in a number of judgments during the 1950s and 1960s.[32] In its *Sgarlata* judgment in 1965 for instance, the Court confirmed that arguments relating to the protection of basic rights 'cannot be allowed to override the clearly restrictive wording of Article 173, which it is the Court's task to apply',[33] while Advocate General Roemer in his opinion for that case argued that 'it clearly cannot fall within the powers of the Court of Justice to amend the Treaty on this point.'[34] Such statements were in part made in resistance to the idea that *national* human rights protection should apply to Community measures or action, but altogether during this earlier

---

28   The turning point was the litigation arising from *Internationale Handelsgesellschaft* v. *EVSt,* comprising successive rulings by the European Court of Justice (Case 11/70, (1970) European Court Reports (ECR) 1125), the *Verwaltungsgericht* of Frankfurt ((1972) Common Market Law Reports (CMLR) 177), and the *Bundesverfassungsgericht (Solange I)* ((1974) 2 CMLR 564).

29   This is, of course, true of a number of 'leading' cases in EC law. For instance, both *Van Gend en Loos* and *Costa* v. *ENEL* arose from relatively trivial disputes. But then, this is a main point of the argument – that 'trumping' results from the stakes being raised, by invoking in such cases either basic constitutional principles or fundamental rights, in order to win the legal point in the case in hand.

30   For instance, in *Frontini* v. *Miistero delle Finanze* (1974) 2 CMLR 372, the Italian Constitutional Court handed down a ruling similar to that of *Bundesverfassungsgericht* concerning the need to monitor the EC system of protection of fundamental rights.

31   See in particular the discussion in Chapter 5 below.

32   See, for instance: Case 1/58, *Stork v High Authority* (1959) ECR 17; Cases 36–8, 40/59, *Geitling* v. *High Authority* (1960) ECR 423; Case 40/64, *Sgarlata and others* v. *Commission* (1965) ECR 215.

33   Note 32 above, (1965) ECR, at 227.

34   Ibid., at 235.

period the human rights argument was neither pressed by applicants nor discussed by the Court with any vigour. When the matter arose, it did so incidentally, and was easily met with a disclaimer of any judicial power of Treaty amendment. In contrast, the *Internationale Handelsgesellschaft* litigation comprised a frontal assault, and then a response from the Court of Justice that shifted doctrine. As stated above, the stakes were raised by moving the question of fundamental rights protection to the centre of the stage and constitutionalising the issue, in particular probing the basic transfer of sovereign power to the Communities. The Frankfurt Administrative Court appeared to produce a trump card in the form of the German Basic Law, provoking the Court of Justice to respond by producing two European trump cards. The first card was the principle of supremacy of Community law, irrespective of the status of any conflicting national provision. But as a trump card, this had to be played with the second card. This second card was a neat trick, trumping the German trump on its own terms:

> However, an examination should be made as to whether or not any analogous guarantee inherent in Community law has been disregarded. In fact, respect for fundamental rights forms an integral part of the general principles of Community law protected by the Court of Justice. The protection of such rights, whilst inspired by the constitutional provisions common to the Member States, must be ensured within the framework of the structure and objectives of the Community. It must therefore be ascertained, in the light of the doubts expressed by the Verwaltungsgericht, whether the system of deposits has infringed rights of a fundamental nature, respect for which must be ensured in the Community legal system.[35]

This was an impressive trump, cleverly incorporating the Member State system of protection into the EC order, which by a marvellous act of judicial discovery was found to have inherently contained the protection of fundamental rights as something which *must be ensured*. But the Member States, although important shareholders in this enterprise of European-level protection, were not controlling shareholders – the Community would have the final word on this legal development through a sense of its own structure and objectives. In a single move, the Court of Justice had ensured the application of the supremacy principle in the most challenging situation, whilst inaugurating a new system of supranational fundamental rights protection, which would eventually lead to treaty amendment (such as the appearance of Article 6 of the Treaty on European Union[36]) and the EU Charter of Fundamental Rights. Whatever the subsequent reservations regarding the *adequacy* of this EC/EU system of protection,[37] there had been an irreversible shift in the respective European and

---

35 (1970) ECR, at 1134.

36 In particular, Article 6(2) provides: 'The Union shall respect fundamental rights, as guranteed by the European Convention for the Protection of Human Rights and Fundamental Freedoms … And as they result from the constitutional traditions common to the Member States, as general principles of Community law.'

37 As expressed for instance in such cases as *Re Wünsche Handelsgesellschaft,* decision of the *Bundesverfassungsgericht* of 22 October 1986, (1987) 3 CMLR 255 (*Solange II*); and *Brunner* v. *The European Union Treaty* (another decision of the *Bundesverfassungsgericht*) (1994) 1 CMLR 57.

national positions, such that the burden of showing any weakness in the EC system of protection would now lie with Member State critics.

Corporate Power in the Courtroom

The third example of the trumping effect of human rights argumentation, bringing about a major shift in legal policy, is based on the recent ruling of the European Court of Human Rights in what has become colloquially known as the 'McLibel' case,[38] involving the use by the McDonald's Corporation of English defamation law to quieten a vociferous and critical campaign against the company's policies. Although the defending party in the legal proceedings before the Human Rights Court was the British Government, the saga of litigation[39] preceding the final ruling was very much concerned with the balance of legal and economic power between large corporations and their critics.

In 1986, the organisation London Greenpeace[40] issued a 'factsheet' entitled 'What's Wrong with McDonald's', which was critical of the company's employment practices and the nutritional value of its products. In 1990, the company brought legal proceedings against two of the people distributing this literature, Helen Steel and David Morris, claiming damages for libel. The two defendants were denied legal aid, but contested the claim, representing themselves and supported only by some help from volunteer lawyers. After a record-breaking 313-day trial, it was held that, although many of the statements made about McDonald's were true,[41] some statements were libellous and £60,000 damages were awarded to the company. This judgment was largely upheld on appeal, although the damages were reduced to £40,000. The defendants were refused further leave to appeal, and then brought their own claim against the UK under the European Convention on Human Rights, alleging violations of their right to a fair trial under Article 6(1), and to their freedom of speech under Article 10. These claims were upheld in February 2005.

In effect, the libel action had already damaged the company, despite its legal outcome and the company's original belief that English defamation law would provide it with the trump card. The crusading resilience of the two campaigners and the demonstrated accuracy of some of the key critical comments in the leaflet, damaged the public image of the company, leaving it wary of trying to enforce its award of damages. Already the argument between the two sides had been hugely

---

38   *Steel and Morris* v. *United Kingdom,* application no. 68416/01, Judgment of 15 February 2005; 41(2005) *EHRR* 403. See also the discussion in Chapter 8 below.

39   The writ for libel was issued in 1990; the trial took place between June 1994 and December 1996 (at 313 days, the longest trial in English legal history); there was a 23-day appeal in 1999; the ECHR case was lodged in September 2000, and final judgment given by the Human Rights Court in February 2005. Clearly, few individuals would possess the stamina for such sustained litigation.

40   Not associated with the global NGO Greenpeace.

41   Mr Justice Bell ruled for instance that McDonald's marketing 'pretended to a positive nutritional benefit which their food did not match', that the company's advertising strategy 'exploited children', and that the company 'paid low wages, helping to depress wages in the catering trade'.

dramatised; the stakes had been raised by the company's decision to invoke its rights under the libel law, and were then further raised by the Steel and Morris's decision to invoke their more fundamental rights, and play a card which might trump the libel card. At the end of the libel case, the outcome of the game might have been termed an uncertain draw, as a legal victory for the company, but a moral victory for the campaigners. By the end of the Strasbourg proceedings, playing the human rights trump had resulted in not only a legal victory for the campaigners but also in a redrawing of the legal map. By 2005, McDonald's were shy of publicity, pointing out that they were not a party to the Strasbourg proceedings and that the earlier case related to practices of the 1980s, from which the company had 'moved on'.

The wider and longer-term significance of the 'McLibel' case resides in the impact of human rights argument on the legal and political strategies respectively of large corporate actors on the one hand and of critical NGOs and individuals on the other hand, and the balance of resources between these types of player on the legal and political stage. English libel law, which had made it difficult for small campaigners to defend critical statements against major corporate interests, may no longer be played as a trump card. The absence of legal aid in a case of this kind was found by the Human Rights Court to be in violation of Article 6(1), as denying a right to a fair trial: in a case of such complexity, the denial of legal aid had deprived the applicants of the opportunity to present their case effectively and resulted in an unacceptable inequality of arms.[42] Equality of arms was also an important consideration in deciding on the application of the guarantee of free speech under Article 10 of the Convention. The Court found that, if a State was willing to provide to a corporate body a remedy such as substantial damages for defamation, it was then essential, for purposes of free expression and open debate, to ensure equality of arms, both through the provision of legal aid and proportional limits on the amount of damages.[43] Underlying this ruling was a concern to promote the free circulation of information about the activities of powerful commercial entities, and to counteract the possible 'chilling effect' on other potential critics of such companies. The Court's ruling therefore represents – through the dealing of a trump constitutional card – a fundamental determination of the balance of these competing interests. It also provides high drama, not only in the courtroom, but also more generally in the contemporary media.[44]

The Impact of Human Rights Argument at the Judicial Level: Avoiding Devaluation

The discussion so far has demonstrated the potential impact of the resort to human rights argument in a number of different contexts, in bringing about 'meta-level' changes in policy and law: the abolition or non-implementation of certain kinds of penal measure, the incorporation of human rights protection into EC law, and

---

42   Para. 72 of the judgment.

43   See paras 59–72 of the judgment.

44   For instance, through the making of a documentary film, *McLibel* (Spanner Films, 2005, directed by Franny Armstrong and Ken Loach), televised in the UK in June 2005.

the disablement of English defamation law as a corporate weapon against critical comment. This may read as an impressive achievement of developing legal entitlement and of protection of the individual against more powerful corporate and collective interests. How then should more sceptical comments, such as that of Koskenniemi quoted above, be viewed against such a survey?

It may be useful at this point to explore a lurking doubt in relation to this picture of progressive legal achievement. This is the problem of the expansion of legal entitlement and its possible extent. In simple terms: may claims to fundamental rights be made without limit and encroach infinitely on opposing interests? Or, to put the question somewhat differently: at what point does the increasing legal entitlement of individuals undermine the 'fundamental' nature of that entitlement? Certainly, the protection of all individual interests cannot be viewed as fundamental, and this may be argued to be particularly so in the context of economic activity. This point is related to that concerning the currency of rights claims, mentioned above – that playing the trump card raises the value of the game, but winning the game more frequently in the longer term affects the value of the winning hand. There is thus an inherent puzzle in the progressive use of such argument, in that the more often that it is used successfully, the less potent it may prove to be in the future. As Alston has commented:

> As the perceived usefulness of attaching the label 'human right' to a given goal or value increases, it can be expected that a determined effort will be made by a wide range of special interest groups to locate their cause under the banner of human rights … such a proliferation of new rights would be much more likely to contribute to a serious devaluation of the human rights currency than to enrich significantly the overall coverage provided by existing rights.[45]

Therefore, to retain its currency there must be some limit imposed on the use of such argument. We need to appreciate how this is achieved.

One solution of course would be to draw a line against allocating new substantive areas of entitlement – for instance, to say 'We have gone far enough, there is a right to health, but not a right to sleep.' But such an approach may be insufficiently sensitive to the changing needs of society.[46] In practice, new substantive categories of fundamental rights have been recognised (such as the rights of disabled persons, or of consumers). Rather, what may be seen to operate as a limiting device is the practical qualification of the entitlement with reference to specific circumstances. With a few exceptions (such as the right to life, or the prohibition of torture), most fundamental rights are not regarded as literally fundamental, but they are often subject to a qualification in favour of other (usually more general) interests. A glance at most human rights instruments will reveal the insertion of such general-interest qualifications in relation to most guaranteed rights, and certainly those categorised

---

45 Philip Alston (1984), 'Conjuring up New Human Rights: A Proposal for Quality Control', *American Journal of International Law* 78:607, at 614.

46 As Alston, note 45 above, argues: 'both the validity and necessity of a dynamic approach to human rights, as well as the expansion, where appropriate, of the list of recognized human rights, cannot reasonably de disputed' (at 607).

as economic and social in character. As will be shown below, this is a commonly used device to limit in practice the scope of the entitlement and in that way retain the currency of the 'core' element of what is guaranteed in the award of the right. To return to gaming metaphor, this may be seen as a sleight of hand, since what at first sight might have been regarded as a substantial legal entitlement may in practice amount to a limited right. But this is an important feature of human rights discourse and practice to take on board. It is also what Koskenniemi refers to in the above quotation, as an important process of 'contextual assessment' of proportionality and administrative balancing 'through which priorities are set among conflicting conceptions of political value and scarce resources are distributed between contending social groups'.[47] This process of limiting the actual scope of such rights may be carried out in various ways, sometimes, for instance, through judicial decision in human rights litigation, or sometimes as the result of practical barriers.

The judicial limitation of basic rights claims is particularly evident in the context of economic rights and the way in which this has been carried out in the context of European law will be discussed in more detail in Chapter 5, in relation to both trading rights and corporate defence rights in the context of competition regulation. But for present purposes, the outcome of the *Internationale Handelsgesellschaft* case, referred to just above, provides a good illustration of this process. Having made its impressive meta-level 'discovery' of the EC system of fundamental rights protection in its ruling in that case, the European Court of Justice went on to balance the company's fundamental trading rights against the broader public and Community interest in an efficient system of economic management. This balancing of interests entailed a classic application of the principle of proportionality, itself already well-developed under German constitutional law: that basic rights should only be limited in the public interest to the extent strictly necessary to serve that wider interest.[48] The specific question in this case was therefore the necessity for restricting the trader's basic right to carry out an export (inspired by such provisions as Articles 2, 12 and 14 of the German Constitution)[49] by means of the system of advance security payments for export licences. The Court concluded that the security system was an infringement of economic freedom that was proportional to the public interest needs in this situation:

> ... knowledge of the market situation is essential for allowing the competent authorities to judiciously exercise their ordinary or exceptional power of intervention. Such authorities

---

47   Note 12 above.

48   For an application of this principle in the context of German law, see the *Apotheken* decision of the *Bundesverfassungsgericht,* BVerfG 7, 377, 11 June 1958.

49   Article 2 guarantees the free development of personality, or 'personal self-determination' (in this context the right to develop a business); Article 12 guarantees the right to choose an occupation ('freedom of commerce'); Article 14 guarantees the right to property ('freedom of disposition'). All three rights are subject to qualification – thus Article 2(1) reads: 'Every person shall have the right to the free development of his personality in so far as he does not violate the rights of others or offend against the constitutional order or against morality'.

needed to be supplied not only with statistical information on the market situation but also with a detailed prediction of future imports and exports.[50]

The payment of a security acted as a kind of guarantee that the export would in fact be carried out. In the Court's view, simple declarations by traders of the extent to which they had carried out exports and used licences would not provide reliable data on the future flow of exports. This kind of information was necessary for the Commission to manage the market effectively; moreover, the cost to the trader in paying (and potentially forfeiting the security) was not disproportionate in view of the total value of the proposed transaction.[51] Although this application of the concept of proportionality was subsequently contested by the Frankfurt Administrative Court,[52] the German *Bundesverfassungsgericht* in its turn agreed with the analysis of the Court of Justice, arguing that the security system was 'not only appropriate in the present stage of development of the European Community, in which economic relations cannot function without planning and effective control, but is indispensable and not replaceable by a different, similarly effective and simple ... system'.[53]

This kind of analysis carried out by all the Courts in the *Internationale Handelsgesellschaft* litigation therefore fits well into Koskenniemi's description of 'administrative balancing', and at that specific level does not resonate so much with the high rhetoric of fundamental rights discourse. The principle of proportionality (the real determinant of such questions) is both more technical and more mundane than fundamental rights talk.

Taking again the example of the 'McLibel' case, the eventual judgment of the European Court of Human Rights was also in itself an exercise in balancing competing interests in a specific context: freedom of expression was being weighed against protection of reputation, in the context of the need for a level playing field in the market, comprising both information and transparency for consumers and fair judgment of the goods on offer. Similar arguments were deployed by the Human Rights Court in the earlier case of *Markt Intern* in balancing the supply of information through freedom of expression against a supplier's right to a 'fair hearing in the market place':

> However, even the publication of items which were true and described real events might under certain circumstances be prohibited. An isolated incident might deserve closer scrutiny before being published; otherwise an accurate description of one such incident could give the false impression that the incident was evidence of a general pattern.[54]

In addition to formally worked out judicial limitations on the scope of fundamental rights protection, there may also be practical limits on the opportunity actually to

---

50   (1970) ECR, at 1135.

51   Ibid., at 1136.

52   (1970) CMLR 294.

53   (1974) CMLR 540, at 557.

54   *Markt Intern Verlag and Klaus Beerman* v. *Germany*, 12 (1990) *European Human Rights Reports* 161, App No 10572/83, judgment of 20 November 1989, para. 35 of judgment.

invoke legal protection. It is clear enough now, following the judgment in *Steel and Morris*, that the circumstances in which the English law of defamation was used to stifle critical comment amounted to a violation of rights under the Human Rights Convention. However, this finding was dependent in the first place on the exceptional determination and stamina of the applicants in that particular case. Problems of cost, motivation, energy and knowledge determine in a mundane but decisive way the actual extent to which human rights argument is deployed. The existence of rights on paper may not translate into action; just as McDonald's declined, for political reasons, to enforce the award of damages in their favour, the extent to which rights-holders are able or willing to assert their rights is very dependent on a range of circumstances.

Understanding the Leverage of Rights Argument

The discussion in this chapter has probed the appeal of human rights argument and explored in more general terms its political and legal impact. Starting with the analogy of a large-scale, publicly staged protest and demonstration, the argument used here has sought to emphasise the *dramatic* and *rhetorical* impact of a resort to fundamental rights argument, and how such argument may then be used as a legal and ethical 'trump' card against opposing positions. To some extent, this may be seen as a natural and expected outcome of being able to make use of a higher currency. Yet, some more sceptical views have also been expressed regarding the value of this kind of legal argument. For instance, Koskenniemi has also agued that in the EU context: 'The European Court's judicial everyday is the banal exercise of coping with conflicts of (most commonly economic) interests, and allocating scarce resources. The fact that those interests are dressed in rights language does not change this pattern, but it does obscure the political nature of the task.'[55]

However, we should also take care not to be overly distracted by the 'banal' character of many specific adjudications which admittedly often involve a technical balancing of competing claims for priority and resources. That is very much the nature of particular disputes. It has been argued here that it is helpful to view the matter at different levels and so assess the impact of 'fundamental rights talk' at a more general or 'meta' level, as well as that of resolving particular disputes.

Indeed, the impact of human rights argument may differ at the meta-level and at the more specific level and context of individual cases. Care should be taken not to assume that what happens at the meta-level is no more than empty rhetoric. Undoubtedly at that level, as shown above, there may be movement: some change in the normative landscape which is more concretely evident in shifts in attitude and culture. Powerful actors may alter their position, if only in subtle ways: they make think twice about asserting their formal rights and they may modify their policies (as McDonald's claimed following their litigation); they may reallocate resources in favour of the practical realisation of particular rights (for instance, investment in or requirement of measures to help the situation of disabled persons), or they may

---

55   Koskenniemi, note 12 above, at 110.

tighten up administrative practice in order to ensure a higher level of respect for the rights and interests of certain parties. It will be argued later, for example, that in the context of EC competition regulation, companies subject to investigation rarely demonstrate in court serious violations of their rights of defence. But the fact that such rights may be invoked in the first place may well have ensured that regulators aim at a higher standard in the conduct of investigations, so as to avoid formal determinations of rights infringement. Thus, at the meta-level, a 'chill factor' may operate, deterring potential violations and inculcating a different general culture[56] and standard of behaviour.

There is a further important critical point to consider in relation to the resort to fundamental rights argument. In crude terms, the availability of such argument is a rich resource and in a sense must be paid for.[57] Apart from the material cost (good money for lawyers, but undoubtedly the costs of litigation are passed on, and some is met from the public purse), there are more abstract costs. One such cost, in legal terms, is the elevation of the party who is accorded fundamental rights entitlement, and that party's interest. A crucial point to remember – and here we return to the subject of both the context of market actors and their interests, and of corporate and consumer identity – is whether such persons and such interests deserve such rich entitlement.

---

56   For instance, the EU introduction of a moratorium in relation to generically modified foodstuff (see Chapter 6 below).

57   See, for instance the concluding reflections in the discussion by Christopher Harding and Alun Gibbs (2005), 'Why Go to Court in Europe? An Analysis of Cartel Appeals 1995–2004', *European Law Review* 30:349.

PART II
Testing Grounds

Chapter 5

Antitrust Recidivists as Rights Crusaders: Fashioning Producer Rights in Europe

Hoechst and its Rights of Defence

Hoechst AG (since 1999, when it merged with the French company Rhône-Poulenc, part of the Aventis corporation) had been for a long time one of the most significant producers of chemicals and pharmaceuticals on the global market for those products. The company was founded in Frankfurt in 1863 and was one of the co-founders of the pressure group IG Farben in 1916, and was part of IG Farben from 1925 when the latter became a corporate conglomerate, notoriously associated with Nazi war production and the use of slave labour.[1] Hoechst regained its separate corporate identity in 1951 and emerged in the post-Second World War period as a major international player in chemicals and pharmaceuticals. In that role, it has been subject to both official criticism (in the form of criminal convictions) and unofficial censure, as both an antitrust recidivist and in relation to some of its products which have been found to be damaging to human health and the environment. For example, the company was Number 12 in Russell Mokhiber's 'Top 100 Corporate Criminals of the 1990s',[2] on the basis of the $36 million fine imposed for its participation in the 17-year-old price-fixing and market-sharing Sorbates Cartel. The company had pleaded guilty to involvement in the cartel, and one of its marketing managers, Bernd Romahn, was also convicted under the US Sherman Act and paid a personal fine of $250,000. The company's subsidiary, Hoechst-Roussel, was blacklisted in 1990 by the US Generic Pharmaceutical Industry in relation to a number of alleged fraudulent and deceptive policies. These included its recommendation of the drug dipyrone for trivial pains, and its marketing of the molluscide 'Brescan', which is dangerous to human health, in the Philippines. In 1992, the US Federal Drugs Agency fined the company $292,000 for failing to disclose that its anti-depressant drug 'Nomifenine' had caused several deaths in Europe. The company therefore was no stranger to litigation and criminal prosecution.

At the beginning of 1987, the EC Commission opened an investigation of alleged price-fixing and delivery quota cartels in the European markets for the thermoplastic

---

1 For further information on the history and role of IG Farbenindustrie, see: George W. Stocking and Myron W. Watkins (1946), *Cartels in Action: Case Studies in International and Business Diplomacy* (New York: The Twentieth Century Fund); Joseph Borkin (1979), *The Crime and Punishment of I.G. Farben* (London: André Deutsch).

2 See Russell Mokhiber and Robert Weissman (1999), *Corporate Predators* (Monroe, ME: Common Courage Press) <www.corporatepredators.org>.

products PVC and polyethylene.[3] Hoechst was an alleged participant in these two (not to mention other) cartels and, late in January of that year, the Commission, exercising powers under Article 14 of EC Regulation 17/62, authorised an unannounced inspection and search of the company's offices in Frankfurt-Main.[4] The company refused to allow either Commission officials or accompanying officials from the German *Bundeskartellamt* (BKA) to enter its offices without a judicial warrant.[5] Following three unsuccessful attempts to carry out the search, the Commission adopted a decision on 29 January imposing a daily penalty payment of 1000 ECUs for as long as the company refused to allow the search to take place. In the meantime, the BKA applied for a search warrant, but its initial request was refused by the *Amtsgericht* of Frankfurt on 12 February, on the ground that insufficient evidence had been presented to justify suspicion of Hoechst's involvement in the cartels. A warrant was eventually granted on 31 March and the search finally took place on 2 and 3 April. By that time, the Commission had lost the advantage of surprise for a period of about ten weeks and Hoechst had paid 55,000 ECUs in periodic penalty payments. Hoechst then challenged the legality of the Commission's decision imposing the penalty payments before the European Court of Justice (ECJ). Eventually, the company was found to be in violation of Article 85(1) of the EC Treaty in relation to its involvement in the cartels and subject to heavy fines.[6]

In challenging the legality of the penalty payments for non-compliance with the search, Hoechst raised arguments concerning the violation of its fundamental rights. In particular, it alleged a violation of the fundamental right to protection of the home (*Wohnung,* guaranteed under both the German Federal Constitution and Article 8 of the European Convention on Human Rights). Hoechst – supported by an expert report prepared by Professor J.A. Frowein of the University of Heidelberg[7] – argued that this protection applied by analogy to business premises, and required a court order for the search of such premises, issued in advance and specifying the limits of any such search. This argument was considered fully by Advocate General Mischo in his opinion to the Court of Justice, which included a detailed comparative analysis of Member State law on this issue. Both Advocate General and Court came to a broadly similar conclusion that the right was protected but not violated in the circumstances of this case, at least once the search was carried out under judicial warrant (the penalty payment decision had been finally computed and confirmed after the search took place under the warrant).

---

3   For further discussion of the legal process relating to these cartels, see: Christopher Harding and Julian Joshua (2003), *Regulating Cartels in Europe: A Study of Legal Control of Corporate Delinquency* (Oxford: Oxford University Press), especially at 132–4.

4   A so-called 'dawn raid', a strategy developed during this period as a crucial means for gaining evidence of involvement in cartels. See Harding and Joshua, note 3 above, at 165–6.

5   For details of this episode, see the account given in the report of Hoechst's appeal: Case 46/87, *Hoechst* v. *Commission* (1989) European Court Reports (ECR) 2859.

6   Commission decision relating to the PVC Cartel (1970) 4 Common Market Law Reports (CMLR) 435.

7   Interestingly, Advocate General Mischo pointed out in his opinion that Professor Frowein had in an earlier commentary published in 1985 argued against the assimilation of the protection of the home and of the office: (1989) ECR, at 2893. This provides an insight into the use of expert testimony in such cases!

The survey of Member State law on the question was indecisive,[8] nor was there clear precedent for the assimilation of private home and business premises in this context. The ECJ was willing to extend protection to companies and business premises but not explicitly on the basis of the guarantee specifically laid down in Article 8 of the Convention, but following the EC principle which provided protection against arbitrary and disproportionate intervention on the part of public authorities. Thus, at the general level, the basic protection was recognised, without much discussion of the nature of the claimant's legal personality and substantive need for protection of the office rather than the home. The right was assimilated and to that extent Hoechst appeared to have played a trump card. But on the more specific issue of whether the right had in fact been violated, the Court recognised the strength of the broader interest in the effective application of the competition rules. It ruled that the Commission's countervailing right of access to the premises

> ... would serve no useful purpose if the Commission's officials could do no more than ask for documents or files which they could identify precisely in advance. On the contrary such a right implies the power to search for various items of information which are not already known or fully identified. Without such a power, it would be impossible for the Commission to obtain information necessary to carry out the investigation if the undertakings concerned refused to cooperate or adopted an obstructive attitude.[9]

But, at the same time, these powers of search must be carried out in such a way as to 'respect the undertaking's rights as laid down by national law'. Thus, in the context of a German company with its office within German jurisdiction, a judicial warrant of a certain kind must be used for such a forcible search to be carried out.

This narrative presents just one episode within a saga of litigation involving a major corporation in relation to alleged anti-competitive behaviour, but it is instructive in what it reveals about the deployment of human rights argument in this commercial context. In the first place, the judgment of the Court of Justice on the single issue of the legality of the periodic penalty payments allowed for an exploration of the underlying constitutionality of the Commission's powers of search and the conditions under which such investigatory powers could be exercised. These are important practical legal questions, but the stakes were raised in the legal argument by playing the fundamental rights trump card, involving the sanctity of the home (and the office). *At the level of general principle*, the outcome was a significant gain for corporate interests. It was ruled that companies and their offices should benefit from legal protection in a way analogous to that of human individuals in the home. Moreover, the specific requirement for a judicial warrant, and respect for national rules on the carrying out of forcible searches, was also confirmed. In this respect the argument relating to the entry into Hoechst's office in Frankfurt had moved the law forward in a significant way. But, as a second observation, it may be argued that the gain was largely illusory. In the final analysis, *at the particular level*, the Court of Justice was clear in its view that the fundamental protection of business premises was qualified by the wider public interest requiring an effective

---

8   See in particular the analysis of Advocate General Mischo (1989) ECR, at 2893.
9   (1989) ECR, at 2926.

application of competition rules, so in effect balancing Hoechst's basic rights against those of consumers and other traders. In that sense, the gain in legal principle was at Hoechst's expense, since the company lost the case and was required to pay the legal costs as well as the penalty payments. Admittedly, following the ruling the Commission would have to tighten up its investigatory procedure, but that was mainly a question of ensuring that it had the national judicial warrant ready for the date of the dawn raid.

The third observation relates more specifically to Hoechst's role as a fundamental rights 'crusader' (a role that it shares with a number of other large corporate antitrust recidivists). There is some irony in the fact that so much legal development in relation to arguments concerning basic legal entitlement in the economic context should be driven forward in particular by companies with a delinquent record in legal and ethical terms. But, in another perspective, that is a simple reflection of the realities and practicalities of the legal world. Important players, such as transnational companies, have both the resources and the economic and political motivation to engage in high-stakes legal argument, which by its nature is likely to be a motor of legal development. The interesting question which now deserves further consideration relates to what more exactly may be gained, in either the shorter or longer term, by large corporate actors who so willingly enter this legal arena.[10]

The Construction of Producer Rights Under EU Law: Ordoliberal Logic

From the discussion so far, it should be clear that an examination of how producers, as economic and legal actors, have been able to exploit European human rights discourse to protect their interests should proceed from the context in which the EU legal order itself has developed. Although on the one hand, the market liberalisation policies which underlie the EU (and indeed now the global economic order) work to the advantage of producers, opening up their trading opportunities and conferring expansive market rights, on the other hand, the European market environment is also a regulated environment. Thus while producers have been able to assert expansive trading (free movement) rights, typically against Member States, at the same time European-level regulation has sought to constrain producer activity in the interest of broader economic policy, sometimes by sector (as in the case of agriculture, or coal and steel), sometimes more generally, as in the case of competition. The outcome for the producer, being liberalised and regulated at the same time, is an essential element within the 'ordoliberal' logic upon which the European Common Market was founded – a theory of the market within which 'market freedoms are seen as intrinsic to the notion of human dignity'.[11] This underlying philosophy, associated in particular with the 'Freiburg School', has been summarised by Gerber in the following terms:

---

10   See, on this point, the study by Christopher Harding and Alun Gibbs (2005), 'Why go to court in Europe? An analysis of cartel appeals 1995–2004', *European Law Review* 30:349.

11   Sionaidh Douglas-Scott (2002), *Constitutional Law of the European Union* (Harlow: Longman), at 457.

The Freiburg School thinkers agreed with earlier conceptions of liberalism in considering a competitive economic system to be necessary for a prosperous, free and equitable society. They were convinced, however, that such a society could develop only where the market was imbedded in a 'constitutional' framework. This framework was necessary to protect the process of competition from distortion, to assure that the benefits of the market were equitably distributed throughout society and to minimise governmental intervention in the economy. This interpretation of legal and economic ideas was the essence of the Freiburg School and of the 'ordoliberal' school of thought into which it developed.[12]

In this way, the characteristic condition of entrepreneurial power under the EC and EU systems has been one of being set free and then reined in. Some of the main legal arguments regarding producers' rights at the European level have therefore arisen from this latter experience of containment, leading to a contest between producer power and market regulation. The producer response to market regulation may be analysed in three main aspects. First, in substantive terms, it has entailed a broad assertion of rights of economic self-determination. Secondly, in terms of process, it has involved claims of defence rights against the procedures of regulation. Finally, in so far as these claims have been worked out in litigation, the latter has been of a particular character: supranational proceedings involving powerful actors and with transnational implications.

Economic Self-Determination

The entrepreneurial assertion of economic freedom, as a constitutional entitlement, has been a notable feature of European-level litigation. For the European Court of Justice, this kind of claim has been a major trigger for the development of its jurisprudence on human rights. There is now a familiar legal story within textbook accounts: the slow start giving way to a burst of judicial activity in the 1970s as the Court of Justice became energised, mainly by German judicial misgiving, into forging an EC system of legal protection.[13] Indeed, in the context of trading rights, it is interesting to note both the impact of the German legal challenge and the energy of German litigants. In comparative constitutional terms, as Craig and de Búrca note: 'Germany's *GrundGesetz* ... gives strong protection to economic rights and to the freedom to pursue a trade or profession.'[14] Thus German courts,

---

12   David J. Gerber (1998), *Law and Competition in Twentieth Century Europe* (Oxford: Oxford University Press), at 232; see generally his discussion of ordoliberalism in Ch. 7 of that work.

13   For a useful overview of these legal developments, see Paul Craig and Gráinne de Búrca (2007), *EU Law: Text, Cases and Materials* (Oxford: Oxford University Press, 4th edn), Ch. 11; and see the discussion in Chapter 4 above.

14   Ibid., in the third edition of that work (2002), at 330. In particular, Article 2 of the *Grundgesetz* guarantees the free development of personality (including the development of business – economic self-determination); Article 12 guarantees the right to choose an occupation ('freedom of commerce'), and Article 14 guarantees the right of property ('freedom of disposition'). Contrast the British tradition: Marshall, writing at the start of the 1970s, stating that 'one might well wish to exclude or reserve judgment' on economic

German companies[15] and German writers have been vigorous in promoting the issue of economic freedom, or more precisely the rights of producers and traders, before the European Courts (notably in cases such as *Internationale Handelsgesellschaft* (1970), *Nold* (1974), *Hauer* (1979), *Wunsche* (1986), *Wachauf* (1989), *Schräder* (1989), and also the claim by the German Government (1994)[16]). The argument and outcome in this line of cases has been consistent, invoking basic rights of economic freedom, which are confirmed by the Court of Justice, but subject to qualification in a wider (Community) interest, the latter then usually prevailing over the exercise of that right. Here is a classic statement of the Court of Justice's jurisprudence on such trading rights:

> The Court has recognised in particular, notably in the judgment in Case 44/79, that both the right to property and the freedom to pursue a trade or profession form part of the general principles of Community law. However, these principles do not constitute an unfettered prerogative, but must be viewed in the light of a social function of the activities protected thereunder. Consequently, the right to property or the freedom to pursue a trade or profession may be restricted, particularly in the context of a common organization of a market, provided that those restrictions in fact correspond to objectives of general interest pursued by the Community and that they do not constitute a disproportionate or intolerable interference which infringes the very substance of the rights guaranteed.[17]

This illustrates very well the established judicial response to claims based on economic freedom at the EC level: what is important, in the final analysis of each case, is less the rhetoric of rights protection than the more specific calculation of proportionate and tolerable interference with such freedom of action. Both limbs of this argument are inspired by other systems – proportionality has been emphasised by the European Court of Human Rights, while protecting the 'very substance of the right' derives from the German constitutional principle *Wesensgehaltsgarantie.* But it has been commonly alleged that in making such calculations the Court of Justice is more likely to veer towards the Community than the individual interest, certainly as compared to the kind of assessment which might be made by German courts.[18] The thrust of much of this criticism has been summed up by de Witte:

---

protections (Geoffrey Marshall (1971), *Constitutional Theory* (Oxford: Oxford University Press), at 134).

15   See Christopher Harding (1992), 'Who Goes to Court in Europe? An Analysis of Litigation Against the European Community', *European Law Review* 17:105, for discussion of the high profile of German litigants before the European Court of Justice.

16   Case C-280/93, *Germany* v. *Council* (1994) ECR I-4973.

17   Case 265/87, *Schräder* v. *HZA Grönau* (1989) ECR 2237, at 2268. The reference in the quotation is to Case 44/79, *Hauer* v. *Rheinland-Pfalz* (1979) ECR 3740.

18   See in particular: Jason Coppel and Aidan O'Neill (1992), 'The European Court of Justice: Taking Rights Seriously?', *Common Market Law Review* 29:669; U. Everling (1996), 'Will Europe Slip on Bananas?', *Common Market Law Review* 33:401 (Everling is a former judge at the Court of Justice); P. Huber (1997), 'Das Kooperationsverhältnis zwischen BVerfG und EuGH in Grundrechtsfragen', *EuZW* 517; T. Stein (1998), 'Bananen-Split? Entzweien sich BVerfG und EuGH über den Bananenstreit', *EuZW* 261. Much of the critical discussion has been usefully analysed and summarised by Bruno De Witte (1999), 'The Past and Future

... it has been argued that the reference made to the international human rights treaties and to the common constitutional principles of the Member States is rather ritual and does not denote a willingness of the Court of Justice to subject itself to the human rights standards developed elsewhere.[19]

The sharper point of such criticism would seem to concern the more specific interpretation of the level of rights protection, and more particularly in the context of economic rights, the way in which the Court of Justice has appeared to favour a 'hands-off' approach to economic regulation.[20] This has frequently manifested itself in a willingness to concede a large measure of unassailable discretion to Community regulation of trading. De Witte, for instance, cites the approach taken in relation to the German Government's challenge in 1993 of the 'Banana Regulation'[21] as being a lenient exercise of control, when the Court stated:

> ... while other means for achieving the desired result were indeed conceivable, the Court cannot substitute its assessment for that of the Council as to the appropriateness or otherwise of the measures adopted by the Community legislature if those measures have not been proved to be manifestly inappropriate for achieving the objective pursued.[22]

The words 'manifestly inappropriate' clearly set a high threshold for intervention, and one that would be higher in particular than that adopted in German constitutional law (though perhaps not higher than that of the European Court of Human Rights, as discussed below). But, as de Witte points out, the German standard is probably more legally exacting than that used in some other Member States and if the Court of Justice was expected to adopt a 'maximalist' approach it would thereby be privileging, for instance, the German over the more restrained Swedish approach, without a compelling reason for doing so.[23]

Another view of the Court of Justice's jurisprudence on such rights is therefore that it does take such rights 'seriously' but draws the line further along the spectrum towards the regulatory interest.[24] In this way, it would appear to have adopted a constitutional *position* on the protection of economic rights which is at variance

---

Role of the European Court of Justice in the Protection of Human Rights', in P. Alston (ed), *The EU and Human Rights* (Oxford: Oxford University Press), at 859.

19   De Witte, note 18 above, at 878.

20   See, for example, the discussion in Ch. 6 of J.A. Usher (1998), *General Principles of EC Law* (Edinburgh: Longman).

21   Case C-280/93, *Germany* v. *Council,* note 16 above.

22   Ibid., at para. 94 of the judgment.

23   De Witte, note 18 above, at 880–81. A contrary argument, in favour of a maximalist approach, is put forward by L. Besselink (1998), 'Entrapped by the Maximum Standard: On Fundamental Rights, Pluralism and Subsidiarity in the European Union', *Common Market Law Review* 35:629.

24   The term 'seriously' has been used in an interesting and particular way in rights discourse. 'Taking rights seriously' in this context usually means giving preference to those rights rather than subjecting them to rigorous scrutiny. On the other hand, it is possible to use the term somewhat differently in the sense of taking the subject seriously by applying rigorous argument.

with that for instance used in Germany, and this helps to explain the low rate of success for such claims by traders before the Court of Justice: in effect, a handful of cases over the years, most of which have succeeded on grounds of unjustifiable discrimination.[25] Yet, this more 'restrictive' position should not necessarily be open to criticism simply because it is relatively restrictive of traders' rights. The important question is deeper: how much protection should be accorded to the rights and interests of *traders as traders*, rather than more generally as persons exercising economic rights, in the context of the competing interests protected by the regulatory system? This question is less frequently posed by those critics of the Court of Justice who tend to present the matter as one of abstract rather than competing rights.

What is required, therefore, is a more penetrating analysis of how such economic rights are protected in practice. A number of related questions come to mind in performing such an exercise:

- Given that trading rights are virtually always subject to some qualification in favour of other interests, how is this limitation applied across jurisdictions – similarly or differentially?
- If there are differences in approaching this aspect of the matter (as there does appear to be between EU Member States), what does this mean for the underlying philosophy of rights protection? For instance, does this imply that the German legal system in effect provides greater legal protection for large traders and producers than for smaller traders and consumers, and the EC system the reverse?
- If the majority of successful claims before the Court of Justice are based on a certain level of unjustifiable discrimination, how does this then inform the content of traders' rights as worked out at the European level?
- Finally, if the majority of claims in relation to a particular right do not succeed, does it follow that the right is not being taken 'seriously' by those adjudicating, or should we instead be asking questions about the context, profile and motivation of those parties typically litigating in that area?

In addressing these particular questions, the nature of this kind of economic right may be further clarified. First, it is evident that this clutch of trading rights and the overarching concept of 'economic self-determination' are not a matter of absolute protection and indeed are very much contingent upon underlying political and economic ideology. As Weiler and Lockhart state in their robust demolition of Coppel and O'Neill's critique of the Court of Justice's jurisprudence: 'that rights are not absolute in this sense seems to us so banal as hardly worth illustrating.'[26]

---

25   See the summary in de Witte, note 18 above, at 881–2. An example of a successful claim of this kind comprises Case C-122/95, *Germany* v. *Council* (1998) ECR I-973 and Joined Cases C-364, and 365/95, *T Port GmbH* v. *HZA Hamburg-Jonas* (1998) ECR I-1023 (later challenges of the 'Banana Regulation').

26   J.H.H. Weiler and N. Lockhart (1995), '"Taking Rights Seriously" Seriously: The European Court and Its Fundamental Rights Jurisprudence', *Common Market Law Review* 32:51 and 579, at 585. It is an interesting reflection on the published discussion on this subject

The boundary of acceptable limitation at the legislative level was proposed by the European Court of Human Rights, in relation to the right of property and freedom of disposition as laid down in Article 1 of the First Protocol to the European Human Rights Convention. The Court stated, referring to the customary qualification in the public interest:

> ... the notion of 'public interest' is necessarily extensive ... the Court, finding it natural that the margin of appreciation available to the legislature in implementing social and economic policies should be a wide one, will respect the legislature's judgment as to what is 'in the public interest' unless that judgment be manifestly without reasonable foundation.[27]

What emerges from a preliminary glance at contemporary human rights practice is a sense that the unassailable 'core' content (or *Wesensgehaltsgarantie*) of trading and property rights is both relatively small and itself not so fixed in its boundaries. It may be true that there is a larger core area under German constitutional law than under European (EC or ECHR) law, but that may reasonably follow from differing ideologies of political and economic organisation and market regulation. The emphasis may shift from one jurisdiction to another. As Gerber has noted:

> A new form of liberalism that emerged after the Second World War, most prominently in Germany, sought ... to use legal and constitutional means to protect economic freedom from disintegration and attack ... An important strand of German thought and scholarship has continued to emphasize the goal of economic freedom as a value in competition law decisions, and that message has often resonated with legislators and judicial decision-makers.[28]

To appreciate the subject in such terms enables us to reinterpret apparent differences. Thus, variation in the level of legal protection in a particular context is seen, not so much as one system (that of the EC) falling short of another (the German), but an unsurprising divergence arising from differing underlying political and economic objectives. This serves to shift the perspective of critical evaluation.

A closer examination of the few cases in which the Court of Justice has found a violation of substantive trading rights is also instructive. Frequently, and naturally enough, such allegations of violation entail an attack on legislative-level policy decisions which are by their nature less susceptible to judicial review. This fact informs much of the jurisprudence of the Court of Justice (hence the 'hands off' approach) and indeed that of courts in other jurisdictions. In public law terms, this is a classic 'margin of discretion' zone. In such a context, it is generally easier to find grounds for legal criticism in relation to the manner of implementation and enforcement of policy rather than of policy choices as such. This point is made by de Witte and also by Weiler and Lockhart, the latter arguing for instance:

---

that Coppel and O'Neill's paper (having already been published in two journals – *Legal Studies* and the *Common Market Law Review*) has been so widely and sometimes uncritically cited, after being hit far out of court by Weiler and Lockhart.

27   Judgment of 21 February 1986, *James and others*, A. 98 (1986), 32.
28   Gerber, note 8 above, at 418.

... violation of human rights by primary legislatures and the principal legislator is relatively rare. Most violations take place in the process of governance – by the executive branch and public administration elaborating primary legislation and administering and executing primary and secondary legislation. We would expect, then, that most complainants against the Community would be in areas where it operates in that administrative-executive function.[29]

It may be added that it is also in that area of public activity that we should expect a higher number of *successful* claims based on alleged human rights violations. This helps to explain the outcome within the jurisprudence of the Court of Justice: that most successful challenges in terms of basic rights violations have been in relation to enforcement procedures (notably the competition cases, discussed below) or the manner in which policy has been implemented, the latter giving rise typically to claims regarding fair and equal treatment. This is well illustrated by the later challenge of the 'Banana Regulation'. This claim succeeded on a particular point about unjustified discrimination in the application of policy, but not on an infringement of the core content of trading freedom. The Court of Justice stated first:

> The Council ... has not provided the Court with sufficient information to explain why the increase in the tariff quota and its division into country quotas, together with the concomitant lowering of customs duties, were not sufficient to offset the limitations which Regulation No. 404/93 had imposed on the marketing of bananas from the third countries party to the Framework Agreement and why that objective had therefore to be achieved by the imposition of a financial burden on only some of the economic operators importing bananas from those countries.[30]

The failing, therefore, was essentially in relation to the method of implementing the policy. On the other hand, the policy itself was not vitiated by any violation of guaranteed economic freedom. The Court confirmed that

> ... restrictions on the right to import third-country bananas resulting from the opening of the tariff quotas and the machinery for its sub-division were inherent in the objectives of general Community interest pursued by the establishment of a common organisation of the market in the bananas sector and therefore did not properly impair the freedom of traditional traders in third-country bananas to pursue their trade or business.[31]

Indeed, it might be said that the essence of legal protection in this context relates not so much to substantive economic freedom as to the manner in which that freedom is restricted (see Table 5.1 below). As Barents puts the matter: the essential function of the principle of non-discrimination, in the context of trading activity, 'its very substance in the words of the Court – for the operator, is to protect him from arbitrary treatment.'[32] Such a conclusion is perhaps even more evident in the

---

29   Weiler and Lockhart, note 26 above, at 85.
30   Case C-122/95, *Germany* v. *Council,* note 16 above, (1998) ECR I-973, at 1018.
31   Ibid., at 1019.
32   René Barents (1994), *The Agricultural Law of the EC* (The Hague: Kluwer), at 352. Thus it might be said that, under EC law, the *Wesensgehaltsgarantie* of trading rights is the right not to have economic freedom regulated in an arbitrary manner.

context of competition regulation, discussed immediately below. Reflection on the area of guaranteed economic freedom also leads to some consideration of the nature of trading activity itself, and how that informs the degree of protection, and this will be discussed thereafter.

Table 5.1 *Wesensgehaltsgarantie* **Model A: Trading rights (economic self-determination) under EU law**

Core statement	Area subject to general interest limitation
Right to pursue a trade or profession, right to use and dispose of property and assets, free from any arbitrary, disproportionate or discriminatory regulation	Reasonable exercise of discretionary powers to achieve a common organisation of the Market

The Enforcement of Economic Policy and Rights of Defence

One of the most impressive areas of development of EC jurisprudence on fundamental rights has been in relation to rights of defence, for the most part in the context of competition proceedings. Since the European Commission has direct powers of enforcement in relation to competition infringements and has been using those powers energetically since the end of the 1970s, a number of legal issues concerning the exercise of investigatory powers, the conduct of hearings and the imposition of sanctions have naturally come to the fore. The fact that such competition proceedings typically concern the activities of large companies with the resources and motivation for litigation challenging the Commission's enforcement, has stimulated legal argument and in turn the opportunity of the Court of Justice and the Court of First Instance to develop a jurisprudence on defence rights.[33]

This jurisprudence has focused on four principal aspects of the Commission's enforcement procedure:

- the legal character of the whole process, as an 'administrative' procedure, and the appropriate level of legal protection for those subject to the procedure;[34]
- the conduct of investigations;
- the presentation of defence arguments, and
- the imposition of sanctions.[35]

---

33   The development as a whole is discussed and analysed by Harding and Joshua, note 3 above, Chs 5 and 7.

34   Guiding judgments on this element of the discussion have been those of the Court of Justice in Cases 100-103/80, *Musique Diffusion Francaise* v. *Commission* (1983) ECR 1880, and Case T-1/89 etc, *Rhône-Poulenc* v. *Commission* (1991) ECR II-867, especially the opinion of Judge Vesterdorf as Advocate-General.

35   More recently, many of the appeals against Commission competition decisions have concerned predominantly points about the justification for or the amount of fines. For a

Although the Court of Justice and Court of First Instance have carefully confirmed the character of the process as administrative, some analogy with criminal proceedings has in effect still been taken on board in working out the legal entitlement of companies subject to investigation and sanctions. In this way, a number of defence rights have been extrapolated from relevant international instruments and Member State constitutional law and confirmed as an element of EC law, although carefully presented as an EC version of such rights. There has been some criticism of the resulting level of protection, especially in so far as it may be compared with analogous protection under the European Human Rights Convention.[36] None the less, the fact remains that companies have been able to exploit human rights discourse, at least for purposes of establishing a system of regular legal control, which in fact, through the role of the Court of First Instance, now monitors in some detail the Commission's enforcement powers in this context.

For purposes of presenting a summary, it may be said that the defence rights established in this way can be identified in relation to two main phases of the Commission's procedure: broadly speaking, investigations and hearings. In the first place, the exercise of the Commission's investigatory powers has provoked a series of arguments relating to rights based on privacy, confidentiality and other grounds for withholding evidence, and the manner in which companies, their employees and property may be dealt with in the course of investigations. In constitutional terms, many of these arguments have centred on ideas relating to the inviolability of business premises and assets, and the right of silence in relation to questioning procedures. In another sense, this is a new law of evidence, concerning the categories of evidence which may be justifiably withheld in the course of this kind of legal investigation. Without going into detailed account of this area of jurisprudence, it may perhaps be said that there have been two main constitutional achievements for companies asserting defence rights in the context of competition investigations: confirming *a kind of inviolability of the office*, and a *kind of right of silence*. The latter to some extent follows on from the former and the underlying rationale of this protection is indicated in the well-known *Hoechst* judgment of the Court of Justice:

> … in all the legal systems of the Member States, any intervention by the public authorities in the sphere of private activities of any person, whether natural or legal, must have a legal basis and be justified on grounds laid down by law, and, consequently, those systems provide, albeit in different forms, protection against arbitrary and disproportionate intervention. The need for such protection must be recognized as a general principle of Community law.[37]

---

critical study of the presentation of such argument, and the outcomes before the Court of First Instance, see Harding and Gibbs, note 10 above.

36   See, for example, A. Clapham (1990), 'A Human Rights Policy for the European Community', *Yearbook of European Law* 10:309; D. Spielman (1999), 'Human Rights Case Law in the Strasbourg and Luxembourg Courts: Conflicts, Inconsistencies and Compementarities', in P. Alston (ed), *The EU and Human Rights* (Oxford: Oxford University Press), Ch. 23.

37   Case 46/87, *Hoechst* v. *Commission* (1989) ECR 2859, at paras 17–19 of the judgment. Note the Court's reference to 'arbitrary and disproportionate intervention' as the

Such protection has entailed more specifically: respect for the confidentiality of lawyer-client communications,[38] the prohibition of 'fishing expeditions',[39] and forcible search being subject to the conditions laid down by the relevant national law,[40] though not a prohibition of 'dawn raids'.[41] Regarding the right not to respond to certain questions, a kind of right of non-self incrimination, this was laid down in its essential form by the Court of Justice in its *Orkem* judgment, when it stated that the Commission must not undermine the rights of defence and therefore could not 'compel an undertaking to provide it with answers which might involve an admission on its part of the existence of an infringement which it is incumbent on the Commission to prove'.[42] The scope of this protection was explained at a later point in the judgment, when the Court distinguished (using examples) between questions of fact, which must be answered, and 'leading questions', which need not be answered.

Secondly, another clutch of arguments have concerned the procedural rights of companies in relation to the 'hearing' stage of the procedure, after the Commission has issued a formal statement of objections and is receiving defence argument before adopting a decision on the case. Such defence rights established in this regard include the provision of reasonable time in which to present a defence,[43] and general 'equality of arms' rights, ensuring a fair balance in the presentation of both sides of the case. The latter has included in particular the provision of access to the Commission's file, for purposes of securing any information there which may be of value to the defending company's case. Such access to the file was confirmed in an arguably extensive form in the Court of First Instance 1995 *Soda Ash* judgment.[44]

It is probably true to say that this rights-building jurisprudence has now, for the most part, reached its limits. In recent years, most litigation relating to competition proceedings has involved the assertion of established defence rights rather than developing further the scope of protection. What may be noted for the present is the extent of the 'core' content of this area of legal protection. As noted already, this comprises a body of protected information – evidence or material which cannot be used against defending companies – alongside a number of procedural guarantees relating to the way in which cases are investigated and legally constructed by the Commission as a 'prosecuting' authority. To some extent, this area of core protection

guiding criteria, which recalls the vocabulary of core legal protection used in the economic freedom cases discussed above.

38 Case 155/79, *AM&S Europe* v. *Commission* (1982) ECR 1575.

39 Case 374/87, *Orkem* v. *Commission* (1989) ECR 3283, per Advocate General Darmon, at 3320.

40 *Hoechst* v. *Commission*, note 37 above, (1989) ECR, at 2927.

41 Case 136/79, *National Panasonic* v. *Commission* (1980) ECR 2033.

42 Cases 375/87 and 27/88, *Orkem, Solvay* v. *Commission* (1989) ECR 3283. See also Case T-112/98, *Mannesmannröhren-Werke* v. *Commission* (2001) ECR II-729.

43 Cases 6 and 7/73, *Commercial Solvents* v. *Commission* (1974) ECR 223.

44 Cases T-30/91 etc, *Solvay and others* v. *Commission*, Case T-36/91, *ICI* v. *Commission* (1995) ECR II-1847. See the discussion by Harding and Joshua, note 3 above, at 197–201, where comparisons are drawn with the more restrictive approach under both British and American law.

bears some analogy with that provided at the national level in relation to criminal proceedings, despite the disclaimers about 'administrative' procedure. As Judge Vesterdof observed, the substance of these cases 'broadly exhibits the characteristics of criminal law' so that 'in many instances the parties' submissions can only be understood with the help of the terminology and the concepts in criminal law and procedure.'[45]

In this sense, the scope of the protection is, despite a certain amount of criticism, not inconsiderable. For the Commission, certain categories of evidence are out of reach and certain procedures must be complied with and to this extent companies have succeeded in establishing a more substantial zone of protection than in the case of freedom of trading discussed above (see Table 5.2 below). This conclusion may well serve to confirm Weiler and Lockhart's argument that legal protection is more naturally and readily granted in relation to enforcement activity than regulation at the legislative level.

Table 5.2　　*Wesensgehaltsgarantie* **Model B: Defence rights (enforcement of economic regulation) under EU law**

Core statement	Area subject to general interest limitation
Protected information: 　•　lawyer-client confidential 　•　self-incriminatory answers 　•　outside the scope of authorised 　　　investigation	Powers to carry out inquiries and investigation : 　•　questioning 　•　search 　•　unannounced inspection
Procedural entitlements: 　•　adequate time to prepare defence 　•　forcible search subject to national 　　　regulation 　•　access to prosecution file 　•　adverse decision to be reasoned, 　　　evidence-based and authenticated 　•　judicial review of regulatory 　　　process	Confidentiality for third parties Power to impose sanctions

The Rights-Building Arena: The Character of the Litigants

Finally, in this section of the discussion, it may be helpful to make some observations regarding the socio-legal context of these legal developments. In relation to both substantive economic freedom and defence rights within the process of regulatory enforcement, the construction of such rights and the exploitation of rights discourse

---

45　(1991) ECR II, at 884.

for that purpose has been largely a product of litigation involving two main kinds of actor. On the one side, there are 'decision-taking' Community institutions (the Council and the Commission)[46] acting either as legislators or engaged in the implementation and enforcement of policy and legislation. On the other side, for the most part, there are large trading companies[47] acting out a role as the primary and direct subjects of regulation. This is therefore a significant regulatory battleground. Other interested players – smaller companies, competitors and consumers, for instance – may be the ultimate beneficiaries of Community policies and proceedings in this context, but occupy the sidelines in the crucial arena of argument. The rights discourse is deployed within, and the rights development emerges from, an arena staging litigation and judicial resolution. The legal outcome is therefore the product of formal adversarial argument and a public and principled balancing of interests, expressed through such justice-based concepts as proportionality and fair treatment.

A consequence of this whole area of legal development has been a fleshing-out of the legal personality of corporate actors. In so far as producer rights have been developed – at least in form and on paper – this has entailed a more mature notion of the producer-company, as a right-holder, as a beneficiary of rights discourse, and as a supranational litigant. Put another way, in the EU context, the legal relationship between EU institutions and large companies has emerged as more characteristic and in some respects distinctive in terms of its dialogue and representation of interests.

One specific indication of this role for the corporate producer is the way in which rights entitlement has been confirmed for corporate actors. In some of the cases discussed above, there was some debate concerning the availability of rights, originally designed for individual human actors, to companies. This issue arose in particular in the context of defence rights, having their origin in criminal procedure and concepts such as privacy and the inviolability of the home. Despite the fact that doctrine on this matter appeared somewhat uneven across the Member States, in practice the Court of Justice was happy enough to award a comparable legal protection to corporate actors. As the Court stated in its *Hoechst* judgment:

> ... in regard to undertakings ... there are not inconsiderable divergences between the legal systems of the Member States in regard to the nature and degree of protection afforded to business premises against intervention by the public authorities ... Nonetheless, in all the legal systems of the Member States, any intervention by the public authorities in the sphere of private activities of any person, whether natural or legal, must have a legal basis and be justified on grounds laid down by law ... The need for such protection must be recognized as a general principle of Community law.[48]

---

46   In the last ten years or so, the European Parliament may appear more frequently as a co-legislator with the Council. In many of these cases, the Commission appears as the defending party in litigation.

47   With a few exceptions: for instance, Hauer (Case 4/79, note 17 above) was an individual-as-trader rather than a company-as-trader. Some of these companies have a transnational character and are actively and regularly involved in substantial litigation.

48   *Hoechst v. Commission*, note 37 above, paras 17–19 of the judgment. See also the fuller discussion, including some comparative survey of Member State law by Advocate General Mischo: (1989) ECR at 2893; and also the discussion in Chapter 2 above.

But it is interesting to note that the Court's award of *comparable* protection to companies, rather protection *equivalent* to that given to the 'home' under Article 8 of the Human Rights Convention, has excited critical comment. So, for example, Spielmann has commented that 'Rick Lawson submits rightly that the "level of protection offered under Community law as interpreted by the ECJ in *Hoechst* is in danger of falling below the requirements of Article 8 ECH."'[49]

But then little is offered to substantiate more precisely why there is a danger of a lower standard, while at the same time the assumption that there should be the same standard for individuals in the home and for corporate actors seems to be argued too easily from the European Court of Human Rights' later *Niemietz* judgment,[50] which focused upon the position of *individuals* in the office. The more difficult question appears to be less frequently addressed: whether a *large transnational corporate actor* is entitled to the same kind of protection as an *individual human being* (the issue explored more fully in Chapter 2 above). It would seem that the Court of Justice has answered the question by accepting that the company does have a fundamental right of office inviolability, but that the degree of protection contained therein may not be the same as that accorded to the individual in the home, under other jurisdictions. But, as de Witte has noted, it is ironic that Article 13 of the German *Grundgesetz* has been more recently reformed, in 1998, so as to reduce considerably the degree of protection for all persons, natural and legal, in terms of inviolability of the home![51]

Thus it may be argued that, especially through the jurisprudence of the EU courts, we do have a fuller idea of the corporate producer as a rights holder, but this idea may not be very explicitly conveyed. The expression of the Court of Justice, for instance, tends to be elliptic, not directly stating that it views the entitlement of a large company as following from its role and position *as a large company*. But in effect this may be the outcome, if the degree of protection actually accorded to corporate producers within the scope of their rights is examined more closely. This is the more specific question of how much legal protection such actors require or deserve, within the actual context of their commercial activity, which will be considered next.

Outcomes: Taking Rights Seriously?

Any critical rights analysis needs to consider not only the design of rights protection and how it is formulated, but also how that system of protection is applied at a concrete level. The *Wesensgehaltsgarantie* models used above supply therefore a template, but more may be learnt from the way in which individual cases are judicially decided and how the broad concepts of rights protection are applied to

---

49   Spielman, in Alston (ed), note 18 above, at 769, referring to R. Lawson (1994), 'Confusion and Conflict? Diverging Interpretations of the European Convention on Human Rights in Strasbourg and Luxembourg', in R. Lawson and M. de Bloijs (eds), *The Dynamics of the Protection of Human Rights in Europe* (The Hague: Kluwer), iii, 219 at 228.

50   *Niemietz* v. *Germany,* Application 13710/88, judgment of 16 December 1992, 16 (1992) *EHRR* 97. See also the discussion in Chapter 2 above.

51   De Witte, note 18 above, at 879.

particular circumstances and facts. In this way, the kind of picture which has been presented above, which supplies an idea of the framework of protection, may be modified through the examination of actual outcomes of litigation.

Economic Self-Determination

First, in relation to the economic rights of trading and disposition of property, the template of protection under EU law appears at first sight rather ambiguous. On the one hand, there is an impressive-sounding guarantee of basic economic freedom. On the other hand, this is clearly subject to limitation in the general public or Community interest in having a measure of economic regulation. From judicial statements, we then learn that the balance is struck by allowing the regulator to push back the limits of individual freedom subject only to a prohibition against doing so in a manner that is arbitrary or manifestly disproportionate or unjustifiably discriminatory. From the jurisprudence, therefore, we would expect that – if the regulator is careful – few claims that economic freedom has been violated would succeed. And indeed, this proves to be the case. As already noted, only a handful of claims have succeeded over the years, usually on the ground that regulatory measures have been applied in an unacceptably discriminatory manner.[52]

But does that imply that the EU judicial approach is tender towards EU regulatory interests? Superficially perhaps, this may appear to be the case, yet we need to remember that *such regulatory interests represent other interests and rights* and that many of these cases on closer analysis involve a balancing of rights. This may be seen clearly from one example of this kind of litigation, concerning a claim by traders to the right to supply meat which had been treated with hormones (the *Fedesa* case).[53] Council Directive 146 of 1988 prohibited the use of certain hormonal substances in livestock farming – a classic regulatory limitation of economic freedom – and this was challenged on a number of grounds asserting an unlawful and unjustifiable limitation of that freedom, by a number of manufacturers[54] and distributors of veterinary medicines, associations in the field of animal health, a veterinarian and a farmer. Formally, the claim was defended by the Council, since the national-level litigation questioned the legality of the Council's directive. But in the proceeding before the Court of Justice, the Council was supported by the Commission, and some Member State governments (the UK, Spain and Italy). Less directly, the European Parliament, the EC Economic and Social Committee and a number of consumer organisations were ranged behind the Council, indicating more exactly the provenance of the measure under attack as ultimately serving consumer interests. Consumer interests and concerns had been filtered through both the

---

52   See for instance de Witte's summary: de Witte, note 18 above, at 881.

53   Case C-331/88, *R* v. *Minister of Agriculture, Fisheries and Food, ex parte Fedesa and others* (1990) ECR I-4023.

54   Including Hoechst UK. The Hoechst company, as explained above, has been a frequent subject of EC regulation and is a well-known litigant at the European level.

Parliament[55] and the Economic and Social Committee[56] and the Council appeared to be concerned both by the consumer concerns and the economic impact of those concerns (consumer boycotts and declines in sales).[57]

In dealing with the claim, the Court of Justice first of all restated its familiar principle of judicial control of discretionary regulatory power: having regard to the Council's discretionary powers in the field of regulating agriculture, judicial review would be limited to examining whether there had been a manifest error, misuse of powers or other action beyond the limits of discretion.[58] Then, turning to the mix of public health and economic arguments which informed the Council's exercise of discretion, the Court stated:

> ... faced with divergent appraisals [of scientific evidence relating to safety] by the national authorities of the Member States, reflected in the differences between existing national legislation, the Council remained within the limits of its existing discretionary powers in deciding to adopt the solution of prohibiting the hormones in question, and respond in that way to the concerns expressed by the European Parliament, the Economic and Social Committee and by several consumer organisations.[59]

At one level, the Court was saying that it was a valid exercise of discretion. But at another level, the judgment is also acknowledging the fact that the Council had the task of balancing competing producer and consumer interests and rights and had done so in a fair way, taking into account the balance of opinion on the matter. In this context, the Council's task was to ensure good management of the agricultural market in accordance with the guiding principles and objectives of market organisation as laid down in the EC Treaty. Fulfilment of this task might entail some restriction of the economic freedom of some parties but this could be justified by reference to the overriding needs and interests of other parties or sections of the market. The evidence, in the Court's assessment, supported the degree of restriction adopted by the Council. Consumer organisations had called for boycotts of hormone-treated meat and such campaigns had twice already resulted in a decline in meat consumption. Advocate General Mischo suggested that these campaigns were motivated not only by fears concerning the harmful nature of hormone-treated meat but also by a more general trend in public opinion: 'a growing aversion on the part of the public to the

---

55   Opinion of 11 November 1985, OJ 1985, C 288/158.

56   OJ 1985, C 44/14. See also the discussion in Advocate General Mischo's opinion ((1990) ECR I, at p 4046), which refers to negative opinions on the use of hormones for animal livestock from the European Bureau of Consumers' Unions, the Consumer Federation of America and the Public Voice for Food and Health Policy.

57   The Council states, in the preamble to the Directive: 'Whereas distortions to competition and barriers to trade must be removed ... And these products correspond to [consumer] anxieties and expectations in the best possible manner; whereas such a course of action is bound to bring about an increase in consumption of the product in question' (OJ 1988, L 70). It is of course open to argument whether the Council's predominant concern was for consumer interests or for market damage. This aspect of the matter will be addressed again later in the chapter.

58   (1990) ECR I, at 4061.

59   Ibid., at 4062.

use of chemical products in agriculture'.[60] The Council could therefore anticipate that the legalisation of hormone treatment would result in greater protest, leading to further reduction in consumption, with in turn negative consequences for the market and for farmers. In this context, the Council's response was judged to be a fair and proportionate restriction of trading freedom.

The value of this closer analysis is that it serves to demonstrate that, despite the formal language of such judgments, cases of this kind are mainly decided by a weighing of particular competing interests rather than the evaluation of abstract rights. It may then be misleading to suggest, as does some of the critical legal commentary, that legal rights are drawn narrowly or, if unsuccessfully invoked, not taken seriously by legislators and courts. It is important to remember that rights do not exist in the abstract but are located in a correlative space in which different and sometimes competing interests have to weighed together. To some extent, the language and structure of the process of judicial review obscures this fact, so that writers are tempted to talk about 'an active human rights scrutiny of Community measures'[61] by the Court of Justice (or complain about an insufficiently active scrutiny). What a case such as *Fedesa* reveals is a very active scrutiny of rights, and a strong enforcement of rights – however, not those of producers to supply a certain kind of product, but those of consumers to exercise choice and to safeguard health, and of other parties with an interest in market stability. Within that perspective, the narrow producer interest in hormone-treated meat is a very small section of the total domain of rights protection to be considered by law-making or judicial bodies.

Rights of Defence

Turning then to the outcome of claims made in the context of defence rights, particularly in the context of EC competition proceedings, there would seem at first sight to have been a higher degree of success on the part of producers in their litigation. In the first place, the template in Table 5.2 suggests a larger area of guaranteed non-interference, in terms of untouchable evidence or strict procedural requirements. But, apart from those ground-breaking cases (such as *Orkem*, or the *Soda Ash Cartel*) in which the domain of guaranteed protection was established, to what extent have producers successfully demonstrated a violation of their rights in terms of a trespass on that protected domain?

There is, in fact, a substantial body of litigation and jurisprudence to assess in this way in the EU context, since (especially since the 1970s) there have been a large number of appeals by individual companies, often alleging several grounds of violation of rights, before the EU courts. However, measurement of the 'success' of such claims is problematic in that different aspects of regulatory activity may be used as 'units' of challengeable action: for instance, whole decisions or parts of decisions, the establishment of infringements, fines, the amount of fines. Then, the significance of a successful claim may be difficult to measure – for instance, how does a 10 per cent reduction in the amount of a fine compare with the annulment of

---

60 Ibid., at 4046.
61 For instance, de Witte, note 18 above, at 881.

part, or the whole of the substantive decision? Grappling with such methodological problems, a recent study by Harding and Gibbs[62] attempted to assess the outcome of a particular (though significant) sector of EC competition appeals, in relation to anti-competitive cartels, over a ten-year period. The study found that, out of a sample of two hundred appeals before either the Court of Justice or Court of First Instance, 6 per cent were wholly successful (in that the whole decision was annulled), 33 per cent were wholly unsuccessful, and 61 per cent were 'partly successful' in that they achieved some measure of fine reduction. However, the authors are very cautious about the interpretation of the outcome for this last category of case. In that the fine reductions were sometimes small, and that in all of these cases the principal finding against the company was upheld, the category could just as well be relabelled 'largely unsuccessful'. Moreover, the great majority of cases involving a fine reduction were on grounds of insufficient evidence in relation to part of the alleged conduct, and were not indicative of any violation of constitutionally significant rights in connection with the conduct of investigations and hearings. The authors conclude by speculating on who gains what from this appellate activity:

> On the whole the appellants would seem to gain little directly, apart from some reasonable prospect of some reduction in the amount of fines. It seems rare now for the Commission to be defeated on major issues of legal principle and its seminal setbacks ... are receding into history. Most of the appellant arguments are knocked down, by both the CFI and the ECJ.[63]

Certainly, the findings of that research do not (again, contrary to the view of some critical commentators)[64] suggest any significant judicially established level of rights violation in this area.

In the context of EC competition proceedings, it is clear that companies do possess a number of established defence rights (largely worked out by the EU courts), that they frequently complain that such rights are violated, but with a small degree of success before the Court of First Instance and Court of Justice. Again, it may be asked whether this demonstrates some judicial softness towards the regulatory interest. A closer examination of the facts and circumstances of the cases suggests that this is unlikely.

For instance, there is some evidence of pointless legal claims by companies, in relation to pleas that are on the facts very unlikely to succeed, or in relation to instances of 'harmless error' (or immaterial illegalities). An example of the latter occurred in the second *PVC Cartel* appeal.[65] During the investigation of this

---

62   Note 10 above.

63   Ibid., 30 (2005) *European Law Review*, at 368. By 'seminal setbacks', the authors are referring to 'landmark' judgments which established the right in question, thereby entailing (in a somewhat retroactive fashion) the annulment of the enforcement measure at issue in that particular case.

64   See, for instance, some of the literature referred to in Ch. 7 of Joshua and Harding, note 3 above, especially at 206–209.

65   Cases T-305/94 etc, *LVM and others* v. *Commission* (1999) ECR I-931. An example of another 'harmless error' decision is provided by Case 107/82, *AEG* v. *Commission* (1983) ECR 3151.

infringement, the companies had properly invoked their *Orkem* 'right of silence' in relation to certain questions but then sought annulment of the subsequent decision by the Commission since the questions had been asked in the first place. However, the Court of First Instance stated:

> ... it is ... undisputed that the questions contained in the decision requiring information and which are challenged by the applicants in this part of the plea are identical to those annulled by the Court of Justice in *Orkem*. These questions are therefore likewise unlawful. However, as the Commission has emphasised, the file shows that the undertakings either refused to answer those questions or denied the facts upon which they were being thus questioned. In the circumstances, the illegality of the questions does not affect the legality of the Decision.[66]

While it may be argued that there is still some value in the judicial confirmation of the Commission's impropriety, it may be questioned whether it is an appropriate point for litigation when the improper questions have not resulted in any damage.

But once more it should be emphasised that the judicial role in many of these cases is very much one of weighing competing interests and rights and this role is often performed in a very thorough manner. In a general sense, defence rights in competition proceedings are usually being balanced against the general interest in ensuring effective enforcement of the EC competition policy, which is in the interest and so ultimately protecting the rights of a range of market participants, such as competitors and consumers. But sometimes the rights-balancing exercise is more directly evident in the arguments before the Courts. One specific example may be cited, in relation to disclosure of evidence and access to the file. In one of the *Soda Ash Cartel* appeals,[67] there was considerable discussion concerning the extent of such access to the Commission's file, and whether it should extend to material which was not actually used by the Commission in its formal case against the party concerned, was not exculpatory and also contained confidential information. The Commission argued that the company did not have a strong claim for access to such immaterial evidence: 'undertakings have no right to peruse, on a wholly speculative basis, the internal documents of their competitors, which are not used against them.'[68] Moreover, the Commission asserted that any such claim should be outweighed by the competing third-party claim to confidentiality, urging for instance that 'the applicant's interest in examining documents which the Commission has not relied on against it is even less than a [third-party] complainant's interest in examining in examining documents upon which the Commission has in fact relied.'[69]

This takes the discussion into interesting territory. Such an argument brings into the picture a range of different interests and rights, jostling with each other: the defence rights of the defending company, competitor's rights of confidential treatment of evidence supplied to the Commission, and the rights of third-party complainants,

---

66   Ibid., at 1063.

67   Case T-36/91, *ICI* v. *Commission* (1995) ECR II-1847.

68   (1995) ECR II, at 1872. Put in such terms, it is an argument against the defending party's freedom to conduct a 'fishing expedition'.

69   Ibid., at 1872.

who may be for instance competitors, consumers, or other official agencies. The Court of First Instance cut short this potentially interesting essay in rights protection by sweeping the whole matter into a broad entitlement of defendant access to the file, as a matter of 'equality of arms'. The Court justified this partly by criticising the Commission's self-appointed role of sole judge of what may be material, exculpatory, or inculpatory. The Court stated that, although the Commission had decided not to use certain documents in order to prove the infringement, 'equality of arms nevertheless required that the applicant should have the opportunity likewise to decide whether or not to use them in its defence.'[70] Regarding the problem of confidential material, the Court suggested procedures by which the full file, or at least an itemised version, could be communicated to the defendant without breaching confidentiality owed to other parties.[71]

This *Soda Ash* judgment therefore provides an instructive example of rights delimitation and balancing with reference to a very specific situation and set of circumstances. Once more, contrary to some critical commentary, it demonstrates an EU court 'taking rights seriously'. The judgment does not really allow a defendant fishing expedition, but it is a conscientious exercise in achieving 'equality of arms'. It explores practical issues of legal process,[72] while also developing doctrine on defence rights and access to information. Although not all the arguments raised in the pleadings are fully explored in the judgment, as a judgment it is decisive in its reconfiguration of legal roles, enabling both parties in this kind of litigation to assess the character of evidence. In this respect, it suggests an even-handed approach at ground level to the issue of rights evaluation.

Producer Rights: Rhetoric, Rule and Practice

At first glance, it would seem that large corporate producers have made good progress under the European basic rights protection regimes: their entitlement has been accepted in principle. But on closer examination, practice does not entirely match the rhetoric. Such companies, in relation to claims regarding both economic self-determination and defence rights, have won few of their well-resourced actions. Yet, at the same time, the rhetoric has not been without impact, especially in establishing a kind of rule of law, or set of standards, which are increasingly rigorous and serve to govern and inform the regulatory decisions and judgments which balance the competing economic and other types of interest in this context. It will be seen that, at the other end of the spectrum, the emergence and impact of consumer claims are less transparent, and remain more buried in a complex regulatory domain.

---

70   Ibid., at 1898. Note, however, that this degree of access to the prosecution file is more generous than that provided for instance under US or UK law: see Harding and Joshua, note 3 above, at 200. This is an example therefore of a *broader* rights entitlement under EU law relative to some other jurisdictions.

71   Ibid., at 1893–4.

72   For instance, the Court recognises the administrative burden for the Commission in performing a fuller disclosure of material but concludes that legal and technical difficulties are outweighed by the need to recognise rights of defence: (1995) ECR II, at 1897.

Chapter 6

The European Laboratory:
The Construction of Consumer
Rights in Europe

GMOs and Consumer Safety: The Tale of Syngenta's B*t*10 Maize

In March 2005, the science journal *Nature* published an article entitled 'US launches probe into sales of unapproved transgenic corn'.[1] This article detailed a case of mistaken identity that led to one variety of genetically engineered maize developed by Syngenta known as *Bt*10 – *a variety that had not been approved for commercial use anywhere in the world* – being inadvertently distributed and planted as if it were another, licensed variety, *Bt*11.[2] By the time the matter came to light, not only had several hundred tonnes of the unlicensed maize been grown and harvested across the US and Canada over a four-year period, between 2001 and 2004, but consignments of the unlicensed grain had been commercially exported to various other states, including a number of EU countries. Interestingly, despite the fact that the US authorities were notified that there was a problem in December 2004, they failed to alert the European Commission until three months later – just two days before the publication of the *Nature* article.

Unsurprisingly, Syngenta sought to play down both the scale and implications of the mix-up. The total amount of *Bt*10 maize involved would, according to the company, amount to enough seed to plant an area equivalent to just 0.01 per cent of the annual total US corn acreage – a mere 37,000 acres.[3] Thus, contamination of maize consignments destined for the domestic market would inevitably only be at low concentrations. Moreover, as just 18 per cent of the US corn harvest is exported, only 'very small volumes' of the rogue maize could possibly have entered third countries' markets.[4]

---

1   C. Macilwain (2005), 'US launches probe into sales of unapproved transgenic corn'. *Nature*, 434:423.

2   *Bt*11 has been used for some time in the US and has been approved for consumption in the EU.

3   In total, around 80 million acres of corn are planted annually in the US. GeneWatch UK and Greenpeace International (2005), *GM Contamination Report 2005: A review of cases of contamination, illegal planting and negative side effects of genetically modified organisms* <http://www.gmcontaminationregister.org>. Reported contamination incidents from around the world are regularly added to the online register maintained by NGOs.

4   'Syngenta agrees to settlement with USDA on unintended Bt10 corn', *Syngenta Press Release*, 8 April 2005, quoted in GeneWatch UK and Greenpeace International, ibid. (emphasis added*).*

Any possibility that this protracted contamination incident might present a threat to human or environmental health was also dismissed by Syngenta. Jeff Stein, the corporation's head of regulatory affairs was quoted in the *Nature* article as having stated 'What makes this [incident] somewhat unique is that *Bt*10 and *Bt*11 are physically identical and the proteins are identical.'[5]

The two GM maize lines may well be very *similar* in character but it is misleading to describe them as being *identical*. Syngenta would have been fully aware of the fact that *Bt*10 bears at least one notable feature that distinguishes it from *Bt*11[6]: *Bt*10 contains a gene that gives resistance to the antibiotic ampicillin.[7] The company would also have been aware of the EU's opposition to the use of such markers in the development of GMOs as well as, no doubt, the antipathy of the international food standards body, the Codex Alimentarius Commission which, due to concerns over potential risks to human and animal health, has also recommended that the commercial use of antibiotic resistance marker genes should be avoided.[8] Despite the controversy surrounding the use of these genes (or possibly because of it), there was some delay in informing the European Commission about the presence of this gene in the *Bt*10 line.[9] Syngenta also issued assurances to the European Commission

---

5   Macilwain, note 1 above, at 423.

6   This statement is rather surprising bearing in mind that in 2003, in its submissions to the UK's Advisory Committee on Releases into the Environment, Syngenta used *Bt*10 as the comparator to demonstrate that *Bt*11 did not contain an antibiotic resistance marker gene: Advisory Committee on Releases to the Environment (ACRE) (2003), *Advice on a notification for marketing of insect resistant and herbicide tolerant GM maize*, 11 September <http://www.defra.gov.uk/environment/acre/advice/pdf/acre_advice35.pdf>.

7   That is, in addition to the gene from the soil microorganism *Bacillus thuringiensis* and the PAT gene (also from a soil microorganism) that confers herbicide tolerance.

8   The risk of unintentional horizontal transfer of antibiotic resistance to bacterium and the potential repercussions of such transfer for human or animal health has led both the European Food Safety Authority and the international food standards body, the Codex Alimentarius Commission, to recommend that the commercial use of such genes should be avoided. See 'Opinion of the Scientific Panel on Genetically Modified Organisms on the use of antibiotic resistance genes as marker genes in genetically modified plants', *The EFSA Journal* (2004) 48:1–18. Note also, the *Statement of the Scientific Panel on Genetically Modified Organisms on the safe use of the nptII antibiotic resistance marker gene in genetically modified plants*, adopted on 22–23 March 2007. Both EFSA documents are available at <http://www.efsa. europa.eu/en/science/gmo/gmo_opinions.html>. At the EU regulatory level, *Directive 2001/18/EC of the European Parliament and of the Council on the deliberate release into the environment of genetically modified organisms and repealing Council Directive 90/220/ EEC* [2001] OJ L106/1 requires that the use of antibiotic resistance marker genes be phased out. For the Codex Alimentarius position, see *Principles for Risk Analysis and Guidelines for Safety Assessment of Foods Derived From Modern Biotechnology*, Codex Alimentarius Commission, CAC/GL, 44-2003, at section 5, 20–21. Document available via <http://www. codexalimentarius.net/web/index_en.jsp>.

9   This delay was noted by GeneWatch and Greenpeace International, note 3 above, at 17.

that none of the rogue *Bt*10 maize that had entered the market had been used in sweetcorn varieties destined for human consumption in the EU.[10]

It is estimated that about a thousand tonnes of *Bt*10 maize may have been unlawfully imported into Europe between 2001 and 2004.[11] However, the accuracy of this figure is impossible to determine. A full assessment of the scale of contamination within the EU was hampered not just by the timescale of the incident – four years is a long time for any contamination incident to continue unnoticed – but also by Syngenta's reluctance to list the specific countries that had 'accidentally received' the *Bt*10 seed;[12] its tardiness in coming up with a validated detection test for *Bt*10, and its insistence that access to the *Bt*10 reference material (needed to confirm the identity of suspect maize) should be restricted to state authorities and just one commercial laboratory on grounds of commercial confidentiality, all of which rendered independent verification of Syngenta's claims highly problematic.[13] Ultimately, the reality is that it was not possible to trace and recall all of the rogue maize that may have been planted, harvested, exported and processed between 2001 and 2004.

The *Bt*10/*Bt*11 fiasco is just one of many incidents that have fuelled the GM debate since 1996 when the importation of mixed consignments of conventional and Monsanto's genetically engineered Roundup Ready soybeans into Europe triggered the first wave of public outrage and opposition to GM foods.[14] Perhaps the most widely publicised incident to have occurred prior to 2005 concerned the unintended (and unlawful) release of another *Bt* maize known as *StarLink* into the environment, onto the market and, ultimately, into taco shells sold for human consumption in

---

10   C. Sondermann (2005), 'EFSA Follows Up On Bt10 Maize', *EFSA Press Release*, 9 June. Available at <http://www.efsa.europa.eu/en/press_room/press_statements/953.html>.

11   GeneWatch UK and Greenpeace International, note 3 above, at 15. This report provides a detailed review of the *Bt*10 incident and its implications. See at 14–21.

12   Macilwain, note 1 above.

13   GeneWatch UK and Greenpeace International, note 3 above, at 15–17.

14   The importation of mixed GM/conventional soya attracted significant media attention and provided the impetus for a widespread, energetic and enduring campaign against the introduction of genetically engineered foods in some EU Member States and demands for stringent regulatory controls to protect consumers and the environment. Opposition was particularly strong in the UK. Examples of media and NGO reports and commentaries from the latter half of the 1990s include, G. Monbiot (1997), 'Watch These Beans', *The Guardian*, 17 September, at 17; 'Frankenstein Food Companies Named and Shamed', Friends of the Earth Press Release, 26 April 1998 <http://www.foe.co.uk/resource/press_releases/19980426140249. html>; The controversial special edition of *The Ecologist* published in 1998 under the title, 'The Monsanto Files: Can We Survive Genetic Engineering?', September/October, 1998; Author unknown, 'Monsanto Apologises Over GM Soya Bean', *Farmers' Guardian*, 22 May 1998; 'Shoppers Say "No!" To Genetically Modified Food', Friends of the Earth Press Release, 25 April 1997 <http://www.foe.co.uk/resource/press_releases/19970425112530.html>; J. Sheppard (1997), *From BSE to Genetically Modified Organisms: Science, Uncertainty and the Precautionary Principle* (London: Greenpeace); J. Sheppard (1996), *Spilling the Genes: What we should know about genetically engineered foods* (London: Genetics Forum).

2000.[15] Following the accidental commercial cultivation of *StarLink* in US fields, traces of this GMO – which due to concerns over its possible allergenic properties has only been approved for use in animal feed – were found in food products across the world. It has been estimated that the clean-up operation after this incident cost to the food industry around $1 billion.[16]

The Online GM Contamination Register[17] (established and maintained by GeneWatch and Greenpeace International) provides an alarming indication of the scale of GM contamination of the food and feed chain over the last ten years that extends far beyond the highly publicised examples noted above. In total, the 2005 Report[18] lists 113 incidents affecting thirty-nine countries across five continents. Predictably, the vast majority concern the four major commercial GM crops – maize, soybean, oilseed rape and cotton – but some (around 10 per cent) involve less familiar or experimental GMOs, including grass, plum, potato, rice, pigs and tomatoes.[19] Moreover, the negative impacts reported are varied and as the online Register demonstrates, errors have occurred at every stage of development – from the laboratory, to the field, to the plate'.[20] The NGOs assert:

> Cases of misidentification, poor quality control and lack of awareness of proper controls in laboratories have led to GM tomato, zucchini and maize seed being distributed around the world and meat from GM pigs entering the food chain. Seed used for GM trials, even the high-profile scientific farm-scale evaluations in the UK has been found to be contaminated by other GM crops. Experimental trials have led to contamination of neighbouring and subsequent crops. Cross-pollination and poor quality control have led to non-GM seed and food aid being contaminated. Illegal large-scale growing of GM crops in Brazil, India and Romania, together with scientists conducting illegal trials or failing to contain them properly, show that GM organisms are often out-of-control even when claimed to be 'strictly contained.[21]

---

15   Similarly to the importation of Monsanto's Roundup Ready soyabeans in 1996, the Starlink incident attracted a significant amount of publicity. See, for example, J. Borger (2000), 'Banned GM Corn Reported in Taco Snack', *The Guardian*, 19 September, at 14; M. Dejevsky (2000), 'GM Maize Linked to Allergic Reactions', *The Independent*, 6 December, at 9; A. Clark and J. Martinson (2001), 'Aventis Chiefs in GM Blunder Sacked', *The Guardian*, 13 February, at 23; for a pro-GM perspective see, for example, T. Hoban (2000), 'Tacogate: There Is Barely A Kernel of Truth', *Washington Post*, 26 November. The following, from the NGO Food First, also provides an informative overview of this contamination incident and the wider controversy: Rosset, P. (2000), 'Anatomy of a "Gene Spill": Do We Really Need Genetically Engineered Food?', *Food First, Institute for Food and Development Policy, Backgrounder*, 6(4).

16   Macilwain, note 1 above.

17   GeneWatch UK and Greenpeace International, note 3 above.

18   Ibid.

19   Ibid., at 4.

20   Ibid. The report lists negative impacts as follows: eighty-eight cases of contamination, seventeen cases of illegal releases into the environment and eight reports of negative agricultural side-effects.

21   Ibid., at 12.

The credibility of (anti-biotech) NGO reporting and the research findings of critical commentators from within the scientific community are often hotly disputed by industry and regulatory authorities. None the less, it is difficult to dismiss entirely the evidence linking the cultivation and consumption of genetically modified food and feed and contaminated food and feed with adverse environmental and human health impacts.[22]

Returning briefly to the *Bt*10 incident, the European Food Safety Authority's (EFSA) (cautiously reassuring) conclusion that the inadvertent contamination of imported maize grain with *Bt*10 was 'not considered likely'[23] to present a risk to animal or human health was certainly fortuitous – bearing in mind that the incident went unnoticed for four years and the evident pervasiveness of these organisms once released into the environment and the food chain.[24] However, as more products

---

22   The following represent no more than a very small sample of the varied discussion about the environmental and human health risks associated with agricultural and food biotechnology: S. Nottingham (2002), *Genescapes: The Ecology of Genetic Engineering* (London: Zed Books); The Royal Society (2002), *Genetically Modified Plants for Food Use and Human Health – An Update*, Policy Document 4/02 (London: The Royal Society); M. Gundula and H. Warwick (2002), *Seeds of Doubt: North American Farmers' Experiences of GM Crops* (London: The Soil Association); H. Sampson, (2003), 'Environmental Risk Assessment of GMOs under Directive 2001/18: an Effective Safety-Net or a Collective Illusion', *European Intellectual Property Review*, 25(2): 79–90; N. Salmon (2005), 'What's "Novel" About It? Substantial Equivalence, Precaution and Consumer Protection 1997–2004. Monsanto Agricoltura Italia SpA v Presidenza del Consiglio dei Ministri (Case 236/01, 9 September 2003)', *Environmental Law Review*, 7(2):138; M. Teitel and K. Wilson (2000), *Changing the Nature of Nature: All You Need to Know About Genetically Engineered Food* (London: Vision Paperbacks); N. Salmon (2002), 'A European Perspective on the Precautionary Principle, Food Safety and the Free Trade Imperative of the WTO', *European Law Review* 27(2):138–55; J. Smith (2004), *Seeds of Deception: Exposing Corporate and Government Lies About the Safety of Genetically Engineered Food* (Dartington: Green Books) (note in particular, Chapter 2, 'What Could Go Wrong? A Partial List', where Smith sets out his concerns about the safety of food biotechnology); B. Toker (ed.) (2001), *Redesigning Life? The Worldwide Challenge to Genetic Engineering* (London: Zed Books), in particular Part 1, Chapters 1–8. For a readable explanation of the scientific and technical aspects of GM crop production, as well as discussion of the background to, and future prospects of plant biotechnology, see A. Slater et al. (2003), *Plant Biotechnology: The Genetic Manipulation of Plants* (Oxford: Oxford University Press).

23   Sondermann, note 10 above.

24   M. Partridge and D.J. Murphy (2004), 'Detection of genetically modified soya in a range of organic and health food products: Implications for the accurate labelling of foodstuffs derived from potential GM crops', *British Food Journal*, 106: 166–80; J. Orson (2002), 'Gene Stacking in Herbicide Tolerant Oilseed Rape: Lesson From the North American Experience', *English Nature Research Reports*, 443; D. Quist and I.H. Chapela (2001), 'Transgenic DNA Introgressed into traditional landraces in Oaxaca, Mexico', *Nature* 414:541–42; M. Metz and J. Futterer (2002), 'Suspect Evidence of Genetic Contamination', *Nature*, 416: 600–601; D. Quist and I.H. Chapela (2002), 'Reply to Letters', *Nature*, 416:602; P.J. Dale et al. (2002), 'Potential for Environmental Impact of Transgenic Crops', *Nature Biotechnology*, 20:567–74; Greenpeace International (2007), *Bayer CropScience Contaminates Our Rice* (Amsterdam: Greenpeace International).

reach the market and the industry moves into the commercial production of crops coding for drugs or other biologically active compounds,[25] the law of statistics dictates that the likelihood of a major problem arising at some future time must, inevitably, increase. NGOs with an anti-biotech agenda may, on occasion, be guilty of exaggeration and alarmist reporting, and it is reasonable to caution that claims of rampant contamination of the food and feed chain and corporate recklessness should not be accepted unquestioningly as wholly accurate or representative of the wider picture. By the same token – bearing in mind the significant interest the beleaguered biotech industry and EU and Member State authorities have in avoiding politically and economically costly food scares and protecting their respective shares of biotech 'Golden Egg'[26] – the reassuring platitudes issued by these key stakeholders must also be treated with some caution.

Notwithstanding the scope for differing perspectives on such matters, the fact remains that NGO predictions of widespread contamination of the food chain have proven to be credible; although only a handful of GMOs have been approved for food and feed use in the EU, low-level contamination of the food and feed chain has already become an uncomfortable fact of life.[27] In light of this, it has to be acknowledged that even a qualified acceptance of the anti-biotech lobby's claims that GM crops and foods present a threat to both the environment and human health, must raise important questions about both the short and longer term safety of agricultural and food biotechnology.

---

25   See, for example, S. Dibb and S. Mayer (2000), *Biotech – The Next Generation. Good for Whose Health?* (London: The Food Commission and Genewatch UK); J. Adam (2001), 'Down on the Pharm', *The Guardian*, 30 April.

26   According to the ISAAA (International Service for the Acquisition of Agri-biotech Applications), global plantings of GM crops exceeded 100 million hectares in 2006. Coverage is predicted to increase to 200 million hectares by 2015: *ISAAA Brief 35-2006: Press Release* <http://www.isaaa.org/resources/publications/briefs/35/pressrelease/default. html>. For a detailed review of industry progress, see the full report: G. Brookes, and P. Barfoot (2006), ISAAA Brief 36, *GM Crops: The First Ten Years – Global Socio-Economic and Environmental Impacts* (UK: PG Economics Ltd). For the official EU perspective, see the Communication from the Commission of the European Communities, *Life Sciences and Biotechnology: A Strategy for Europe*. COM (2002) 27. Here the Commission identified the life sciences industry as key to the European Union's future: 'Life sciences and biotechnology are widely recognised to be, after information technology, the next wave of the knowledge-based economy, creating new opportunities for our societies and economies'. at 3. Note also, the publication of two related 'Progress Reports' by the Commission in the intervening period: COM (2004)250 final and COM(2003) 96 final.

27   See the Online GM Contamination Register maintained by Greenpeace and GeneWatch UK, note 3 above. It is worth noting here that these NGOs have stated that it is impossible to know the extent to which their 'register' of *reported* incidents provides a full account of GMO contamination. It is entirely possible that some accidental releases and contamination events may never have been reported at all and that details of others may have kept out of the public domain.

The EU's adoption of the 2003 regulations governing the authorisation, marketing and traceability of genetically engineered food and feed products,[28] and the subsequent lifting of the five-year *de facto* moratorium on new GM approvals, marked the end of problematic stand-off between the EU and the major GM producer states. Whilst capitulation in the face of mounting pressure and formal complaints proceedings in the WTO[29] has certainly diffused a politically tense and potentially costly trade dispute, the shift in policy also says something about priorities. The moratorium was lifted despite continued disagreement and uncertainty about the possible longer-term impacts of GMOs, and ongoing public opposition to GM foods. The protection of consumer interests is not the sole, nor necessarily the primary, objective of Community policy and law. In fact, it seems that ultimately, when the going gets tough, the free trade agenda wins. As Scott has recently observed, the EU's revamped GM food and feed framework

> ... has been shaped in fundamental ways by the SPS context in which it emerged. In important respects the continuing concerns of many Member States have been silenced in the face of the trade imperative. For some, the new regime forces Member States to account for the external effects of their domestic policies in a disciplined way; others see it as sacrificing democracy and other tangible values to trade.[30]

The food biotechnology market, and indeed the food sector generally, provide a fertile ground for an analysis of European consumer policy. Today, the majority of EU citizens are wholly dependent upon the industrialised and globalised food market. The BSE/vCJD epidemic and official responses to both the bovine and the human variants of this shocking brain disease shattered consumer confidence in the safety and integrity of the food chain in the first half of the 1990s.[31] The rapid rise of the food biotechnology industry in the second half of the decade, typically characterised by controversy, contamination, what many consider to be a reckless disregard for safety and also a blatant bulldozing of public opposition, has done little to restore public confidence in the intentions of either the industry itself or those who regulate it. A Special Eurobarometer Survey, *Europeans and Biotechnology in 2005: Patterns and Trends* found that 'overall, a majority of Europeans think that GM food should not be encouraged. GM food is seen by them as not being useful, as morally unacceptable and as risky for society.'[32]

---

28 *Regulation (EC) No. 1829/2003 on genetically modified food and feed* [2003] OJ L268/1 and *Regulation (EC) No. 1830/2003concerning the traceability and labelling of genetically modified organisms and the traceability of food and feed produced from genetically modified organisms and amending Directive 2001/18/EC* [2003] OJ L268/24.

29 WTO Dispute Settlement Cases DS293, DS292 and DS291, *European Communities: Measures Affecting the Approval and Marketing of Biotech Products*. All related documents and the Panel's final report are available via <http://www.wto.org/english/tratop_e/dispu_e/find_dispu_cases_e.htm#results>. See also the discussion in Chapter 7 below.

30 J. Scott (2007), *The WTO Agreement on Sanitary and Phytosanitary Measures: A Commentary* (Oxford: Oxford University Press), at 2.

31 For an overview of the BSE/vCJD crisis see Chapter 3 above.

32 G. Gaskell et al. (2006), *Special Eurobarometer. Europeans and Biotechnology in 2005: Patterns and Trends*. Final Report on Eurobarometer 64.3, at 4.

In this market-driven and market-dependent society, it is unsurprising that the various crises and controversies affecting the food chain in recent years have provided a key impetus for the evolution of a more robust consumer policy at both the national and the European levels. Consumer policy, the body of law (both soft and substantive) that aims to protect the interests and rights of the individual sitting at the end of the supply chain, impacts on the interests of all market stakeholders and is thus is of key importance to all.

The next part of this chapter traces the evolution of European consumer policy and the emergence of the consumer as a right-bearing stakeholder at the supranational level, before moving on to focus on the special case of food policy and the all-important issue of food safety. Building upon this analysis, the latter half of the discussion moves on to assess the consumer-protective value of Community food law via an analysis of both the General Food Law Regulation that was adopted in 2002[33] and the revamped sector-specific GM food and feed regulations that entered into force in 2004.[34] Ultimately, the objective here is to determine the extent to which the rhetoric of consumer rights – specifically this actor's right to safe food – is reflected in the reality of EU policy and law.

The Evolution of European Consumer Policy, 1957–2006

When the original Treaty of Rome was agreed fifty years ago, the signatories' goal was to create a regulatory framework within which a mutually beneficial borderless, integrated Common Market (later Single Market) could flourish. Within the context of this original 'Community vision', the emphasis was very much on the *economic*. In part, this was due to the context in which negotiations on the Treaty took place, for although by the late 1950s the concept of 'the consumer' as an active beneficiary of regulatory protection and holder of rights had taken hold in the US economic and social context, such a conception of this economic actor had yet to pervade the European consciousness.[35] Consequently, when the six original Member States came together in 1957, there was no perceived need to broker a broad-based consumer policy within which consumer 'rights' or interests might be *directly* identified

---

33   *Regulation (EC) No 178/2002 laying down the general principles and requirements of food law, establishing the European Food Safety Authority and laying down procedures in matters of food safety.* [2002] OJ L31/1.

34   Focusing particularly on the core measures: [2003] O.J. L268/1 and [2003] O.J. L268/24, note 28 above. The former measure regulates the entry onto the market of food and feed consisting of, containing or produced from GMOs, whilst the latter introduces comprehensive traceability and labelling requirements across all stages of the production chain. For a list of other key measures governing the development, cultivation, processing and marketing of GMOs see the list provided at note 119 below.

35   The more sophisticated concept of 'the consumer' that emerged initially in the US is reflected in the five basic consumer rights identified by President Kennedy in March 1962. These were: a) right to protection of health and safety; b) right to protection of economic interests; c) right of redress; d) right to information and education, and e) right to representation. John F. Kennedy, Congressional Address, Consumer Bill of Rights, *Special Message on Protecting the Consumer Interest*, 1962 Cong. Q. 458.

and protected; the end-consumer simply provided the final (economic) link in the production and distribution chain.

That is not to say that Community law did not, even in its infancy, bestow notable benefits upon this key stakeholder; it clearly did. Regulatory interventions directed at harmonising product standards or promoting reliability of supply across Member States' markets have always been a central tenet of the Community project, and such measures will often have some consumer protection value – whether by design or fortuitous coincidence. The pursuit of the European free market ideal has always necessitated at least some consideration of the consumer interest, and consumer protection – at least in the more passive sense of the term – has necessarily been long recognised as one aspect of the integrative process. Importantly though, under the original scheme, the Community's agenda was driven primarily by the combined *State* interest in uniform market regulation rather than by an overriding concern for the *rights* of the end-consumer. Whilst the overarching objectives set out in the original text of the EC Treaty spoke generally of 'a harmonious development of economic activities, a continuous and balanced expansion, an increase in stability, [and] an accelerated raising of the standard of living', none of this was couched in terms that acknowledged the status and entitlements of the consumer as a key stakeholder in the European Project.[36] As Weatherill explains:

> The assumption of the original Treaty pattern is that the consumer will benefit from the process of integration through the enjoyment of a more efficient market, which will yield more competition, allowing wider choice, lower prices and higher quality products and services. The substantive provisions of the Treaty, such as those designed to remove barriers to the free circulation of goods, persons and services … are designed *indirectly* to improve the lot of the consumer.[37]

Despite the universality of consumerism and the crucial role played by this actor, the emergence of a free-standing supranational consumer policy has proven to be a rather slow and faltering process; a process that has been variously encouraged and guided by numerous soft law measures,[38] and realised via incremental amendments

---

36   This agenda was expressed in Article 2 of the *EC Treaty* which, in its original form stated that 'The Community shall have as its task, by establishing a common market and progressively approximating the economic policies of Member States, to promote throughout the Community a harmonious development of economic activities, a continuous and balanced expansion, an increase in stability, an accelerated raising of the standard of living and closer relations between the States belonging to it.'

37   S. Weatherill (1997), *EC Consumer Policy and Policy* (London: Longman), at 5 (emphasis added). Much of the background information relating to the emergence of Community consumer policy is drawn from this text.

38   The first of these was the *Council Resolution of 14 April 1975 on a preliminary programme of the European Economic Community for a consumer protection and information policy*, [1975] OJ C 92/1. Relevant measures adopted in the intervening years are too numerous to list here. However, a detailed review of the evolution and character of Community consumer policy, including reference to the various soft law measures that have helped to shape this key area of Community activity is provided by S. Weatherill (2005), *EU Consumer Law and Policy* (Cheltenham: Edward Elgar Publishing Ltd), Ch. 1.The following

to the EC Treaty. These amendments began with the insertion of Article 100a into the Treaty by the Single European Act 1986 – formalising the Commission's obligation to 'take as a base a *high level of protection*' in the drafting of market harmonisation measures concerning health, safety, environmental protection and consumer protection[39] – and culminated in the formal mainstreaming of consumer policy following the Amsterdam amendments to Article 129(a) (now Article 153) in 1997.

By this stage, what Justin Greenwood has described as the 'high, crisis politics' resulting from consumer concerns over the integrity and safety of the European food supply chain, and the EU's struggle to achieve and maintain 'output legitimacy', had significantly raised the profile of consumer protection issues across the EU.[40] In the midst of the various crises over product safety, the emergent 'Consumer Society' populated by an increasingly vocal, demanding and concerned community of consumers was playing its part in focusing official attention on the needs of this particular 'economic link' in the supply chain.[41] Overall, the *status quo* on consumer protection and particularly the more active rights of the consumer was rapidly becoming untenable. The need for a more effective Community consumer policy that could more readily accommodate and provide for both the passive and active rights of the consumer (that is, related rights to safety and autonomy) was

---

may also be of interest: S. Weatherill (1999), 'Consumer Policy', in P. Craig and G. De Búrca (eds) (1999), *The Evolution of EU Law* (Oxford: Oxford University Press); J. Stuyck (2000), 'European Consumer Law After the Treaty of Amsterdam: Consumer Policy in or Beyond the Internal Market?', *Common Market Law Review* 37:367–400.

39   EC Treaty, Article 100a(1) and 100a(3). The insertion of the 'high' baseline requirement does not in itself guarantee high standards in terms of product quality, value for money, or consumer safety. In fact, the consequences of this standard can sometimes be perverse; for some Member States, harmonisation may well result in lower standards than those previously guaranteed under pre-existing domestic legislation. Note also Article 100a(4) which allows Member States to maintain more stringent rules than those agreed a European level *so long as they do not constitute a disguised restriction on trade.*

40   J. Greenwood (2007), *Interest Representation in the European Union* (Hampshire: Palgrave Macmillan, 2nd edn), at 140.

41   Greenwood takes the view that crises in *the market* – such as BSE – have provided the main impetus for the general trend towards a stronger consumer policy at EU level. In his view, 'High politics and a search for output legitimacy have done more to drive consumer policy to center-stage of the EU agenda than 40 years of continual effort by EU consumer organizations could' (Greenwood, ibid., at 139–40). Though valid to a point, this rather sweeping dismissal of these actors' influence can be challenged. In recent years, consumer awareness of 'the market' has increased. This is, in part, a direct consequence of various safety crises, but it is also attributable to the high profile campaigns of, and public engagement with, key NGOs. Such groups have certainly played an important part in the shaping of both Community consumer policy and the market environment itself. Note, for example, the extent to which public opposition to GM food (largely generated by energetic consumer group campaigns and media coverage) provided the key trigger for the EU's five-year de facto moratorium on new GMO approvals. The power of consumer (and environmental) NGOs to influence the character and regulation of the market should not, therefore, be so easily dismissed.

now widely acknowledged.[42] As the Commission observed in 2001, 'The last few years have certainly been years of transition, with consumer policy moving to centre stage there has been a belated realisation, at both EC and national level, that consumer policy is not a luxury but rather an essential element of overall EU policy and development.'[43]

Thus, responding to the shifting sands of market relationships, and building upon earlier Treaty amendments that had gone, some way at least, towards acknowledging the basic rights of this core stakeholder, the Amsterdam Treaty finally dragged consumer policy onto centre stage in an attempt to improve the credibility of EU market governance. Article 153 of the EC Treaty (previously Article 129(a)) provides that:

1. In order to promote the interests of consumers and to ensure a high level of consumer protection, the Community *shall* contribute to protecting the health, safety and economic interests of consumers, as well as to promoting their *right* to information, education and to organise themselves in order to guard their interests.
2. Consumer protection requirements *shall* be taken into account in defining and implementing other Community policies and activities.
3. The community shall contribute to the attainment of the objectives referred to in paragraph 1 through:
   a) measures adopted pursuant to Article 95 in the context of the completion of the internal market;
   b) measures which support, supplement and monitor the policy pursued by the Member States.[44]

---

42   Building upon its first consumer policy 'Action Plan' – *Communication from the Commission of the European Communities, Three Year Action Plan of Consumer policy in the EEC (1990–1992)* COM (90) 98 – the Commission continued to develop its consumer protection agenda in the years between the adoption of the Maastricht Treaty and the Amsterdam Treaty and beyond. The following 'Action Plans' were key soft law measures adopted by the European Commission in the years between the adoption of the Maastricht Treaty and the entry into force of Amsterdam Treaty in 1999: *The Second Commission Three-Year Action Plan 1993/1995 on Consumer Policy— Placing the Single Market at the Service of European Consumers.COM (93) 378; Communication from the Commission of the European Communities, Priorities for Consumer* Policy – 1996–98. COM (95) 519; *Communication from the Commission of the European Communities, Consumer Policy Action Plan 1999– 2001.* COM (1998) 696. The increasing awareness of the centrality of the consumer within the market place and the need to develop the rights and protection enjoyed by this actor is clearly reflected in these illuminative documents.

43   *Report from the Commission on the 'Action Plan for Consumer Policy 1999–2001' and on the 'General Framework for Community Activities in Favour of Consumers 1999– 2003'.* COM(2001) 486 final, at pp. 2–3, 21, quoted by Greenwood, note 40 above, at 139.

44   Emphasis added. EC Treaty Article 153 (ex 129a). Article 95 of the EC Treaty is also important here as it sets out the legal base for market harmonisation measures. The third paragraph of Article 95 provides that: 'The Commission, in its proposals envisaged in paragraph 1 [that is, market harmonisation measures] *concerning health, safety, environmental*

Following the Amsterdam Treaty, the EC Treaty requires law makers at least to consider the broader interests and rights of the consumer across all fields of policy development and law making. Aside from the most obvious issue of consumer safety, the consumer's (fundamental) right to information[45] was finally elevated from a mere 'interest' to a firm *right*[46] along with the right to 'education' and what Stuyck has since described as the consumer's fundamental right to freedom of association.[47]

Overall, the remoulding of the consumer from 'mere economic link'[48] to autonomous key player has taken more than twenty years, but as will be seen as this chapter progresses, even now, the *substantive* characterisation of this actor as an autonomous rights-bearing player continues to fall some way short of what consumers might reasonably expect and demand in the context of the all-encompassing global market place of the twenty-first century. The simple act of mainstreaming of the consumer interest does not, of itself, transform the essential character of the Single Market: for all the talk of consumer rights and consumer autonomy, the EU continues to be underpinned by an unerring faith in the free trade system.

European Consumer Policy and the Food Market

EU food policy provides an ideal focus for a consideration of the realities of Community consumer policy and analysis of the way which competing stakeholder interests are mediated under this regional free trade system. With annual production in the food and drink, and agricultural sectors being worth around €600 billion and €220 billion respectively, the EU agro-food sector is clearly of major economic importance.[49] Food is big business, and this being the case, it should come as little

---

protection and consumer protection, will take as a base a high level of protection, taking account in particular of any new development based on scientific facts. Within their respective powers, the European Parliament and the Council will also seek to achieve this objective' (emphasis added). Thus, this paragraph also reflects an intention to define consumer protection broadly. Market harmonisation measures, whether concerned with health, safety, environmental protection, or directly with issues of consumer protection must, ostensibly, provide a good level of protection of the consumer interest.

45   Stuyck, note 38 above, at 384.

46   Alongside health, safety and economic interests under Article 129a of the EC Treaty.

47   Stuyck, note 38 above, at 385. The right to freedom of association in the general sense has been recognised by the ECJ. See, for example, Case C-415/93, *Union Royal Belge des Societès de Football Association* v. *Bosman* [1995] ECR I-4921; Case C-325/92, *Montecatini* v. *Commission* [1999] ECR I-4539.

48   The original characterisation of the consumer as a 'mere economic link' and this actor's evolution into something more than this, was recognised and commented upon by the Council in its first *Resolution on a preliminary programme of the European Economic Community for a consumer protection and information policy,* adopted in 1975. See note 38 above.

49   According to figures relied upon by the European Commission in its *White Paper on Food Safety,* at that time, the EU's food and drink sector accounted for around 15 per cent of total manufacturing output; the EU is the world's largest producer of food and drinks; EU

surprise to find that the food market – production and supply – has consistently attracted significant attention from policy makers and legislators at both the national and European levels.[50] Indeed, Community intervention in this core market sector goes right back to the earliest days of the Common Market. Of necessity, many of the earliest harmonisation measures were food-related consumer protection measures designed to establish and enforce the consistent standards of quality and safety that were a prerequisite of the envisaged borderless Community-wide free market.[51] Inevitably, as the European free-market project has progressed, a complex and elaborate system of Community-level food quality and food safety provisions has evolved to meet the challenges of rising consumer expectations and ever expanding markets.

Traditionally, Community food policy and law has been developed in a rather haphazard and incremental manner, with action being taken, and law being made, as and when the need has arisen. For many years, food policy was simply one aspect of the broader market harmonisation agenda, and similarly to other market sectors consumer protection and thus the consumer protection value of the law, was determined in accordance with the needs of the market itself – on the basis of what might be necessary to create and maintain the 'level playing field' of a smoothly functioning internal market. Any implied consumer policy coming out of this process was simply a fortuitous consequence of the free trade agenda. However, as already noted earlier in this chapter, the series of high-profile food crises that characterised the late 1980s and 1990s – particularly the BSE epidemic and the furore over the arrival of GM food on the European market – ensured that by the mid-1990s, both national and Community food policy had been moved out of the wings and into the spotlight. In the wake of various clear and incontrovertible failures in the governance of the food chain – widely publicised by a sensationalist media keen to make the

---

exports of agricultural, and food and drink products are worth around 50 billion euros a year: Commission of the European Communities, *White Paper on Food Safety*. COM (1999) 719 final, at 6.

50 Early UK statutes dealing with food-related issues include the Bread Acts 1822 and 1836. The first general food law introduced in the UK was the Adulteration of Food or Drink Act 1860. For an informative and readable historical review and evaluation of the UK food law, see M. French and J. Phillips (2000), *Cheated Not Poisoned? Food Regulation in the United Kingdom 1875–1938*. (Manchester: Manchester University Press). This book provides an insightful historical perspective on the evolution of national food safety law and the enduring challenges facing legislators striving to protect both consumer and commercial interests. For a more recent and very comprehensive review and critique of EU food law, see C. MacMaoláin (2007), *EU Food Law: Protecting Consumers and the Health in a Common Market* (Oxford: Hart Publishing).

51 Early food-related measures include: *Council Directive 64/54/EEC of 5 November 1963 on the approximation of the laws of the Member States concerning the preservatives authorised for use in foodstuffs intended for human consumption* [1964] OJ L12/161; *Directive 65/66/EEC of 26 January 1965 concerning criteria of purity for authorised preservatives*. [1965] OJ L22/373. An important measure from the consumer information perspective was the first general labelling directive: *Directive 79/112/EEC on the approximation of the laws of the Member States relating to the labelling, presentation and advertising of foodstuffs*. [1979] OJ L33/1.

most of stories about 'mad cow disease'[52] and 'Frankenstein foods'[53] – consumer confidence in the ability of national and EU regulators to *effectively* manage and regulate the food chain had plummeted to an all-time low. A fearful and distrustful consumer is bad for business and the EU food sector was now in a state of crisis: urgent action was needed to create a more coherent and systematic approach to food safety policy and food policy generally – for the sake of the market as much as for the sake of the end-consumer.

In 1997, the European Commission's *Green Paper on Food Law*[54] was published, wherein for the first time the increasing complexities of, and challenges presented by, the contemporary EU food market were aired with a view to initiating change. Almost three years later, at the beginning of 2000, this paper was followed by the Commission's *White Paper on Safety*.[55] Here, the Commission finally presented its vision for a 'radical new approach' to food policy; an approach that would strengthen governance across all aspects of the food production chain 'from farm to table'.[56] In the Commission's words, the overarching policy objective here was to 'transform EU food policy into a proactive, dynamic, coherent and comprehensive instrument to ensure a high level of human health and consumer protection'.[57]

The hope was that programme of reforms addressing the various weaknesses that a decade of high-profile food and feed emergencies had exposed within existing

---

52   The following represent no more than a very small, random sample of the thousands of reports published across the mainstream media since the initial emergence of BSE and vCJD in the 1980s: J. Erlichman (1988), 'Butchers Selling Diseased Meat', *Guardian Unlimited*, 28 June; S. Goodwin (1996), 'Official Secrecy Blamed For BSE Crisis Worsening', *The Independent*, 19 November; P. Brown (1999), 'New Research Raises CJD Fears', *The Guardian*, 21 December; Author unknown (2000), 'From BSE To CJD And What We Were Told At The Time', *The Guardian*, 27 October; P. Lashmar (2000), 'Exports of BSE-Contaminated Cattle Feed Continued For Eight Years After UK Ban', *The Independent*, 11 December; I. Sample (2007), 'Should We Still Be Worried?' *The Guardian*, 10 January.

53   Media coverage of GM food and feed-related issues has been extensive and rather mixed. A brief perusal of the BBC or major news websites will provide a long list of hits, and the following represent no more than a sample of some of the less than enthusiastic UK coverage of the topic from the late 1990s onwards: P. Brown (1999), 'GM risk in daily food of millions: Scientists claim new tests needed on soya', *Guardian Unlimited*, 24 May; Author unknown (1999), 'Who has the liability if GMO pollen corrupts a non-GMO crop?' *Guardian Unlimited*, 24 August; T. Radford (1999), 'Pollen from GM maize shown to kill butterflies', *Guardian Unlimited*, 20 May; J. Borger (1999), 'How The Mighty Fall', *The Guardian*, 22 November; J. O'Sullivan (2000), 'US Covered Up Warnings From Its Scientists On Dangers Of GM Foods', *The Independent*, 29 February; G. Tansey (2000), 'Words of Warning: when scientists talk of "absence of evidence" of risk, take cover', *The Guardian*, 5 January; J. Vidal (2002), 'GM Genes Found in Human Gut', *The Guardian*, 17 July.

54   Commission of the European Communities, *Green Paper on Food Law*. COM (97) 176 final.

55   COM (1999) 719 final.

56   Ibid., at.3.

57   Ibid., at 8.

regulatory systems would 're-establish public confidence in its food supply, its food science, its food law and its food controls'.[58]

The Commission proposed to tackle the shortcomings of EU food policy and the attendant crisis of public confidence from two angles. On the one hand, basic issues of safety and quality across the food supply chain were to be addressed via an extensive overhaul and general upgrading of food safety legislation and a renewed emphasis on science-led risk analysis. A key aspect of the Commission's strategy in this regard was to enhance consumer protection via the separation of (science-based) risk assessment and (more political) risk management functions. This was to be achieved via the hiving-off of responsibility for risk assessment to a new, independent Community-level food safety body, the European Food Safety Authority (EFSA),[59] with responsibility for risk management remaining with the Commission.[60]

The *White Paper* also acknowledged the need to make some provision for (and concessions to) the 'informed consumer' within the revamped system of European food law and policy.[61] In this regard, the Commission sought to move beyond the more traditional characterisation of the consumer as a primarily passive and vulnerable beneficiary of protective regulatory interventions to a more positive characterisation as an autonomous and confident actor operating at the frontlines of the market and beyond. Thus, the Commission's programme of reforms addressed the related issues of informed choice and food labelling, as well as the broader issue of transparency in policy development and the need to facilitate public scrutiny in order to promote democratic control and accountability.[62]

Real and perceived failures in food safety and quality controls as well as controversial developments in the field of agricultural biotechnology had, by this stage, engendered a heightened sensitivity to food-related risks amongst consumers, rendering unaccountable or opaque decision-making increasingly politically and economically unaffordable. Circumstances dictated that the only viable and legitimate way forward was to proactively cultivate a more open, transparent and accountable system of governance wherein the citizen-consumer – as a legitimate and, ostensibly, equal stakeholder – could more easily be informed about, understand and contribute to, the development of food policy. Thus, the Commission characterised risk communication as an interactive and participatory process and stressed the

---

58   Ibid, at 7. (emphasis added).

59   Ibid., at 14–21. The EFSA was established in 2002 by Regulation 178/2002, note 33 above.

60   It was neither possible nor appropriate to transfer responsibility for risk management from the Commission to the new authority for the following reasons. First, a transfer of regulatory powers to an independent body would dilute the democratic accountability of EU decision making (and this would certainly have been counter-productive); secondly, it was considered essential for the Commission to retain both its regulatory and risk management responsibilities in order for it to be able to continue to discharge the responsibilities placed upon it under the founding Treaties; third, current institutional arrangements imposed by the existing provisions of the Treaties precluded the creation of a new *regulatory* authority. See, the *White Paper on Food Safety*, note 49 above, at 14–15.

61   Ibid., at 31–33.

62   Ibid., at 31–32.

importance of promoting a more open dialogue with consumers across *all* aspects of food policy and policy development:

> In all aspects related to food safety, it is essential that the consumer is a fully recognised stakeholder and that consumer concerns are taken into account by
>
> * consulting the public on all aspects of food safety
> * providing a framework for discussions (public hearings) between scientific experts and consumers
> * facilitating trans-national consumer dialogue both at European and at global level.
>
> It is important that all steps in policy making are taken in full openness ... Transparency will result in the necessary public scrutiny and ensure democratic control and accountability.[63]

The *White Paper on Food Safety* certainly represented an important landmark in the evolution of a more consumer-oriented approach to governance of the EU food market, but, as the proverb says, 'the proof of the pudding is in the eating.' In order to assess the extent to which EU food policy has, *in reality*, now been transformed into 'a pro-active, dynamic and comprehensive instrument [designed] to ensure a high level of human health and consumer protection'[64] in the broader sense, it is necessary to look at the fruits of the Commission's ambitious programme of reforms. There are certainly some questions that would benefit from further consideration in light of developments since 2000. Focusing generally on the key issue of safety and with reference to key legislation, in particular Regulation 178/2002[65] (the General Food Law Regulation) and Regulations 1829/2003 and 1830/2003 (the key GM Food and Feed/Traceability Regulations),[66] the rest of this chapter assesses the *real* value of EU consumer policy and consumer rights in the context of the twenty-first-century food market.

The Rhetoric and Reality of Food Safety: Regulation 178/2002

Two years after the *White Paper on Food Safety*[67] was published, Regulation 178/2002[68] was adopted. This overarching legislation established the European Food Safety Authority[69] and set down, in a single measure, the general principles and requirements of Community food law applicable across all stages of the food production and supply chain. In line with the Commission's vision, the Regulation has been drafted to strengthen and introduce a greater coherence to Community

---

63   'Risk communication should not be a passive transmission of information, but should be interactive, involving a dialogue with and feedback from all stakeholders', ibid., at 31.

64   Ibid., at 8.

65   [2002] OJ L31/1, note 33 above.

66   [2003] OJ L268/1 and [2003] OJ L268/24, note 28 above.

67   COM(1999)719 final, note 49 above.

68   [2002] OJ L31/1, note 33 above.

69   See Article 1(2) and Chapter III of Regulation 178/2002, note 33 above.

governance of the food market. It pursues this goal by placing particular emphasis on regulatory uniformity across Member State markets, and via the promotion of a unified and objective science-based approach to the assessment and management of food-related risks – in order to protect both consumer and commercial interests across the Internal Market.[70]

Food is defined broadly so as to include 'any substance or product, whether processed, partially processed or unprocessed, intended to be, or reasonably expected to be ingested by humans. "Food" is expressly taken to include "drink, chewing gum and any substance, including water, intentionally incorporated into the food during its manufacture, preparation or treatment …".'[71]

Moreover, reflecting the reality of the complex and non-linear nature of food production and supply, including the link between animal feed and food safety, the legislation expressly states that it 'lays down procedures for matters with a direct *or indirect* impact on food and feed safety'.[72] Thus, the reach of this timely regulatory overhaul is maximised. Overall, the legislation is careful, comprehensive and very thorough in both its scope and its determination of the manner in which food production and marketing is to be managed from 'farm to table'.[73]

Whilst it is clear from both the tone and substance of Regulation 178/2002, that *one* of the core objectives here is to ensure that consumers are able to enjoy the (mandatory) high level of protection provided for under Articles 95 and 153 of the EC Treaty, predictably, the free market ethos underpinning the EU project is also clearly reflected in the provisions set out therein. Regulation 178/2002 is very much a product of a *market-oriented* decision-making structure. Here, as is the case with other market sectors, the consumer interest is accommodated within a regulatory

---

70   The impact of inconsistent national approaches to food law and the need to develop a common basis for Community food law via the approximation of inconsistent national concepts, principles and procedures is highlighted at several times in the recitals to the Regulation. See, recitals (3), (4), (5) and (66). The dual goals of the new regime – market protection and consumer protection – are very clearly reflected in the first recital to the Regulation which reads: 'The free movement of safe wholesome food is an essential aspect of the internal market and contributes significantly to the health and well-being of citizens, and to their social and economic status', [2002] OJ L31/1, note 33 above.

71   Article 2, Regulation 178/2002 [2002] OJ L31/1, ibid.

72   Article 1(2), ibid. Reflecting the important link between animal feed and consumer protection, animal feed is expressly brought within the scope of the new regime. Note for example, Articles 1, 4 and 15 of *Regulation 178/2002*. The general sentiment that food and feed must be considered in tandem, that sits at the heart of the regime, is nicely expressed in recital (12) which makes the point that 'in order to ensure the safety of food, it is necessary to consider all aspects of the food production chain as a continuum from and including primary production and the production of animal feed up to and including sale or supply of food to the consumer because each element may have a potential impact on food safety.'

73   As per the Commission's *White Paper on Food Safety*, note 49 above, at 8. Regulation 178/2002 sets a timescale for the programme of reforms; Article 4(3) provides that a wide-ranging reinforcement and upgrading of European food law should be achieved by 1 January 2007: [2002] OJ L31/1, note 33 above.

framework that doggedly presupposes the desirability, benefits and legitimacy of a borderless internal market in food.[74]

Therefore, the assessment and management of food risks in the EU market place is essentially a balancing act: regulators seek to balance the base-line requirement of 'a high level of consumer protection' against the overarching objective of maintaining a free flow of goods around the internal market. Community food law seeks to create and maintain a rigorous regulatory environment within which objectivity, predictability and transparency provide adequate consumer protection whilst also effectively mediating against all manner of trade-disruptive problems that might arise between farm and table.

Establishing and maintaining a 'high level' of protection and communicating that level of protection to the consuming public in a manner that both promotes stakeholder confidence and facilitates the free movement of goods around the EU (and internationally) is naturally a key objective of EU market regulation. Thus, the notion of safety necessarily sits at the heart of the legislation – Article 14 of the Regulation sets down what appears to be, at first glance, a very clear and stringent 'general standard' for food safety:

1. Food shall not be placed on the market if it is unsafe.
2. Food shall be deemed to be unsafe if it is considered to be:
    (a) injurious to health;
    (b) unfit for human consumption.[75]

The subsequent paragraphs of Article 14 go on to elaborate upon this basic safety standard, extending it to encompass both the short *and long-term* health implications of food, including the potential implications of food consumption for the health of future generations.[76] Thus, paragraph 4 expressly requires that the 'probable cumulative toxic effects' of foods and the 'health sensitivities' of particular categories of consumers are factors that *must be considered* when determining whether or not a food should be deemed to be 'injurious to health' in this broader sense of the term.[77] In respect of the bar on the marketing of food that is 'unfit for human consumption', paragraph 5 offers a fairly expansive definition of this term, stating that it covers 'contamination, whether by extraneous matter or otherwise, or through putrefaction, deterioration or decay'.[78] Moreover, even where food reaching the market ostensibly complies with the fundamental requirement of safety, the legislation provides

---

74   See recital (1) and Article 1(1) of Regulation 178/2002. Article 1 reads: 'This Regulation provides the basis for the assurance of a high level of protection of human health and consumers' interest in relation to food, taking into account in particular the diversity in the supply of food including traditional products, whilst ensuring the effective functioning of the internal market', [2002] OJ L31/1, ibid.

75   Articles 14(1) and 14(2), ibid.

76   Article 14(4), ibid.

77   Ibid.

78   Ibid.

that it may still be removed from the market if the competent authorities deem it necessary.[79]

The general safety requirement set down in Article 14 certainly appears to impose an exacting and stringent standard. Indeed, notwithstanding the fact that in the context of the food market (as elsewhere) it is generally accepted that a 'zero risk' policy is both unachievable and undesirable,[80] on the face of it Article 14 appears to aspire to something approaching this. In reality of course, life is an inherently risky business and the reality of EU food safety policy mirrors the reality of the concept of 'safety' itself. 'Safety' cannot be pinned down to a single universal definition or be taken to imply a single universally applicable standard. In the real world of food production and consumption, as in other fields of human activity (and dependency), 'safety' is a highly context–sensitive and relative concept. The requirement that food marketed in the EU must be 'safe' for human consumption certainly does not imply that all foods reaching the shop shelves must be *absolutely* safe in the sense that consumption of those products must entail no risk whatsoever. The Regulation itself, and the rhetoric of EU food policy more generally, may aim to offer a reassuring veneer of near-absolute safety (an assurance of something approaching zero risk), but in fact, the obligation to ensure that foodstuffs placed on the market are 'safe' simply translates into an obligation to ensure that the risks associated with them do not exceed those that have been deemed to be acceptable. In the context of the Internal Market in foodstuffs, this benchmark of 'acceptability' is determined on the basis of a (sound) scientific risk assessment – the concept of 'sound science' being, in itself, highly controversial, particularly as applied in the public sphere. Robin Grove-White has expressed, very clearly, the contentious character of 'sound science' in the context of policy development and official responses to contemporary risks:

> Again and again, unambiguous official assertions of what constitutes 'sound science' in relation to particular policy commitments at one moment are replaced by equally unambiguous assertions of scientific justification for quite different policy positions, as

---

79   Article 14(8), ibid. Similar requirements are applied to animal feed intended to be fed to food-producing animals. See Article 15, ibid.

80   In some circumstances, consumers might feel that a zero-risk policy is both desirable and possible and indeed, in some cases, at least, a complete avoidance of risk may well be feasible – on either the individual or a broader societal basis. Individual consumers may seek to avoid certain categories of product on grounds of risk; for example, some individuals exclude all bovine products from their diet in order to avoid the perceived risk of contracting vCJD – at least via ingestion of infective material. Nowadays, of course, conscientiously risk-averse consumers might also seek to avoid blood products too, in order to minimise their risk of exposure. GMOs provide another useful example. These organisms have now pervaded the food and feed chain to such an extent that it no longer possible to effectively regulate for zero risk. The use of emergent nanotechnologies in food production is, on the other hand, still a new phenomenon and thus it *could* still be possible for the EU to regulate in accordance with a zero-risk policy in respect of foods produced using these technologies. For an overview of the use of nanotechnologies in agriculture and food production, for example, ETC Group (2004), *Down on the Farm: The Impact of Nano-Scale Technologies on Food and Agriculture,* Ottowa, Canada, November <http://www.etcgroup.org>. (The ETC group – the Action Group on Erosion, Technology and Concentration – was formally known as RAFI).

circumstances change … Science in the public policy world needs to be recognised again for what it truly is – properly a servant, not a master. This has nothing to do with whether or not particular scientific findings are 'true', but everything to do with the way in which the problems on which scientists come to focus are shaped and framed. In crises of political credibility like those which in recent years have surrounded issues such as the Brent Spar, BSE, and genetically modified crops and foods, Ministers have been heard repeatedly to invoke the prevailing state of 'scientific knowledge' in support of their favoured policy stances, as if somehow the involvement of scientists put their pronouncements above the fray, and were therefore to be regarded by the rest of us as carrying unique social authority.[81]

Returning to the specific question of 'acceptable risks' and food consumption, there are two key points to consider: First, consumers consciously and unconsciously accept exposure to the (un)certain risks that are part and parcel of human life on a daily basis, and, as with so many things in life, food is inherently hazardous, and exposure to some level of risk is unavoidable. Thus, from the consumer perspective, the task of regulators is to identify and where possible remove hazardous products from the food chain and where this is either impossible or impractical, their role is to *assess, manage and effectively communicate risks*.

The second point, or angle, that must be considered is that the regulatory vision of a food market within which 'the free movement of safe and wholesome food' is assured, is based in a *common Community-led and 'sound science'-based approach* to risk and risk analysis – risk analysis being the umbrella term used to denote the 'process consisting of three interconnected components: risk assessment, risk management and risk communication'.[82] Regulatory reliance on (ostensibly objective) 'sound science'-based risk analysis engenders uniform and objectively defensible – *and thus trade-friendly* – approaches to risk at both the national and the supra-national levels and across the whole of the EU's food production and supply chain.

In order to gain a clearer understanding of the tone of Community risk analysis, it is useful to consider briefly exactly what is implied by the three core elements identified above. First: 'risk'. The Regulation explains the notion of 'risk' as meaning 'a function of the probability of an adverse health effect, consequential to a hazard'.[83] A 'hazard' in turn is defined as 'a biological, chemical or physical agent in, or condition of, food or feed with the potential to cause an adverse health effect'.[84] 'Regulatory risk assessment' is described in Article 3(11) of the legislation as being 'a scientifically based process consisting of four steps: hazard identification, hazard characterisation, exposure assessment and risk characterisation'.[85]

---

81   R.G. White (1999), 'Afterword: On "Sound Science", the Environment, and Political Authority', *Environmental Values*, 8:277–82.

82   Article 3(10) of Regulation 178/2002, [2002] OJ L31/1, note 33 above.

83   Article 3(9), ibid.

84   Article 3(14), ibid.

85   The nature of the risk assessment procedure is further reinforced in general terms in Article 6(2) of the Regulation which requires that 'risk assessment shall be based on the available scientific evidence and undertaken in an independent, objective and transparent manner,' [2002] OJ L31/1, ibid.

Risk management – the second element – becomes relevant once the nature and extent of risk has been assessed. It is then possible to make a determination as regards the threshold for 'acceptable risk' and to decide upon strategies for the practical management of identified risks in the real world of production and consumption. Risk management then, is explained in Article 3(12) as being 'the process, distinct from risk assessment, of weighing policy alternatives in consultation with interested parties, considering risk assessment and other legitimate factors, and, if need be, selecting appropriate prevention and control options'.[86]

As per the Commission's *White Paper*,[87] 'risk communication' – the third component of risk analysis – is presented as an integral and *inclusive* part of the overall process via which food-related risks are mediated within the EU. Article 3(13) conceives this as a 'two-way' (or perhaps even a circular) process within which the consumer is expected to participate as an apparently equal 'interested party', standing shoulder to shoulder with other key stakeholders:

> 'Risk communication' means the interactive exchange of information and opinions throughout the risk analysis process as regards hazards and risks, risk-related factors and risk perceptions, among risk assessors, risk managers, consumers, feed and food businesses, the academic community and other interested parties, including the explanation of risk assessment findings and the basis for risk management decisions.[88]

Notwithstanding this very accommodating and egalitarian representation of risk communication, the reality is that market-oriented regulatory risk analysis remains an essentially linear process. The overriding objective of the legislation, and thus, the primary objective of regulatory risk analysis (in this context, at least) is to facilitate the free movement of foodstuffs within and between Member State markets; to get products from A to B – from producer to table – with as little disruption to the free flow of goods as possible, and without falling foul of the free-trade rules governing the international arena. Hazards are identified; the risks consequential to that hazard are assessed and evaluated; then, the acceptability or unacceptability of these quantified risks can be determined and appropriate risk-management strategies put in place. The latter stage of this process is essentially a matter of *policy* to be decided in accordance with the specifics of the overarching free-trade agenda.

Ostensibly, Community risk analysis requires that all stakeholders (including consumers, directly or indirectly) are to be consulted and informed about said hazards, risks and risk-management strategies. Importantly however, the fact of risk 'communication' does not in itself imply any degree of active or participatory consultation between consumers (or consumer interest groups) and regulatory and industry actors. It certainly cannot be construed as providing any sort of guarantee that consumers' less scientific but arguably *equally valid* perceptions of risk will, in the end, influence determinations of 'acceptable risk' or inform or direct EU food

---

86   Ibid.,
87   COM (1999) 719 final, note 49 above.
88   Regulation 178/2002, [2002] OJ L31/1, note 33 above.

safety policy in any substantive way.[89] The consumer voice is neither the only nor the most powerful voice competing to be heard in the market place, and beyond the threshold of narrowly construed, basic safety requirements, the consumer protection agenda, important as it is, will certainly not always be considered to be *the* most important agenda. Beyond base-line safety, economic viability holds sway.

When a Member State does move to implement controversial protective (safety) measures, its chances of successfully defending its actions will certainly be rather higher in respect of identifiable and *objectively quantifiable* risks. Thus, overtly trade-restrictive measures that have been adopted on the basis of a rational, sound scientific risk assessment and that have as their aim the mitigation or reduction of *scientifically proven* risks should stand a reasonable chance of being deemed legitimate in the face of a formal challenge.[90]

---

89   When considering technologically induced risks – such as those associated with agricultural and food-related applications of modern biotechnologies – consumers will not typically rely primarily on 'sound science' as the benchmark against which risks and benefits should be assessed. Consumer evaluations of risk in this, and other contexts, will tend to accommodate a range of non-linear, qualitative factors that lie outside the remit of expert-led scientific risk assessment. The disparity that exists between expert assessments of risk and non-expert (consumer) perceptions of risk has often led 'frustrated scientists and industrialists [to] castigate the public for behaviours they judge to be based in irrationality or ignorance': P. Slovic (1993), 'Perceived Risk, Trust and Democracy', *Risk Analysis*, 13(6):675–82, reprinted in R. Lofsted and L. Frewer (eds) (1998), *The Earthscan Reader on Risk and Modern Society.* (London: Earthscan), 81–192. However, lay perceptions of risk should not be dismissed in this manner for as Marris commented in 2003, 65 per cent of the public may not be well informed enough to know that both ordinary and GM tomatoes contain genes, but this does not mean that their concerns about GM foods are not based on 'knowledge'. As she explains, public perceptions may not be based on expert or scientific knowledge, but they are, none the less, based on *knowledge* – 'knowledge derived from common sense and every day experiences, especially about the behaviour of institutions' (C. Marris (INRA), The French National Institute for Agronomic Research, Research Unit TSV, Social and Political Transformations Associated with Life Sciences, comments made during her presentation entitled 'Risk Perception – Sociological Perspectives', given at the conference on risk perception and public policy hosted by the European Commission – *Risk Perception: Science, Public Debate and Policy Making*, Brussels, 4–5 December 2003. Presentation slides available at <http://europa. eu.int/comm/food/risk_perception/sp/marris.pdf> (last accessed, 11 February 2004)). Marris also noted here that although the UK Government would, no doubt, beg to differ, in the public mind, institutional responses to BSE are seen as a *typical* example of institutional responses to risk rather than an *exceptional* example. Much has been written on the relative validity of expert and lay perceptions of risk. See generally, for example, P. Slovic (ed.) (2000), *The Perception of Risk* (London: Earthscan), or Lofsted and Frewer (eds), above.

90   See Article 6, Regulation 178/2002, which stresses the science-led character of Community risk analysis, [2002] OJ L31/1, note 33 above. It is perhaps useful here to note that the relationship between the European and the international market arenas and related rules cannot be ignored. The emphasis on science-led risk analysis at EU level is entirely in line with that employed under the *WTO Agreement on Sanitary and Phytosanitary Measures*. For a comprehensive consideration of the place of science within the SPS regime see Scott, note 30 above, at Chapter 3, 'Science and the SPS', 76–138.

It is also worth being aware of the fact that even where risks are quantifiable, the 'high' level of consumer protection required by the EC Treaty will still sometimes lose something in the course of translation into 'on the ground' (market) policy. The following comment from MacMaoláin expresses clearly the (negative) potential of Community law in this regard:

> The promotion of free movement of goods throughout the 25 Member States of the European Union (EU) has been coupled with concerns about depreciating food quality levels, brought about by the high degree of protection accorded to the principle of mutual recognition … Furthermore, where the Community has set harmonised standards for generic foodstuffs, these have tended to be set at the lowest common level. Traditional, locally and regionally produced products that have sustained communities for generations now come under threat from mass produced and nutritionally inferior substitutes manufactured from poor quality ingredients by different methods of production.[91]

This inherent tendency of Community law to shift national food safety controls towards a lowest common denominator inevitably impacts across all aspects of food regulation. It is not just an issue in the context of what might be termed 'primary' food safety regulation. For example, EC controls relating to more general or 'secondary' issues of food quality or nutritional standards may have a similar impact on consumer protection standards at the national level. Although such matters might arguably be considered less significant than more direct issues of food safety, the depreciation of food quality and nutritional standards certainly has repercussions for consumer health and well-being in the longer term.

It is increasingly the case that hazards and risks are neither fully identifiable nor quantifiable in terms of the guiding light of objective 'sound science'. Moreover, as the *Bt*10 case reviewed at the beginning of this chapter illustrates, in the context of a complex globalised market environment, even where regulators have concluded a particular product should not be permitted to enter the EU food chain on grounds of risk (to human, animal, or environmental health), incidences of unlawful distribution or unwitting consumption of an offending product will not always easily come to light. This makes the reality of associated risks can be extremely difficult to assess with any degree of confidence.[92]

On the whole, the increased prevalence of what are often termed 'technological risks' – risks that are characterised by their inherent uncertainty – tends to lend a certain complexity and ambiguity to risk management. In circumstances where uncertainty prevails, defensive *trade-friendly* decision making is generally a safer option for States than the adoption of overtly (consumer) protective measures, whether they are acting individually or cooperatively under the banner of the European Community. Defending

---

91   On Community law relating to food safety and quality, see generally, MacMaoláin, note 50 above, especially Chapters 1, 3, 5, 6 and 7. For more general discussion of EC harmonisation rules and consumer protection, see, for example, Weatherill, note 38 above.

92   Note the fact that the party best placed to identify and notify such inadvertent lapses/breaches of Community law will often have a significant interest in playing down the implications of their acts/omissions, and may possibly even seek to conceal a potentially damaging incident altogether; after all, bad publicity is generally bad for business.

restrictive regulatory interventions can be problematic enough at the best of times, but where scientific uncertainty prevails and objective and comprehensive 'sound scientific' evidence supporting restrictive measures is in short supply, disproving claims of disguised protectionism and anti-competitive behaviour becomes all the more difficult.

From the perspective of a concerned Member State, or indeed, the individual consumer, this difficulty is exacerbated by the Community's insistence that, even in the face of scientific uncertainty, the legitimacy of any national measures will be measured against the ever-present benchmark of scientific evidence. Article 7 of Regulation 178/2002 reflects the 'economically conscious' approach to precaution adopted in Article 174 of the EC Treaty.[93] Thus, it demands not only that any national recourse to precaution will be of a provisional nature 'pending further scientific information for a more comprehensive risk assessment', but also that all such measures will be 'proportionate and no more restrictive of trade than is required to achieve the high level of protection chosen in the Community, regard being had to technical and economic feasibility and other factors regarded as legitimate in the matter under consideration'.[94]

The precise meaning and scope of 'other factors regarded as legitimate' that might supplement a scientific risk assessment in this context remains somewhat unclear, and notwithstanding this rather ill-defined concession to the more qualitative aspects of uncertain risks, ultimately, the lawfulness of (trade-restrictive) precautionary measures will be determined against the backdrop of the EU's free-trade Constitution and agenda.[95] Therefore, national measures adopted in response to consumer concerns about the (uncertain) longer-term environmental or human health impacts of GM products, for example, will be highly unlikely to pass the legitimacy test.

As noted above, the notion of objective, 'sound science'-led risk analysis is, in itself, rather controversial, and in areas where some tension exists between the consumer's broad interests and those of other stakeholders and a degree of scientific uncertainly prevails, reliance on this ostensibly objective, but reductionist approach to market regulation can prove to be highly contentious and problematic. The consumer interest inevitably extends beyond the fundamental issue of scientifically determined 'acceptable risk'; aside from the fact that consumer perceptions of risk are often at odds with expert or regulatory conceptions of risk, when it comes to certain aspects of the food market, consumers are also concerned with rather more subjective and contextual issues of morality and principle. The general legitimacy of 'sound science' as the mainstay of regulatory risk analysis – particularly in situations of scientific uncertainty

---

93   The precautionary principle also finds expression in Article 5.7 of the WTO Sanitary and Phytosanitary Agreement (the SPS Agreement). The position on precaution adopted in the SPS Agreement is broadly similar to that reflected in the EC Treaty.

94   Article 7 of Regulation 178/2002, [2002] OJ L31/1, note 33 above.

95   The EU's interpretation of such factors will naturally be strongly influenced by that of the WTO. On Article 5.7 of the SPS Agreement and the application of precautionary measures, including an explanation of the extent to which qualitative factors are relevant, see Scott, note 30 above, Chapter 3, and in particular at 119.

– such as in the context of food biotechnology is certainly open to question. Here, the application of such a restrictive and untextured approach to the determination of acceptable risk can prove to be highly unpalatable for the end-consumer.

Mediating Uncertainty: Food Safety and the Precautionary Principle

The manner in which uncertainty is regulated within the dominant free-trade system reveals a lot about contemporary trends in trade and law, the status of the consumer as a key stakeholder and the nature and scope of consumer rights. In recent years, the increased prevalence of technological risks – risks that are at once both unfamiliar and novel in their character – has added to the challenges inherent in market-oriented regulatory risk analysis. How can and how should national and European authorities determine, manage and communicate 'acceptable risk' in the face of scientific uncertainty? In those circumstances where a dearth of solid scientific data and a lack of past experience of novel hazards and their associated risks render traditional cost-benefit-based risk analysis inadequate, how might commercially conscientious regulators legitimately balance the consumer protection/market protection books?

The concept of precaution provides at least a partial solution to the challenge of technological risks. In law, this familiar (common-sense) concept is encapsulated in the precautionary principle, a policy tool that has steadily gained ground over the course of the last thirty years or so.[96] Although it continues to defy attempts to develop a single, universally accepted definition, 'the' precautionary principle[97]

---

96   The precautionary principle originally emerged as a key principle of German environmental law in the 1970s. As the principle has gained wider credibility and authority, much has been written about both its history and contemporary significance. An in-depth consideration of this important and often controversial policy tool is not possible here. The following represent a small sample of the vast literature available on both the principle's general significance and its relevance in the more specific context of the regulation of GMOs: T. O'Riordan and J. Cameron (eds) (1994), *Interpreting the Precautionary Principle.* (London: Earthscan Publications); C. Raffensperger and J. Tickner (eds) (1999), *Protecting Public Health & the Environment: Implementing the Precautionary Principle* (Washington, DC: Island Press); J. Morris (ed.) (2000), *Rethinking Risk and the Precautionary Principle.* (Oxford: Butterworth Heinmann); Communication from the Commission of the European Communities, *Communication on the Precautionary Principle*, COM (2000) 1 final; M. Matthee and D. Vermersch (2000), 'Are the Precautionary Principle and the International Trade in Genetically Modified Organisms Reconcilable?' *Journal of Agricultural and Environmental Ethics*, 12:59–70; P.H. Sand (2000), 'The Precautionary Principle: A European Perspective', *Journal of Human and Ecological Risk Assessment* 6(3):445–58; Salmon (2002), note 22 above; C. MacMaoláin (2003), 'Using the Precautionary Principle to Protect Human Health: Pfizer v Council', *European Law Review*, 28(5):723–34, at 723; A. Nucara (2003), 'Precautionary Principle and GMOs: Protection or Protectionism', *International Trade Law and Regulation*, 9(2):47–53; Salmon (2005), note 22 above.

97   To refer to *the* precautionary principle is, in itself, somewhat problematic as it has been subject to various formulations. In essence though, it can be broadly defined as the principle that in situations of uncertainty, where risks defy full objective assessment and quantification, policy makers should err on the side of caution.

has now achieved notable recognition both regionally and internationally as 'a fully fledged principle of international law'.[98]

At the regional level, the principle has featured (both implicitly and explicitly) within EU policy and law for many years now,[99] and since 1992 it has enjoyed the status of a legally binding principle of Community law. Following the Maastricht amendments to the EC Treaty, Article 174 (previously, Article 130r) now provides that:

> Community policy on the environment shall aim at a high level of protection taking into account the diversity of situations in the various regions of the Community. It shall be based on the precautionary principle and on the principles that preventive action should be taken, that environmental damage should as a priority be rectified at source and that the polluter should pay.

---

98   Since the 1980s, the precautionary principle has featured in a number of regional and international legal instruments. See, for example, Ministerial Declarations adopted at the North Sea Conferences 1984, 1987 and 1990, reprinted in D. Freestone and T. Ijlstra (eds) (1991), *The North Sea: Basic Legal Documents on Regional Environmental Co-operation,* (Dordrecht: Graham Trotman), at 3–89; UN General Assembly Resolution on the World Charter for Nature, GA Res. 37/7, UN GAOR, 37th Session, Supp. No. 51, at 17, UN Doc. A/37/51 (1982) reprinted in 22 *ILM* 455 (1983). Note in particular the much cited and highly influential Principle 15 of the Rio Declaration on Environment and Development, adopted by the UN Conference on Environment and Development in June 1992 which reads as follows: 'In order to protect the environment, the precautionary approach shall be widely applied by States according to their capabilities. Where there are threats of serious or irreversible damage, lack of full scientific certainty shall not be used as a reason for postponing cost-effective measures to prevent environmental degradation.' The version set down in Article 174 of the EC Treaty can be seen to mirror the tone of this international statement on the general formula of the precautionary principle. Note also, the Cartagena Protocol on Biosafety to the United Nations Convention on Biological Diversity, UNEP/CBD/Ex COP/1/L.5, 28 January 2000.

Relevant international case law includes the following Judgments from the International Tribunal for the Law of the Sea: *Southern Blue Fin Tuna Cases* (New Zealand v. Japan; Australia v. Japan) (Provisional Measures) (27 August 1999) 38 *ILM* 1624 (1999). In relation to scientific uncertainty and precaution in the specific context of sanitary and phytosanitary measures as regulated by the WTO SPS Agreement see EC-Biotech: EC-Measures Affecting the Approval and Marketing of Biotech Products (DS291, DS292, DS293); *Hormones: EC Measures Concerning Meat and Meat Products (Hormones)* (DS26, DS48); *Hormones II: United States/Canada-Continued Suspension of Obligations in the EC-Hormones Dispute* (DS320, DS321); *Japan Apples: Japan-Measures Affecting Importation of Apples* (DS245); *Japan Varietals: Japan-Measures Affecting Agricultural Products* (DS76); *Salmon: Australia-Measures Affecting Imports of Salmon* (DS18). For a discussion of the key WTO case law concerning the relationship between science and precaution in the context of agricultural and food products, including the recent WTO ruling in the *EC-Biotech* case, see Scott, note 30 above.

99   Sand has described the incorporation of the principle into the EC Treaty in these terms. He noted the development as being 'a logical consequence and formal recognition of the [international] trend towards precaution'. Sand, note 96 above, at 449.

This first paragraph of Article 174 serves to entrench the precautionary principle within the constitutional structure of the European Community, with the specifics of the base-line Community formulation being prescribed by the qualifying text contained in the rest of the Article. Notwithstanding the absence of detailed guidance as to the precise meaning, scope and application of the principle, a broad sense of the limits of the Community's 'broad brush' precautionary obligations can be gleaned from the text of Article 174 generally, and in particular from its third paragraph which provides that:

> In preparing its policy on the environment, the Community shall take account of:
> – available scientific data,
> – environmental conditions in the various regions of the Community,
> – the potential benefits and costs of action or lack of action,
> – the economic and social development of the Community as a whole and the balanced development of its regions.

Clearly, the (mandatory) exercise of precaution as a policy response to *uncertainty* is subject to *certain* qualifications. Importantly, and in contrast to the overtly risk-averse formulations of the principle commonly advocated by environmental and consumer NGOs (that are uncompromising in their prioritisation of safety) and that have, on occasion, been accommodated within more targeted regional and international legal instruments,[100] the base-line Community formulation of the principle set down in the Treaty errs firmly on the side of what might be termed 'economic precaution'.[101] In addition to reiterating the leading role of science-led risk analysis within the Community system – even in the face of scientific uncertainty – the provision also incorporates an unambiguous cost-benefit proviso for potentially trade-restrictive and politically contentious precautionary responses to environmental risks. From the industry perspective, such an approach is useful for whilst it imposes certain restrictions and controls on risky activities, Article 174 also builds a degree of scientific and economic objectivity, and thus, *predictability* into regulatory responses to uncertainty. Importantly, in contrast to the stronger formulations of the principle commonly advocated by environmental NGOs 'economic precaution' does not impose an unqualified requirement that

---

100   A selection of international Declarations, Conventions, Treaties and other pre-1995 statements wherein various formulations of the precautionary principle feature are listed in O'Riordan and Cameron (1994), note 97 above, at 243–6. Some of these instruments incorporate a relatively strong and overtly precautionary version of the principle, whilst others are more cautious (trade friendly) and include a 'cost-effectiveness' proviso. As a general benchmark, it can be seen that the stronger formulations of the principle tend appear within instruments with a more limited geographical and/or economic impact – as in the case of, for example, the Ministerial Declarations arising out of the 1984, 1987 and 1990 North Sea Conferences. These Declarations are reproduced in Freestone and Ijlstra (eds), note 99 above, at 3–89.

101   A term utilised by Salmon in, for example, Salmon (2005), note 22 above, at 145.

When an activity raises threats to the environment or human health, precautionary measures should be taken, even if some cause and effect relationships are not fully established scientifically. In this context, the proponent of the activity, rather than the public, should bear the burden of proof [of the safety of the activity]. The process of applying the precautionary principle must be open, informed and democratic and must include potentially affected parties. It must also involve an examination of the full range of alternatives, including no action.[102]

By requiring that any recourse to precaution within the EU must be tempered by reference to the legitimising benchmarks of sound science and economic expediency,[103] the market-oriented Community formulation of precaution seeks to be both reassuring and accommodating; a risky balancing act indeed.

Since its incorporation into the EC Treaty, the precautionary principle has gained ground across a number of other fields of Community competence. As its profile has been raised, its essentially pro-trade premise has been variously confirmed and to some extent clarified by the Community institutions. Early in 2000, seeking to define the meaning, scope and appropriate role of precaution within EU law, the Commission published a highly influential *Communication on the Precautionary Principle*.[104] Here, the Commission expressly acknowledged the wider utility and relevance of precaution beyond the implied limits of Article 174 of the Treaty:

The precautionary principle is not defined in the Treaty, which prescribes it only once – to protect the environment. But *in practice*, its scope is much wider, and specifically where preliminary objective scientific evaluation, indicates that there are reasonable grounds for concern that the potentially dangerous effects on the *environment, human, animal or plant health* may be inconsistent with the high level of protection chosen for the Community.[105]

At the same time though, the potential impact of precaution was tempered by the Commission's insistence that (a) measures based upon the precautionary principle should be viewed as provisional,[106] and (b) that 'far from being a way of evading obligations arising from the WTO Agreements, the envisaged use of the precautionary

---

102   Commonly, formulations of the precautionary principle advocated by environmental and consumer NGOs will be akin to that adopted at the Wingspread Conference 1998 – the formulation provided in the text above. The Conference was organised by the Science and Environmental Health Network and brought together academic scientists, grass-roots environmentalists, government researchers and labour representatives from the US, Canada and Europe for the purpose of discussing how the principle could be formalised and brought to the forefront of environmental and public health decision making. See Raffensperger and Tickner (eds), note 96 above, particularly at 8–9, 166, 208, 345–55. The *Wingspread Statement on the Precautionary Principle* is reproduced at 353–4 therein.

103   Article 174(2) of the EC Treaty.

104   COM (2000) 1 final, note 96 above.

105   Ibid.

106   The Communication expressly states that measures based upon the precautionary principle are to be viewed as provisional (essentially, temporary). The idea is that the necessity of such measures will be reconsidered as new scientific evidence becomes available. See ibid., at 20.

principle complies with these obligations.'[107] Neither the Community's insistence on a 'high' level of environmental and consumer protection nor its apparent willingness to embrace the precautionary principle were intended to displace in any way the standard legitimising benchmarks of sound science and cost-effectiveness. In the years since the publication of the Communication, the legislative institutions and the European courts have continued to hone the Community formulation of the precautionary principle to fit the needs and aspirations of the EU – without displacing the basic premise of this economic, (free-trade obsessed) Union of states.[108] In the end, despite the EU's popular reputation as the 'primary promoter' of the precautionary principle, and supporter of 'a version which is so "strong" [as] to border on the absurd',[109] in real terms there is little to choose between the EU and WTO approaches to precaution.[110] However, it is interesting to note (bearing in mind the traditional reputations of the two regimes) that Scott has recently suggested that as the EU approach to precaution has become 'increasingly circumscribed' in recent times, it may now be the case that the WTO will now offer Member States more regulatory latitude in respect of precautionary risk management than the EU. In her view, the regional stance on precaution has now shifted to such an extent that if the European Court was to hear the Beef Hormones case today, the outcome would be entirely different: 'Were Hormones to be decided before the European courts today, such are the substantive and procedural safeguards which have come to surround the application of the precautionary principle that the measure would in all likelihood be annulled.'[111]

What then, of the general role of precaution in the context of Community food safety policy? The Commission's *White Paper on Food Safety*[112] – published shortly before the Communication on the Precautionary Principle – expressly identifies the precautionary principle as a risk management tool within a 'proactive, coherent and comprehensive' European food policy aiming to provide 'a high level of human health and consumer protection'.[113] Significantly – bearing in mind the extent to which uncertainty characterised the major food crises of the latter years of the twentieth century – although this sectoral affirmation of the principle speaks of the Community's desire to 'clarify and strengthen the existing WTO framework for the use of the precautionary principle',[114] it fails to challenge, in any way, the hegemony of sound science-led risk analysis. Notwithstanding various references to the right of

---

107   Ibid., at 9.

108   See in particular, T-13/99 *Pfizer*; Case C-236/01 *Monsanto Agricoltura Italia*; Case C-192/01 *Commission* v. *Denmark*. For discussion of key case law and further references see generally, J. Scott, 'The Precautionary Principle Before the European Courts', in R. Macrory (ed.), *Principles of European Environmental Law* (Groningen: Europa Law Publishing, 2004); MacMaoláin (2003) note 96 above, at 723; Salmon (2005), note 22 above.

109   Scott (2007), note 30 above, at 128.

110   As Scott observes, recent case law shows that overall, 'there is more to unite the EU and the WTO [on the question of precaution] than there is to divide them', ibid., at 128.

111   Ibid. For a summary of the Beef Hormones dispute, see Chapter 7 below.

112   COM (1999) 719 final, note 49 above.

113   Ibid., at 8.

114   Ibid., at 34.

(WTO and EU) Member States to establish and maintain a high level of public health protection,[115] the Commission's view of precaution (both here and in the subsequent Communication) is deliberately designed to sit comfortably alongside the market-empathetic approach advocated by the WTO.[116]

Unsurprisingly, being born out of the reforms set forth in the *White Paper*, Regulation 178/2002 also fails to challenge the established Community stance on the precautionary principle. Identifying the role of precaution and the overriding importance and legitimacy of scientific evidence of risk in contemporary food safety policy, Article 7 of the Regulation first provides that

> In specific circumstances where, following an assessment of available information, the possibility of harmful effects on health is identified but scientific uncertainty persists,

---

115   For example, ibid., at 34, where the Commission states that 'The Community plays an active role in the SPS Committee, and in other WTO committees, to ensure that the international framework encourages and defends the rights of countries to maintain high public health standards for food safety.' See also, the Commission's *Communication on the Precautionary Principle,* note 96 above, at 3, where the Commission comments that it, 'considers that the Community, like other WTO members, has the right to establish the level of protection – particularly of the environment, human, animal and plant health – that it deems appropriate. Applying the precautionary principle is a key tenet of its policy, and the choices it makes to this end will continue to affect the views it defends internationally, on how this principle should be applied.'

116   The WTO Sanitary and Phytosanitary Agreement (SPS) limits the scope for autonomous State action in order to minimise the risk that SPS measures might be employed as a means of justifying (disguised) protectionist measures. Thus, although Member States may implement SPS measures designed to provide a higher level of protection than that provided under other national systems, they are required to minimise negative impacts on trade and ensure that any measure adopted is adequately supported by scientific evidence. The possibility that precautionary measures may legitimately be implemented in some circumstances is accommodated by Article 5.7 of the SPS Agreement which provides that 'in cases where relevant scientific evidence is insufficient, a Member may provisionally adopt sanitary or phytosanitary measures on the basis of available pertinent information, including that from the relevant international organizations as well as from sanitary or phytosanitary measures applied by other Members. In such circumstances, Members shall seek to obtain the additional information necessary for a more objective assessment of risk and review the sanitary or phytosanitary measure accordingly within a reasonable period of time.' The Commission explains the scope for precautionary action under the SPS Agreement, at p. 12 of its *Communication on the Precautionary Principle* (note 96 above) as follows: 'The concept of risk assessment in the SPS leaves leeway for interpretation of what could be used as a basis for a precautionary approach. The risk assessment on which a measure is based may include non-quantifiable data of a factual or qualitative nature and is not uniquely confined to purely quantitative scientific data. This interpretation has been confirmed by the WTO's Appellate body in the case of growth hormones, which rejected the panel's initial interpretation that the risk assessment had to be quantitative and had to establish a minimum degree of risk.' For a brief explanation of the WTO's approach to risk analysis and the precautionary principle under the SPS Agreement, see, for example, Salmon (2002), note 22 above, at 146–50. For a more comprehensive commentary on the WTO SPS Agreement, including the Beef Hormones case, see Scott (2007), note 30 above.

provisional risk management measures necessary to ensure the high level of health protection chosen in the Community may be adopted, pending further scientific information for a more comprehensive risk assessment.

Then, mirroring the format adopted in the EC Treaty, the potentially strong interpretation of the principle is immediately and effectively qualified and its potential impact on the free movement of goods around the market place restricted by the following *caveat*:

> Measures adopted on the basis of paragraph 1 shall be proportionate and *no more restrictive of trade than is required* to achieve the high level of health protection chosen in the Community, regard being had to technical and *economic* feasibility and other factors regarded as legitimate in the matter under consideration. The measures shall be reviewed within a reasonable period of time, depending on the nature of the risk to life or health identified and the type of scientific information needed to clarify the scientific uncertainty and to conduct a more comprehensive risk assessment.[117]

The version of the precautionary principle found in the EC Treaty, advocated in the Commission's Communication, confirmed by European case law and accommodated within the general food law regulation, entrenches a base-line market-friendly formulation of the precautionary principle; a formulation that can be seen to be relatively 'safe' – at least in economic and political terms. Bearing in mind the fundamental objectives and priorities driving the EU agenda, and the wider world of international trade and WTO regulation, any general accommodation of an overtly 'strong' precautionary principle within Community law would undoubtedly be highly problematic and confrontational. The routine pre-emption of uncertain risks to environmental, human, animal, or plant health through recourse to uncompromising and truly risk-averse (precautionary) protective measures would both imply, and invite charges of, protectionism. Therefore, inevitably, although the rhetoric of precaution is certainly reassuring in its tone (as seen in Article 174 of the EC Treaty and Article 7 of Regulation 178/2002), the principle's potency is sorely undermined by the qualifications and conditions imposed upon its use.

GM Food and Feed and the Regulation of Risk

The contested and uncertain character of the risks associated with the agri-biotech sector, and the way in which Community law addresses these risks, demonstrates the extent to which (*and the certainty with which*) the free-trade agenda ultimately drives regulatory compromise within the food market. Thus, the Community regulation of risk in this specific context provides a practical and highly topical insight into, and illustration of the limits of, the consumer's right to safety on the front-lines of the market, that is, at the supermarket shelf.

---

117 Article 7(2) of Regulation 178/2002, note 33 above (emphasis added).

There has been some sort of Community-level supervision of this sector since the beginning of the 1990s,[118] and since then the law governing this area has evolved incrementally in response to the challenges presented by the burgeoning life sciences industry – not least the significant and persistent public wariness of, and opposition to, food-related applications of modern biotechnologies. Today, EU trade in GM food and feed is governed by a comprehensive regulatory framework designed to ensure that the risks associated with the importation, cultivation and consumption of GMOs are assessed and managed in a manner capable of both promoting safety *and* facilitating the effective functioning of the internal market.[119]

Sitting at the very heart of the current framework are Regulation 1829/2003 on GM Food and Feed and its partner, Regulation 1830/2003 on the traceability and labelling of genetically modified food and feed.[120] Whilst the former measure sets out the rules and procedures governing pre-market assessment and authorisation of food and feed products consisting of, containing, or produced from genetically modified organisms, the latter imposes stringent traceability and labelling controls upon all such products in order to facilitate:

---

118 Key measures adopted at the beginning of the 1990s to regulate this sector were Directive 90/219/EEC on the contained use of genetically modified organisms [1990] OJ L117/1 and Directive 90/220/EEC on the deliberate release into the environment of genetically modified organisms: [1990] OJ L117/15. The entry of GM foods onto the EU market was initially regulated by Regulation (EC) No 258/97 concerning novel foods and novel food ingredients: [1997] OJ L43/1.

119 The key legislation now governing this area includes: Directive 90/219/EEC [1990] OJ L117/1 as amended by Directive 98/81/EC, on the contained use of genetically modified organisms [1998] OJ L330/13 (regulating the first stage of a GMOs passage to market – the laboratory based/controlled closed environment research and development); Directive 2001/18/EC on the deliberate release into the environment of GMOs [2001] OJ L106/1 (governing experimental releases of GMOs – that is, products consisting of or containing GMOs – into the environment as well as the placing on the market of new GMOs for example via importation or cultivation); Regulation (EC) No 1829/2003 on genetically modified food and feed [2003] OJ L268/1 (regulating the entry onto the market of food and feed consisting of, containing or produced from GMOs); Regulation (EC) No 1830/2003 concerning the traceability and labelling of genetically modified organisms and the traceability of food and feed produced from genetically modified organisms and amending Directive 2001/18/ EC [2003] OJ L268/24; Regulation (EC) No 1946/2003 on transboundary movements of genetically modified organisms [2003] OJ L287/1. There are also various other supplementary measures in force including Commission Regulation (EC) 65/2004 establishing a system for the development and assignment of unique identifiers for genetically modified organisms. [2004] OJ L10/5 and Commission Regulation (EC) 641/2004 of 6 April 2004 on detailed rules for the implementation of Regulation (EC) 1829/2003 of the European Parliament and of the Council as regards the application for the authorisation of new genetically modified food and feed, the notification of existing products and adventitious or technically unavoidable presence of genetically modified material which has benefited from a favourable risk evaluation [2004] OJ L102/14.

120 [2003] OJ L268/1; [2003] OJ L268/24, ibid., and note 28 above.

(a) accurate labelling;
(b) effective post-market monitoring of environmental, animal and human health impacts of GM food and feed, and
(c) the implementation of appropriate risk management measures including, where necessary, the withdrawal of (unsafe) GMOs and GM products from the food and feed chain.

Together, with their extended reach and comprehensive coverage of the food and feed chain, these core regulations (along with the various other associated measures) build upon and reinforce the pre-existing GMO framework, strengthening somewhat its general precautionary value.[121]

The following brief overview of and comment upon the coverage and tone of the regulations should serve to provide the reader with a general sense of how the law perceives and addresses both the predictable and unpredictable risks associated with the use of GMOs in food and feed production.

Here, as in other fields of Community competence, one key concern of European law is the assessment and management of 'acceptable risks' and the preservation of the 'high level' of consumer protection demanded under Articles 95 and 153 of the EC Treaty. In line with the pro-trade and pro-technology ethos underpinning the EU, the foundational assumption upon which the whole corpus of legislation governing this area is built is that the agricultural biotechnology industry and its products are desirable and beneficial to both Member States' economies *and* consumers – regardless of the weight of public opinion[122] and conflicting views regarding the longer-term environmental, social and human health risks.[123]

---

121   The new framework builds upon pre-existing legislative controls – both those specifically directed at GMOs and those directed at addressing potential risks associated with conventionally produced food and feedstuffs. Thus, for example, the GM Food and Feed Regulation expressly refers to key legislation governing flavourings, additives, animal nutrition, and so on, and draws these aspects of food and feed control under the umbrella of the sector-specific GMO regime. Importantly, from the environmental perspective in particular, both the GM Food and Feed, and the Traceability Regulations expressly incorporate key principles set out in the essentially precautionary Deliberate Release Directive adopted in 2001, [2001] OJ L106/1, notes 8 and 119 above.

122   Public opinion polls have consistently found that a significant proportion of Europeans are opposed to the wide-spread commercial development and marketing of GM food and feed in the EU. For a general view of trends in public opinion in relation to GM food and other applications of genetic engineering technologies, see, for example, the following Eurobarometer Surveys: *Eurobarometer 46.1. The Europeans and Modern Biotechnology.* European Commission, Directorate-General Science, Research and Development. Luxembourg: European Commission, 1997; *Eurobarometer 55.2. Europeans, Science and Technology*. European Commission, Directorate General for Press and Communication, Public Sector. Brussels: European Commission. 2001; G. Gaskell et al. (2003), *Eurobarometer 58.0. Europeans and Biotechnology in 2002*, 21 March, 2nd edn. A report to the EC Directorate General for Research from the project 'Life Sciences in European Society', QLG7-CT-1999-00286; Gaskell et al, note 32 above.

123   See Greenpeace and GeneWatch UK, note 3 above; see also, the various references provided at notes 22, 24 and 25 above. On the social and economic impact of GM agriculture

The most notable change brought about by the GM Food and Feed/Traceability Regulations must surely be the extension of mandatory pre-market assessment, traceability and labelling requirements to include animal feed consisting of, containing, or produced from genetically modified organisms.[124] As regards pre-market assessment, previously, although the use of GMOs for animal feed was subject to approval under the Deliberate Release Directive (governing deliberate releases of GMOs into the environment), such products escaped the more rigorous controls applied to GM foods intended for human consumption.[125] Now, under the new system, operators seeking to bring a GMO or GMO-derived product to market for *either* use are required to obtain authorisation for *both* uses.[126] Bearing in mind that a significant proportion of all GMOs entering the EU market are destined for the animal feed chain, this development is certainly significant. Then, once a GMO or GMO-derived product has been approved for commercial use, the traceability system – enforced across 'all stages of the placing on the market' – comes into play, 'facilitating accurate labelling, monitoring [of] the effects on the environment and, where appropriate, on health, and the implementation of the appropriate risk management measures including, if necessary, withdrawal of products'.[127]

Other significant amendments to the pre-existing regime include (a) the removal of the controversial 'notification' route to market that was previously available to operators seeking to market 'substantially equivalent' GM food products under the Novel Foods Regulation 1997,[128] and (b) the general shift from *GM content* to *product origin* as the trigger for mandatory labelling via the inclusion of food and feed 'produced from' GMOs.[129] The requirement that *all* new products should be subjected to the full force of the centralised risk assessment and pre-market approval procedure – regardless of whether or not they might objectively be described as being 'substantially equivalent'[130] to, or in layman's terms, materially 'the same as'

---

in the developing world and issues relating to the ownership and theft of genetic resources and traditional knowledge, see also, for example, V. Shivá (2000), *Stolen Harvest: The Hijacking of the Global Food Supply* (London: Zed Books); C. McManis (ed.) (2007), *Biodiversity and the Law: Intellectual Property, Biotechnology and Traditional Knowledge* (London: Earthscan).

124   See Regulation 1829/2003, [2003] OJ L268/1, notes 28 and 119 above, Article 1 and Chapter III, and Regulation 1829/2003, note 34 above, particularly Articles 1 and 2 setting out the objectives and scope of the traceability and labelling regime.

125   Under Regulation 258/97, [1997] OJ L43/1, note 118 above.

126   By means of a single application under Regulation 1829/2003, [2003] OJ L268/1 (notes 28 and 119 above) in accordance with the 'one door, one key' policy, or via a split application submitted under both Directive 2001/18 [2001] 106/1 (notes 8 and 120 above) and Regulation 1829/2003. So far as the issue of deliberate release into the environment is concerned, approvals issued pursuant to the 'one door, one key' policy comply with the environmental risk assessment criteria set down in Directive 2001/18.

127   Article 1 of Regulation 1830/2003, [2003] OJ L268/24, notes 28 and 119 above.

128   Articles 3(4) and 5 of Regulation 258/97, [1997] OJ L43/1, note 118 above.

129   Article 1, 12–14 (food) and 24–6 (feed) of Regulation 1829/2003, [2003] OJ L268/1 and Articles 1 and 4 of Regulation 1830/2003, [2003] OJ L268/24, notes 28 and 119 above.

130   For background on the development of 'substantial equivalence as a safety assessment tool, see the World Health Organisation, *Strategies for Assessing the Foods*

a conventionally produced counterpart – certainly enhances the precautionary bias of Community governance in this area. Similarly, by increasing the visibility and traceability of GMOs across the supply chain, the upgrading of the industry-friendly labelling requirements that had previously, in practice, permitted the vast majority of GMO-derived foodstuffs to be marketed across the EU without any GM labelling is also broadly reflective of an increased allegiance to precaution.[131]

Strategically, this shift to a combined approach to pre-market assessment and approval (supported by the 'one door, one key' application under the GM Food and Feed Regulation) alongside the new traceability paper-trail serves two closely related purposes. By treading a careful path between weak precaution and strong precaution, and between protection and protectionism, the EU seeks to *adequately* protect consumer and environment, whilst also (hopefully) reassuring the sceptical European consumer, *and* legitimising Community regulation of this sector in the eyes of important trading partners (particularly the US) and the WTO.

Therefore, the reach of Community-level regulatory oversight of the GM food (and feed) sector is now more extensive than was the case under the Novel Foods Regulation, and the tone of the new regime is, undoubtedly, *more* precautionary than that it succeeds; but just how legitimate is the new regime from the perspective of the concerned, rights-bearing consumer? How well does the new and ostensibly rigorously protective regime mediate competing stakeholder interests to provide consumers with a 'high' level of protection? How is the determination and management of 'acceptable risk' dictated under this regime? A brief critique of the legislation, focusing (a) on what is *excluded from*, rather than what is included

---

Produced by Biotechnology (WHO: 1991); OECD, *Safety Evaluation of Foods Derived by Modern Biotechnology* (OECD: 1993); Report of a Joint FAO/WHO Consultation, *Biotechnology and Food*, FAO Food and Nutrition Paper 61, 1996. Various commentators have argued (convincingly) that regulatory controls underpinned by the concept of substantial equivalence cannot effectively mitigate the potential risks presented by genetic modification. Some have gone so far as to argue that products already approved for commercial release and widely marketed throughout the Community may not be safe. See, for example, E. Millstone, E. Brunner and S. Mayer (1999), 'Beyond Substantial Equivalence', *Nature*, 401(7):525–6; E. Diamand (2001), *The Great Food Gamble: An Assessment of Genetically Modified Food Safety.* (London: Friends of the Earth). The Royal Society of Canada produced an interesting report on precautionary regulation of food biotechnology in 2001. This report devoted some space to a consideration of the concept of 'substantial equivalence.' See Chapter 7 of the Report: *Elements of Precaution: Recommendations for the Regulation of Food Biotechnology in Canada: An Expert Panel Report on the Future of Food Biotechnology prepared by The Royal Society of Canada* (Ontario: Royal Society of Canada). The full report can be accessed via <http://www.rsc.ca>.

131   GM feed was, of course, entirely exempt from mandatory labelling by virtue of its exclusion from the scope of Regulation 258/97 (note 118 above). For a summary of the pre-2003 regulatory framework, including details of the labelling requirements see D. Lauterburg (2002), *Food Law: Policy and Ethics* (London: Cavendish), Chapter 6. On the specific issue of labelling, see in particular ibid., at 173–6, where there is a brief description of Regulation (EC) No 1139/98. [1998] OJ L159/4, Regulation (EC) No 49/2000 [2000] OJ L6/13 and Regulation (EC) No 50/2000 [2000] OJ L6/15 – the various measures which served to strengthen progressively the labelling requirements under the novel foods regime.

within the scope of the authorisation and traceability schemes, and (b) the character of the risk analysis applied here, exposes the limits of trade-oriented environmental and human protection.

The Scope of the GM Food and Feed/Traceability Framework

The prior exclusion of animal feed from the novel foods regime, and reliance on substantial equivalence as a benchmark against which the need for a full pre-market safety assessment was determined, fuelled opposition to agricultural biotechnology across Europe through the 1990s. Ostensibly, these particular glitches in GMO safety controls have now been dealt with. However, the reality is that despite the extended reach of Community governance of this controversial market sector, there is still some scope for scepticism. Although the prohibition on 'single-use' market entry (for feed) under the new regime, and the introduction of fairly comprehensive traceability requirements certainly increase the protective value of Community law and enhance its precautionary bias, governance of this sector still suffers from some notable weaknesses.

First, the possibility that (GMO)-contaminated food and feed products might enter the EU market – that is, that another *Bt*10-type event may occur again in the future – remains a very real risk. *Bt*10 was, after all, an experimental GMO that (unlike StarLink) had not been approved for commercial use of any kind; yet, as explained earlier, it still managed to find its way into the human food chain where it was distributed (and quite possibility consumed) for several years before Syngenta finally notified the authorities. As the Online GM Contamination Register illustrates, although the duration of the *Bt*10 incident may render it unique (or at least, relatively unusual), the fact of contamination is not, of itself, so uncommon. GMO-contaminated food and feed products are still finding their way through the supply chain on a fairly regular basis. The fact that various incidents have been formally identified and recorded does, to some extent at least, confirm the effectiveness of EU and Member State border controls as well as NGO commitment to consumer and environmental protection. However, bearing in mind the grand scale of food and feed production, processing, import and export across the EU, perhaps – similarly to national crime detection figures – it is more realistic to view such incidents is as representing just the tip of the iceberg.

Secondly, so far as the general consumer protective value of the regulations is concerned, the 'produced with' exemptions provided for within the GM Food and Feed/Traceability legislation can be seen to be somewhat at odds with a comprehensively precautionary approach to uncertain technological risks. The practical impact of this controversial distinction is that key foods such as meat, eggs, or milk produced from animals fed on GM feed, as well as food or feed produced using a GM processing aid are not directly subject to the centralised risk assessment procedure, mandatory labelling, or the traceability requirements laid down in the regulations.[132] Bearing in mind that the foundational position adopted by the

---

132   Recital (16) and Article 3 of Regulation 1829/2003, [2003] OJ L268/1; Article 2 of Regulation 1830/2003, [2003] OJ L268/24, notes 28 and 119 above.

legislation is that full traceability of *all* GM food and feed products is necessary to provide the high level of protection demanded by the Treaty, the distinction drawn between produced 'with' and produced 'from' appears both arbitrary and a 'contradiction'.[133] This limitation undoubtedly has rather more to do with market efficiency than any rationally informed assumption that traceability of certain kinds of products is unnecessary; it highlights the boundary that exists between the *genuine* EU consumer protection agenda and the rhetoric of industry-oriented regulatory PR.[134] As Friends of the Earth Europe (FoEE) commented during the negotiations on the legislation, foods such as meat, milk and eggs produced from animals fed on GM feed are 'clearly produced from GMOs'.[135]

Some commentators have questioned the regulatory assumption that the use of GM feed will not give rise to any safety concerns further down the production line. For example, during the run-up to the adoption of the GM Food and Feed/Traceability Regulations, FoEE lobbied against the 'produced with' exemptions on grounds of consumer protection and food safety,[136] whilst in a similar vein the Consumers' Association observed that 'While the … proposals will allow for environmental monitoring through a requirement for traceability of GMOs, this will not extend to the end product. It is essential that mechanisms for monitoring any adverse health consequences are also developed.'[137]

In any case, whether their objections are rooted in doubts over safety, or ethical objections to agri-food applications of these technologies, from the perspective of the conscientiously objecting consumer this gap in the coverage of the new controls is undesirable as it makes it impossible to determine whether or not meat or dairy products have, in fact, been produced from animals fed on GM feed.

GM Food and Feed: Determining Acceptable Risk

Bearing in mind the generally optimistic EU view of the life sciences industry and its potential,[138] it would be surprising indeed to find legislators adopting a fundamentally

---

133   Friends of the Earth Europe (FoEE) (2002), *Position Paper on GM Food and Feed Position Paper*, Brussels, March, at 1.

134   According to FoEE (citing a National Consumer Council (NCC) public opinion survey), a large majority of consumers (nearly 80 per cent) wanted to see meat and other products obtained from animals fed on GM feed labelled. Friends of the Earth Europe (2002), *Position Paper on Traceability and Labelling*, Brussels, March, at 2. Consumer ambivalence towards GM foods is also reflected in the 2005 Eurobarometer survey, Gaskell et al., note 32 above, which reported that although attitudes varied between Member States, overall, 58 per cent of respondents remained opposed to GM food.

135   Friends of the Earth Europe, note 133 above, at 1.

136   Ibid.

137   Consumers' Association (2002), *Policy Report: GM Dilemmas – consumers and genetically modified foods*. (London: Consumers' Association). at 113–14.

138   See, European Commission, COM (2002) 27, note 26 above. This Action Plan placed the life sciences at the forefront of the EU drive to achieve its long-term strategic goal of becoming a leading competitive and dynamic 'knowledge-based economy'. (This strategic goal was set by the Lisbon European Council in March 2000.) The Commission has recently

distinct position on the question of risk analysis and 'acceptable risk' in the context of agri-food biotechnology. Predictably, despite significant consumer opposition to, and concern about, GM food and feed, the basic approach to GM food and feed safety mirrors that advocated under Regulation 178/2002.[139]

Thus, the starting point for risk analysis in the context of GM food and feed is 'sound scientific' risk assessment, supported by risk management strategies legitimised with reference to objectively defensible scientific evidence. To a certain extent (or perhaps, in this case, to an *un*certain extent), the legislative emphasis on evidence-based regulation of this food and feed sector makes perfect sense – at least in so far as the associated risks are (a) identifiable and (b) scientifically assessable. However, it can be argued that the *uniquely contentious and inherently uncertain* nature of the technological risks associated with the use of modern biotechnologies in food production and processing renders allegiance to such an approach untenable in this particular context – at least in so far as risk analysis strays into the realms of the uncertain and the unknowable. Of course, the importance accorded to uncertainty, and views as to the specific point at which the preferred evidence-based approach should give way to an overtly precautionary approach, will vary according to the perspective of the stakeholder making these assessments.

Interestingly, although the GM Food and Feed/Traceability Regulations are key components of what is, after all, an essentially precautionary corpus of sectoral legislation, the precautionary principle itself features *just once* in the Traceability Regulation – and then only in a recital.[140] There is no direct reference to it whatsoever in the GM Food and Feed Regulation.[141] In terms of general principle, the legitimate role of precaution is alluded to rather than expressly advocated, with recital (32) of this Regulation allowing for the possibility that 'In some cases, scientific risk assessment alone cannot provide all the information on which a risk management decision should be based, and that [in such cases] *other legitimate factors* relevant to the matter under consideration may be taken into account.'[142]

---

published a mid-term review of the progress made towards achieving this goal since 2002: *Commission Communication on the mid term review of the Strategy on Life Sciences and Biotechnology.* COM (2007) 175 final. Although the mid-term review notes the ambivalence of European consumers and some Member States towards GM foods, the Commission does not propose any notable change in EU policy. See COM (2007) 175 final, at 5–7.

139   [2002] OJ L31/1. On GM food and feed, see recital (9) of Regulation 1829/2003 (notes 28 and 120 above). The text of this recital is reproduced in the text above. The approach adopted under the GM Food and Feed Regulation reflects the EU's support of a 'field to table' approach to safety that encompasses human, animal and environmental health protection. Note the general requirements – or safety standards – set down in Articles 4(1) (GM food) and 16(1) (feed) of Regulation 1829/2003.

140   Recital (3) of Regulation 1830/2003 [2003] OJ L268/24 (notes 28 and 119 above) provides that 'Traceability should also facilitate the implementation of risk management measures in accordance with the precautionary principle.'

141   [2003] OJ L268/1, notes 28 and 119 above.

142   Recital (32), Regulation 1829/2003, [2003] OJ L268/1, notes 28 and 119 above (emphasis added). See also, Articles 7 and 19 of this Regulation which make formal provision for the Commission to give consideration to such 'other legitimate factors relevant to the

Substantively, lawful recourse to precautionary risk management in the face of scientific uncertainty is provided for through the linking of GM food and feed approval procedures to the Deliberate Release Directive[143] and the General Food Law Regulation[144] – both of which *do* contain direct references to the precautionary principle.[145] Thus, the position adopted is that

> The new authorisation procedures for genetically modified food and feed should include the new principles introduced in Directive 2001/18/EC. They should also make use of the new framework for risk assessment in matters of food safety set up by Regulation (EC) No 178/2002 of the European Parliament and of the Council of 28 January 2002 laying down the general principles and requirements of food law, establishing the European Food Safety Authority, and laying down procedures in matters of food safety. Thus, genetically modified food and feed should only be authorised for placing on the Community market after a scientific evaluation of the highest possible standard, to be undertaken under the responsibility of the European Food Safety Authority (Authority), of any risks which they present for human and animal health and, as the case may be, for the environment. This scientific evaluation should be followed by a risk management decision by the Community, under a regulatory procedure ensuring close cooperation between the Commission and the Member States.[146]

The drafters of the legislation have ensured that (economic) precaution will guide market approvals, and in achieving this have successfully avoided any explicit elaboration of this regulatory concept which might expose the real limits of its (consumer and environmental) protective value. In light of the ongoing controversy colouring perceptions of and attitudes towards GM food and feed, the adoption of a loosely precautionary tone that, whist having some legal clout, does not draw undue attention to the limitations of the relatively weak Treaty formulation of the principle was probably wise. Any unequivocal reference to scientific uncertainty and the precautionary principle within the text detailing risk assessment and risk management procedures would have highlighted the sound-science basis for precaution as well as the cost-benefit proviso for recourse to such pre-emptive measures. This would have rendered their basis much more immediately obvious, inviting the obvious question: to what extent can sound science provide the benchmark against which the legitimacy of *precautionary* measures might be determined? Moreover, such explicit references could have easily been interpreted as some sort of acknowledgment that

---

matter under consideration' when making decisions relating to the authorisation of GM food and feed products.

143   Directive 2001/18 [2001] OJ L106/1, notes 8 and 119 above.

144   Regulation 178/2002, note 33 above. Note Article 1 of Regulation 1829/2003, [2003] OJ L268/1 (notes 28 and 119 above) and the alignment of this regulation's objectives with those of the General Food Law Regulation.

145   See recital (8), Articles 1 and 4, and Annex 2 of Directive 2001/18 [2001] OJ L106/1 (notes 8 and 120 above) and note how the environmental safety requirements set down in this Directive – including the role of precaution – are incorporated into the GM Food and Feed Regulation (Regulation 1829/2003) (notes 28 and 119 above) by virtue of Articles 6(4) (*re* GM food) and 18(4) (*re* GM feed).

146   Recital (9) of Regulation 1829/2003, [2003] OJ L268/1, notes 28 and 119 above.

current understanding of the potential impacts of these technologies is, in some way, lacking, thus fuelling the fire of consumer opposition.

The revamped EU regime is certainly stringent when compared to those in force elsewhere. This being the case, it must be conceded that European consumers benefit from a *comparatively high* level of protection. None the less, from the perspective of the large body of ambivalent consumers – 58 per cent according to the 2005 Eurobarometer Survey[147] – the negotiation of 'acceptable risk' against the backdrop of 'economic precaution' remains somewhat less than satisfactory. *Some* precaution is better than none, but in the face of hotly disputed technological risks, regulatory precaution lacks the potency to ensure that where uncertainty prevails, the interests of the environment or the consumer will automatically be prioritised over competing interests of state and market. In those cases where precaution is advised but the implementation of decisively precautionary risk management measures is considered to entail *excessive* costs (economic or, indeed, political), it is entirely possible, if not highly probable, that Community and Member State determinations of 'acceptable risk' will be at odds with those of the consumer. Inevitably, the *reality* of the 'high'-level consumer protection promised by the EC Treaty will fall some way short of what consumers themselves might deem to be appropriately precautionary, thus exposing these individuals to what they would, no doubt, consider to be an *unacceptable* level of risk.

Conclusion

There is no escaping the inherent tensions of a market-based regulatory system; whilst the free movement of goods within and between states is crucial for the success of the Single Market, effective protection of consumer interests will tend to necessitate restrictions on such movements. Inevitably then, the 'highest' level of protection boasted by the Commission in respect of GM foods must be understood as implying no more than the highest *practicable* level of consumer protection feasible within a system that is also fundamentally concerned with protecting the European stake in a profitable biotech future.[148]

In the case of the GM food and feed sector, it was the increasingly explosive and contradictory combination of economic and political pressures and ambition that finally drove the institutions to agree upon a new regulatory framework. Consumer mistrust of, and opposition to, GM food on the one hand, and US-led WTO complaints proceedings against the EU moratorium on the other, compelled the Community institutions to introduce new legislation to facilitate the controlled (and *relatively 'safe'*) entry of GM products onto the EU market. These very same economic and

---

147   Gaskell et al., note 32 above.

148   Article 1 of Regulation 1829/2003 [2003] OJ L268/1 (notes 28 and 120 above) effectively mirrors Article 1 of Regulation 178/2002 (note 33 above). It states: 'The objective of this Regulation, in accordance with the general principles laid down in Regulation (EC) No 178/2002, is to: (a) provide the basis for ensuring a high level of protection of human life and health, animal welfare, environment and consumer interests in relation to genetically modified food and feed, whilst ensuring the effective functioning of the internal market … .'

political pressures also, of course, ensured that legislators took care to adequately protect 'the market' – not least by ensuring that (economic) precaution prevails and that key secondary products supported by the GM animal feed sector did not suffer an overly onerous (and economically and politically damaging) regulatory burden.

In the final analysis, it is very clear that in contrast to the uncertainty surrounding the human health and environmental risks associated with GM food and feed, there was very little uncertainty surrounding the significant economic and political risks associated with the embargo on new GM approvals. By the time the new GM food and feed legislation was adopted, GM-related trade disputes had been rumbling on for several years and the EU was fielding problematic and potentially expensive complaints from three major GM producer countries – Canada, the US and Argentina – all of which claimed that the EU moratorium constituted a serious breach of WTO free-trade rules.[149]

It is also worth noting here that the wisdom of regulating to restart GMO approvals in the EU should, perhaps, be assessed from a rather broader perspective than the purely sectoral. As Bernauer suggested in 2003,[150] a failure to negotiate a workable regulatory compromise on GM food and feed could have had important implications for EU risk management policies more generally. Referring to recent statements from US policy makers,[151] he commented that the US-led action against the EU's regulation of agricultural biotechnology was, in fact, symptomatic of a much broader dissatisfaction with the way in which Europe deals with risks to consumer and environmental health. Writing just before the new regulations were agreed and the moratorium lifted, he expressed concern that US objections to risk regulations based on the precautionary principle could lead to the sector-specific agri-biotech dispute escalating into a much 'larger and fundamental conflict over appropriate regulatory models for [the mitigation of] environmental and consumer risks'.[152]

The thorny issue of GM food and feed 'safety' demonstrates very clearly the character and priorities of the supranational system of market regulation. In this, as in other sectors, the consumer protection value of regulatory risk analysis is wholly dependent upon, and determined by, the priorities of those responsible for leading the process of assessment, management and communication, and the relative weight accorded to alternative scientific opinions and the views of particular stakeholders. In

---

149   For further discussion about the WTO complaints, see Chapter 7 below. See also, Scott (2007), note 30 above.

150   T. Bernauer (2003), *Genes, Trade and Regulation: The Seeds of Conflict in Food Biotechnology* (Princeton, NJ: Princeton University Press), at 167.

151   Bernauer refers readers to the web site of the US National Foreign Trade Council (NFTC) (<http://www.nftc.org>) where the publication of the following NFTC report, would have just been announced: *Looking Behind the Curtain: The Growth of Trade Barriers That Ignore Sound Science*, NFTC, June 2003. The NFTC press release announcing publication of this report states that it 'offers powerful evidence of a deliberate strategy to invoke the need for "precaution" in order to protect ailing or lagging industries and block market access'. This Report is available at <http://www.nftc.org/default/white%20paper/TR2%20final.pdf>. The associated press release can be found at <http://www.nftc.org/newsflash/newsflash.asp?Mode =View&articleid=1630&Category=All>.

152   Bernauer, note 150 above, at 167.

the context of the EU – wherein policy is largely shaped by the underlying 'free-trade' agenda – regulatory risk analysis is inevitably firmly oriented to the facilitation of the free movement of goods. Ultimately, despite conflicting evidence and significant consumer concerns regarding the possible risks associated with the importation, cultivation, processing and consumption of GM food and feed, the constitutional standard of a 'high' level of consumer protection entrenched in the Treaty had to be interpreted sympathetically; there was little option but to interpret it in such a way as to permit the *de facto* moratorium on GM food and feed to be finally lifted.

The *highest* level of consumer safety protection provided by the EU-wide ban on new GM food and feed products has been replaced by an alternative high – *but not so high* – level of protection that is compatible with both the regional and global free-trade environment, and the biotech ambitions of the European Union and its Member States. The cost-benefit proviso that runs through the heart of the EU (and by implication, through the heart of Community consumer policy) ensures that there can be no guarantees that the reality of GM food and feed safety will consistently live up to the reassuring rhetoric spouted by institutions such as the European Commission. Here as elsewhere across the internal market, it seems inevitable that the high level of protection guaranteed by Community law will, oft-times, fall at least some way short of the (*highest*) level of protection that consumers might, themselves, consider to be appropriate.

Chapter 7

Transatlantic Trade Wars: Producer and Consumer Rights on the Global Stage

The Beef Hormones Dispute: North America versus Europe

Hormones may be used in the meat industry as a means of improving productivity, profit and competitiveness by accelerating the growth or fattening rate of animals. Hormones of this kind have included, for example oestradiol-17, progesterone and testosterone (all of which are naturally occurring), and trenbolone acetate, zeranol and melengestrol acetate (which are synthetic). Such hormones have been used in the US meat industry since the 1970s, but concerns in relation to the effect of such meat consumption on human health have led to a stricter regulation of the marketing of meat from hormone-treated animals in Europe, where there also appears to be a strong consumer preference in principle for non-hormone-treated meat.[1] In some countries, such as the US, Canada and Argentina, there is a significant economic interest in the free production and international marketing of hormone-treated meat, and this interest has collided with European resistance in what have in effect become a series of transatlantic trade wars.

The more restrictive European regulation – at both national and EU levels – dates from 1981 and applies to both the use of growth hormones by EU farmers and to the import into the EU of meat and meat products deriving from animals which have been given these hormones. By the 1990s, the differing positions on the subject had become a policy and legal issue at the international level. The earlier focus of disagreement was within the body charged with determining international foods standards, the Codex Alimentarius Commission.[2] The Codex debated the acceptability of levels of hormones in meat, and an earlier vote against allowing residue levels of hormones was narrowly overturned by an exceptional secret ballot (under American chairing of the relevant committee) in 1995. The significance of the

---

1 The European debate on competing producer and consumer interests and rights was played out in European Community litigation during the 1980s: see the discussion in Chapter 5 above, and arguments presented in Case C-331/88, *R* v. *Minister of Agriculture, Fisheries and Food, ex parte Fedesa and others* (1990) European Court Reports (ECR) 1-4023. The judgment of the European Court of Justice in 1990 provides a good insight into the balancing act being carried out in the EC context, and how the EU position within the broader international context has been arrived at.

2 The Codex Alimentarius Commission was established in 1963 by the Food and Agriculture Organisation (FAO) and World Health Organisation (WHO) to develop food standards, guidelines and codes of practice under the Joint FAO/WHO Food Standards Programme.

Codex decision lay in the use of Codex standards as benchmarks by the World Trade Organisation (WTO), which then became involved in the debate and argument when the US and Canada began to argue that EU restrictions on hormone-treated meat was in violation of World Trade Agreement (WTA) obligations relating to free trading. The North American claim was that the EU measures were unjustifiable in that the risk to health was insufficiently proven, and were in fact discriminatory in seeking to protect the less competitive European meat industry from imports from outside the EU, particularly from the US and Canada. More specifically it was alleged that the EU was in breach of the Agreement on Sanitary and Phytosanitary Measures, which permits only non-discriminatory restrictions on imports, based on adequate risk assessment, and of the Agreement on Technical Barriers to Trade, which requires the application of international standards where they exist. Both these Agreements are annexed to the WTA.

The US Government, following lobbying from farming interest groups and the Monsanto Corporation as a major supplier of the hormones, lodged a formal complaint concerning EU measures against beef hormones with the WTO in 1996, and Canada followed suit. The issue was dealt with by a WTO Panel, which ruled in 1997 that the EU position was in breach of the Agreements on a number of counts. The EU's appeal against this ruling was heard by the WTO Appellate Body early in 1998;[3] the latter modified some of the Panel's findings but still found the EU position to be unlawful in that it had not provided an adequate assessment of the risks to human health.[4] The EU then strove to provide the adequate assessment, while the US and Canada subsequently in 1999 imposed trade sanctions against the EU for failing to remove its restrictions. The EU claimed that a new directive adopted in 2003 implemented the WTO Appellate Body's ruling by requiring a sufficiently rigorous assessment of the risks associated with meat consumption.[5] The new measure was officially described as embodying 'a thorough risk assessment based on current scientific knowledge, fully respecting ... international obligations'; it was argued that 'public health and consumer protection are at the core of [the EU] approach to food safety guided by independent scientific advice.'[6] The EU then called upon the

---

3   WTO (1998), *EC Measures Concerning Meat and Meat Products (Hormones): Report of the Appellate Body (AB-1997-4)*. Ruling of 16 January 1998. Geneva, Switzerland, World Trade Organisation.

4   The Appellate Body found that the scientific material used by the EU was too general in nature, since it did not specifically evaluate the risks arising from hormone residues in meat products.

5   For an account of the risk evaluation see European Commission Press Release IP/03/1393, 15 October 2003. Directive 2003/74/EC, entering into force on 14 October 2003, imposed strict control over the use of the hormone oestradiol 17 alpha, which should be considered a carcinogen, and maintained a provisional prohibition of five other hormones while more complete scientific information was being sought to clarify the present state of knowledge. See also, R. Ancuccanu (2003), 'Maximum Residual Limits of Veterinary Medicinal Products and their Regulation in European Community Law', *European Law Journal*, 9:215.

6   Health and Consumer Protection Commissioner David Byrne, Press Release IP/03/1393, note 5 above.

US and Canada to lift the trade sanctions, which consisted in increased tariffs on selected products, totalling over US$116 million and CDN$11 million annually.

With the trade sanctions still in place, the EU decided later in 2004 to formally challenge the sanctions at the WTO, and two WTO Panels were set up to hear these claims against the US and Canada. In August 2005, the two Panels agreed to open their hearings to public observation,[7] in response to a growing debate on the level of wider participation in WTO dispute resolution. While the WTO bodies have in the past accepted unsolicited legal argument and *amicus curiae* briefs from interested third parties, it has also been argued, especially by developing countries, that public hearings would add further transparency and access to the process, and ultimately confer greater legitimacy on WTO decision making. Both the US and the EU have supported such moves towards greater transparency and have welcomed the innovation of public hearings in this case. As the narrative of the beef hormones dispute continues as a saga, it is also being observed as a kind of rehearsal for a similar transatlantic confrontation in relation to genetically modified organisms (GMOs), also involving issues of corporate interest, consumer choice and scientific uncertainty.[8]

The beef hormones dispute is an illuminating legal conflict for a number of reasons. In the first place, it demonstrates the progression of argument through a number of legal levels, most especially the European and the global. While the interplay of interests and competing legal claims is in some respect similar in both contexts, the process of debate and resolution can be seen to be different. For instance, the main actors on the stage at the European level included a number of individuals, such as specific traders, but in the global context the drama appears as more intergovernmental in character, as actors such as the US and the EU cross swords. Similarly, argument at the European level (as discussed in Chapter 5) is more directly rights based, whereas at the global level discourse is based rather on the treaty obligations of governmental entities. Secondly, the dispute reveals that the nature of the balancing act being carried out at both levels, by adjudicatory institutions such as the European Court of Justice, and the WTO Panels and Appellate Body. This balancing act is not simply the weighing of free-trade imperatives against health and environmental protection imperatives. It involves more specifically the often tricky application of principles such as that of precaution, which in turn raises questions of scientific assessment, and standards of the latter. Finally, and consequentially, there are also important questions lurking in this narrative regarding subjectivity: the issue of more precisely whose interests are at stake and how these interests are being represented. At the individual level, it is possible to identify a range of players, such as livestock farmers, corporate suppliers of hormones, meat consumers, technical experts and civil society representative groups. At the governmental level, there is also a range of actors, including conventional State governments, and international organisations, performing different roles and intergovernmentally representative

---

7   WTO Panel Meetings: WT/DS320/8, and WT/DS321/8.

8   See Chapter 6 above for the European legal background to this issue, and also further in this Chapter below.

to different degrees. Such modalities of process and representation merit further exploration.

The Intergovernmental Dimension: the WTO, the EU, the US – Whose Interests?

It is a truism – but also increasingly perhaps an over-simplification – to say that the international (or global) legal domain is largely a matter of intergovernmental relations, while the European legal domain comprises legal relations between governments, individuals and European institutions. Thus the same beef hormones narrative has rather different actors in Chapter 5 compared with some of its presentation in this chapter. The former account focused upon litigation between mainly corporate persons and a governmental agency,[9] which attracted the interest of a number of European institutions and was resolved by a European tribunal. The latter appears more as an account of intergovernmental feuding (although a major protagonist is an organisation (the EU) representing a group of States rather than the latter individually). But it is very instructive to trace the narrative through its successive legal stages: national litigation (companies, trade associations and veterinarians versus a UK government department), European litigation (the same complainants versus a number of EU institutions and bodies, consumer associations and Member State governments), and global litigation (the governments of the US and Canada versus the European Union) – see Figure 7.1.

The interests at stake and the policy and legal issues remain constant throughout the saga of litigation: freedom of trading and marketing versus the protection of human health, animal welfare and consumer preference (broadly speaking, 'life protection' interests). At each stage, there is also some kind of adjudication which comprises a balancing of these competing interests. The important question for purposes of the present discussion involves a comparison of that balancing process at the European and global levels (by the European Court of Justice and the WTO Appellate Body). In so far as the outcomes were different, to what extent is this explicable in terms of context, and to what extent does it follow from the modalities of argument? Further analysis would suggest that it is a matter of both, since the two are closely interconnected.

The context is not so much a matter of geography (European or transatlantic) as *dramatis personae*. The participants in the respective EU and WTO processes are, as indicated above, different and this is very much a reflection of the differing character of the organisations themselves, as respectively supranational and intergovernmental. As Slotboom has pointed out,[10] in comparing the dispute resolution mechanisms

---

9   To be precise, corporations and others associated with the animal medicine industry – (Fedesa – *Fédération européenne de la santé animale*; Pitman-Moore, Distrivet and Hoechst (producers of pharmaceuticals); the National Office of Animal Health (representing the British animal medicines industry); Donald Haxby (a politically active veterinary scientist)) – aligned against the Ministry for Agriculture, Food and Fisheries (MAFF).

10   Marco M. Slotboom (2006), 'Participation of NGOs before the WTO and EC tribunals: which court is the better friend?', *World Trade Review*, 5:69.

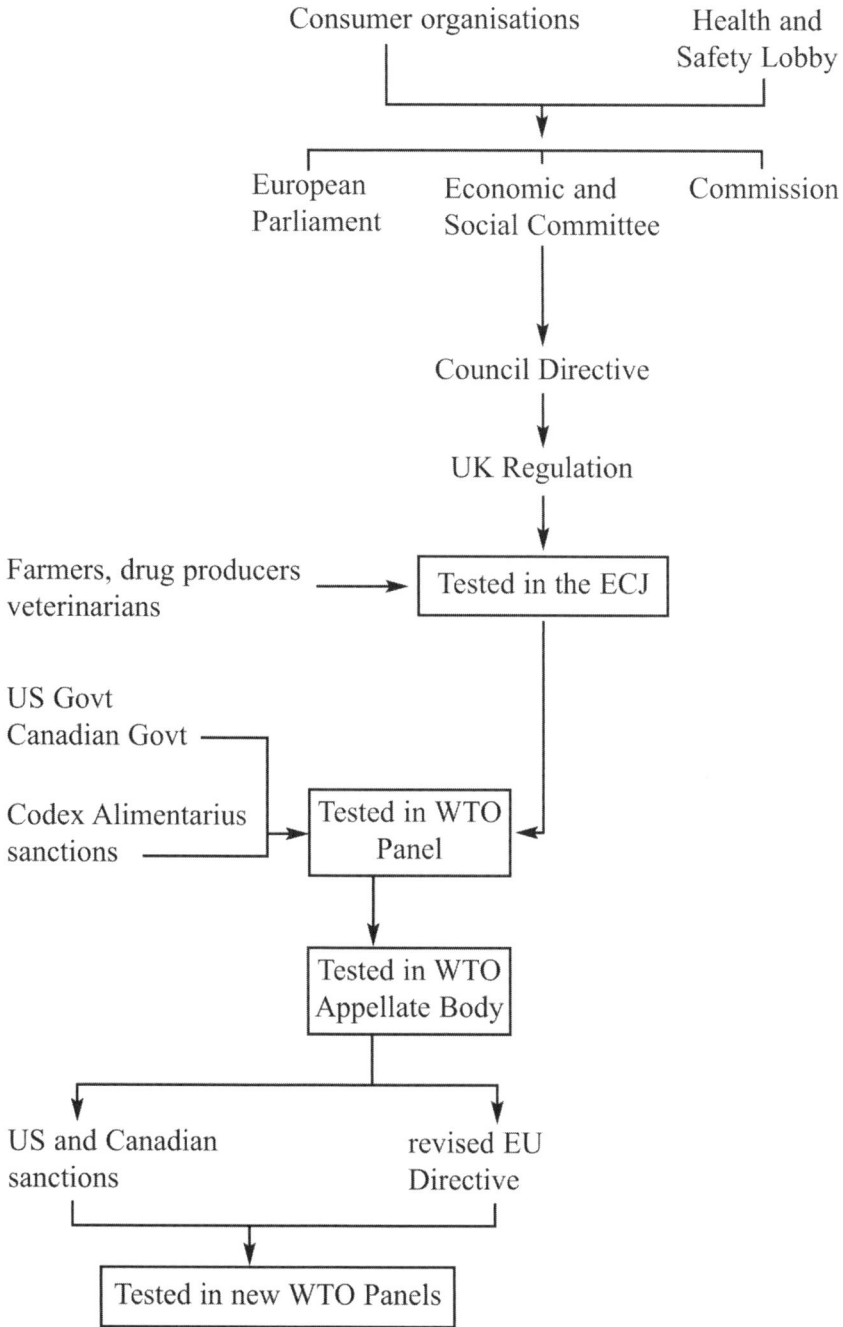

Figure 7.1   The trajectory of the beef hormones dispute

of the two organisations, that of the EU appears both more elaborate and more democratic than that of the WTO. EU (or to be more precise, EC) measures have a democratic basis in the way in which they are adopted and accountability via the scrutiny which may be carried out by the European Court of Justice (ECJ). The jurisdiction of the ECJ is responsive to claims on the part of EU citizens, Member State governments and European institutions. In this way, a claim being heard by the ECJ is in effect a forum for discussion for a number of different actors – individuals, corporate persons, representative organisations, governments and EU institutions and bodies, as demonstrated by the *Fedesa* case. In particular, the access to legal argument afforded to individuals and representative organisations has encouraged the direct representation of individual interests and the formulation of argument by reference to the rights (including the fundamental human rights) of such actors. In this sense, the EU forum, and especially that provided by the ECJ, is the site for an increasingly richly textured legal discourse relating to the market interests of a wide range of actors. The multi-dimensional system of accountability within the EU system has important consequences for the level of participation in legal debate and for the formulation of legal argument with reference to a range of entitlements.

In contrast, the WTO is as yet at an intergovernmental stage of evolution, with a more limited dispute settlement mechanism open only to WTO State parties. Despite opportunities for lobbying and *amicus curiae* briefs, formal representation of any interests is carried out by governmental actors who may be a number of stages removed from 'original' producer or consumer interests, and national-level interests are likely to prevail in any jostling for attention in the dispute resolution process. WTO procedures are therefore noticeably less participatory and less democratic than those within the EU; this fact is interestingly reflected in growing calls for more transparency in WTO dispute resolution, resulting in the recent decision referred to above to have public WTO Panel hearings. Opportunities for legal argument are correspondingly restricted since WTO adjudicators may only rule upon the compliance of States (or the EU as a representative of its Member States) with treaty provisions which relate to and bind States rather than individuals or companies. Thus the main questions relate to such matters as the legality of trade sanctions or trade restrictions adopted as international measures and as they are experienced by other State actors, rather than considering directly their impact on individual traders or consumers. The latter remain 'ghost' actors, hovering in the wings of the legal stage. For purposes of WTO adjudication, talk of basic human rights is tangential and cannot be taken on board directly, but must rather be filtered through intergovernmental relations and the injury done by one State to another. The situation is similar to the *ancien régime* of international law, that of diplomatic protection, when injury to individuals abroad was taken up at the international level by their governments and there was hardly any opportunity for an individual to assert a violation of rights directly before an international legal forum.

The foregoing analysis would therefore suggest that, in relation to the same conflict of interests, the legal outcomes could well differ at European and global levels, since the possibilities of participation in legal argument, and hence the modalities of argument are at present quite different. But before moving on to consider more closely the outcomes of legal argument on the global stage, it would be useful to consider the range of interests and entitlements which underlie and feed into that global legal argument.

Ghosts in the Machine: The Underlying Rights

The familiar dichotomy of 'producer' and 'consumer' rights may be recast somewhat at the global level. Although the main categories of competing rights may still be broadly associated with the respective positions of producers and consumers, it may be seen that the interests underlying these positions cluster around two main substantive objectives: the opportunity for economic exploitation on the one hand, and life protection on the other hand. It may be helpful for purposes of analysis to identify the underlying interests and rights in these terms. In addition, all market place actors have, in a more procedural sense, an interest in securing some participation in policy and decision making, which gives rise to claims in relation to a clutch of democratic entitlement rights.

Free-Trading and Economic Exploitation Rights

Producers and suppliers, who at the global and transnational level are inevitably large corporate actors, have a common broad interest in exploiting economic opportunity, or what might be termed 'free trade'. In this respect, such actors stand to benefit from the free-trading and larger open market policies of organisations such as the EC, the WTO, NAFTA and other regional free-trade organisations.[11] The commitment of such organisations to establishing larger and more accessible marketing areas involves in a number of ways the dismantling and prevention of barriers to trading activity, so as to allow companies to exploit 'foreign' territories and markets within the larger free market area to the full. To that extent, the assumption might be made that free-trade organisations are inevitably sympathetic to economic self-determination claims by large companies. But, although this is frequently the starting point for such organisations, the history of the EC and EU has shown how these organisations can also take on board some different and competing values, such as consumer and environmental protection, and so become more of an arbiter of disputes between different economic actors. That this may not be so much the case for less supranational organisations, such as the WTO and NAFTA, is an issue to be explored further at a later point in this chapter. For the present, the main supplier interests and rights which have been promoted by free-trade policies may be broadly indicated. Without attempting to be exhaustive, some prominent claims to entitlement may be listed: access to markets, exploitation of intellectual property, the opportunity to invest, access to raw materials, and participation in policy making. As legal claims, these may be based upon broadly drafted guarantees laid down in a number of international instruments. For instance, the Charter of Fundamental Rights of the European Union refers in Article 16 to the freedom to construct a business, and

---

11   For an overview of the role of the various organisations, see: Gerhard Loibl (2006), 'International Economic Law', Ch. 23, in Malcolm D. Evans (ed.), *International Law* (Oxford: Oxford University Press, 2nd edn).

in Article 17 to the right to property (to own, use, dispose of and bequeath lawfully acquired possessions, and the protection of intellectual property).

The *right of access to markets*, in order to supply goods and services and compete in those markets in the most basic sense, is perhaps the most obvious entitlement to be claimed by producers and suppliers. Free-trading policies promote such economic opportunities by seeking to remove obstacles to such access, typically in the form of fiscal barriers and non-fiscal restrictions such as quotas and other trading requirements which may hinder the easy supply of the territory in question. The Beef Hormones case, as outlined above, provides a classic illustration of the claim to freedom of trading, on the part of suppliers of meat treated with hormones, which had been restricted by preventive measures put in place by the EC in the interest of health protection and consumer preference.[12] Thus it was argued that the rights of access to markets on the part of farmers, suppliers of hormones and the veterinary sector were subject to disproportionate and discriminatory restriction.

The *exploitation of intellectual property* is perhaps a less obvious aspect of economic freedom, but certainly one of significance in the global market. Forms of intellectual property such as patents and copyright allow to some degree the marketing of commodities without competition, or for payment through licensing arrangements, representing a return for investment and opportunity for conventional profit. In so far as such legal protection restricts consumer access to goods and services (for instance, through high prices or availability), the exercise of intellectual property rights may conflict with different claims, for instance, to fair economic dealing or provision of health care. This was the issue famously tested before South African courts, when legislation was introduced by the South African Government in 1997 allowing for the curtailment of patent rights to ensure the availability of certain drugs in the context of an HIV/AIDS epidemic. That matter was taken before the South African Constitutional Court,[13] while countries such as Brazil and Thailand have adopted a very assertive stance in favour of compulsory licences, provoking ongoing argument about WTO compliance.[14] The outcome and impact of these legal disputes will be considered later in this chapter; for present purposes, they serve to illustrate the kind of policy and legal confrontation which may arise between intellectual property-based 'exploitation' claims and opposing claims based on 'protection of life' argument.

Alongside the exploitation and protection of intellectual property in the global context may be set the subject of '*investor protection*'. Once again, at a transnational level, reference to investment for the most part relates to large-scale corporate activity, and often means the economic exploitation of vulnerable 'developing' economies;

---

12   In some respects, this case involved an interesting reversal of roles, in that the ECJ has often to test the legality of Member State protectionist measures (argued to be justified under Article 30 of the EC Treaty) set up against the EC policy of free movement (guaranteed by Article 28 of the Treaty).

13   Case 4183/98, *Pharmaceutical Manufacturers Association of South Africa* v. *Republic of South Africa*.

14   See for instance, European Parliament Press Release, 7 May 2007, *Decision by Brazil to Allow Production of Anti-AIDS Drug*.

one way of viewing the matter in international terms is to see it as the relation between capital-exporting and capital-importing countries. As such, 'international investment' has become an important section of international law in its own right. As Evans explains:

> The expansion of Western economies since the nineteenth century has resulted in considerable levels of investments in other States, both developed and developing. But the degree of control over local economies that follows from this has given rise to conflicts between capital exporting and capital importing countries. On the one hand, capital exporting countries require protection and security for the investments made by their nationals whilst, on the other hand, the capital importing countries demand the ability to regain or retain control over certain (key) parts of their economies, and numerous countries, both developing and developed, have expropriated foreign property to achieve this.[15]

In very broad terms therefore, the international legal battle-line has been drawn up between investor countries, promoting their own economies and representing their nationals as corporate investors, and investment-importing countries, concerned to protect their economic sovereignty and sustainability, and representing the interests of their national businesses and labour forces. The substantive and procedural rules developed at the international level to balance these interests and resolve conflicts have evolved through a number of stages: the exercise of 'diplomatic' protection in specific cases, the use of bilateral investment treaties, and more recently, attempts to establish a multilateral investment agreement (MIA) as a global mechanism for dispute resolution.[16] The recent history of stalled attempts to agree upon such a MIA brings into sharp relief the opposing claims, interests and rights in this particular market place context. The initiative for an MIA has arisen in particular in the investor country camp and an attempt was made, from 1995 to 1998, to negotiate an agreement under the auspices of the OECD.[17] The secretive nature of these negotiations and what was eventually revealed as a strong bias towards the interests of investor countries, led to the breakdown of the negotiations and a subsequent attempt to revive them under the WTO and the UN Conference on Trade and Development (UNCTAD). These moves were also strongly criticised, particularly by NGOs, and there have been calls to relocate such discussions to the UN, as a fairer and more transparent forum for such legal development.[18] The attempt to introduce an MIA at the WTO Ministerial Meeting in Cancun in 2003 was again unsuccessful,[19] leading to something of a continuing deadlock on the issue.

Another significant area of economic exploitation, and one that may have significant international and transnational implications, relates to the issue of *access*

---

15   Evans, note 11 above, at 708.

16   For an account of these developments, see: Malcolm Shaw (2002), *International Law* (Cambridge: Cambridge University Press, 5th edn), at 737–52.

17   Evans, note 11 above, at 711.

18   Ibid., at 711–12.

19   ActionAid International (2003), *Beyond Cancun: Key Issues Facing the Multilateral Trading System,* December.

to raw material. Such raw material may be scarce, geographically inaccessible, expensive to extract, or located in environmentally sensitive environments,[20] so that its exploitation may then run counter to interests and claims which have both a national and international dimension. Such a collision arose in the context of the regime for the deep seabed, when this matter was being negotiated as part of the package for the 1982 Law of the Sea Convention. Exploitation of the mineral resources of the deep seabed involved on one side the interests of developed countries and companies who had invested in the technology to make such exploitation feasible, and on the other side the interests of those (represented mainly by the governments of 'developing' countries), who were likely to miss the benefit of exploitation and become yet further disadvantaged in an unequal international economic order. The idea of the deep seabed as the 'common heritage of mankind',[21] which was eventually incorporated in the 1982 Convention, was advanced to encapsulate a bundle of economic development and fair treatment rights which could be asserted against the industrial exploitation rights of (affluent and advantaged) 'investor' States and companies. The argument resulted in a kind of deadlock which delayed ratification of the whole Convention on the part of a number of States, despite some concessions being made to 'pioneer investors', until a breakthrough was achieved in the early 1990s, and the 1994 Implementation Agreement persuaded more States to ratify the Convention. But the resolution of the argument owed a great deal to important shifts in economic reality: a shifting of interest away from mineral resources located outside the reach of national jurisdiction to those (such as polymetallic sulphides) more commonly found on the seabed of the continental shelf, so that the potential rewards of deep seabed exploitation had become less obvious.[22] Without such a change in the economic circumstances, the balance of interests (economic power as against political conscience) had appeared sufficiently even as to produce a continuing 'rights deadlock'.

A similar alignment of interests and arguments appears in the now long-running saga of commercial whaling activity. In this situation, a small number of national fishing industries (notably those of Iceland, Norway and Japan) have for economic, and perhaps also to some extent cultural reasons, favoured a continuation of the practice of killing whales, while majority opinion at the global level favoured a moratorium, on environmental and ecological grounds. The International Whaling Commission (IWC)[23] established a moratorium on commercial whaling in relation to all species of the great whale in 1985. Norway is not bound by this, having lodged an

---

20　A significant example would be Antarctica, in relation to which there is a ban on mineral resource activity, except for scientific research: see Annex V to the 1991 Protocol on Environmental Protection, to the 1959 Antarctic Treaty.

21　On the emergence of this concept, see: Christopher C. Joyner (1986), 'Legal Implications of the Concept of the Common Heritage of Mankind', *International and Comparative Law Quarterly*, 35:190.

22　Malcolm D. Evans, 'The Law of the Sea', Ch. 21, in Evans (ed.), note 11 above, at 645–6.

23　An international body set up under the 1946 International Convention for the Regulation of Whaling, The IWC monitors the application of the measures set down in the Schedule to the Convention on the conduct of global whaling.

objection within the specified period, and has continued to catch minke whales for commercial purposes. There are also exceptions in favour of 'aboriginal subsistence whaling' (in practice relating to small aboriginal communities in Alaska, Greenland and northern Russia), and for purposes of scientific research. Japan has exploited the latter exception, but to a controversial extent (some seven hundred whales killed each year), and whale meat and other products from this 'scientific' whaling are sold on the Japanese market. Iceland was not a member of the IWC when the moratorium was established and was therefore not legally bound by the measure, and entered a reservation[24] when rejoining the IWC in 2002. Under this reservation, Iceland stated that it would not engage in commercial whaling before 2006, but did indeed resume commercial whaling in October 2006. The controversy surrounding Iceland's decision to do so illustrates well the competing claims in relation to this issue. On the one hand, twenty-five anti-whaling countries, led by the UK, condemned Iceland's decision in a *démarche* issued on 1 November 2006.[25] This critical position is based principally on concern for a number of kinds of whale as an endangered species, on the view that whaling is unacceptably cruel to the animals, and the argument that there are now cheaper synthetic alternatives to whale products so that commercial exploitation is no longer justifiable (with the narrow exception of the dependent position of small indigenous societies). Pro-whaling countries on the other hand have supported Iceland's return to commercial whaling by contesting the scientific evidence in relation to the risk to whale populations and putting forward the claim that 'controlled whaling is environmentally sustainable, and a right of whaling communities.'[26] Thus, as in other instances of trade versus environmental and health arguments, much would seem to rest upon the role of scientific risk assessment and interpretation of its results. That process is used to balance the competing claims of justifiable economic exploitation, scientific research and the protection of indigenous culture on the one side, and environmental sustainability and animal welfare on the other side.[27]

Life Protection Rights

In substantive terms, the category of rights which are frequently asserted against the freedom of trading are largely concerned with human welfare, the material position of human individuals, and broadly what might be described as individual self-determination – aspects of life, manifested for example in claims to health and health care, subsistence, a fair standard of living and fair economic treatment, and an independent exercise of political and economic choice. At a more general and communal level, such life protection interests increasingly entail a concern for the environment in which we live as human beings, and find expression in the assertion

---

24   This reservation was subject to formal objection on the part of nineteen States.

25   See Defra News Release, 1 November 2006, Ref. 496/06.

26   Official statement by Hideki Moronuki, Japanese Fisheries Agency official, 18 October 2006.

27   For a useful overview of these arguments, see Defra Fact sheet: *Whales, Whaling and the International Whaling Commission*, February 2006.

of principles of sustainability, environmental protection, biodiversity and animal welfare. Some of this list may be attached directly to the human role as consumer, as in the case of the right to health or consumer preference, while other forms of entitlement reflect not so much the risk of direct injury to the consumer *qua* consumer, as the risk to civil society arising from environmental depletion and degradation. Examples of these various categories of entitlement may be quickly drawn from the discussion in the chapters above, especially from rights discourse in the European legal arena. In summary, this considerable range of rights can be grouped into some main categories, along with some examples of their legal guarantee, as indicated in Table 7.1 below.

Table 7.1   Main categories of life protection rights

Protection of human health and provision of health care *Art 12 ICESCR* Guarantee of food safety *EU Regulation 178/2002*	Subsistence *Art 11 ICESCR* Freedom from poverty Minimum standard of living *Art 11 ICESCR* Non-discrimination (removal of the distinction between rich and poor) *Article 3 ICESCR*	Economic self-determination Right to development *Arts 1,2 Declaration on Right to Development* Exercise of consumer choice and preference Fair treatment of consumers Right to work and enjoyment of just and favourable conditions of work *Arts 6, 7 ICESCR*	Sustainability Protection of the environment against degradation Biodiversity Animal and plant welfare	Protection of cultural diversity and indigenous ways of life *Art 15 ICESCR*

Democratic Participation Rights

Finally, in a more procedural sense, reference may be made to the *ability to participate in policy and law formulation as a kind of democratic opportunity* at the global level. The growing body of international regulation of economic and trading matters is in formal terms largely the product of intergovernmental discussion and decision making. But of course other parties may contribute to such processes and large corporate actors commonly do so through lobbying both national governments on the position they may adopt at international meetings and also organisations such as the EU and WTO. Access to officials and policy makers, whether within national governments or international organisations, and transparency in discussion and the adoption of measures therefore comprise an important means of ensuring a degree of democratic governance at the supranational level. This issue has given rise to an increasing amount of discussion and argument, and in particular the assertion that there is a significant imbalance in the degree of access as between large corporate actors on the one hand and individuals and public interest groups on the other hand. This has led to the allegation, especially on the part of a number of NGOs, that intergovernmental organisations such as the OECD, the WTO and even the EU are dominated by corporate interests, either through direct lobbying or indirectly when large companies have the ears of governments. In political terms, this is a matter of policy construction and interest representation; in legal terms, the issue is translated into a question of participation in governance, and is centred upon a collection of democratic rights – in particular, equal representation, transparency, consultation, and access to information. As matters stand, it is strongly argued that large producer companies have enhanced opportunities for participation at the global level in this respect, especially compared to public interest groups. In short, there is not a level democratic playing field. Much of this discussion has been rehearsed in Chapter 3 above.

Terms of Engagement

As argued already, any attempt to judge the relative legal positions of consumers and producers at the global level must take into account the context of legal process. Comparison with the legal context in the EU is instructive. The legal structure of the EU is distinctive: there is a compulsory jurisdiction, and also a developed culture of basic rights protection (which draws upon that of the European Human Rights Convention (ECHR)). Perhaps most importantly, it is a supranational structure which enables non-State actors – whether corporate, human individual, or public interest bodies – to engage in direct legal argument with governments and supranational institutions. While it may yet be argued that large corporate interests still command a strong position in the EU political process, there is an important sense in which there may be said to be a more level playing field for purposes of legal engagement.

The global or more broadly international situation remains different in these respects. Both political and legal processes are still predominantly intergovernmental rather than supranational in character, so that governments and intergovernmental organisations (IGOs) retain the key roles in terms of both political and legal initiative and discourse. In legal terms, non-State actors have an inferior *locus standi*, and consequently political weight and leverage assumes a greater significance, or, to be more specific, access to and influence with governments and IGOs counts for more since the legal dialogue is much more a matter of engagement between the States and the organisations. The battle lines in such intergovernmental legal engagement may be variable: in relation to hormone-treated meat and GMOs, the EU is drawn up against the US; on intellectual property and investment protection, developed States face developing States; on the issue of whaling, States such as the UK, the US and

Australia oppose the position adopted by Iceland, Norway and Japan. The constant factor is the way in which governments and international organisations serve as a kind of proxy for individual interests, whether corporate or human, or whether producer or consumer. In legal terms, therefore, basic or human rights discourse occupies a shadowy position, hovering in the background of intergovernmental argument. The terms of engagement are different from the European and the national context.

The Outcome for Producers and Consumers at the Global Level

Having said that about the context of legal argument, what conclusions may be drawn as to how producer and consumer interests and their 'shadowy' rights fare at the global level? A reasonable working hypothesis might be that, in so far as corporate producer interests appear at present to be better placed to gain the attention of intergovernmental negotiators, such interests will tend to dominate in the outcome of such negotiations or even in intergovernmental judicial processes such as those now employed within the WTO. In juristic terms, economic exploitation, market access and investment rights might be expected to prevail over countervailing health or environmental protection rights, or consumer preference or fair dealing rights. This hypothesis could be tested in relation to some recent and ongoing controversies: biotechnology and food supply (for instance, hormone-treated meat or genetically modified products); intellectual property and the supply of drugs and medicine; and the proposed multilateral regime for dealing with investment disputes.

Biotechnology and Food Supply

The issue of the application of biotechnology to food production and supply provides an important contemporary battleground for the contest between producer and consumer interests. The examples of hormone-treated animals destined for human consumption and the use of genetically modified organisms (GMOs) in the food chain bring into sharp relief the potential conflict between claims to freedom of trading and the protection of human health and the environment. Two particular instances of legal and political argument may be used here to test the outcome of such arguments as they have been deployed in a number of international fora: first, the Word Health Organisation/Food and Agriculture Organisation evaluation of food standards programmes, especially as worked out by the Codex Alimentarius Commission; and secondly, the challenge of the EU moratorium in relation to GMOs, mounted by the US, Argentina and Canada before a WTO Panel.

Evaluation of Codex Standard Setting It may be recalled that the Codex Alimentarius Commission (Codex) is an intergovernmental body established in 1963 by the World Health Organisation (WHO) and the Food and Agriculture Organisation (FAO), both of which are specialised agencies of the UN. The Codex is intended to play a major role in the protection of consumer health and fair dealing for consumers and carries out this function by working out standards, which are then offered to governments for adoption in relation to both the domestic supply of food and its export and import. However, at the same time, the Codex standards have now become presumptively authoritative for purposes of WTO decision making (for instance, through WTO panels), and in particular in relation to the WTO Agreement on the Application of Sanitary and Phytosanitary Measures (the SPS Agreement). In so far as the WTO is required to mediate disputes involving the facilitation or freedom of trading and barriers to trade arising from safety standards, the Codex standards have thus become important reference points in the resolution of such disputes. The way in which the Codex arrives at its standards has therefore emerged as a significant element in the resolution of such disputes. In April 2002, the WHO and FAO launched a joint evaluation of their food standards programmes, including the Codex Alimentarius, 'so that the programme best serves the concerns of all (the rich and poor), regarding health, safety and trade in food'.[28] The evaluation was carried out by an independent Evaluation Team, advised by an Expert Panel, by conducting consultation with both governments and other stakeholders.[29]

One of the misgivings expressed about the evolving role of the Codex centres on a perceived shift in the emphasis in its work, from the 'life protection' concerns of its parent organisations towards the 'trade facilitation' concerns of the WTO, via the way in which the WTO has requisitioned Codex standard setting for purposes of applying its own treaties, especially the SPS Agreement. For instance, it was argued in a Consumers International (CI) briefing paper:

> Rights – such as consumers' right to know about what they are consuming – are not recognised as a legitimate factor in how Codex elaborates food standards. Codex does, however, take into account the economic impact of food standards on Codex member governments and their national food producers. The pressure to elaborate standards to minimise trade barriers, rather than to maximise consumer protection, has been overwhelming since the SPS Agreement came into force. Standards to protect consumer health and prevent unfair trade practices have increasingly come under attack as 'disguised' non-tariff barriers to trade. Most major exporting countries are united in their opposition to ethics playing a role in standard setting or in trade dispute settlement. They have opposed revision of a Draft Code of Ethics for International Trade in Food.[30]

This argument – that Codex work is being steered away from a concern for consumer protection towards taking into account the economic impact of food standards – tends to centre on two particular mechanisms which may be used in the crucial standard-setting process. First, there is the above-mentioned role for a code of ethics in relation to international trade in food. This is a subject which has polarised views within Codex, as may be seen from the report on the debates at the twenty-seventh session of the Codex (June–July 2004) – some countries, such as Brazil, urging that work on the draft code be stopped, while some EU and developing countries

---

28 Press release, 22 April 2002.

29 For a fuller account of the methodology of the evaluation, see World Health Organisation (2002), *Report by the Director-General, Joint FAO/WHO evaluation of the work of the Codex Alimentarius Commission,* EB111/29, 15 December, paras 2–3.

30 Consumers International briefing paper, *Codex Alimentarius Commission Governance* (2005), based on a report by Steve Suppan.

argued in favour of its continuing revision. At the twenty-seventh session, the WTO representative, arguing against the possibly dominating role of a code of ethics, asserted that all Codex texts would be equally relevant under the SPS Agreement and the way in which a particular text could be interpreted by a WTO Panel should be determined in the framework of a particular trade dispute.[31]

Secondly, there is the matter of how scientific evidence and expertise is used, which raises questions relating to both 'precaution' and 'sound science'.[32] The process of risk assessment is crucial to decisions which seek to balance claims for economic freedom against those for health or environmental protection, whether the decision-making context is judicial resolution or intergovernmental negotiation. The key question is the cogency and persuasiveness of the scientific argument and evidence regarding the risk to health or the environment and this issue remains controversial. For instance, in the Beef Hormones dispute, the WTO Panel's acceptance in 1998 of the findings of a FAO/WHO Joint Expert Committee on Food Additives report (on the maximum level of hormone treatment that could be tolerated without harm to human health) was contested by the EU, on the basis of concerns regarding the scientific integrity of the report and conflicting, less conclusive evidence resulting from EU risk assessment.[33] The question of scientific evidence was also addressed in the evaluation of the Codex, in so far as many Codex standards are necessarily based on risk assessment, and a need for greater rigour was identified:

> Expert advice to the Codex Alimentarius Commission needs to have greater identity and coordination and significantly increased resources. Its independence and transparency need to be further reinforced within FAO and WHO … It is recommended that FAO and WHO establish a scientific committee of eminent scientists to provide, to the Codex Alimentarius Commission and the two organizations, overarching scientific advice, including on emerging challenges, and to provide guidance and quality control to existing and ad hoc committees.[34]

The perceived role of the Codex in balancing competing interests depends very much, therefore, on the quality of its own information for standard-setting purposes and how its standards are taken into account by other bodies (for instance, the relative weight given to a code of ethics compared to quantified risk-assessment

---

31 *Report of the 27th Session of the Codex Alimentarius Commission,* ALINORM 04/27/41, para 158.

32 The phrase 'sound science' is used here in the sense of scientific investigation and findings which are ostensibly objective and politically neutral and is widely referred to as an underpinning principle of both industry and regulatory approaches to risk analysis. However, the idea is problematical given the reality of the sources of and methods of funding of scientific work. In the context of scientific uncertainty, and hence the need for precaution, the idea of sound science may serve an important legitimating function, as 'a rational and accepted basis for decision-making' (see Jane Hunt (1994), 'The Social Construction of Precaution', 117 in Timothy O'Riordan and James Cameron (eds), *Interpreting the Precautionary Principle* (London: Earthscan Publications), at 122).

33 See note 5 above.

34 World Health Organisation, note 29 above, at paras 12–13.

results).[35] At present, much of this debate is still very much in the melting-pot. A major recommendation of the assessment of standard setting concerned the speed of decision making. The first main area for improvement identified by the evaluation was the speed of Codex work and the provision of expert scientific advice. This may be seen as playing into the hands of the trade facilitation lobby, a major concern of which is not only the existence of technical and scientific barriers to trading, but also the chilling effect of the amount of time taken to decide upon the legality of such barriers. Overall, the evaluation of standard setting, and particularly of the role of the Codex, serves to illustrate the way in which the debate on competing interests takes place at the 'legislative' standard-setting level.

GMO Approval   In the more specific context of adjudicatory settlement, the recent WTO ruling on GMO produce[36] may serve similarly to demonstrate the interplay of interests and their resolution. The debate on the acceptability of genetically modified or engineered organisms has been referred to already,[37] but in legal terms recently came to a head when the US, supported by Argentina and Canada, filed a complaint with the WTO in May 2003 against the EU's *de facto* moratorium on GM organisms and the ban which had also been imposed by a number of EU Member States. Once again, in broad terms the conflict involved lost trading opportunity (a considerable reduction in exports for the GM-producing countries) and protection of human health, and a crucial factor was risk evaluation and scientific evidence. In particular, the US and the EU apply different standards in risk evaluation. On the one hand, the practice of the US Food and Drug Administration (FDA) is to use companies' own summaries of safety and nutritional assessments as a basis for finding that a GM food variety is generically safe and so may be approved for commercial exploitation. On the other hand, the EU approval process is much more demanding. In the words of the European Commission:

> In the EU, GMOs can only be placed on the market after having undergone a stringent science-based risk assessment on a case by case basis. This approach is fully in line with international standards, in particular with the Cartagena Protocol on Biosafety as well as with the relevant Guidelines adopted by the Codex Alimentarius Commission in 2003 and by the International Convention on Plant Protection ... The EU approval process may appear to be lengthy for some countries which adopt a more lenient approach to food and environmental safety issues. The longer times to assess the safety of GMOs in the EU are due to the complexity of the science involved as well as delays incurred by biotech companies to provide suitable data demonstrating the safety of their products.[38]

---

35   See for instance, the critical discussion by Steve Suppan of the Institute for Agriculture and Trade Policy (2004), 'Consumer International's Decision-Making in the Global Market', Codex Briefing Paper, August.

36   WTO Panel decision: *European Community: Measures Affecting the Approval and Marketing of Biotech Products* (WT/DS/291, 292 and 293); preliminary report, 6 February 2006, approved 10 June 2006.

37   See the discussion in Chapter 6 above.

38   European Commission Press Release, *Europe's Rules on GMOs and the WTO*, MEMO 06/61, 7 February 2006.

Indeed, the complexity of these issues was further borne out by the time taken by the Panel in this case to reach a decision (almost three years).[39] Although hailed as a legal reverse for the EU, in fact the scope of the Panel's finding against the EU was narrow. Strictly speaking, what was condemned was a *de facto* moratorium on EU approvals between 1999 and 2003 (which resulted in 'undue delay' in twenty-four out of twenty-seven contested approval processes) and the ban imposed by a number of EU States. While the moratorium and bans were found to be contrary to the WTO's SPS agreement, crucial aspects of the EU regulatory framework were not condemned: the underlying principle that the safety of human and animal health and of the environment requires assessment before marketing, the science-based case-by-case method of risk assessment, and the post-marketing monitoring of GM products through mandatory labelling and traceability rules, all of which are criticised by the US as barriers to trading opportunities and rights. Also, it is important to realise that the Panel's decision does not directly rule on the safety or otherwise of GM products, apart from implicitly accepting that they are not inherently unsafe but that there are legitimate interests requiring their assessment for approval and further monitoring.

It is clear that this recent Panel decision represents just one stage within an ongoing global argument regarding the extent of any need to test the safety of GMOs, and thereby restrict trading opportunity. The EU (or more strictly, the European Commission[40]) subsequently decided not to appeal against the Panel decision. In so far as the latter related to the *de facto* moratorium, this is a matter of largely historical relevance. However, the question of the national bans remains contentious,[41] and it may be that the US will next question the legality of EU traceability and labelling requirements under the WTO rules.[42] What is likely therefore is a continuing

---

39   In 2004, the Panel decided that it would require independent scientific advice; further delays appear to have been associated with problems of resources.

40   The decision whether to appeal appears to lie with the Commission, taking a consensus opinion on the matter from the Member States. In this case, despite the efforts of States such as France, Austria and Greece which maintain bans on GMO imports, there did not appear to be sufficiently wide support across all EU members for an appeal. The decision may well have been influenced the narrow scope of the Panel decision and the perception that little could be gained in an appeal.

41   At present, bans (national safeguard measures) have been imposed by Austria, France, Germany, Greece, Hungary, Luxembourg and Poland. The bans are legally based on EU directives. In June 2005, the Commission brought forward a proposal to lift the bans but the proposal was defeated by an adverse vote of twenty-two out of twenty-five Member States in the Council. The President of the Council Lucien Lux commented, 'In the light of the subsidiarity and precautionary principles and taking into account the uncertainties about the lifting of several of these bans, we are happy to have sent a clear message to the Commission … these bans will remain in place, until more data is available' (Council Communiqué, 24 June 2005). In these debates, the European Commission may be seen as occupying a middle position on the political and legal spectrum, with GMO-producing companies and exporting States and the WTO on one side, and a number of European States and environmental NGOs on the other side. In WTO terms, the legality of national bans depends on the compatibility of the risk assessment, on which the bans are based, with WTO norms.

42   In 2004, a number of American companies were known to be seeking legal advice on the compatibility of EU traceability and labelling requirements with WTO rules.

assault on the part of the 'GMO-exporting' countries against whatever mechanisms or rules are employed by the EU or individual European States to impede in any way that export. The US's argument is cast in terms of criticising science-based and precautionary European measures as disguised economic impediments to US, Argentinian and Canadian exports. In crude terms, the argument may then be seen in terms of an American preference for trade facilitation and a European preference for precaution. What complicates the deployment of such argument is the fact that using even 'purely' motivated scientific, health, or environmental argument has economic consequences. Genuine concerns about health and the environment appear to be affecting consumer economic preferences in Europe,[43] which then translate into natural concerns on the part of American corporate and governmental interests.

In the longer term, consumers may possess an *economic* trump card in this context. It is then interesting to speculate whether traders and exporters can find their own trump card in a legal form, based on a basic right to trading activity (a 'WTO trump'), which is capable of defeating other basic rights to health and environmental protection. Alternatively, 'life interest' claims may provide the trump card. Another recent skirmish on the field of risk assessment demonstrated the strength of the synergy of arguments relating to democratic governance, precaution and values of health protection and biodiversity. In April 2006, the European Commission proposed some changes to the EU procedures for approving GMOs,[44] providing greater weight for critical assessments presented by Member States at the scientific evaluation phase. It is envisaged that the European Food Safety Authority (EFSA)[45] should liaise more fully with national scientific bodies to resolve divergent opinions, and that the EFSA should justify more fully any decision not to accept scientific objections raised by national bodies, while also addressing more explicitly potential long-term effects and biodiversity issues. The underlying argument in favour of this shift towards precaution and 'critical science' was explained in the following terms by the EU Environment Commissioner, Stavros Dimas:

---

43   For information on consumer perceptions of risk in relation to food, see the 2006 Eurobarometer survey commissioned by the Commission and the EFSA (EFSA Press Release, 7 February 2006 <www.efsa.eu.int>). Judgments relating to fluctuating trade flows must be made carefully, however. US assertions that restrictive EU rules on GMOs have adversely affected American exports have been countered by the European Commission: 'US soybean and soy meal exports have steadily declined over the last ten years because of a decline of competitiveness of US agriculture on the global market. The trends in EU maize imports further confirm that US farmers are no longer low-cost producers and are less and less able to compete with emerging countries such as Brazil and Argentina on global commodity markets. EU trade data show clearly that EU rules on GM are not affecting the imports of more competitive GMO producers.' (Commission Press Release, *Europe's Rules on GMOs and the WTO*, MEMO 06/61, 7 February 2006.)

44   Commission Press Release IP/06/498, 12 April 2006. The changes comprised 'practical changes' to the EFSA approval process.

45   EFSA is an EC agency established by the European Parliament in 2002, with a remit to provide scientific advice on food and feed safety. See Chapter 6 above.

In an area in which public opinion is so strong, as is GMO policy, it is the duty of the Commission to work together with member States to ensure that the rules for the authorization and use of GM crops respond to the concerns of citizens and protect biodiversity in our natural environment whilst at the same time complying with the functioning of the internal market.

Interestingly, Dimas then converted this policy argument into a statement of rights talk, by asserting:

Farmers must be able to choose the crops they grow, whether conventional, or organic, or other, and have confidence in the quality and purity of their harvested products. Consumers need to know what they are putting in their shopping baskets and what ends up on their plates. And last but not least, the impact of cultivation of certain crops on biodiversity and the environment must be clearly established.[46]

Put another way, this may be understood as a listing of *equal* claims to (a) producer freedom of *safe* cultivation, (b) consumer information, preference and safety, and (c) biodiversity and environmental protection, underpinned by democratic governance (official engagement with public opinion and concerns).

A number of main points may be drawn from these particular examples of the deployment of trade freedom and consumer protection argument, as crucial interrelated issues of engagement: (a) how priorities may be adopted within standard-setting and evaluation processes; (b) participation and representation within such processes and any resolution procedures, and in particular the role of independent advice and decision making; (c) the speed and efficiency of decision making and its relation to the 'trade imperative'; (d) the differing positions (or even cultures) on these issues across different countries. The trade facilitation versus consumer protection debate, whether cast in terms of interests or rights, inevitably resolves itself in processes of standard setting and risk evaluation. Such processes themselves depend upon the way in which certain emphases or priorities (such as impact on trade, or ethical concerns) may be adopted and on issues of participation (such as the degree of independence of those conducting risk assessment and the representative role of those taking part in risk management). The broader context for all of this is the political response to the increasing perception of scientific uncertainty (the need for greater speed pitched against the need for greater caution). Finally, there is the complex political issue of how political preferences and responses are geographically distributed: at present, there is clearly a stronger European support for precaution, facing a stronger American support for freedom of trading. This may to some extent reflect differing regulatory and consumer cultures, and in particular a more vigorous assertion of certain consumer interests and rights within Europe. Overall, this suggests a very fluid global picture, within which it is difficult to see, at the present, any clear outcome in terms of any prevalence of either producer or consumer interests or rights.

---

46 Statement at Vienna Conference on policies of coexistence of GM crops with traditional and organic crops, 4–6 April 2006.

Intellectual Property and the Supply of Drugs and Medicine

The clash of interests arising in the context of patent protection and the supply of drugs and medicine also illustrates clearly and topically the way in which competing claims to legal entitlement collide in the market place. Once again, the matter may be cast in terms of the right to property and trade versus the right to health. The latter, or more specifically, the right to health care, may be interpreted as requiring access to drugs and medicine at an affordable price. Set against this claim, the exercise of patent protection, by establishing a monopoly which drives up prices, may be seen as a legal device which jeopardises the real enjoyment of a right to adequate health care. On the other hand, the patent protection may also be traced back to a fundamental and desirable value embodied in the protection of property and economic activity: encouragement of the incentive to innovate by providing a fair economic return on the investment and effort required for innovation. Put in more practical terms, effective health care requires the development of new medicine, so that the right to health is itself contingent to some extent on respect for the right to property. On such a view, the respective legal claims are not so much competing but interrelated, and the essential task is one of ordering and weighing priorities within what should be a virtuous loop of welfare provision. However, the politics of the market place tend to cast the issue in terms of a battleground, in this case populated by large transnational pharmaceutical companies and poor and needy citizens in less developed countries.

The legal and political clash is well illustrated by the litigation which ran between 1998 and 2001 in the South African courts, as a kind of global test case on the extent of patent protection and the supply of drugs to deal with the HIV/AIDS pandemic in Africa. The broader legal background to this dispute comprises the resort to compulsory licensing by some States in order to provide affordable medicine. Compulsory licensing is the legal process which enables a government to allow somebody else to produce within that State a patented product or process without the consent of the patent owner. It is permitted by Article 31 of the WTO Agreement on Trade-Related Aspects of Intellectual Property Rights (TRIPS), in force since 1995, provided that certain conditions are met.[47] In its original form, Article 31(f) of TRIPS allowed such licensing only in relation to supply to the domestic market, but not for purposes of export to other 'needy' countries. Compulsory licensing in this way provides some relief for those countries in which many potential purchasers of medicines would not be able to afford the prices resulting from normal patent protection and thus in itself attempts to balance the claims of trading protection and health care provision.

In 1997, in an attempt to deal with the considerable problem of HIV and Aids among its population, the South African Government introduced the Medicine and Related Substances Control Amendment Act, which allowed for compulsory licences and parallel imports. This legislation was challenged in the South African courts as unconstitutional by the Pharmaceutical Manufacturers Association of

---

47 Most importantly, that the person applying for the compulsory licence must first of all have attempted to negotiate a voluntary licence, and that the patent holder is still entitled to receive adequate remuneration, as decided by the State authorising the compulsory licence.

South Africa and almost forty major producers of medicine, in what was effectively a concerted transnational corporate attack on the South African attempt to broaden the legal scope of compulsory licensing.[48] In this legal context, the applicants invoked fundamental rights argument, alleging in particular breaches of Article 25 of the South African constitution (which guarantees the right to property, prohibits the arbitrary deprivation of property and limits expropriation) and Article 44 (on legislative authority, arguing that the legislation was discriminatory in relation to the enjoyment of patent rights in the pharmaceutical field, conflicting with Article 27 of TRIPS and its South African implementing legislation). On the other side of the constitutional debate, Article 27 of the Constitution guaranteed the right to health care. In the event, the claim was unconditionally withdrawn in April 2001, by which time the litigation had become a global public relations disaster for the companies. [49]A large number of NGOs had rallied global public opposition to the claim and many of the companies were clearly happy to negotiate a face-saving accord with the South African Government. A Joint Statement of Understanding between the Republic of South Africa and the Applicants[50] affirmed that all parties to the case agreed that 'the challenges of accelerating access to care and treatment of the diseases that affect the health of the South African population require co-operation and partnership from all stakeholders' and on that basis, the applicant companies recognised the need and legality of the South African legislation, while on its side the Government reiterated its commitment to its international obligations and TRIPS.

There are two important points to note regarding the outcome of this South African litigation, both of which relate to the rhetorical and political impact of such dramatic and high-profile legal argument. The first point concerns the way in which the litigation mobilised broader political debate, resulting not only in an abandonment of the formal proceeding but also in an unforeseen political reverse for corporate interests who had initially exploited considerable legal resources (in a way not dissimilar to the 'McLibel' litigation discussed in Chapter 2 above and Chapter 8 below). One level of engagement was the classic courtroom battleground, but playing the constitutional rights and 'health-care crisis' cards had then led to another kind of engagement, more moral and political in character, on the field of civil society debate. In the latter arena, the political and economic value of reputation counted for more than strict legalities. Murray, for example, points to the significance of good commercial reputation in European public opinion, even though the immediate issue may have been health-care provision in South Africa:

---

48   Case 4183/98, *Pharmaceutical Manufacturers Association of South Africa* v. *Republic of South Africa*. There were many well-known names among the list of coprporate applicants: for instance, Bayer, Bristol-Myers Squibb, Glaxo Wellcome, Hoechst, Hoffman la-Roche, Rhône-Poulenc, Smithkline Beecham and Boehringer-Ingelheim. The case was heard by the High Court of South Africa in Pretoria (Transvaal Provincial Division).

49   Two hundred and sixty thousand concerned citizens and 140 organisations from 130 countries had signed a 'Stop the Case' Petition: Joint Press Release from MSF, Oxfam and TAC (Treatment Action Campaign), 19 April 2001.

50   South African Government, 19 April 2001.

... many pharmaceutical companies are based in Europe. They value their reputation in Europe. With the US and Japan, Europe holds the key to access to essential medicines in developing countries. Public opinion, or consumer opinion, matters more and has more political weight in Europe than in many other parts of the world. The EU has an important influence in developing, implementing and interpreting international trade rules.[51]

Certainly, in the global context, we should remain aware of the different levels and modalities of legal and political engagement.

The second point concerns a more specifically legal outcome. The global rhetoric generated by the litigation in Pretoria had an impact on the WTO agenda, forcing the issue of compulsory licensing and Article 31 of TRIPS on the attention of the fourth WTO Ministerial Conference in Doha in November 2001. There, the question of access to essential medicines for countries which lacked the capacity for their own domestic production and so relied on imports from other States which had made use of compulsory licensing, came to the forefront of discussion. The conference recognised the problem (in paragraph 6 of the Doha Declaration),[52] but could not itself agree on a solution. After a further period of heated debate, agreement among WTO members was finally achieved two years later, when the Agreement on the Implementation of paragraph 6 of the Doha Declaration on the TRIPS Agreement and Public Health was adopted.[53] This measure allowed any developed or less developed countries which lacked the capacity to manufacture their own medicines to import cheaper generic drugs made under compulsory licences elsewhere, effectively providing a waiver in relation to the obligation under Article 31(f) of TRIPS. This waiver mechanism was subsequently embodied in another WTO General Council Decision in December 2005,[54] agreeing on a formal amendment of Article 31 of TRIPS to incorporate the waiver into the treaty itself.

But the story continues. While in one sense the 2003 WTO Agreement and 2005 decision to amend Article 31 signalled a significant shift in the governing legal arrangements at the global level, in another sense this has meant that the site of engagement has shifted from the issue of principle (the application of compulsory licensing to exports as well as domestic production of medicine) to the way in which the waiver of Article 31(f) is being implemented. Indeed, despite the rhetoric at the legislative level, the issue of implementation remains controversial. In the first place, it should be noted that a number of States have opted out of the opportunity to import generic drugs,[55] which not only affects the position of consumers in those countries

---

51   Jim Murray, Director of BEUC (European Consumers Organisation), Address to the conference to mark the Third Annual European Consumers' Day, 15 March 2001.

52   WTO Declaration on the TRIPS Agreement and Public Health, 20 November 2001, WT/MIN (01)/DEC/2.

53   Decision of the General Council, 30 August 2003, WT/L/540.

54   WT/L/64, General Council Decision of 6 December 2005.

55   In 2003, twenty-three developed countries immediately announced that they would not use the system to import drugs; the ten acceding States to the EU in 2003 joined that list. Eleven other WTO members have stated that would only use the system as importers in situations of national emergency or other circumstances of extreme urgency.

but is also argued to have a chilling effect[56] on the willingness of other States to act upon the waiver and import cheaper generic drugs. Secondly, it is also argued strongly that the waiver mechanism is itself complex and dissuasive, and in practice has not been used. The organisation Médecins Sans Frontières (MSF) for example has asserted, in relation to the 2005 decision to amend TRIPS, that:

> ... the decision shows that the WTO is ignoring the day-to-day reality of drug production and procurement. The amendment has made permanent a burdensome drug-by-drug, country-by-country decision-making process, which does not take into account the fact that economies of scale are needed to attract interest from manufacturers of medicines ... The amendment does not allow for the procurement of medicines through international tendering, which is the most common and efficient way of purchasing drugs.[57]

MSF itself has itself sought to test the efficacy of the waiver process by placing its own orders with a generic drug manufacturer, and found the process to be long and resource intensive.[58] There is a clear gap between the upbeat rhetoric emerging from governmental and intergovernmental sources and pragmatic scepticism expressed by civil society sources.[59] At one level, the WTO, EU and various governments may well believe that they are recognising the fundamental right to health care[60] but (as is often the case in rights discourse) practice (that is, implementation and actual take-up of opportunities) may not match the belief in legal provision. Such an outcome may be partly the result of cynical governmental and corporate calculation,[61] or partly

---

56   The argument is based on media presentation of compulsory licensing in countries such as Brazil and South Africa as a form of piracy or theft of property, so effectively intimidating potential compulsory licensing. Conversely, it is argued that instances of developed countries taking action to deal with abuses of the patent system send out an encouraging signal for compulsory licensing elsewhere.

57   See the summary prepared by Michael Palmedo for CPTech (Consumer Project on Technology), *How reporters covered the 6 December 2005 WTO deal* <www.cptech.org./ipwto/p6/wtoreporting-table.html>.

58   Ibid.

59   Ibid. Palmedo's table compares directly the reported statements of the WTO, governments and NGOs.

60   Thus, WTO General Council Chairperson Amina Mohamed informed Intellectual Property Watch that although the waiver had not been used by any country, it had 'delivered': she argued that the success of a WTO regulation could not be judged by the frequency of its use, since the fact that the system is in place could provide comfort; moreover it had worked to lower prices for medicines for diseases such as HIV/AIDS (Palmedo, note 57 above). Such arguments clearly require further social scientific testing. But penetration of the subject remains very complex. For instance, account should be taken of the fact that until 2005 it had been possible to import cheap medicines from India, which only then introduced patents for pharmaceuticals; arguably, that may have reduced the need to resort to the waiver.

61   After all, governments, IGOs and corporate actors are likely to be well aware of the economic and political complexities of the operation of the patent system. Corporate actors also seek the higher moral ground. Between 1999 and 2002, the pharmaceutical industry contributed $1.9 billion to the global campaign against poverty and disease (Jean Jacques Bertrand, Chairman of Aventis Pasteur, at a forum conference, 'Global Healthcare and Development, Brussels, 4 June 2002). But how does this compare with the level of profit? At

due to a failure to think through practicalities. It is not easy to disentangle these two possible causes, and this also raises the question of whether the problem is as much a matter of finding adequate resources and infrastructure for a meaningful right to health as curbing rapacious claims to the right of property and free trading. Or, to put the matter more abstractly, when should the emphasis shift from promoting one right to restricting another right?

The Resolution of Investment Disputes: The Corporate Right to Roam

In the global context of international trade, 'investment' means 'foreign direct investment' (FDI), which in turn means the freedom of large transnational companies to establish and develop their business in other (which means, increasingly, 'developing') countries. In legal, political and economic terms, the battleground of the debate on foreign investment is one on which large corporate actors and the governments of some developed countries are ranged against the governments of developing countries and NGOs concerned about environmental protection, labour standards, and the political and economic independence of regions and less powerful countries. In 1997, a *Friends of the Earth Fact Sheet* summed up the argument in these terms:

> Proponents of free trade and globalization have turned their sights to the next target for liberalization and deregulation – foreign investment. Recognizing that foreign investment has become the main force behind economic integration, multinational corporations and industrialized countries are advocating a Multilateral Agreement on Investment (MAI). The MAI – which is being negotiated at the Organization for Economic Cooperation and Development (OECD) – would 'open' all sectors of countries' economies, strip nations and localities of their right to differentiate between local and foreign companies, and let corporations directly challenge our[62] laws.[63]

At present, the subject remains internationally regulated by a large number of bilateral treaties (BITS),[64] so that a multilateral treaty would not only provide, in a functional sense, a tidier overall regime at the international level, but, depending on its content, would serve to generalise certain values and policies, by incorporating the latter into a powerful international regime such as those now contained in WTO multilateral treaties such as TRIPS. It is this potential for an international regime favouring certain interests and policies and capable of overriding national and local interests which has provoked concern about and resistance to the MAI project.[65] In terms of legal

---

the same time, companies engage in other tricks: Bristol-Myers Squibb was subject to legal action in several US jurisdictions for abusing its patent powers in order to delay production of the generic from of the drug Taxol (see FTC Press Release, 7 March 2003 <www.ftc .gov>; claims were brought against the company in thirty-two US State jurisdictions in 2002).

    62   That is, national.

    63   *Fact Sheet*, Friends of the Earth US, 19 February 1997.

    64   The number of BITS has increased rapidly, for instance from 385 in 1989 to 2181 in 2002.

    65   The first draft of a multilateral investment agreement was drawn up by the International Chamber of Commerce and intended for the Uruguay Round of the GATT.

rights, the thrust of the proposed MAI has been the protection of foreign investor rights to equal treatment with local enterprise, and to undertake legal challenge of restrictive national legislation (for instance, concerning environmental protection or labour conditions). The underlying principles of the MAI may be summarised as non-discrimination between foreign investors and local companies, the removal of entry conditions for foreign investors, and the removal of 'performance requirements' for foreign investors. On the other side, such local and national interests find their legal expression in the form of rights relating to the protection of the environment, labour, cultural diversity and economic self-determination. In this context, it is therefore only partly a matter of conflicting supplier and consumer interests – there is a wider field of conflict also involving the interests of workers, other (smaller and more local) producers and enterprises, and civil society more generally. The subject also raises the question of global democratic governance and participation in the formulation of policy and law at the international level. Much of the controversy concerning the MAI project has related to the site of its discussion, with objection being mounted successively against the 'closed club' negotiations within the OECD and WTO, and argument in favour of a more open and widely participative debate within UN fora. In short, the objection to the MAI has centred on the perception that it has been dominated by the interests of a small number of large transnational corporations[66] and threatens the interests of vulnerable developing countries and civil society generally.

There is at the present time scope for judicial resolution of such investment issues, principally at the national level, and occasionally at a regional supranational level (for instance, within NAFTA[67]), bearing in mind that such judicial resolution is frequently carried out according to the terms of bilateral investment-protection treaties. Such judicial resolution thus comprises a major site for the playing-out of argument concerning competing rights. The appearance of a MAI would affect the substantive content of such judicial resolution, and in a WTO context would shift some of the debate to the level of WTO dispute resolution. The fact that this has not yet happened, after two major attempts to bring about a MAI infrastructure, is part of the ongoing narrative of contest between the conflicting interests referred to above. The failure of the attempts to establish a MAI, first under the auspices of the OECD between 1995 and 1998, and then at the WTO Ministerial meeting at Cancun in 2003, is therefore instructive.

The collapse of the largely secret OECD negotiations for a MAI became evident early in 1998, following mounting critical pressure from a large number of NGOs and a number of governments beginning to waver in response to the mounting public concern. An illustrative expression of this concern was the adoption by the European Parliament of a resolution in March 1998, with a large vote against

---

66   For instance, the estimate that the hundred largest multinational companies control more than half of FDI.

67   For an example of such dispute resolution under NAFTA, see the final award of the NAFTA Chapter Eleven Tribunal in *GAMI Investments Inc* v. *Government of the United Mexican States*, November 15 2004.

the MAI being negotiated at the OECD in its existing form.[68] The Parliament set out thirty-seven conditions for the adoption of a MAI and in particular expressed its concern regarding the imbalance between the position of large companies and governments wishing to legislate in favour of national interests,[69] and the level of democratic control over the negotiation and outcome of the MAI. Following the demise of the OECD negotiations in 1998, the EU and Japan promoted an attempt to negotiate a WTO agreement, and this was strongly endorsed at the WTO Ministerial meeting at Doha in 2001. A decision was adopted at Doha, stating that there was a 'case for a framework to secure transparent, stable and predictable conditions for long-term cross-border investment, particularly FDI, that will contribute to the expansion of trade'.[70] The Ministerial meeting at Cancun in September 2003 then became the focus of the effort to establish a WTO investment agreement and there was vigorous debate on the issue preceding the conference. Illustrative of this phase of the debate was the joint NGO report,[71] issued in June 2003, by Friends of the Earth International and the World Development Movement, which addressed the thirteen main arguments put forward by the EU in support of a WTO agreement. The report advocated an alternative strategy in the form of UN rules on the conduct of FDI in developing countries, so as to ensure the promotion of indigenous policies on sustainable development, poverty and environmental protection. For example, it argued that:

> Principles for a fair agreement on investment have been developed by a United Nations expert working group. These could form the basis of a set of core principles and an eventual agreement on international investment. These criteria for the development friendliness of investment frameworks emphasise the role of rule-based systems in allowing the discrimination of investment according to its 'quality', particularly the contribution that it

---

68   Resolution containing the Parliament's recommendations to the Commission on negotiations within the framework of the OECD on a multilateral agreement on investment, 11 March 1998, OJ 1998, C 104.

69   For example, see the view of MEP and rapporteur Dorfler, who was concerned about new environmental standards being compromised, the loss of any real sovereignty on the part of States to safeguard national and civil society interests, and the arbitration structure foreseen by the MAI, which would allow companies to challenge State activity, but not the contrary. See also the European Parliament Resolution on European standards for European enterprises operating in developing countries, 15 January 1999, OJ 1999, C104/180.

70   For many countries, however, the commitment to work for a MAI was seen as being extracted by force. According to Ambassador Chidyausiku of Zimbabwe, the developed countries 'said that if you don't agree to the inclusion of new issues, you don't get the TRIPS and Health Declaration and the ACP waiver. The other source of pressure was that no minister was prepared to be blamed for the failure of Doha, or standing in the way of fighting terrorism. There was so much pressure during the negotiations …' (A. Kwa, *Power Politics in the WTO*, 2002 (Focus on the Global South)).

71   Friends of the Earth International and the World Development Movement (2003), Briefing Paper: *Busting the Myths*, June.

makes to development aims. The criteria also call for a balance between the rights and the responsibilities of both government and investors.[72]

This approach thus shifts the emphasis from the protection of investor company rights to the imposition of investor company obligations.[73] The fact that such arguments contributed to the failure to agree[74] on a WTO agreement at the Cancun conference indicates the force of 'life protection' and democratic legitimacy arguments in this context. This at least suggests some balance (or, it may be said, stalemate) as between the competing arguments, but it is significant that the MAI project, which was widely perceived as tilting the balance one way, appears for the present to have fallen from the global legal agenda.[75] Thus the important site for debate and specific legal argument remains for the most part at the national judicial level within the framework of the large number of bilateral treaties on investment protection.

Differences Between the EU and Global Contexts

It is clear that the differing global (international) and European legal infrastructures, processes and methods affect the way in which argument, and consequently rights discourse, may be employed in the market place context. At the global level, despite the emergent legal regime of the WTO, there are elements of political and legal infrastructure lacking, compared to what may be observed within the order of the EU. First, the EU is based upon a unified legal system (despite its complex relationship with the legal orders of the Member States), which comprises a single policy and law-making process and a compulsory jurisdiction. The EU order possesses (despite its critics on this point) a clear measure of democratic legitimacy and indeed prides itself on its involvement of non-State actors in its law-making and other legal processes. Finally, the European system has increasingly taken on board a rights discourse, which has been embedded in the more long-standing culture of the European Human Rights Convention. The outcome is a system in which the interplay of market interests readily finds expression in the vocabulary and argumentation of basic rights, whether that entitlement is being claimed by large corporate actors or individual citizen-consumers.

In contrast, in terms of formal legal structure and process, the global context is one of international law and the formal interplay is still largely intergovernmental. The

---

72   Ibid., at 25. The UN expert working group is the UNCTAD Commission on Investment, Technology and Related Financial Issues; see its report, *Criteria for the development friendliness of investment frameworks*, UNCTAD, October 1997.

73   See also the EP Resolution on standards for European enterprises, note 69 above.

74   India was a significant critic of the planned agreement; its permanent representative to the WTO, Ambassador Chandrasekhar urged that no convincing arguments for multilateral investment rules had yet been put forward.

75   Also of note is the view of the World Bank: 'an international agreement that seeks to substantially increase investment flows by increasing investor protections seems destined, on the basis of available evidence, to fall short of expectations' (Friends of the Earth International/World Development Movement (2003), 'Investment and the WTO: Busting the Myths', June).

main actors with legal *locus standi* are governments and international organisations, who often act as the proxy for individual players, whether corporate or human. The interests of individual actors, with their various market place roles, provide an important well-spring for legal activity, but the position of the individual players remains shadowy when much of that legal action occurs. Thus, the manoeuvring of large corporations and public interest NGOs in the corridors of power is as significant, if not more so, than formal courtroom contests. This is not to say that rights argument has little value in the global context; rather, its use and impact are less transparent and perhaps more subtle. Partly for that reason, it appears less easy to play a rights trump card – such a move is not appropriate when the rules of the game do not include a single constitutional structure, a generally applicable bill of rights, or a court of compulsory jurisdiction with power to rule finally on the question within that order. At the present stage of global legal development, the trump card takes more the form of an appeal to legitimacy, underpinned by the economic and market place value of good reputation. Appeals to fundamental rights take place, but given the kind of legal structure and process described above, they serve to inform rather than determine outcomes.

There is evidence, however, that human rights arguments may prove forceful and influential at the global level, especially via the increasingly playable legitimacy trump card. From the survey carried out above, it appears that argument based upon citizen-consumer and civil society interests may moderate or block the apparently well-resourced claims of large corporate actors and governments committed to expansive trading. In such a context, stalemate may not be a bad outcome for individuals, and public interest groups are well able to fire warning shots in the direction of corporate ranks. Two examples may be provided of how such shots may be fired, one of which is directly international, and the other more indirectly so.

First, in 1998, at the time of the MAI negotiation within the OECD, the UN's Commission on Human Rights' Sub-Commission on the Prevention of Discrimination and Protection of Minorities took up the cause of human rights in the global market place and adopted a resolution on human rights as the *primary* objective of trade, investment and financial policy.[76] The Sub-Commission was concerned about

> … the possible human rights implications of the Multilateral Agreement on Investment, and particularly about the extent to which the Agreement might limit the capacity of States to take proactive steps to ensure the enjoyment of economic, social and cultural rights by all people, and in the process creating benefits for a small privileged minority at the expense of an increasingly disenfranchised majority.[77]

The Sub-Commission's concerns on this particular issue thus served to shift the debate on economic interests and rights into the wider fields of both political and

---

76   Sub-Commission on the Prevention of Discrimination and the Protection of Minorities, 50th Session, Agenda item 4 (a), Resolution of 20 August 1998: *The Realization of Economic, Social and Cultural Rights – The International Economic Order and the Protection of Human Rights – Human Rights as the Primary Objective of Trade, Investment and Financial Policy* (adopted by consensus).

77   Recital (8) of the Resolution.

moral legitimacy and also of large-scale discrimination. The Sub-Commission's resolution, which is addressed to UN agencies such as the IMF and the World Bank, and organisations such as the OECD, as well as governments, emphasises in a number of ways the primacy of human rights norms and standards and how the latter may better inform international trading policy and activity. While such a resolution formally constitutes 'soft law', it aspires to trump-card status and does provide ammunition for NGOs, and to sympathetic IGOs and governments, in their deployment of political and legal argument. Moreover, it should be remembered that the proposal for a MAI did indeed fail, not only within the OECD in 1998, but also within the framework of the WTO in 2003.

Secondly, but more indirectly and prospectively, there is the possibility that rights arguments may be employed to hinder or prevent governmental adoption or commitment to international trading instruments which are cast as violating rights. For instance, the ratification of WTO agreements may be affected in this way. As Petersmann has argued, 'Human rights law offers WTO rules moral, constitutional, and democratic legitimacy that may be more important for the parliamentary ratification of future WTO agreements than the traditional economic or utilitarian justifications.'[78]

Alternatively, governments might find their support for allegedly rights-violating international instruments subject to legal assault under their own law or under regional human rights protection systems such as that of the European Human Rights Convention.[79] While a WTO instrument might not yet be subject to attack directly under international law for violating basic rights, State members of the WTO may be more locally challenged for their participation in the adoption and implementation of such an instrument. Such indirect potential routes of legal challenge raise, of course, the prospect of colliding legal orders, but none the less suggest a means for bringing the issue of rights protection closer and more sharply to the centre of the stage of global legal argument.

---

78   Ernst-Ulrich Petersmann, 'Constitutionalism and WTO law: From a state-centred approach to a human rights approach in international economic law', Ch. 2 in Daniel L.M. Kennedy and James D. Southwick (eds) (2002), *The Political Economy of International Trade Law* (Cambridge: Cambridge University Press), at 67.

79   For instance, consider the way in which the UK was successfully challenged under the First Protocol to the European Human Rights Convention, for its participation in an EU Council decision to disenfranchise the voters in Gibraltar from participating in European elections: *Matthews* v. *UK,* judgment of the Court of Human Rights, 18 February 1999, 28 *EHRR* 361.

Chapter 8

Freedom of Expression
in the Market Place

Lone Consumer Warriors

Consumer warriors – maybe they are the modern Robin Hoods, robbing the rich to feed the poor, fighting injustice; maybe they are the outlaws of the twentieth and twenty-first centuries who take on the modern tyrants: multinational companies like the McDonald's and the Nikes of this world. But then again, maybe not.

The McLibel saga[1] finally came to a close in 2005, after almost twenty years, with the verdict of the European Court of Human Rights in favour of the consumer activists, Dave Morris and Helen Steel. It will be recalled that Morris and Steel had since the mid-1980s campaigned against McDonald's, distributing leaflets in which they attacked many aspects of McDonald's business practices and products. McDonald's sued them in 1990 for libel. Seven years, 313 hearing days and 400,000 pages of documentary evidence later, Justice Bell of the High Court found that Steel and Morris – who had represented themselves as legal aid is not available for defamation actions – had not been able to prove the truth of most of their allegations and ordered them to pay McDonald's £60,000 in damages.[2] McDonald's had won in law, if not in popularity.[3] But then Morris and Steel enjoyed a legal victory of sorts: the European Court of Human Rights held that the UK had breached Morris and Steel's human rights to a fair trial and to freedom of expression by failing to provide them with legal aid to fight their cause.

Across the Atlantic, Nike had to fight a similar battle, although in this instance it was at the receiving end of the litigation. Nike had decided to respond to a wave of damaging television and newspaper reports from the mid-1990s about its labour

---

1 For background information, see <http://www.mcspotlight.org/case/index.html>; see also discussion in Chapter 4 above.

2 For key judgments of the 'McLibel' case see: *McDonald's Corp. & Anor* v. *Steel & Morris* [1997] EWHC QB 366 (Bell J, 19 June 1997) (finding that the truth of most of the allegations made by Steel and Morris were not proven); *Steel* v. *McDonald's Corp. & Anor* [1999] EWCA Civ 1144 (31 March 1999) (allowing part of the appeal: reduction of damages from £60,000 to £40,000); European Court of Human Rights: *Steel and Morris* v. *the United Kingdom* [2005] ECHR 103 (15 February 2005); 41 (2005) *EHRR* 403 (finding that the UK had breached Steel and Morris's right to a fair trial and freedom of speech).

3 For background literature: Marlene Arnold Nicholson (2000), 'McLibel: A Case Study in English Defamation Law', *Wisconsin International Law Journal*, 18:102; Adam Nash and Giles Crown (2005), 'McLibel: the Last Supper for denying legal aid?', *New Law Journal*, 316.

practices in its Third World factories with a full-blown PR campaign.[4] To Marc Kasky, a Californian corporate vigilante, the company presented too rosy a picture and so, in 1998, he availed himself of a statute which allows private citizens to bring a prosecution against a business for false and misleading advertising. In 2002, the Californian Supreme Court held that Nike's speech, although not advertising in the strict sense, was still commercial speech, and thus it could be challenged under the local legislation if it was not truthful. The consumer lobby, spearheaded by Kasky, had won this round.

These are 'speech' cases.[5] In McLibel, it was the consumer's speech about a corporation that was at issue. *Nike* concerned a corporation's speech to its consumers and investors, who are consumers of sorts.[6] Both cases concerned the consumer-corporation relationship and their battle of words. Mere words and yet, the stakes are high. Companies invest millions each year on branding, image creation, on choosing the right words and pictures to compel consumers to view their products in the most favourable light possible. Accusations of bending reality, being economical with the truth, or outright lying can have devastating repercussions not just for the company's profits and thus its shareholders, but its employees and the community at large. At the same time, being seduced by a company's projected image does not simply entail choosing its products, but also implicitly condoning its business practices – its sale techniques, its labour practices, its environmental and human rights record.[7] In short, mere words make and break our economic powerhouses and affect society far beyond the narrow sales or even wider commercial context.

The courts in the above cases were faced with the difficult task of determining the legitimate limits of company and consumer speech *vis-à-vis* each other. Companies or businesses more generally 'speak' in a variety of ways. They speak when they file information with government departments, when they communicate with their investors, suppliers, or employees and sometimes they speak, rather more quietly, with their competitors. Whatever relationships companies entertain, these relationships require, and are defined by, communications. Their primary relationship is with their customers, often consumers, and it is those communications that are under the microscope in this chapter. What are the rules of the game? Ought both sides be equally committed to the truth? Should their speech be measured with the same yardstick? And to what extent should practical considerations inform normative expectations? McDonald's won the libel case, not because its business practices were beyond reproach or because Morris and Steel were necessarily

---

4   *Kasky* v. *Nike Inc* 27 Cal 4th 939, 946f (2002). The case went to the Supreme Court which decided that leave to appeal had been improvidently granted: *Nike Inc* v. *Kasky* 539 US 654 (2003).

5   The phrases 'free speech' (US) and 'freedom of expression' (Europe) are here used interchangeably.

6   For a discussion on the spectrum of market players, see Chapter 1 above.

7   There is now a vast amount of academic and popular literature on corporate social responsibility or, more accurately, its absence: Joel Bakan (2004), *The Corporation* (London: Constable); Ike Okonta and Oronto Douglas (2003), *Where Vultures Feast* (London: Verso), Janet Dine (2005), *Companies, International Trade and Human Rights* (Cambridge: Cambridge University Press).

lying, but because Morris and Steel's task of proving the truth of their allegations was an onerous one indeed, requiring extensive resources far beyond their means. This chapter explores how even-handedly the law deals with consumer speech and corporate speech, in particular, the speech by large companies, often transnational companies (TNCs). How does the human right to freedom of expression reflect and affect their relationship? Does the law strike the right balance between the legitimate commercial interests of companies and the legitimate commercial and other interests of consumers? The discussion compares the UK approach as informed by the European Convention of Human Rights, with that taken in the US based on the First Amendment to the US Constitution.

The Company's Freedom of Expression

The following examines the protection accorded to, and restrictions imposed on, corporate speech – via the 'commercial speech' concept – with particular focus on the equality or inequality it creates in relation to consumer speech and its repercussions.

Higher Expectations in Relation to 'Commercial Speech'

Most market economies have extensive rules on advertising,[8] principally prohibiting any false or misleading marketing practices,[9] but also at times banning certain advertisements considered harmful altogether.[10] Such regulation recognises that unbridled *laisser-faire* economic policy does not sufficiently protect the consumer's economic and other interests, such as health and safety, and undermines fair competition as well as general confidence in the market. In human rights terms, this State interference has been justified on the basis that greater governmental inroads into commercial than non-commercial speech are permissible (to protect human rights such as the right to life and the right to health[11]), rather than on the principally legitimate basis that 'commercial speech' is not a protected human right – a matter which will not be raised below.[12]

8　For example, EU: Articles 6 and 7 of the Unfair Commercial Practices Directive 2005/29/EC; Australia: Part v. of the Trade Practices Act (1974) (Cth); US: Fair Packaging and Labelling Act, 80 Stat. 1296, 15 USC §§1451–61.

9　Lying *per se* is not normally prohibited but only when linked with an intention to gain financially or to cause financial loss to another; see, for example, s.2 of the UK Fraud Act 2006 ('fraud by false representation').

10　An obvious candidate would be tobacco advertisements. For its rocky legislative history in the UK, Canada and the US see David Feldman (2002), *Civil Liberties and Human Rights in England and Wales* (Oxford: Oxford University Press, 2nd edn), at 829ff.

11　See the discussion in Chapter 3 above.

12　See Chapter 2 for a critique of corporate human rights. Marius Emberland (2006), *The Human Rights of Companies* (Oxford: Oxford University Press), at 119ff, on how uncomfortable 'commercial speech' fits into the classic rationales for the human right to free speech, that is, democracy, self-fulfilment and pursuit of truth.

In the US, commercial speech is a category of protected speech under the First Amendment to the US Constitution.[13] However in contrast to non-commercial speech, commercial speech is never protected if false or misleading and thus can be prohibited.[14] But even truthful commercial speech may be restricted more than non-commercial speech. Such governmental restrictions have to withstand only 'intermediate judicial scrutiny' rather than 'strict judicial scrutiny' applicable to non-commercial speech.[15] That 'intermediate judicial scrutiny' involves an assessment whether there is a substantial governmental interest in curbing the speech, and then whether the restrictions imposed advance that interest and are no more than necessary.[16]

The same categorisation of commercial versus non-commercial speech has also been adopted in Europe,[17] and again commercial speech is given protection under Article 10 of the European Convention of Human Rights,[18] but again less than non-commercial speech. The European Court of Human Rights (ECtHR) has held that

---

See also Eric Barendt (2005), *Freedom of Speech* (Oxford: Oxford Univeristy Press, 2nd edn), at 399ff.

13   It is protected under the First Amendment to the US Constitution (*Virginia Bd of Pharmacy* v. *Virginia Citizens Consumer Council Inc.* 425 US 748, 770 (1976)) on the basis that consumers can best look after themselves in the market if they are well informed about the products and services. This makes the unwarranted assumption that advertisements are informative. Robert L. Kerr (2005), 'Subordinating the Economic to the Political: the Evolution of the Corporate Speech Doctrine' 10 *Communication Law and Policy*, 10:63; Elizabeth Blanks Hindman (2004), 'The Chickens Have Come Home to Roost: Individualism, Collectivism and Conflict in Commercial Speech Doctrine', *Communication Law and Policy*, 9:237; on the Canadian approach see: Karla K. Gower (2005), 'Looking Northward: Canada's Approach to Commercial Expression', *Communication Law and Policy*, 10:29.

14   *Central Hudson Gas & Elec. Corp.* v. *Public Serv. Communication of New York* 447 US 557, 563 (1980); *Kasky* v. *Nike Inc* 27 Cal 4th 939, 45 P 3d 243, 247 (2002).

15   *Central Hudson Gas & Elec. Corp.* v. *Public Serv. Communication of New York* 447 US 557, 566 (1980). A critical difference is that under the intermediate scrutiny test, the government need not adopt the least restrictive means, but merely one 'reasonably fit' to achieve the government's purpose: *Board of Trustees, Sate University of New York* v. *Fox* (1989) 492 US 469, 480.

16   *Central Hudson Gas & Elec. Corp.* v. *Public Serv. Communication of New York* 447 US 557, 565f (1980); refined in *Board of Trustees of State University of New York (SUNY)* v. *Fox* 492 US 469, 479 (1989).

17   Note that the Human Rights Court does not prima facie for speech protection entitlement distinguish between different forms of expression, see *Müller* v. *Switzerland* [1988] 13 *EHRR* 212, para. 27. Creating different categories for speech is by no means universally accepted, see, for example, Maya Hertig Randall (2006), 'Commercial Speech under the European Convention on Human Rights: Subordinate or Equal?', *Human Rights Law Review*, 6:53, 54f; or judgment by Justice Stevens in *Rubin* v. *Coors Brewing Co* 514 US 476, 491ff (1995). For other discussion of the 'commercial speech' doctrine particularly in Europe see Colin R. Munro (2003), 'The Value of Commercial Speech', *Cambridge Law Journal*, 62:134; Emberland, note 12 above, at 117ff; Alan J. Dingham and David Allen (2000), *Company Law and the Human Rights Act 1998* (London: Butterworths), Chapter 11.

18   *The Church of Scientology and Another* v. *Sweden* [1979] ECC 511; *Markt Intern Verlag und Klaus Beerman* v. *Germany* [1989] ECHR 21, paras 25, 26.

States have 'a wide margin of appreciation' in the case of commercial speech – in contrast to a much smaller margin when 'what is at stake is not a given individual's purely "commercial" interests, but his participation in a debate affecting the general interest'[19] or political debate.[20] Giving States more leeway means that they can impose greater restrictions on commercial speech than 'political' or broadly 'general interest' speech. Comparable to the US, this has meant that States can forbid untruthful commercial speech and limit truthful speech where that would be 'necessary in a democratic society'.[21] As it is, once speech has been categorised as commercial, the ECtHR has not scrutinised the governmental restriction beyond its reasonableness.[22] This freedom given to States in respect of commercial speech would by itself not be problematic, if 'commercial speech' was narrowly defined. But, as shown below, it is not and includes much speech beyond its core (that is, advertising).

For the moment though, what is significant is that 'commercial speech' is singled out for special treatment both in the US and Europe, being ranked as a lower form of expression than political or general interest speech. As these restrictions are first and foremost directed at the promotional speech by companies, this would seem to create an unequal speech field for consumers and companies – giving consumers greater speech freedoms. This matter was addressed by Justice Breyer of the US Supreme Court in his dissent in *Nike Inc.* v. *Kasky*.[23] He expressed concern that the insistence on truthfulness of commercial speech – regardless of intent and regardless of whether it was pure commercial speech or not – not only has a chilling effect on desirable public discussion (in this case, on the labour practices of TNCs in the Third World),[24] but gave rise to an unfair speech inequality between companies and consumers. This inequality is compounded where consumers are entitled to instigate private prosecutions:

> The delegation of state authority to private individuals authorises a purely ideological plaintiff, convinced that his opponent is not telling the truth, to bring into the courtroom the kind of political battle better waged in other forums. Where that political battle is hard fought, such plaintiffs potentially constitute a large and hostile crowd freely able to bring prosecutions designed to vindicate their beliefs, and to do so unencumbered by the legal and practical checks that tend to keep the energies of public enforcement agencies

---

19   *Vgt Verein Gegen Tierfabriken* v. *Switzerland* [2001] ECHR 412, para. 71, citing *Hertel* v. *Switzerland* (1998) 28 EHRR 534.

20   *Vgt Verein Gegen Tierfabriken* v. *Switzerland* [2001] ECHR 412, para. 66.

21   See note 10 above. See also *Casado Coca* v. *Spain* (1994) 18 *EHRR* 81, discussed in Randall, note 17 above, 61ff, and for a US example, *Rubin* v. *Coors Brewing* Co 514 US 476 (1995).

22   Randall, note 17 above, at 62, 74f. *Karner (Free movement of goods)* [2004] EUECJ C-71/02 (25 March 2004), para. 51: 'When the exercise of the freedom does not contribute to a discussion of public interest … review is limited to examination of the reasonableness and proportionality of the interference.' This refusal to interfere is illustrated, for example, by *Casado* v. *Spain* (1994) 18 *EHRR* 1, where the speech in question concerned the prohibition of factual advertising of the applicant's name, qualification as a lawyer and contact details, but was still upheld by the Human Rights court.

23   539 US 654 (2003).

24   *Nike Inc* v. *Kasky* 539 US 654, 676 (2003).

focused upon more purely economic harm ... That threat means that a commercial speaker must take particular care – considerably more care than the speaker's non-commercial opponents – when speaking on public matters ... the commercial speaker engaging in public debate suffers a handicap that non-commercial opponents do not.[25]

Justice Breyer went on to argue that governmental restrictions on speech by trading companies should be subject to stricter judicial scrutiny than currently afforded; companies ought at least in limited circumstances be given First Amendment protection for negligently made false statement. So rather than levelling the field by requiring consumer speech to be truthful, company speech ought to be judged less harshly when it contributes to a public debate and the false statement was honestly but negligently made.[26]

Whether there is indeed an *unfair* inequality between company and consumer speech depends, first, on the definition of commercial speech and to what extent it includes consumer speech, and, secondly, on the rationale for such inequality.

'Commercial Speech': Advertisements?

In Europe as well as in the US, commercial advertising – that is, speech designed to promote sales – forms the heart of the 'commercial speech' concept.[27] Controversial is whether there can be commercial speech without the sales motivation and whether its existence always turns speech into commercial speech? In other words, is commercial advertising a sufficient and necessary element of commercial speech?

In the US, *Kasky* v. *Nike Inc.*[28] illustrates that speech designed to promote sales is commercial speech even if it raises issues of political or general interest. Such accompanying interests do not transform its essential commercial character. The Californian Supreme Court held that Nike's attempt to refute allegation of its involvement in disreputable labour practices abroad was not political speech, as Nike had tried to make out. The court assessed the three accepted commercial indicators,[29] that is, the speaker, the intended audience and the content of the message:

In typical commercial speech cases, the speaker is likely to be someone engaged in commerce – that is, generally, the production, distribution, or sale of goods or services ... [Furthermore it is] directed to an audience of persons who may be influenced by that speech to engage in a commercial transaction with the speaker or the person ... Finally, the factual content of the message should be commercial in character ... this typically

---

25   *Nike Inc* v. *Kasky* 539 US 654, 679f (2003).

26   *Nike Inc* v. *Kasky* 539 US 654, 676 (2003).

27   *Kasky* v. *Nike Inc.* 27 Cal 4th 939, 960f (2002), see text accompanying note 30 below. *Vgt Verein Gegen Tierfabriken* v. *Switzerland* [2001] ECHR 412, para. 57: speech for the purpose of 'inciting the public to purchase a particular product'.

28   27 Cal 4th 939 (2002). For a contextual discussion of see Bakan, note 7 above, Ch. 6.

29   *Central Hudson Gas & Elec. Corp.* v. *Public Serv. Communication of New York* 447 US 557, 562 (1980): 'speech proposing a commercial transaction'.

means that the speech consists of representations of fact about the business operations, products, or services of the speaker ... *made for the purpose of promoting sales* ... .[30]

Nike's attempt to set the record straight on its labour practices was still commercial speech (and thus legitimately subject to the strict truth requirement under the unfair competition statute) because it was speech from a commercial speaker about Nike's business operations and directed at a commercial audience for the purposes of promoting sales.[31] The fact that it formed part of a wider public debate on the issue of Third World labour did not transform its essential character from commercial to political or general interest speech.[32] Generally, the requirement that the message must be 'for the purpose of promoting sales' would seem to subsume the other requirements: such messages tend to come from a business or an institution with some business operations and are necessarily directed at potential customers.[33] The latter two criteria are helpful in cases, such as *Nike*, where the communications are not overtly adverts and do not directly propose an economic transaction.[34]

Similarly, in Europe if the message is designed to promote sales, then no other context or subtext can detract from its core commercial character. In *The Church of Scientology and others* v. *Sweden*,[35] the 'religious' nature of the speaker did not turn adverts for the sale of e-meters (measuring one's purification from sins after confession[36]) by the Church of Scientology into general interest speech – unlike statements about a faith or expressing a religious conviction.[37] This was in essence commercial speech and thus Sweden could restrain it under the local 'misleading advertisement' offence. However, the purpose of wanting to promote sales must be the dominant one. That was not the case in *Barthold* v. *Germany*,[38] where, in an interview with a newspaper, a veterinarian criticised the lack of all-night veterinary

---

30   *Kasky* v. *Nike Inc* 27 Cal 4th 939, 960f (2002) [emphasis added, existing emphasis omitted].

31   *Kasky* v. *Nike Inc* 27 Cal 4th 939, 946 (2002).

32   *Kasky* v. *Nike Inc* 27 Cal 4th 939, 964 (2002) and 968f: 'An advertisement to the public that cherries were picked by union workers is commercial speech if the speaker has a financial or commercial interest in the sale of the cherries and if the information that the cherries had been picked by union workers is likely to influence consumers to buy the speaker's cherries. Speech is commercial in its content if it is likely to influence consumers in their commercial decisions. For a significant segment of the buying public, labor practices do matter in making consumer choices.'

33   The commercial character becomes more ambiguous where the advertisement comes from a public institution such as a school or a university.

34   *Kasky* v. *Nike Inc.* 27 Cal 4th 939, 968 (2002) where the Court rejected that 'that commercial speech must have as its only purpose the advancement of an economic transaction'.

35   [1979] ECC 511.

36   Quality assessment knows no boundaries.

37   *The Church of Scientology and Another* v. *Sweden* [1979] ECC 511, where the Commission distinguished 'between advertisements by a religious group which are informational or descriptive in character and those which offer objects for sale and so are commercial'.

38   (1985) 7 *EHRR* 383.

facilities and in the process of doing so incidentally promoted his own facilities. The topic of the article was of general interest and the advertising effect of some of the statements made was secondary. Thus the speech was not commercial.

While both Europe and the US agree that an overt or covert sales motive gives communications a commercial essence, the jurisprudence diverges on the question of whether there can be commercial speech without such motive. In the US, such motive seems to be essential.[39] Certainly, consumers' critical statements have been treated as non-commercial speech.[40] In Europe, there are also some cases which go along the same track. In *Vgt Verein Gegen Tierfabriken* v. *Switzerland*,[41] the ECtHR held that promotions by the meat industry fell within the regular commercial context, while anti-meat commercials by animal welfare groups 'reflected controversial opinions pertaining to modern society in general and also lying at the heart of various political debates'.[42] Just because the subject-matter and the intended audience of the latter advertisements were commercial in the general sense did not mean that the message was 'commercial' in the legal sense. The anti-meat commercials were not designed to increase sales (quite the opposite) or directly or indirectly promote any business activity of the speaker. The same rationale could be applied to the holding in *Hertel* v. *Switzerland*,[43] where the speech in question was again not motivated by the bottom line. Hertel, a scientist, had allowed his research findings to be published in a lay magazine in a sensationalist style. His main claim was that microwaves were unsafe – a claim which he could not prove. The manufacturers' association persuaded a Swiss court to grant an injunction – based on unfair competition law – on the basis that the publication was intended to 'influence the market' and thereby likely to affect competition. The ECtHR characterised the speech as non-commercial and thus worthy of greater protection: 'what is at stake is not a given individual's 'purely "commercial" statements but his participation in a debate affecting the general interest, for example, over public health.'[44] The speech was not inspired by any sales motive. Indeed, even its characterisation under domestic law as *unfair competition* seemed strained: Hertel was *not competing* with the manufacturers.[45]

---

39   *Kasky* v. *Nike Inc.* 27 Cal 4th 939, 969 (2002): 'we conclude that when a corporation, to maintain and increase its sales and profit, makes public statements defending its labor practices ... those public statements are commercial speech.'

40   *Bose Corp.* v. *Consumer Union of US Inc.* 466 US 485, 513 (1984) (on false disparaging statements in a consumer magazine's review of hi-fi speakers). Justice Stevens of the US Supreme Court noted in *Rubin* v. *Coors Brewing Co.* 514 US 476, 494 (1995) that the same content presented by a consumer organisation would no longer be considered 'commercial'.

41   [2001] *EHRR* 412. See also s.321(3)(g) of the UK Communications Act 2003 which, for the purposes of the prohibitions on political advertisements, states 'objects of a political nature and political ends include ... influencing public opinion on a matter which, in the UK, is a matter of public controversy.'

42   *Vgt Verein Gegen Tierfabriken* v. *Switzerland* [2001] ECHR 412, para. 57.

43   (1998) 28 EHRR 534.

44   *Hertel* v. *Switzerland* (1998) 28 *EHRR* 534, para. 47.

45   In fact this was argued by Hertel in all the courts.

The ECtHR did not take objection to that classification.[46] What is of some concern about *Hertel* is that the Court decided that the injunction was a disproportionate response to the offending conduct (not necessary in a democratic society) because, first, the article could barely be attributed to Hertel, secondly, he had merely claimed that the microwaves *might* be harmful and, third, it had no measurable effect on the sales.[47] In other words, being a non-commercial actor did not seem to have helped Hertel to very many speech concessions – apart from the willingness of the Court to actually scrutinise the speech restriction by Switzerland.[48]

When the judges in *Hertel* referred to the speech as not being *purely* commercial (even though it was not at all 'commercial' in the legal sense, that is, being designed to promote sales), they clearly had a wider meaning of 'commercial' in mind and this meaning stems from the case of *Markt Intern Verlag und Klaus Beerman v. Germany*[49](also discussed in Chapter 1 above). While in *Hertel*, the companies tried unsuccessfully to silence their non-commercial detractor, they succeeded in *Markt Intern*. The difference was that in the latter case the speaker was a market player (or at least acting on their behalf): Markt Intern, it will be remembered, was a publishing firm run by journalists set up to protect the 'interests of small and medium retail businesses against the competition of large-scale of large-scale distribution companies'.[50] In one of its bulletins, subscribed to by small traders, it published a critical report by a disgruntled customer of a large-scale mail-order firms, calling for more negative feedback.[51] A mail-order firm applied to a German court for an injunction – again based on unfair competition law – to stop Markt Intern from repeating those criticisms.[52] The Court of Human Rights held (by the bare string of the president's casting vote) that the injunction did not go beyond Germany's wide margin of appreciation, as the article in question 'conveyed information of a commercial nature'.[53] With these words, the Court adopted a definition of commercial speech which virtually includes all speech relating to commerce one way or another.

---

46 *Hertel* v. *Switzerland* (1998) 28 EHRR 534, para. 36.

47 Under these circumstances, it seems Hertel ought to have been exonerated even if he had been a market-player.

48 *Markt Intern Verlag und Klaus Beerman v. Germany* [1989] ECHR 21, para. 33: 'The Court must confine its review to the question whether the measures taken on the national level are justifiable in principle and proportionate.' Note Randall, note 17 above, at 75, where she notes that classification as commercial 'almost automatically result[s] in immunity for the measure under review'.

49 *Markt Intern Verlag und Klaus Beerman v. Germany* [1989] ECHR 21.

50 *Markt Intern Verlag und Klaus Beerman v. Germany* [1989] ECHR 21, para. 9.

51 Other ancillary functions of the association were to provide the less powerful members of the retail trade with financial assistance in test cases, to lobby public authorities, political parties and trade associations on their behalf, and to make proposals to the legislature.

52 *Markt Intern Verlag und Klaus Beerman v. Germany* [1989] ECHR 21, para. 18. The injunction was granted by the first court, overruled by the second, reinstated by the third and left untouched by the fourth.

53 *Markt Intern Verlag und Klaus Beerman v. Germany* [1989] ECIIR 21, para. 26.

The Court also emphasised that although Markt Intern was *not* a competitor,[54] neither was it a 'neutral' third party speaking to the public as a whole, and thus attracting the strong protection normally accorded to the press. Mark Intern 'intended ... to protect the interests of the chemists and beauty product retailers'.[55] So Markt Intern's role was that of a guardian and the beneficiaries were commercial actors. The problem with that argument is that the retailers were also *not* in competition with the large wholesalers, but were in fact consumers in relation to them. The critical difference here is that disparaging speech by competitors is a negative form of advertising and thus within the traditional scope of commercial speech, namely, speech intended to promote sales. But the ruling in *Markt Intern* went beyond that to include not just the speech of suppliers of good and services and their competitors but also of buyers. Admittedly the buyers themselves were businesses, but the large conceptual jump was made.

The next small step to apply the approach to consumer speech was taken in *SRG* v. *Switzerland*.[56] There the ECtHR refused to review a ban on an allegedly 'anti-competitive' consumer television programme purporting to speak about the health hazards of microwaves and painkillers. Although the programme was acknowledged to be a matter of 'general interest', it was not reviewed, given that the expression was made in a 'commercial context' and thus within Switzerland's wide 'margin of appreciation'.

In short, in the EU, the combination of a 'wide margin of appreciation in commercial matters' and an expansive understanding of 'commercial speech' (that is, expression made in the commercial context) means that such speech is vulnerable to significant legal restrictions, whether it comes from companies or any other party broadly involved in commerce, including consumers. This approach to commercial speech could be praised or condemned. Its proponents could argued that Europe – by not confining commercial speech to advertising speech – creates a level playing field for all commercial actors, companies and consumers alike, as broadly in line with the sentiment expressed by Justice Breyer in *Nike*.[57] On the other hand, opponents may assert that companies with the help of the Court of Human Rights have managed to totally pervert the 'wide margin of appreciation in commercial matters', a concept peculiarly designed to restrict profit-motivated speech rather than silence costumers. Far from creating a level speech field, the European jurisprudence exacerbates existing inequalities, and highlights the danger of a loosely defined concept based on a vaguely articulated rationale, especially with aggressive corporate litigators and lobby groups wheeling and dealing in the background.[58] To decide which perspective

---

54   Neither itself, nor as agents for the smaller firms. *Markt Intern Verlag und Klaus Beerman* v. *Germany* [1989] ECHR 21, para. 16 and 18.

55   *Markt Intern Verlag und Klaus Beerman* v. *Germany* [1989] ECHR 21, para. 36.

56   Admissibility Decision of 12 April 2001, Appl. No. 43524/98.

57   The difference is that Justice Breyer argued for giving certain corporate speech more protection, rather than giving consumer speech less protection.

58   Joint dissenting opinion in *Markt Intern Verlag und Klaus Beerman* v. *Germany* [1989] ECHR 21: 'We find the reasoning set out therein with regard to the "margin of appreciation" of States a case for serious concern. As is shown by the result to which it leads

is the better one, let us look at why it might be more acceptable to restrict commercial speech than other speech.

The Rationale for Greater Restrictions on 'Commercial Speech'

The second-class treatment of 'commercial speech' has been justified on a number of grounds. In Europe, for example, States purportedly need more freedom to intervene 'in commercial matters and, in particular, in an area as complex and fluctuating as that of unfair competition'[59] or advertising,[60] or more freedom to accommodate national peculiarities 'to take account of the specific situation in the national market'.[61] Such matters, unquestionably relevant in Europe, fail to explain why the same categorisation, at least in its core, is also adopted in the US.

The most obvious rationale, common to the US and Europe, would be that political, unlike commercial, speech is vital for the maintenance of democracy, provides a check on governmental power and is intrinsically more susceptible to governmental censorship and thus in need of more vigorous protection. Yet even these democracy-based rationales are not entirely persuasive. First:

> Although political expression ... may generally be more important for the democratic process than commercial speech, it would be too simplistic to draw a clear line between [them] ... The interplay between the forces of a free market and democracy are not a one-way street. A free market economy can be both conducive and detrimental to a pluralistic political system.[62]

Secondly, commercial speech may also be susceptible to discriminatory censorship either when industry and government are competitors or when the government has a closer relationship with one commercial actor than another. And finally, democracy-based arguments cannot quite explain why commercial speech should be treated any differently from speech that is only in the widest sense 'political'[63] and only marginally supportive of democratic processes. The statements concerning a vet's efforts of treating animals outside normal working hours, as under consideration in *Barthold* v. *Germany*,[64] would only marginally be helpful to democratic processes.

---

in this case, it has the effect in practice of considerably restricting the freedom of expression in commercial matters.'

59   *Markt Intern Verlag und Klaus Beerman* v. *Germany* [1989] ECHR 21, para. 33.

60   *Karner (Free movement of goods)* [2004] EUECJ C-71/02 (25 March 2004), para. 51; *RTL Television* [2003] ECR I-0000 C-245/01, para. 73.

61   *Markt Intern Verlag und Klaus Beerman* v. *Germany* [1989] ECHR 21, para. 32; *Casado Coca* v. *Spain* (1994) 18 EHRR 1, para. 54; *Vgt Verein Gegen Tierfabriken* v. *Switzerland* [2001] ECHR 412 paras 69–71; *RTL Television* C-245/01 [2003] ECR I-0000, para. 73; *Karner (Free movement of goods)* C-71/02 [2004] EUECJ, para. 51.

62   Randall, note 17 above, at 79ff.

63   As opposed to the heart of political expression, that is, criticism of government: 'interferences with the freedom of political expression of an opposition member of parliament ... call for the closest scrutiny on the part of the Court': *Castells* v. *Spain* (1992) 14 *EHRR* 445, para. 42.

64   (1985) 7 *EHRR* 383.

No doubt, some link with democratic ideals could be made out, but so could it be in the context of classic commercial speech. It is more persuasive to argue that what is indeed so special about commercial speech and justifies greater restrictions can be discerned from its archetypal instance, the core of the commercial speech category both in the US and Europe, and that is advertising.

First, advertising speech is unreliable and inherently so. When years and millions of euros, pounds, or dollars have gone into the development of a drug, it is tempting to understate negative side-effects. For any business, it is tempting to imply that its product is tastier, cleaner, softer, comfier, healthier, longer-lasting, faster, more beauty-enhancing, more environmentally friendly, or fair-trade-conscious than anything else out on the market. Even entirely truthful advertisements cannot detract from the systemic underlying temptation to paint one's products or services in rosier colours than objectively justifiable. While it would be desirable if everyone only ever spoke truthfully, rarely is that desirability turned into a legal obligation.[65] In the case of advertising that does happen, because the tendency to lie combines, first, with the risk of serious harm being caused by such lies to individuals, the community and the market and, secondly, with the ability of the speaker normally to make sure that the statements are accurate.[66] As a side note, in so far as the pursuit of truth is a key rationale for freedom of speech, the susceptibility of commercial speech to be false weakens the case for protecting such speech in the first place.[67]

In contrast, consumers have no natural incentive to lie about their transactions with companies, apart perhaps from the isolated disgruntled consumers or corporate vigilantes with an ideological axe to grind. Although disparaging speech about a company or its product may well cause economic harm to the company, given the consumer's general lack of incentive to lie and greater difficulty to verify the accuracy of his speech, it would seem appropriate for the law to give consumers more leeway. The law ought to counter-balance corporate and consumer natural tendencies by assuming that businesses have a chronic problem with the truth while consumers do not. Such assumptions are in fact consistent with the US imposition of strict liability for misleading advertising by companies, while requiring an intention in respect of false statements by consumers.[68] Justice Breyer's suggestion in *Nike* to

---

65   See note 9 above.

66   In relation to the market rationale, see *Virginia State Board of Pharmacy* v. *Virginia Citizens Consumer Council Inc.* 425 US 748, 764f (1976): 'So long as we preserve a predominantly free enterprise economy, the allocation of our resources in large measure will be made through numerous private economic decisions. It is a matter of public interest that those decisions, in the aggregate, be intelligent and well informed'; *Kasky* v. *Nike Inc.* 27 Cal 4th 939, 955 (2002) where it is noted that advertisements are 'more easily verifiable by its disseminator than ... news reporting or political commentary, in that ordinarily the advertiser seeks to disseminate information about a specific product or service that he himself provides and presumably knows more about than any else.'

67   Emberland, note 12 above, at 122.

68   Consumer speech falls dependant on the public profile of the company within the ruling of *New York Times Co.* v. *Sullivan* 376 US 254, 272 (1964) which requires disparaging false statements to be made intentionally or with reckless disregard as to their truth. *Bose Corp* v. *Consumer Union States Inc.* 466 US 485 (1984).

introduce a mental element for some forms of false advertising would be like inviting an abstinent alcoholic to the pub, both in terms of temptation and protective cover. In large companies with complex hierarchical structures and lines of authority, it would virtually be impossible to prove that a statement was made with the knowledge of its falsity, rather than merely negligently.

Secondly, advertising speech is robust.[69] Businesses have a natural incentive to speak: selling requires advertising, the more the better.[70] Commercial self-interest means that company speech need neither be encouraged nor is easily chilled by restrictions. In contrast, consumers have no inherent self-interest to speak about their past commercial experiences with, or general opinions of, companies. Consumer advocates are far and few between. People such as Morris and Steel make the legal and popular headlines because they are exceptional. Few individuals have the conviction and energy to take on big business,[71] and frequently there is no cost-effective public platform to do so.[72] Yet precisely because consumer speech is not inherently self-interested, it can be, and often is, beneficial for the market generally[73] which indeed makes it speech of 'general interest' par excellence. Thus the law should be slow to create disincentives or hurdles to it. If, for example, it penalises negligent falsehoods, it creates the risk of undue self-censorship and does not give consumer speech the 'breathing space' it needs to survive.[74]

In conclusion, consumer speech is very different from advertising, the classic form of commercial speech. It shares none of the key characteristics of advertising: an inherent unreliability and robustness flowing from its self-serving motivation. These characteristics – rather than the commercial subject-matter of the speech or any general economic interest of the speaker – justify greater governmental restrictions on advertising.

---

69   *Virginia State Bd of Pharmacy* v. *Virginia Citizens Consumer Council Inc.* 425 US 748, 772 (1976); *Kasky* v. *Nike Inc* 27 Cal 4th 939, 955 (2002), where the court also notes as a further reason: 'governmental authority to regulate commercial transactions to prevent commercial harms justifies a power to regulate speech that is linked inextricably to those transactions' [internal marks omitted].

70   As noted by the joint dissent in *Markt Intern Verlag und Klaus Beerman* v. *Germany* [1989] ECHR 21, 'consumers … are constantly exposed to highly effective distribution techniques and advertising which is frequently less than objective … .'

71   Despite Justice Breyer's allusion to hordes of hostile consumers using the courtroom to wage political battles against corporations, *Nike Inc.* v. *Kasky* 539 US 654, 679f (2003), text accompanying note 25 above.

72   Today, an avenue for consumer speech is the Internet. Many gripe sites, set up by disgruntled consumers, have been legally attacked by their corporate targets on the basis of alleged trademark infringement through the use of a domain name related to the company's name, for example, <http://ryanairsucks.blogspot.com>.

73   Indeed, sites such as ebay make their business model dependent upon the value of consumer feedback.

74   *Herbert* v. *Lando* (1979) 441 US 153, 172; *New York Times Co.* v. *Sullivan* (1964) 376 US 254, 272.

Beyond the principled argument based on the underlying speech motivation, there are also practical considerations concerning the respective economic power of companies and consumers, which advocate against any real speech equality of all commercial actors. This shines through the words of Judge Pettiti in his separate dissenting opinion in *Markt Intern*:

> In fact by seeking to support pressure groups ... the State is defending a specific interest. It uses the pretext of a law on competition or on prices to give precedence to one group over another. The protection of the interests of users and consumers in the face of dominant positions depends on the freedom to publish even the harshest criticism of products.[75]

And these practical issues are particularly pertinent when the customer is a mere consumer.

The Consumer's Freedom of Expression

Mirror Images

The 'commercial speech' category is principally aimed at corporate or business speech – it both protects and restricts it. There is no equivalent concept focusing on consumer speech. Consumer speech, unlike business speech, seems to have no special characteristics that set it apart from general speech. Thus *prima facie*, it would seem appropriate to treat it as broadly understood 'political' or 'general interest' expression, that is, 'participation in a debate affecting the general interest'.[76]

This is a relatively uncontroversial premise, but it is equally accepted that rights always fall within a social, cultural, political and economic reality which may work in favour of, or against, their actual assertion and enjoyment. Rights are only as real and effective as the relative interest and strength of the rights holders to defend them against their detractors. Consumer speech by definition has as its subject corporate or business activities, and it is corporations which have an interest in circumscribing consumer speech in so far as it is not favourable about them. The problem is that both in relative and absolute terms the interest of consumers in speaking is significantly weaker than the corporate interest in restricting their speech. The same monumental effort businesses put into speech enhancing their image, they necessarily also put into protecting their products from image-damaging speech. In that respect, consumer speech is exposed to a substantial and systemic horizontal threat – quite unlike general interest or core political speech. This is not to say that, for example, political speech has not also its natural opponents. As it is concerned

---

75   *Markt Intern Verlag und Klaus Beerman* v. *Germany* [1989] ECHR 21, where he continued: 'The problem is all the more serious because often the States which seek to restrict the freedom use the pretext of ... breaches of economic legislation ... to institute proceeding for political motives or to protect "mixed" interests (State –industrial) in order to erect barriers to freedom of expression.'

76   *Vgt Verein Gegen Tierfabriken* v. *Switzerland* [2001] ECHR 412, para. 71.

with governance, it is directed at the State, its institutions and policies,[77] and thus vulnerable to governmental censorship. However, unlike the horizontal private threat to consumer speech, this vertical threat to political speech is squarely acknowledged by human rights law – the classic preoccupation of which is the protection of the individual from the oppressive State.[78] The problem in the commercial context is that corporations and consumers are treated under classic human rights jurisprudence as simply private parties, where an assumption of relative equality leads *prima facie* to equal and reciprocal rights and obligations. That assumption is displaced in respect of corporate speech. The 'commercial speech' concept gives corporations broadly the right to engage in truthful advertising as well as to be protected from untruthful negative advertising by competitors. *Vis-à-vis* consumers, the concept operates as an additional protection – over and beyond the protection they would receive if corporate speech was treated as normal 'general interest' speech.[79] But is that extra protection mirrored in respect of consumer speech, reflecting that consumer speech is as vulnerable to corporate censorship as the consumer is to oppression by commercial speech?

Consumers can only enjoy free speech in any meaningful way – and thereby protect their commercial and non-commercial interests such as health – if the law recognises their vulnerability *vis-à-vis* companies and redresses it through 'positive discrimination'; in other words if there is an acceptance that equality in law can neither provide equality in fact in the corporate-consumer context nor more generally strike a fair balance between the commercial interests of companies and consumer interests. It will be seen – by reference to corporate defamation claims – that in the US significant inroads have been made into corporate censorship of consumer speech, complementary to the US treatment of corporate speech under the 'commercial speech' concept. In contrast, the position in England and Wales, as condoned under EU human rights jurisprudence, is that of an assumption of relative equality between corporation and consumers – also complementary to the misplaced EU interpretation of the 'commercial speech' concept.

---

77   Emberland, note 12 above, at 118: 'Political expression ... comprises statements that ... concern the speaker's participation in a debate affecting the general interest or reflect controversial opinions pertaining to modern society in general' (internal marks omitted), relying on *Vgt Verein Gegen Tierfabriken* v. *Switzerland* [2001] ECHR 412, para. 70 and *Hertel* v. *Switzerland* (1998) 28 *EHRR* 534, para. 47.

78   This is, for example, reflected in the fact that '[t]he limits of acceptable criticism are ... wider as regards a politician as such than a private individual' *Lingens* v. *Austria* (1986) 8 *EHRR* 407, para. 42, or that criticism of government is given the greatest protection. See Feldman, note 10 above, at 754ff.

79   In Europe, only in so far as it applies to the core of commercial speech, that is, advertising, but not in so far as it can be used to uphold restrictions on consumer speech.

Consumer Attack on 'Corporate Dignity'

Under English law, companies have long been able to protect their corporate image from critical comments through defamation claims.[80] Taking this as a starting point, the question is how these corporate claims are and ought to be resolved. How does the corporate plaintiff fit into defamation law, and what effect do corporate claims have on the consumer's freedom of speech? How should the general tension underlying defamation law between the social good of unimpeded open debate and the fairness of compensating those who suffer loss as a result of disparaging statements be resolved when the loss is a corporate loss due to disparaging consumer speech?

The first difficulty arises from the fact that defamation law is rather 'exceptional in the law of tort',[81] with some extraordinary features which present a 'remarkable restriction of the freedom to speak and write',[82] and which have clearly developed with the human plaintiff in mind. So the defamed plaintiff in a defamation action need not prove any loss which the law simply presumes to flow from the defamatory publication. Neither need the plaintiff prove that the offending statement was in fact false. The burden of proving the truth falls upon the defendant, or, in our context, the consumer – in contrast to its closest ally, malicious falsehood.[83] The law's reverence for reputation stems from the Victorian reverence for respectability: 'In the eighteenth century there were still men of honour, proud of their self-esteem; they would call out the man who spoke out; since a suit was better than a duel, a strong remedy had to be provided, and was.'[84] This strong remedy came in the form of a presumption that any slur or critical comment gives rise to a slight on one's respectability (or a mental trauma that this may be the case[85]), proven or not. In any event, it would be difficult to prove such slight. Similarly, the presumption that a negative comment

---

80   *Derbyshire County Council* v. *Times Newspaper Ltd* [1993] AC 534, 547 (Lord Keith): 'a trading corporation is entitled to sue in respect of defamatory matters which can be seen as having a tendency to damage it in the way of its business.' Historically, English law disallowed corporate libel actions for criticism of the products of a business, as opposed to its general operation. In relation to products, 'The desirability of permitting extensive freedom for criticism ... led courts to establish strict preconditions to a successful action' which included the requirement to plead and prove special damages: Casenote 'Libel and the Corporate Plaintiff' (1969) *Columbia Law Review* 69:1496, 1498f.

81   J.A. Weir, 'Local Authority v. Critical Ratepayer – A Suit in Defamation' [1972A] *Cambridge Law Journal* 238, 239.

82   Ibid.

83   The tort of malicious falsehood is committed where the defendant made a false statement about the plaintiff to a third party, knowing that it was false or reckless as to its accuracy, and the plaintiff suffers a loss thereby. For an example, see *Khodoparast* v. *Shad* [2000] 1 WLR 618. But note, s.3(1) of the Defamation Act 1952 extends the common-law defamation rule of presumption of loss to an action of malicious falsehood.

84   Weir, note 81 above, at 239.

85   This is reflected in accepted injuries flowing from a defamatory statement, such as humiliation, mental anguish and suffering. Marc A. Franklin, David A. Anderson and Fred H. Cate (2000), *Mass Media Law* (New York; Foundation Press), at 354.

is false unless the contrary is proven by the speaker suggests that respectability is treated as inviolable – bar contrary evidence.

Today this heightened sense of honour and respectability has gone, but defamation at its core still rests upon the perceived importance of one's good name, conceptualised in modern human rights rhetoric as an essential part of human dignity: defamation reflects 'our basic concept of the essential dignity and worth of every human being – a concept at the root of any decent system of ordered liberty'.[86] As the company, being an artificial person, has no comparable dignity and as its injury to reputation is purely economic, why should it benefit from these extraordinary rules which, after all, cannot but have an extraordinary restrictive effect on free speech and thus ought to be reserved to protecting values of highest importance, such as human dignity? A corporate claim ought to be harder, but is it? 'Corporations have ... claimed and acquired the right to "commercial free speech" as well as a right to reputation and honour, not just as a property right but as a personality interest.'[87]

Presumed Damage   To start with, the notion of presumed damage has been abandoned in the US for all plaintiffs where the defendant was merely negligent because

> Juries may award substantial sums as compensation for supposed damage to reputation without any proof that such harm actually occurred. The largely uncontrolled discretion of juries to award damages where there is no loss unnecessarily compounds the potential of any system of liability for defamatory falsehood to inhibit the vigorous exercise of First Amendment freedoms. Additionally, the doctrine of presumed damages invites juries to punish unpopular opinion rather than to compensate individuals for injuries sustained.[88]

In England, the bastion of presumed damages has withstood repeated challenges in corporate claims. In the early case of *South Hetton Coal Co. Ltd* v. *North-Eastern News Association Ltd,*[89] the defendant argued that a company should only succeed with a defamation claim if 'actual pecuniary damage is proved. It has no feelings which may be hurt or irritated; and it has no moral character which can be defamed.'[90] The Court of Appeal disagreed. Paradoxically, Lord Kay reasoned that it would be unjust not to allow 'a corporation ... [to] maintain an action for a libel by which

---

86   *Rosenblatt* v. *Baer* 383 US 75, 92 (1966). See Emberland, note 12 above, at 37ff. on 'individual dignity' being one of the core values underlying the ECHR, modelled on the Universal Declaration of Human Rights (1948) under which it is taken to be the precondition for justice and freedom.

87   Anna Grear (2007), 'Challenging Corporate 'Humanity': Legal Disembodiment, Embodiment and Human Rights', *Human Rights Law Review*, 7:511, 514, citing Baxi. See also Emberland, note 12 above, at 121, on the misfit between the 'individual self-fulfilment' rationale for the right to free speech and corporate speech. The same argument would appear to be applicable to corporate defamation claims.

88   *Gertz* v. *Robert Welch Inc.* 418 US 323, 349 (1974).

89   [1894] 1 QB 133.

90   *South Hetton Coal Co Ltd* v. *North-Eastern News Association Ltd* [1894] 1 QB 133, 134.

its property is injured'.[91] Exactly. This real, pecuniary loss is the only possible loss
a company can suffer, or in the words of one commentator: 'Its feelings are never
wounded. If it has been injured, the injury must be an economic loss which must in
turn be reflected in the corporate balance sheet.'[92] Or as Weir put it in 1972:

> [A company has] no feelings which might have been hurt and no social relation which
> might have been impaired. The two kinds of presumptive harm could not be presumed
> because they could not have occurred ... the reason for which we absolve the human
> plaintiff from the usual requirement of proving loss cannot and do not apply to the
> inhuman plaintiff.[93]

Thus, in the corporate context, there is no reason to depart from the conventional tort
rule that injury, actual or likely, ought to be proven.

It may be objected that defamation law has long ago embraced less lofty notions
than dignity and allowed individuals to recover for presumed damage to tangible
interests. In fact, this provided the entry ticket for corporate defamation claims:
if individual merchants had the right to bring a libel suit based on injury to trade
or business,[94] then it would seem unjust and inconsistent not to allow companies
similar rights simply on the basis that it had no soul and feelings.[95] Two points may
be made in response. First, immunity for the incorporated artificial person from laws
peculiarly designed for humans, such as 'murder, or incest, or adultery ... corruption
... or assault'[96] have, at least in the past, had easy acceptance. However, no similar
easy acceptance has been forthcoming when it comes to legal benefits peculiarly
designed for humans; suddenly, justice and fairness seem to demand that the law is
the same for all.[97] In the case of defamed merchants, it may indeed be impossible
to draw a neat line between their injured feelings and injured business – a matter
not entirely unrelated to the underlying legal position which does not distinguish
between the trader and the person. Secondly, in so far as an injury to tangible interests
is alleged, it may be argued that actual or likely damage ought also to be proven by
an individual merchant given that it lies outside the rationale for the presumption of
damage.

---

91   Ibid., 147 (Kay LJ).

92   Casenote, note 80 above, at 1510, where the author also argues that the present rule
has 'permitted juries to make outrageous awards'.

93   Weir, note 81 above, at 240, cited with approval by Baroness Hale of Richmond in
Jameel and others v. *Wall Street Journal* [2006] UKHL 44, para. 154.

94   Casenote, note 80 above, at 1497. This was also argued in *South Hetton Coal Co Ltd*
v. *North-Eastern News Association Ltd* [1894] 1 QB 133, 135ff.

95   Ibid.

96   *South Hetton Coal Co Ltd* v. *North-Eastern News Association Ltd* [1894] 1 QB 133,
141. Of course, some of these offences have been taken off this list, for example, manslaughter
and corruption.

97   Ibid., 138 (per Lord Esher MR): 'the law of libel is one and the same to all plaintiffs',
affirmed in *Jameel and Others* v. *Wall Street Journal Sprl* [2006] UKHL 44, para. 100 (per
Lord Hope of Craighead).

Yet the recommendation of the Faulks Committee in its Report on Defamation (1975)[98] – that a trading corporation must establish that 'either it has suffered special damage, or that the words were likely to cause pecuniary damage'[99] – was not adopted. And in a recent challenge in *Jameel and Others v. Wall Street Journal Sprl*,[100] the House of Lords by a majority of three to two decided once more in favour of retaining the *status quo*. They argued that the good name of a company, as that of an individual, is a thing of value, that prompt proceedings may vindicate the victim and prevent any actual loss, which in any case may be difficult to prove or to causally link to the libellous publication.[101] Nobody doubts these matters (although in McLibel, the litigation was much more harmful to McDonald's than the initial leaflet). Yet difficulties of proving damage and causally linking it to the wrongful act are fatal in most other tort contexts (and for good reasons), no matter how disastrous the outcome for the plaintiff. Such difficulties ought only be disregarded when what is at stake is of highest concern, that is, human dignity – it must be remembered that such disregard is at the expense of free speech and other values protected via open debate. To elevate the corporate image to that level of 'top value' seems unfortunate and, according to dissenting judge, Baroness Hale of Richmond, out of tune with the modern commitment of developed democracies to free speech.[102] In Weir's words: 'To prefer the interest in maintaining the corporate image to the right of the citizen to say what he reasonably believes to be true is a grim perversion of values.'[103]

Presumed Falsity As with the presumed damages rule, the common law rule that it is for the defence to prove the truth of the defamatory statement is of long standing, and again unique in tort. It suspends the normal expectation that it is for the plaintiff to establish the cause of action and, more specifically, to prove the inaccuracy of the

---

98   Faulks Committee, *Report of the Committee on Defamation* (March 1975, Cmnd 5909). See also Emberland, note 12 above, at124ff, 130ff, on the difficulty of determining non-pecuniary damage in the corporate context.

99   Ibid., para. 342. Note the second proposition, that is, '*likely* to cause pecuniary damage' would only marginally change existing law, as propounded in *Derbyshire County Council* v. *Times Newspaper Ltd* [1993] AC 534, 547 (per Lord Keith): 'a trading corporation is entitled to sue in respect of defamatory matters which can be seen as having a tendency to damage it in the way of its business.'

100   [2006] UKHL 44, [2006] All ER (D) 132 (dissenting on this issue Lord Hoffman, paras 90–91, and Baroness Hale of Richmond, paras 152–9); affirming *Derbyshire Country Council* v. *Times Newspaper Ltd* [1993] AC 534, 547B–C, and *Shevill* v. *Presse Alliance SA* [1996] AC 959. The rule was also affirmed by the Court of Appeal in *Steel* v. *McDonald's Corp. & Anor* [1999] EWCA Civ 1144, 10, 17–20 on the basis that damage to reputation might be as difficult to prove as damage to the reputation of an individual and not immediate or quantifiable.

101   *Jameel and Others* v. *Wall Street Journal Sprl* [2006] UKHL 44, para. 26 (Lord Bingham), para. 102 (Lord Hope of Craighead), paras 120–23 ((Lord Scott of Foscote).

102   *Jameel and Others* v. *Wall Street Journal Sprl* [2006] UKHL 44, para. 153.

103   Weir, note 81 above, at 240. In practical terms, corporate threat of defamation action is much more easily made (and thus abused at the expense of free speech) when actual or likely damage need not be proven.

injurious statement.[104] While this switch of burden is in most cases not significant, it does become critical where the accuracy or falsity of a statement is difficult or impossible to prove, as was the case in McLibel. The effect of this rule is that expression which is true but cannot (easily) be proven to be true, is penalised and thus discouraged. As noted above, such drastic interference with speech would seem justifiable where what is at stake is an individual's good name and honour, which is to be taken intact until it is positively established not to be so. But should this assumption of good name and honour also apply to companies?

Currently, neither US nor English law creates a different burden of proof in corporate defamation claims from individual ones. Having said that, the traditional position has largely been reversed in the US in the wake of the 'public figure' doctrine (discussed below) which requires the plaintiff to prove that the defamatory statement was made with 'actual malice'.[105] And acting with such malice entails that the 'false statements [were] made with [a] … high degree of awareness of their probable falsity'[106] – a requirement later extended to all claims, whether by a private or public plaintiff, 'against a media defendant for speech of public concern'.[107] This position allows an occasional false statement to slip through the net as the price to be paid for robust discussion on matters of 'public concern':

> … the need to encourage debate on public issues that concerned the Court in the governmental-restriction cases is of concern in a similar manner in this case involving a private suit for damages: placement … of the burden of proving truth upon media defendants who publish speech of public concern deters such speech because of the fear that liability will unjustifiably result.[108]

Although this ruling would not include consumer speech if it is not channelled through mass media,[109] if it goes through such channels most if not all consumer speech would seem to satisfy the 'public concern' requirement, given that consumer speech is invariably of general interest.

Unlike in the US, the law has remained unchanged in good old England. Recently, the English Court of Appeal in the McLibel case rejected tipping the speech balance in the consumer's favour because it was 'not able to change clear and binding law'[110] and the European Court of Human Rights found that the consumer activists' burden

---

104   This is also applies in the case of negligent misrepresentations.

105   *New York Times Co* v. *Sullivan* 376 US 254 (1964).

106   *Garrison* v. *Louisiana* 379 US 64, 74 (1964).

107   *Philadelphia Newspapers Inc.* v. *Hepps* 475 US 767, 776f (1986). So in all cases involving a 'public figure' plaintiff or a media defendant, falsity of the statement must be proven by the plaintiff.

108   Ibid., 777.

109   But see, ibid., 780, per Brennan J: 'I write separately only to note that … I adhere to my view that such a distinction [that is, distinction between media and non-media defendants] is irreconcilable with the fundamental First Amendment principle that the inherent worth of … speech in terms of its capacity for informing the public does not depend upon the identity of the source …' [internal marks omitted].

110   *Steel* v. *McDonald's Corp. & Anor* [1999] EWCA Civ 1144, 20f.

of proof 'was not in principle incompatible with Art 10'.[111] It argued that 'the fact that the plaintiff in the present case was a large multinational company should [not] in principle deprive it of a right to defend itself against defamatory allegations or entail that the applicants should not have been required to prove the truth of the statements made.'[112] Open debate had to give way to the 'interest in protecting the commercial success and viability of companies, for the benefit of shareholders and employees, but also for the wider economic good'.[113] Thus Europe, which otherwise prides itself of a strong consumer-protection tradition, has endorsed a legal position which is infinitely more hard-nosed and less consumer-friendly than the US's.

Even if one disregards the fact that corporate dignity, if existent, is an entirely different animal than human dignity, there are other grounds why the English law's assumption of good name and honour, reflected in the current burden of proof, is much less apt in the corporate context. First, there is ample empirical evidence to suggest that the products and operations of many companies, small or large, are despite their clean façade not beyond criticisms. There is also a growing school of academic and popular thought according to which the corporate institution – due to its inherent characteristics – cannot be expected to act in a socially responsible way of its own free volition and that a robust public debate on, and generally transparency of, corporate operations help to compel better corporate behaviour.[114] Furthermore, as noted above, consumers, unlike competitors, have neither an inherent interest in engaging in such public debate nor any systemic reason to lie about corporate operations. Thus a primary assumption of the truth of critical consumer speech would hardly be unduly cynical as far as companies are concerned nor too gullible or lenient *vis-à-vis* consumers. Finally, such an assumption would be consistent with the 'commercial speech' doctrine which starts from the premise that it is profit-motivated speech, that is inherently untrustworthy and not the speech by consumers, and that it is companies that have better access to accurate information about their operations to prove or disprove the veracity of statements about them. And this holds true whether the company or the consumer is the speaker.

---

111   *Steel and Morris* v. *the United Kingdom* [2005] ECHR 103, para. 93.

112   Ibid., para. 94.

113   Ibid.

114   Bakan, note 7 above, at 60ff. Scott Pegg (2003), 'An Emerging Market for the New Millennium: Transnational Corporations and Human Rights', in Jedrzej George Frynas and Scott Pegg (eds), *Transnational Corporations and Human Rights* (New York: Palgrave Macmillan), 1, 10. On the inadequacy of voluntary reporting by companies on 'corporate social responsibility', see Janet Dine (2005), *Companies, International Trade and Human Rights* (Cambridge: Cambridge University Press), 222ff. This argument of the precise dividing line between a private and public body occurs in various legal contexts. For example, in the context of the International Covenant on Civil and Political Rights, it has been argued that the obligation to disclose information ought not just be applicable to public bodies but to companies when a 'key public interest, such as the environment, is at risk': International Council on Human Rights (2002), *Beyond Voluntarism – Human rights and the developing international legal obligations of companies* (Versix), 41.

Consumer Speech – Quasi-Political Speech?

Another line of argument for a differentiated treatment of corporate claims relies on the economic and quasi-political power of large public companies. In McLibel, the consumer activists argued that TNCs 'are well able to look after themselves without [defamation law]'.'[115] They argued for an extension of the holding in *Derbyshire County Council* v. *Times Newspapers*,[116] which disallows defamation claims by governmental bodies: it is 'of the highest public importance that a democratically elected governmental body, or indeed any governmental body, should be open to uninhibited public criticism'.[117] Steel argued that the invasiveness and influence of TNCs makes them quasi-public and thus unfettered criticism of their actions equally appropriate: 'Their activities are world wide and their commercial power and influence is often as great as government organisations.'[118] In other words, they relied on the key rationale underlying the right to free speech, that is, promoting democratic discourse, to support tight restrictions on the defamation rights of companies.[119]

Yet neither the English Court of Appeal nor the European Court of Human Rights accepted that argument: just because a company is 'a large multinational company should [not] in principle deprive it of a right to defend itself against defamatory allegations'.[120] But both Courts seem to implicitly suggest that speech concerning TNCs ought to be more robust than speech concerning their smaller counter-parts. The Human Rights Court expressly stated that 'large public companies inevitably and knowingly lay themselves open to close scrutiny of their acts ... [and] the limits of acceptable criticism are *wider* in the case of such companies.'[121] What wider limits the Court had in mind remains unclear given that there is no doctrine under English law to that effect. Indeed, the Court of Appeal expressly rejected such wider free speech in respect of multinationals given the difficulty of finding a 'principled basis upon which a line might be drawn between strong corporations and the weaker ones'.[122]

---

115   *Steel* v. *McDonald's Corp. & Anor* [1999] EWCA Civ 1144, 13.

116   [1993] AC 534.

117   *Derbyshire County Council* v. *Times Newspapers* [1993] AC 534, 547. The court also relied on the US case of *City of Chicago* v. *Tribune Co.* (1923) 139 NE 86, 90: 'it is advantageous for the public interest that the citizen should not be in any way fettered in his statements, and where the public service or due administration of justice is involved he shall have the right to speak his mind freely.'

118   *Steel* v. *McDonald's Corp. & Anor* [1999] EWCA Civ 1144, 12.

119   Emberland, note 12 above, at 120f, on the democracy rationale of freedom of expression in the corporate context.

120   *Steel and Morris* v. *the United Kingdom* [2005] ECHR 103, para. 94; *Steel* v. *McDonald's Corp. & Anor* [1999] EWCA Civ 1144, 12f.

121   *Steel and Morris* v. *the United Kingdom* [2005] ECHR 103, para. 94 [emphasis added].

122   *Steel* v. *McDonald's Corp. & Anor* [1999] EWCA Civ 1144, 16, see also 12, where the court also stressed the judicial limitation in respect of creating new legal categories which presented no hindrance in the case of *Derbyshire County Council* v. *Times Newspapers* [1993] AC 534, 547.

US 'Public Figure' Doctrine   This very dividing line is drawn under US law where large companies are presented with significant hurdles to succeed with defamation claims. The US 'public figure' doctrine allows for exactly what the English Court of Appeal sought, namely a principled basis for distinguishing different types of plaintiffs – depending on their public power and influence.[123] If the defamed person is a public figure, governmental or otherwise, the First Amendment's protection allows recovery of damages for defamation only upon proof that 'the statement was made with "actual malice" – that is, with knowledge that it was false or with reckless disregard of whether it was false or not.'[124] In other words, publicly well-known and influential plaintiffs are subjected to the more onerous requirements of showing that the defamatory statement made about them was not just false but also made with malice. In practical terms, public figures can be subjected to less cautious, more robust criticism than private ones. In the case of 'public figures' from the private sector, the more onerous standard has been justified on the basis that

> Increasingly in this country, the distinctions between governmental and private sectors are blurred. Since the depression of the 1930s, and World War II there has been a rapid fusion of economic and political power, a merging of science, industry, and government … While these trends and events have occasioned a consolidation of governmental power, power has also become much more organized in what we have commonly considered to be the private sector. In many situations, policy determinations which traditionally were channelled through formal political institutions are now originated and implemented through a complex array of boards, committees, commissions, corporations and associations, some only loosely connected with the Government.[125]

This reasoning reflects the inadequacy of the strongly vertical focus of classic rights theories in a world where significant and potentially oppressive power is wielded by private actors. Large corporations are the prime example of such quasi-public private actors.

So which companies have been treated as public figures? How do US judges draw the dividing line which according to the English Court of Appeal cannot be drawn? As in the case of individuals, no sharp division between companies that are considered public and those that are not is possible. Each case to some extent turns on its peculiar facts. Nevertheless, companies from highly regulated sectors 'reflecting a special magnitude of public dependence and involvement in the activity'[126] (for example, insurance and banking), or those whose shares are publicly traded, are more likely to fall within the 'public figure' realm.[127] Some courts have suggested

---

123   *Curtis Publishing Co.* v. *Butts* 388 US 130, 163: 'This blending of positions and power has also occurred in the case of individuals so that many who do not hold public office at the moment are nevertheless intimately involved in the resolution of important public questions, or, by reason of their fame, shape events in areas of concern to society at large.'

124   *New York Times Company v. Sullivan* 376 US 254, 279f (1964).

125   *Curtis Publishing Co.* v. *Butts* 388 US 130, 163 (1967) (Warren CJ, concurring).

126   *Jadwin* v. *Minneapolis Star & Tribune Co.* 367 NW 2d 476, 487 (Minn, 1985).

127   *Coronado Credit Union* v. *KOAT Television Inc.* 99 NM 233, 241 (1982) (state-chartered credit union is functionally equivalent to a bank and is a public figure because such institutions are affected with a public interest); *American Benefit Life Insurance Co.*

rigid subcategories to tame the wide factual diversity of companies;[128] some have advocated more fluid tests. For example, in *Jadwin* v. *Minneapolis Star and Tribune Co.*,[129] the 'public figure' status of a corporation was held to depend upon whether

> ... the defamatory material concerns matters of legitimate public interest in the geographic area in which the defamatory material is published, either because of the nature of the business conducted or because the public has an especially strong interest in the investigation or disclosure of the commercial information at issue.[130]

Despite its circularity,[131] this test highlights the underlying concern of the 'public figure' concept in the corporate context: ought the company, in the interest of the public, to be especially closely scrutinised, and 'to [be] probe[d by the media] ... to the depth which is necessary to permit the kind of business reporting vital to an informed public'[132]? In the case of large, multinational corporations, such as McDonald's, one would assume that there is such an 'especially strong interest' in transparency about their operations and products everywhere or wherever they have a presence.

The point here is not to dissect the US 'public figure' concept but to show that there are ways and means of distinguishing between different corporate plaintiffs. Just because the 'public figure' concept cannot avoid borderline cases,[133] it cannot detract from its sound rationale in terms of protecting society from censorship by those who are already in an influential position, may that be political or economic and thus quasi-political. In the US, high-profile companies are not denied a legal remedy for image-damaging speech in form of a defamation claim, but they cannot

---

v. *McIntyre*, 375 So.2d 239, 242 (Ala. 1979) (insurance company is a public figure because closely regulated by the government and is clothed with the public interest); *Reliance Insurance Co.* v. *Barron's*, 442 F Supp 1341, 1348 (SDNY 1977) (insurance company is a public figure based *inter alia* upon state regulation of the industry).

128   Authority according to which such regulation is not necessarily determinative: *Blue Ridge Bank* v. *Veribanc Inc.* 866 F 2d 681, 688 (1989): 'We do not believe that the existence of an ongoing public interest in the stability of society's financial institutions and market, or in the supervision of the gaming industry, or in the regulation of utilities automatically elevates every member of the regulated class to public figure status.' *Bank of Oregon* v. *Independent News Inc.* 298 Or 434, 443 (1985): 'Merely opening one's doors to the public, offering stock for public sale, advertising, etc., even if considered a thrusting of one's self into matters of public interest, is not sufficient to establish that a corporation is a public figure', approved in *Roop* v. *Parker Northwest Paving Co.* 194 Or App 219, 243 (Or App 2004).

129   *Jadwin* v. *Minneapolis Star & Tribune Co.* 367 NW2d 476, 487f (Minn 1985) (footnotes omitted); approved in *Aequitron Medical Inc.* v. *CBS Inc.* 964 F Supp 704 (SDNY 1997).

130   *Jadwin* v. *Minneapolis Star & Tribune Co.* 367 NW2d 476, 487f (Minn 1985) (footnotes omitted).

131   A company is a 'public figure' on the basis that there is an especially strong public interest in transparency about it, which is in fact the very notion embodied by the 'public figure' doctrine, and fails to answer *why* there is such an especially strong public interest.

132   *Jadwin* v. *Minneapolis Star & Tribune Co.* 367 NW2d 476, 487f (Minn 1985).

133   This is necessarily the result of superimposing categories upon 'fluid' reality.

use it to suppress uncomfortable consumer speech regardless of the consumer's good faith. Indeed, the 'public figure' doctrine supplements the 'commercial speech' concept – the former allows robust consumer debate to police corporate honesty required by the latter.

English 'Public Interest' Defence   Curiously, while rejecting the 'public figure' doctrine, a recent development in England and Wales, equally grounded in allowing robust debate on matters of public interest, may signal stronger consumer rights on this side of the Atlantic after all. The House of Lords invented a new 'public interest' defence in *Reynolds* v. *Times Newspaper Limited and Others*[134] – although *pro forma* it was said to arise out of the traditional defence of 'qualified privilege'. In *Jameel* v. *Wall Street Journal Europe Sprl*, Lord Hoffman acknowledged its jurisprudential novelty when he said that it 'might more appropriately be called the *Reynolds* public interest defence rather than privilege'.[135] This new defence protects speakers against liability for false statements where the material is of 'public interest' and 'the steps taken to gather and publish the information were responsible and fair.'[136] While in the above cases, the speakers were journalists of well-established newspapers, Lord Hoffman stressed that the defence applied to any medium[137] and thus presumably to non-media speakers, such Morris and Steel in McLibel, or ordinary consumers voicing their opinions or criticism , for example, on the Internet. If that is the case, it would also be conceivable that such consumer speech would perhaps attract a more lenient interpretation of 'responsible journalism' and 'reasonable and fair fact-finding and information gathering', where the consumers or their advocates act in good faith but without the professional know-how of a journalist. This conjecturing, if anything, shows that this novel defence is still of uncertain definition and only further judicial clarification can provide the assurance necessary to discourage consumer self-censorship beyond the legally required.

Both the US 'public figure' doctrine and the English 'public interest' defence protect the speaker from liability for false statements, where, broadly, there is a public interest in the matter discussed. The marked difference between the two approaches is that that of the US assumes such 'public interest' simply based upon the public standing of the plaintiff, while the English defence looks at the subject matter of the speech in question. Although the outcome may often be comparable, for purposes of this discussion – that is, consumer speech purposes – the American focus on the plaintiff is preferable as it is more clear-cut, predictable and makes any speech concerning large corporations subject to more robust debate. Once a company is held to be a 'public figure', its defamation rights are significantly curbed once and for all. In contrast, the subject-matter focus of the English defence means

---

134   [1999] 3 WLR 1010.

135   *Jameel* v. *Wall Street Journal Europe Sprl* [2006] UKHL44, para. 46. Note that one difference is that this new 'public interest' defence cannot be defeated by actual malice 'because the propriety of the conduct of the defendant is built into the conditions under which the material is privileged' (para. 46).

136   *Jameel* v. *Wall Street Journal Europe Sprl* [2006] UKHL44, para. 53.

137   Ibid., para. 54.

that each speech scenario raises the 'public interest' issue afresh, creating greater uncertainty for the speaker and thus more incentive not to speak.

Rights Determination – Resources and Stakes

So far it has been assumed that, if substantive defamation law makes allowance for the artificial, commercial and often quasi-public character of defamed companies, consumers can freely express their views on corporate activities. The underlying assumption is that legal rights as pronounced by the judiciary or legislators equal their exercise by their beneficiaries – a positivistic confidence that does not take account of the unequal resources at the disposal of corporation and consumers for the purpose of challenging or asserting rights through existing legal avenues. The holding of the European Court of Human Rights in McLibel emphasises precisely this point: rights do not operate in an economic vacuum and the ability to assert and defend them forms an integral part of their enjoyment.[138] As Morris and Steel had not been entitled to legal aid, they had to resort to self-representation against a multinational company that was represented by a high-calibre legal team.[139] In fact, the initial claim by McDonald's was brought against three other members of the London Greenpeace branch who decided to retract the allegations made in the leaflet and apologise to McDonald's, rather than sign their lives over to fighting the economic heavyweight.[140] But even if legal aid had been available, it is doubtful whether their decision not to participate in what turned out to be the longest trial in English history would have been a different one. From their consumer-activist perspective, the issue at stake, albeit central to their mission, was one of principle only and not one of livelihood. In contrast, McDonald's case was about its livelihood; it was about removing a tarnish from its squeaky-clean brand, its most important and valuable asset. From that perspective, the cost of litigation would have been no more than a minor irritation.[141] Where the relative stakes and resources of the disputants are so fundamentally at odds, litigation is no longer about formal rights determination, but becomes an informal censorship tool in the hands of the stronger party.[142] Morris

---

138   *Steel and Morris* v. *the United Kingdom* [2005] ECHR 103, para. 59.

139   Ibid., para. 50.

140   *Steel* v. *McDonald's Corp. & Anor* [1999] EWCA Civ 1144, 4 (31 March 1999).

141   Although in this case, the $16 million that McDonald's spent on the litigation seems somewhat out of proportion to the £40,000 it was awarded in damages. See Scot Wilson (2002), 'Corporate Criticism on the Internet: the Fine Line between Anonymous Speech and Cybersmear', *Pepperdine Law Review*, 29:533, 579. Also the trial was a public relations disaster for the company.

142   But according to the Court of Appeal in *Steel* v. *McDonald's Corp. & Anor* [1999] EWCA Civ 1144, 40 (31 March 1999) that should not deprive the stronger party of its legal rights: 'we cannot … hold it to be an abuse of process in itself for plaintiffs with great resources to bring a complicated case against unrepresented defendants of slender means. Large corporations are entitled to bring court proceedings to assert or defend their legal rights just as individuals have the right to bring actions and defend them.'

and Steel defied the odds and rose to the occasion with an unexpected stamina and capacity.[143] Nevertheless, there is no doubt some truth in their allegation that

> The extensive legal attack by the Plaintiffs on almost the entirety of the issues raised in the Factsheet shows the clear political nature of their legal strategy. Their strategy can only have been that there [sic] were seeking to use the court case as a 'show trial' against the people they thought would be unable to defend themselves, and ... were aiming for a quick judgment which would be publicly used to 'vindicate' their Corporate image.[144]

The threat of litigation is used to induce silence or retractions of speech often beyond what is legally required.[145] Of course, conceding potential legal rights to avoid litigation is not peculiar to the corporate-consumer context, but there are few comparable situations where the available resources and the relative importance of the stakes of the disputants are so routinely and inherently of a different order. The question is to what extent the law can compensate for this dissymmetry. Are there any legal mechanisms to discourage the abusive threat of litigation as a censorship device, short of depriving corporations of the right to make defamation and other speech-restricting claims against their consumer adversaries?

One avenue is to disallow claims against secondary tortfeasors, that is, third-party publishers of defamatory publications. In respect of such neutral intermediaries, the threat of litigation is often even more effective than in relation to the actual speaker as they tend to have no direct interest at all in the speech concerned. Furthermore, as they are vital for the effective distribution of the speech, they make ideal targets for corporate censorship. Thus, for example, in the Internet context such intermediaries have frequently been seized upon by companies to silence their critics.[146] In the case of *ryanair.org.uk*[147] – a consumer site set up in response to Ryanair's total failure to

---

143   *Steel* v. *McDonald's Corp. & Anor* [1999] EWCA Civ 1144, 38 (31 March 1999) where counsel for McDonald's asserts: 'Far from wilting under pressure, the appellants seemed to gather strength during the trial. Their stamina and capacity is demonstrated by the contents of the transcripts.'

144   Ibid., 35. See also Wilson, note 140 above, at 551, 572ff (for a commentary on the US 'anti-SLAPP' statutes designed to deter defamation claims strategically used as scare tactics to suppress uncomfortable speech).

145   *Times Inc.* v. *Hill* 385 US 374, 389 (1967): 'Fear of large verdicts in damage suits for innocent or merely negligent misstatement, even fear of the expense involved in their defense, must inevitably cause publishers to steer ... wider of the unlawful zone' (internal marks omitted). See *Gertz* v. *Robert Welch Inc.* 418 US 323, 340 (1974), for a warning that strict liability for false or misleading speech can 'lead to intolerable self-censorship.'

146   They are also easy targets because they may be more easily identifiable than the primary tortfeasor and, unlike the latter, they may be within the same state as the plaintiff. On some of the advantages and disadvantages of suing third-party publishers , see Wilson, note 140 above, at 552ff.

147   This site has now been subsumed by Ryanair.com, as is the common fate of consumer gripe sites. Mark Paul (2005), 'Ryanair fights to shut complaint websites' *Times Online* (13 February) <http://www.timesonline.co.uk>. Other high-profile examples are or were: FuckGeneralMotors.com, SavageBMWsucks.com, or FuckMicrosoft.com.

deal with consumer complaints[148] – the solicitors acting for Ryanair threatened the Internet Service Provider (ISP) hosting the consumer site with litigation. In response the site disappeared.[149] Of course, the effectiveness of such threats depends upon the potential liability of intermediaries, and here again the American and European positions diverge. In the EU, according to the Electronic Commerce Directive,[150] an intermediary, such as an ISP, may be liable as a third-party publisher (even where it has no editorial control over the content),[151] if the intermediary is aware of the unlawful material and fails to remove or block it.[152] Judging what is defamatory and what is not is often difficult for judges; for an ISP, it is simply too much to expect. Its safest and least costly option to avoid the risk of liability for the content is to remove or block the allegedly offending site. Thus the EU regime of third-party liability encourages voluntary and often excessive self-censorship. In contrast, in the US, online intermediaries are exempted from liability,[153] and neither can they incur liability for removing or blocking content if they consider it appropriate to do so.[154] In short, they are removed as targets for liability; complainants must focus on the actual wrongdoers. For the purposes of this discussion, it means that companies are not deprived of their entitlement to be compensated for a defamatory injury *per se*, but only of one 'quick-fix' ancillary mechanism that is open to abuse given the intermediary's likely disinterest in the speech.

Empowering Consumers

Companies, after all, are companies. It is in the nature of business, part of the corporate survival instinct to sail very close to the wind when it comes to honestly talking and patiently listening to their customers. Should the law treat this conversation between corporations and consumers as no more than a private chat between two equal adults

---

148   Paul, ibid.: 'online complaints forum or customer service e-mail address. It also has no customer service telephone number other than its reservation hotline, which doesn't deal with post-flight queries.'

149   Ibid., although it initially reappeared via a Canadian ISP, receiving thousands of hits within the shortest of time.

150   Articles 12–15 of the Electronic Commerce Directive (2000/31/EC), implemented in the UK by the Electronic Commerce (EC Directive) Regulations 2002, especially Regulations 17–22.

151   See Articles 12(1)(c), 13(1)(a) and 14(2) of the Electronic Commerce Directive, which retains liability where the intermediary has editorial control over the content.

152   Article 13 (caching) and Article 14 (hosting). Whether the Electronic Commerce Directive applies to defamation is currently unclear, but a similar position is created in the UK by Section 1 of the Defamation Act 1996 pursuant to which an intermediary could rely on the defence of innocent publication only if it is (1) not the author, editor, or publishers, (2) took reasonable care in relation to the publication and (3) did not know, and had no reason to believe, that what it did caused or contributed to the publication of a defamatory statement.

153   Section 230(c)(1) of the Communication Decency Act (1996).

154   Section 230(c)(2) of the Communication Decency Act (1996).

perfectly capable of protecting themselves when in possession of the same legal armoury?

The discussion shows that the legal regimes in the EU and the US do not give consistent answers to this question. First of all, US law is consistently, in respect of every aspect examined, more acutely protective of free speech and has overridden or limited traditional common law inroads into it. Secondly, in relation to corporate speech, the law both in the US and also – at least in its origin and core – in the UK and the EU acknowledges that there is something rather different about profit-motivated speech; the commercial speaker ought to be mistrusted. In fact, the speaker is treated with such scepticism that the legal requirement of honesty, regardless of fault, is routinely considered acceptable and necessary to protect the consumer. That same caution and scepticism is thrown into the wind when the company is at the receiving end of speech, as illustrated by the treatment of the corporate defamation claim. However here, both US and English law create legal categories that subsume large quasi-public corporations and facilitate more robust debate about them than would be possible than if the speech merely concerned the private realm. In other words, the law on both sides on the Atlantic is sensitive (albeit arguably insufficiently) to both the commerciality and also the power or influence of certain companies, and they are then treated like other commercial or powerful speakers, giving them more duties and fewer freedoms.

What is conspicuous by its absence is a focus on the artificiality of the company. At no point is the company treated for speech purposes any different than any other full-blooded natural person in business or otherwise. Now it may be argued that incorporation *per se* should not be a ground for any legal discrimination. That would be contrary to the very rationale for the creation of a corporate person – to be treated by the law as nearly as possible as a natural person – which in fact has given rise to 'a tendency to assume that substantive rules of law ... can be applied to companies in the same way, with the same doctrinal tools and consequences, as when applied to individuals'.[155] But, it must be remembered, most legal rules can 'be extended to abstract legal conceptions like the company only by way of an analogy with natural persons'.[156] These analogies are at times accepted and other times not, and these decisions one way or another are not immutable over time and neither are they objectively right or wrong. For example, today there is a widespread (but not universal) acceptance that a corporation can commit manslaughter, a matter which had universally been rejected for years. This change signals a shift of policy and, underlying that, a shift of values away from protecting pure economic success at the expense of health and safety concerns. In the speech context, by stretching defamation concepts (such as presumed damage and falsity) to fit artificial persons, the opposite is the case; economic prosperity is safeguarded at the expense of more liberal consumer speech and all the interests such speech helps to protect – a matter rather out of tune with the heightened consciousness of corporate wrongdoing. There is also the additional principled objection to companies misappropriating human

---

155   Ross Grantham (1998), 'Commentary on Goddard' in Ross Grantham and Charles Rickett (eds), *Corporate Personality in the 20th Century* (Oxford: Hart Publishing), 64, 67.

156   Ibid., 68.

rights: these are rights which do not simply apply to humans, but apply to humans because they are humans.

The corporate and consumer speech case studies provide some more general comments on the debate on human rights in the market place. First, as companies are by far the more active litigants than consumers, they are more often than not the ones who set the legal and rights agenda. With the help of the powerfully seductive but misappropriated and misleading banner of 'equality for all', they can often shift the human rights ground in their favour, exacerbating existing inequalities between them and their adversaries, here consumers. Secondly and interrelated, an empowerment of consumers *vis-à-vis* companies could be achieved 'simply' through a selective legal disarmament of companies based on a clearer recognition of their limited personality and, in the case of large public companies, of their public power. Finally, classic human rights law with its vertical focus on the 'public' power imbalance between the State and the citizens and its attendant assumption of relative power equality in horizontal 'private' relationships quite simply fails all those whose interests do not coincide with the large companies, including consumers.

PART III
Concluding Comments

Chapter 9

Rights Talk in the Market Place: 'Nonsense upon Stilts'?

Rights Talk or Utilitarian Calculus? Bentham's Pitch

The preceding discussion has probed the way in which economic, 'market place' interests and disputes have been addressed through legal argumentation which employs the rhetoric, language and methodology of basic or fundamental rights claims, deriving from the corpus of 'human rights' law. A primary purpose of the discussion has been to evaluate the impact of such resort to human rights talk in this context, in terms of both the actual outcome of argument and disputes but also, more critically, the appropriate use of such an approach. In short, what has been achieved by such attempts to import human rights discourse into the market place context and does it make sense? Does the conversion of economic interests and claims into human right entitlement serve to clarify the process of dispute settlement and provide convincing answers and solutions within that process? Is such 'rights talk' valuable in this context, or, as Bentham asserted in relation to the idea of natural rights, 'simple nonsense … rhetorical nonsense, nonsense upon stilts'?

Bentham took up his argument against the concept of 'natural and imprescriptible' rights, as laid down in Article II of the *Declaration of Rights* issued by the French National Assembly in 1791.[1] His argument in essence was that the concept of a natural and imprescriptible right (listed in the *Declaration of Rights* as the rights of liberty, property, security and resistance to oppression) made little logical sense. He argued that the idea of rights which could never be abrogated by government was a matter of 'terrorist language' and that the notion of indefeasible rights was internally inconsistent ('pretended indefeasible rights in the lump' were inconsistent with each other), and was inconsistent with the existence of government and peaceable society. Applying this argument in relation to the 'natural' and indefeasible right of property, Bentham asserted:

> … whatever proprietary rights, whatever property a man once has, no matter how, being imprescriptible, can never be taken away from him by any law: or of what use or meaning is the clause? So that the moment it is acknowledged in relation to any article, that such article is my property, no matter how or when it became so, that moment it is acknowledged that it can never be taken away from me: therefore, for example, all laws

---

1   Jeremy Bentham (1843), *Anarchical Fallacies*, in Vol. 2 of Bowring (ed.), *Works*. See also: Philip Schofield, Catherine Pease-Watkin and Cyprian Blamires (eds) (2002), *Rights, Representation , and Reform – Nonsense upon Stilts and Other Writings on the French Revolution* (Oxford: Clarendon Press).

and all judgments, whereby anything is taken away from me without my free consent – all taxes, for example, and all fines – are void, and, as such call for resistance and insurrection … .[2]

A modern commentator on human rights law and practice would doubtless respond that very few human rights are regarded as absolute (imprescriptible or indefeasible) in this sense, and certainly not the right to property or any rights classified as economic in character. So much is clearly evident from the discussion above. But, if so, what then does it mean to assert that there is some special quality, whether it be termed 'natural', 'fundamental', 'basic', 'human' or whatever, attaching to any such rights, that provides a superior, 'trumping' character in relation to competing claims? If the conclusion is necessarily that, at the end of the day, it is a matter of pragmatically weighing competing claims against each other,[3] does that not suggest that Bentham's analysis is correct – that the outcome is a matter of utilitarian calculus and that all the grand 'rights talk' is an 'anarchical fallacy' and 'nonsense on stilts'? Or, is there some strategic purpose and value in the resort to the rhetoric and vocabulary of basic human rights?

The Spectrum of Economic Actors and Field Constitution

Importing human rights argument into the market place – into the context of commercial, trading and economic activity – is not a simple matter, since the range of actors under consideration is very different from those at the original site of human rights argumentation. Even if we talk simplistically about just companies and consumers, it is clear that the identity of these actors is problematic when we seek to assess their entitlement to basic rights protection. How do companies compare with 'normal' human individuals, the traditional beneficiaries of human rights claims and argument? The 'consumer' may be a corporate or an individual human person, but in either of these forms, how does consumer identity affect argument about that particular actor's entitlement to legal protection?

Such questions make it clear that some analysis of the identity and role of economic actors is a prerequisite for the application of any human rights law in the market place. It may be useful for this purpose first of all to locate economic actors on a broad spectrum of supply and demand, but also to recognise the complexity of such an exercise. The spectrum of supply and demand is nuanced and overlapping, rather like a rainbow. Moreover, some actors, such as investors, appear in an incidental or tangential way on this spectrum. While locating actors on the spectrum of supply and demand is important for purposes of establishing their economic, political and ultimately legal identity, there is another important exercise which may be labelled 'field constitution', and serves to provide a frame of reference for legal argument.

---

2   *Anarchical Fallacies,* note 1 above.

3   As Koskenniemi has argued, a matter of 'administrative balancing': see Chapter 4 above, and Martii Koskenniemi (1999) 'The Effect of Rights on Political Culture', Ch. 3 in Philip Alston (ed), *The EU and Human Rights* (Oxford: Oxford University Press), at 99.

For instance, as in the *Markt Intern* case,[4] is the relevant field one of competition between traders, or one of freedom of expression? Locating actors on the spectrum of engagement within the market and field constitution are both processes which provide some helpful insight into the practically important balancing acts performed by courts and other bodies in relation to competing rights and claims, for example, as between suppliers and consumers (as discussed in Chapters 5–8), and may also be used in analysing the outcome of such claims.

An important question which underlies this kind of analysis concerns the relative strength and vulnerability of producers and consumers, and their consequent level of need for legal protection. Unsurprisingly, a starting point for most discussion is the assumption that large transnational corporations are more powerful (politically, in economic terms, and legally) than individual human consumers, and a large body of regulatory intervention and law (often referred to as 'consumer law') derives from such a perception. Equally, it may then be thought that some kind of basic rights protection deriving from the ideology of human rights would be a priority for the typical consumer rather than for the typical producer. On the other hand, even politically and economically powerful actors may put forward an argument for equality of opportunity and treatment in the legal arena, and in particular may convincingly claim (and indeed have claimed) an 'equality of arms' in relation to potentially powerful regulatory intervention.[5] By the same token, endowing regulators with considerable legal powers may also serve as an argument against awarding basic rights protection to individuals, at least for purposes of litigation.[6] In the legal context, account should be taken not only of the producer-consumer relationship, but also the producer-regulator relationship, in so far as regulators may be acting protectively on behalf of consumer interests.

Corporations as Rights Holders

When we refer to the use of basic human rights argument in the market place context, we are soon confronted with an underlying (though not always clearly or fully addressed) conundrum. This lies in the inescapable fact that many of the most significant economic actors who may be such rights claimants are not human in the usual sense. Frequently (and this is particularly true of producers and suppliers in the domain of supply and demand), such actors possess a corporate form, such as

---

4 See the discussion in Chapters 1 and 8 above.

5 The notable context for the deployment of this argument is that of competition regulation, especially when the regulatory intervention takes on the character of criminal law or quasi-criminal law, especially for instance in relation to the prosecution of companies alleged to have participated in business cartels. Indeed, it may be possible then for even very large companies to portray themselves as very vulnerable (that is, facing bankruptcy) in the face of regulatory onslaught (for instance, under US law, a combination of Sherman Act prosecution and treble damages litigation): see Andreas Stephan, 'The Bankruptcy Wildcard in Cartel Cases', CCP Working Paper 06-5, March 2006, University of East Anglia Centre for Competition Policy.

6 See the discussion in Chapter 3 above.

the company, are legal and not natural persons, and as such were not the subject in mind when the concept of basic human rights first evolved. A main question which therefore haunts this whole discussion is whether corporate actors (and especially large and powerful corporate actors) should in the first place as a matter of principle be included within the scope of human rights protection. The critical position on this point is summed up, for instance, by Baxi, arguing that the power of human rights discourse has been appropriated by 'global capital', resulting in a shift towards a 'trade-related market-friendly' paradigm of human rights.[7]

There is at present no clear answer to this question. Different human rights protection regimes have come to different conclusions (for instance, a negative answer in the case of the International Covenant on Civil and Political Rights, a positive answer in the case of the European Convention on Human Rights[8] and the EU system of rights protection), arguably without addressing the issue very fully. As Grear has noted, in relation to the European Court of Human Rights: 'The Court simply does not engage in a fully explicated, normative assessment of whether or not companies are appropriate beneficiaries of human rights protection. The Court is content to accept human rights for corporations as unproblematic in principle.'[9]

Doctrine and critical literature on this subject also read like a divided jury. A number of possible justifications for treating corporate persons like humans for purposes of rights protection may be marshalled.[10] It may be argued that it follows from the award of legal capacity and legal personality. It may be argued that corporations are rights holders who derive that character from their human components. It may be argued that corporations are in some sense autonomous rational actors and persons who therefore merit being treated as analogous to human beings. Or it may be argued more pragmatically that the activities of corporations benefit civil society and the economic system, and that on such utilitarian grounds an entitlement to basic rights protection would be justified, and would also serve to establish more convincingly the concomitant imposition of strong obligations upon these corporate actors.

None of these arguments is wholly convincing. Yet it is at the same time difficult to deny the legal reality that companies and other corporate actors have actually engaged in basic rights discourse and argument and been given some degree of recognition. The way out of the conundrum may be to accept some form of basic rights entitlement but not to struggle to accommodate it within a definition or framework of 'human' rights protection. For instance, it may be argued that the 'human' in 'human rights' is a matter of material vulnerability,[11] and that is a major element in the justification for

---

7   Upendra Baxi (2005), *The Future of Human Rights* (Oxford: Oxford University Press, 2nd edn).

8   For a full overview of the treatment of claims by corporate persons under the European Convention, see: Marius Emberland (2006), *The Human Rights of Companies:Exploring the Structure of ECHR Protection* (Oxford: Oxford University Press).

9   Anna Grear (2007), 'Challenging Corporate 'Humanity': Legal Disembodiment, Embodiment and Human Rights', *Human Rights Law Review* 511, at 537. See also Emberland, note 8 above, at 26, referring to a lack of contentiousness in both case law and literature.

10   See Chapter 2 above.

11   Grear, note 9 above: '… it is clear that we suffer from human rights abuses primarily as body-persons. It is also the case that human rights, whether social and economic or civil

some kind of special or higher regime of legal protection. Following that argument, it might then be the case that both human and non-human or organisational actors may assert basic rights, but that their respective basic rights *may not be of exactly the same nature, and so may be said to have a different currency.*

Such a proposition has yet to be explicitly worked out in either the doctrine or the practice of 'human rights law', but may be implicit in some of the solutions which have already been evolved at both the legislative and the judicial levels. Thus it may be a working hypothesis, or even a tentative conclusion, of this study that *if* human life protection rights may ultimately trump corporate freedom of trading claims, that may be read as a differing valuation for 'real' (or perhaps 'embodied') basic *human* rights on the one hand, and *corporate* basic rights on the other hand.

Consumers as Rights Holders

In so far as there may frequently be seen to be an opposition between 'corporate supplier' and 'human consumer' interests and legal claims, the next question to be considered concerns the nature of consumer interests and the character and qualification of consumer rights, especially for purposes of balancing such rights against the typically corporate claims of producers and suppliers. The conversion of economic and political interests into legal claims of entitlement is a central issue in this whole discussion and the process of mediating competing claims through basic rights argumentation requires careful scrutiny of the sense in which any such entitlement should be regarded as 'basic' or 'fundamental' – of such a kind as to trump the adversary's claim. How then do consumption interests and rights compare with the claims to economic freedom on the part of suppliers and producers? In what sense does the situation of the consumer, and any consequent legal claims, translate into a core value within contemporary society, deserving legal protection of a high order? If the typical context is one of opposition between a corporate supplier and a human consumer, is it then possible to argue that the consumer's 'human' right has a superior value in comparison with the supplier's 'corporate' right?

The argument to be tested, therefore, is whether the end-consumer's position and role in the contemporary globalised market place merits a special degree of legal protection. Part of this argument is the issue of effective protection, which arises naturally in the context of an already established and sophisticated framework of regulatory intervention: what kind of process and more specific legal procedure would best serve the protection of such interests – for instance, litigation or administrative standard setting? Given that administrative standard setting is now an inevitable part of market regulation, the crucial consumer interest, and one which may require conversion to a higher-order legal entitlement, is that of having access to, and being heard as, an autonomous actor in that standard-setting process. Finally, it might be considered whether any higher-level entitlement should be coupled with obligation. Recalling the interdependency of the globalised market place, ought the consumer's

---

and political, are addressed to beneficiaries in such a way as to render the presupposition of embodied vulnerability of central importance' (at 542).

protection be connected ethically to other points of vulnerability, such as exploited labour or the degraded environment? In short, ought the deserving citizen-consumer also be a responsible consumer?

A History of Trumping: Basic Rights Protection as a Legal Strategy

What happens, when talking about entitlement to and the protection of rights, when the rights in question are referred to as 'fundamental' or 'basic' rights, rather than just 'rights'? The purpose, and presumed effect of casting the protection as 'fundamental' is to raise its value and produce, in card-playing metaphor, a 'trump' card, which will win the game and defeat opposing claims. In the market place context, in which various economic interests jostle for dominance, to argue a fundamental right claim is to seek to play a trump card which will allow one interest to prevail over another via the discourse of legal rights.

In recent years, fundamental rights arguments have been increasingly deployed in the market place, but with uncertain effect. A preliminary investigation suggests that invoking fundamental rights may well provide a trump at a broad legislative level – for instance, in relation to arguments in favour of penal reform, trading freedom, or the freedom to criticise corporate activity.[12] But while this may produce an impressive rhetoric on that wider stage, care must be taken in evaluating the result in individual cases at a more specific level. In practice, the adjudication of rights claims frequently involves a careful balancing of competing interests, in which apparently broad entitlements are often qualified in favour of an equally broad 'public' or 'general' interest. Indeed, such a practice is necessary to avoid a serious devaluation of the currency of rights protection. The latter cannot follow a trajectory of infinite expansion without risk to the very concept of a fundamental right. This is the irony in playing the trump card. If played too often and too casually, it is no longer a trump, its value is exhausted. Fundamental rights claims are a rich resource which must be paid for in some way – a question to be borne in mind is whether legal systems can sustain a large number of successful claims of that order.

Whereas the trump is a gaming metaphor which fits well into the context of litigation and results by adjudication (the assertion of fundamental right as the winning hand in the contest), the metaphor of dramatisation may be equally helpful in appreciating the levering force and value of appealing to the ideology of basic rights. Some of the examples discussed in Chapter 4 (such as the riots in Seattle and the McLibel saga) demonstrate the way in which a dramatic assertion of such rights may serve, in a broader context and the longer-term view, to bring about changes in the normative landscape – the modification of policy or administrative practice, change in legal culture, the reallocation of resources, or shifts in standard-setting procedures and changes in standards as such. The impact of argument should therefore be tested not only in the courtroom (where the outcome may in any case appear in the end as a compromise, that is, a qualified basic right) but also, and perhaps more significantly, in the legal hinterland of negotiated action, comitology and administrative practice.

---

12   See the discussion in Chapter 4 above.

The European Laboratory (1): The Rise of the Corporate Rights Crusader

The European legal arena, comprising the EU (or primarily the EC) legal order with the ECHR hovering in the wings, has proven to be an important site for invoking basic rights entitlement in the market place. This largely follows from, first, the EC's substantive priorities (economic and trading policy) and, secondly, the distinctive legal structure of the EC. The latter is, in the words of the European Court of Justice (ECJ), '*sui generis*', allowing a direct and frequent legal engagement between supranational and national actors: Member State governments, EU institutions, and individuals, both corporate and human. Within such a structure, the seeds of basic rights argument were eventually able to take root and flourish, especially in the jurisprudence of the ECJ. That Court, once it had admitted the possibility of such argument in the market context, found itself increasingly in receipt of vigorous claims on the part of well-resourced corporate actors, asserting their basic market freedom to supply the market as they saw fit. Producer and supplier self-determination was presented not just as a reality of market power but as a fundamental and legally generated entitlement. Suppliers seized the rights sword with relish.

However, there is another aspect of EU ordering, also a synergy of the confluence of the concepts of the market and of justice. The ordoliberal foundation of the EC, tying the operation of markets to a vision of social justice, both liberated and regulated traders. On the one hand, it guaranteed greater market freedom and opportunity in the growing single European market. But on the other hand it also regulated behaviour within that larger economic space: trading freedom was restricted in favour of other public interests, such as the protection of health and the environment and fair dealing for consumer-citizens. Thus there developed a balancing process, with the ECJ in particular performing the role of referee between the broad interests of trading freedom on the one hand and life protection on the other hand.

Two main battlegrounds have supplied the venue for the European producer and supplier rights arguments. The first concerned the imposition of public-interest restrictions , such as those in favour of human health or environmental protection, on the freedom of marketing. The second arose from the reaction of companies to the imposition of competition regulation and their assertion of 'defence' rights in relation to the investigations and sanctions to which they were subject. These battles present a distinctive picture – of powerful, sometimes recidivist companies, such as Hoechst, going into battle as rights crusaders, waving the impressive banner of basic rights rhetoric, but in the end finding that tactic frequently vulnerable in the process of the judicial balancing of public-interest imperatives, whatever the origins of the latter, be it the risk to human health or a fair deal for consumers or small traders. Ultimately, the crusading zeal has had to contend with a very effective deployment of ordoliberal weaponry, which appears to a large extent to have trumped the suppliers' claims.

The European Laboratory (2): The Rise of the European Consumer-Citizen

Whilst the principal site for the development of producer rights within the EC/EU legal order was litigation before the European Courts, the working-out of consumer rights, as a basic entitlement rather than a public-interest limitation on producer rights, has followed a different trajectory. In the earlier phases of the establishment of the Common Market, the role of the consumer was incidental rather than central. To be sure, consumers stood to gain in some ways from the opening-up of markets and the greater competition facilitated by the free movement provisions, but consumer interests were not thereby necessarily prioritised over the free-trading interests of companies. Thus, for example, public health was regarded as an *impediment* (albeit to some extent a justifiable impediment) to achieving the main aim of free movement and trading freedom.

Consumer protection as a concept did not appear in the original scheme of the EC Treaty. Whereas producer rights had been asserted and developed reactively, in response to market control mechanisms and their enforcement, consumer interests and rights began to be enunciated in a more protective fashion as a factor which should inform market regulation, in Council and Commission soft-law instruments during the 1970s and 1980s. It was not until the Maastricht Treaty amendments in 1992 that consumer protection as such was mainstreamed in the EC Treaty. The further development of consumer protection was as much an outcome of regulatory concern about the potential market damage arising from growing arguments in public opinion and media debate, and criticism and protective action on the part of some Member States, as any assertion by consumers as legal actors claiming specific legal rights. Thus the legal position of consumers has been secured via protective mechanisms, entrusting regulators with the role of invoking a legal entitlement to safety, choice, or information *on behalf of* the actual subjects of that legal entitlement.

The regulation of the food market illustrates the sharp end of that process. Food is naturally a core area of consumer interest and the risk to consumer interests arising from globalisation of the production and supply of food, manifested in particular through a number of high-profile crises and threats, has triggered the development of stronger regulatory control in this sector. Regulation 178/2002 provides the basis for the present European protective regime in relation to food and feed, bringing together regulatory supervision (via the European Food Safety Authority (EFSA)) and an invocation of basic consumer rights (in Article 5(1) of the Regulation). But the real measure of the degree of protection of consumer interests lies in the actual implementation of principle and the working-out of standards by bodies such as the EFSA. A closer study of the process of risk evaluation being carried out in this sector by such agencies suggests that free-trading objectives, which still inspire the guiding spirit of the Single Market, remain influential in the crucial standard-setting procedures. The default position remains the pursuit of market liberalisation, with protection of important consumer interests as a qualification, although an increasingly potent qualification.

The Global Stage: The Search for Legitimacy and the Emergence of Rights

While it is possible to point to interesting and significant developments in the EU legal context and talk in terms of a basic rights-protection regime in the European market place, it should be remembered that the EU does not stand in isolation, especially in relation to trading questions and economic policy. The EU is itself part of the global trading order and in particular, following the establishment of the World Trade Organisation (WTO) in 1995, the issue of the coexistence of trading regimes and legal regimes across the globe needs to be addressed. The Beef Hormones dispute illustrates this point clearly. Any European 'resolution' of this question, any 'final' ruling on the part of the European Court of Justice, is not the end of the story. Issues such as hormone-treated meat or GMOs in food and feed supply are inevitably questions of trade and biotechnology on a global scale. As such, they may give rise to conflicts, not only of trade policy, but also of legal ordering. However, the focus of the present discussion is not so much how to resolve a clash of WTO and EU rules as a comparison of the approaches taken to ethical, political, economic and legal questions within these different orders. In particular, it may be asked: to what extent are answers to these questions worked out with reference to basic rights discourse?

The answer, at least for the present, appears to be – much less so at the global compared to the European level. Tracing the trajectory of the Beef Hormones dispute, it may be said that similar issues, or a similar conflict of interests, arises in both these contexts. But the legal infrastructures, and therefore the modalities of argument, remain different. At the global (international) level, legal relations are expressed predominantly through intergovernmental processes, within which governments and IGOs are the key legal actors. In so far as the interests and rights of individual actors, whether corporate or human, come into play, it is through the proxy of governments or organisations. Any rights discourse is therefore shadowy; the rights are like ghosts in the machine.

But this is not to assert that any rights discourse lacks relevance or impact in the global context. In the final analysis, it is difficult not to see arguments in broad terms as a matter of trading freedom (the agenda of trade liberalisation) pitched against life protection (whether that be cast more specifically as human health, consumer self-determination, cultural preference, environmental protection, or animal welfare). It is possible to identify significant skirmishes across the broad battlefield, such as biotechnology and food supply, patent protection and the availability of drugs and medicines, or the legal framework for investment protection. In an intergovernmental forum, and in the absence of any general and compulsory fundamental rights-protection regime, it is not easy to play a fundamental rights trump card. None the less, as the above case studies demonstrate, it is possible that rights discourse may come more to the forefront, as the proponents of global trading rules come to value and seek legitimacy, and as IGOs such as the UN Human Rights Commission and increasingly influential civil society NGOs scent blood and strike out more confidently into the intergovernmental heartland. It is not impossible that the WTO may undergo a similar transformation to that experienced earlier by the EC and EU

– in the craving for legitimacy becoming constitutionalised and thereby adopting the currency of fundamental rights discourse.

Free Commercial Expression

An interesting example of the interplay of basic rights argument between suppliers and consumers arises from the resort to claims based on the right to free expression in the market place context. This also illustrates the significance of both issues of economic and legal identity, and field constitution in this kind of discussion. The kind of contest which evolved in the McLibel and *Nike* cases discussed in Chapter 8 can be seen variously as one between economic suppliers and consumers, between corporate and human actors, or between defenders of commercial reputation and market place campaigners. Their position on the economic spectrum determines the behaviour of these parties and also their relative positions of strength and vulnerability. But the question also arises, whether this is a matter of competing economic rights, or of competing (political and personal?) rights of defence of reputation and free critical expression – what is the relevant legal field of argument?

The analysis of this kind of contest reinforces some of the themes and argument which have appeared elsewhere in our discussion. Once again, we can point to some 'real world' inequalities of power in the context of the globalised market place; to the way in which large corporate actors reactively seize upon basic rights argument designed in the first place for the benefit of individual human actors;[13] to legal intervention (which seeks to control the overpowering exuberance of commercial advertising and the deployment of defamation claims brought to defend a commercial rather than personal interest), and to the balancing act performed by courts who must resolve competing basic rights claims. In relation to the defence of commercial reputation and the exercise of public critical comment, the necessary legal exercise has been to explore the nature of these competing entitlements and consider the appropriate translation of legal argument from one legal domain (the personal and the political) to another (the economic, market place context). In assessing the value and currency of competing rights, much might be made of the necessity for ensuring a level playing field in any legal contest. But when account is taken of the reality of economic and political power relations, a convincing argument in favour of both regulatory intervention and judicial moderation of strong rights claims becomes evident. In particular, an easy legal assumption of a linear 'horizontal' relationship between suppliers and consumers, as equally situated and equally armed 'private' parties, may be seen as potentially misleading.

---

13   In Grear's words, a process of 'corporate colonisation of human rights': Grear, note 9 above, at 513.

The Lesson: The Importance of Regulation and Derogation

Surveying the law and practice of basic rights argumentation in the market place context, a variable picture emerges. As might be expected, much depends on the more precise context, but a number of main points need to be noted and emphasised:

- First, in geographical terms, within the European Union human rights argument is very much in the forefront of legal activity, whereas in a broader global context, there is not as yet a comparable legal infrastructure to enable and facilitate such a legal strategy.
- Secondly, as economic and legal actors, corporate suppliers are differently placed compared to individual human consumers, in terms of resources and their typical location in legal process.
- Third, the infrastructure of legal regulation has evolved in such a way as increasingly to monitor the activities of producers and suppliers, while adopting a protective stance towards consumers. As a result, the former have tended to assert rights claims *in reaction to* regulation, whereas the latter, as *passive beneficiaries of* regulation, have not been encouraged to think in terms of such a strategy. This has led to something of an ironic outcome, where some of the most vigorous assertion of basic rights and important legal development has originated from powerful corporate actors, rather than the classic beneficiary of rights protection, the vulnerable and obviously damaged individual.
- Fourth, trade liberalisation imperatives, at both a regional (especially EU) and global (especially WTO) level have served to boost large corporate legal claims, sometimes then (ironically perhaps) casting national governments in a protective role regarding individual and consumer interests. But governmental and intergovernmental positions have become complex, involving some juggling of both supplier and consumer interests.

This may then suggest a cynical conclusion. On the one hand, it may be thought that there is little scope for a confident and muscular assertion of legal entitlement on the part of that range of actors at the consumption end of the economic spectrum. Even in the European context, the concept and practical assertion of basic consumer rights is still in its infancy,[14] and beyond Europe there is as yet little in the way of a comprehensive and compulsory infrastructure of rights protection to enable consumers to take the initiative and go to court.[15] Generally, consumer interests are still largely managed by protective regulation and the prevailing culture remains one of passive benefit rather than autonomous legal self-protection. On the other hand, the burgeoning of rights discourse and active resort to legal action has occurred at the other end of the spectrum, as politically and economically powerful corporate actors have seized the opportunity and taken the initiative in exploiting litigation in order to pursue arguments concerning the violation of their basic economic

---

14   See Chapter 3 above.
15   See Chapter 7 above.

freedom, and indeed this development has been stimulated by market liberalisation policy at both the European and the global level. The most cynical interpretation is that powerful corporations have exploited such legal opportunities in an abusive manner (for instance, challenging every possible aspect of competition regulation and diverting limited enforcement resources in the process,[16] or using the concept of libel to stifle criticism). On such a view, it might almost be argued that there is then a legal protection deficit as a consequence of the increasing deployment of basic rights argument, at least from the perspective of some economic actors.

But it should also be recognised (realistically rather than cynically) that some types of interest are less susceptible to protection via basic rights argumentation and that this is true in particular in relation to those interests within the consumption section of the economic spectrum. If the interests comprise such matters as access to a competitive market, or a safe and healthy environment, these are *types of collective good* which by their nature are more susceptible to guarantee through public regulation rather than through individual or private claims. As Koskenniemi has argued:

> Social morality cannot, however, be translated exhaustively into rights language. Such language is based on an ideal of individual autonomy that perceives social conflict in terms of interpersonal relationship … abstract personhood and the conception of individual rights that goes with it cannot address the sense of injustice that arises, for example, from structural (economic/social) causation or from the sense of belonging to an oppressed minority. But also in many other contexts, posing the normative issue in terms of individual rights fails to grasp its social meaning. To take an example from Joseph Raz: I may own a painting by Van Gogh. Nonetheless, I may have a duty not to destroy it even if nobody has a correlative right. The value of art, in this case, cannot be expressed in rights language – just as little as, for instance, the value of a clean environment in a conflict concerning the carrying out of a contract for a large industrial project.[17]

Or, it may be equally well asked how appropriately or effectively the values associated with environmental integrity or public health may be safeguarded against unrestrained trading and industrial activity through the assertion of basic rights by individuals, as compared with regulatory monitoring. There is a related point to bear in mind concerning the nature of different rights. Those rights, usually described as civil and political, often have a more definite and readily adjudicatable character compared to those usually described as economic and social. The latter are often admitted to be 'programmatic' and subject to a more discretionary application of contestable criteria. So we may compare on the one hand something like '*x*' days to prepare an adequate defence, access to an interpreter, or the requirement for a judicial warrant (all of which may call for a 'yes' or 'no' answer), with on the other hand adequate protection of consumer choice, competitive opportunity, or human health, which are dependent on an evaluation of contested expert evidence.

---

16   See Christopher Harding and Alun Gibbs (2005), 'Why go to court in Europe?An analysis of cartel appeals, 1995–2004', *European Law Review* 349.

17   Koskenniemi, 'Effect of Rights', note 3 above, at 102, 104. The reference to Raz is: J. Raz (1986), *The Morality of Freedom* (Oxford: Clarendon), 212–13.

In sum, therefore, it may be said that on the one hand there has been a large amount of activity in terms of both basic rights discourse and legal claims and argument, but on the other hand there are grounds for feeling sceptical about how much has been achieved as a result of this activity: perhaps not 'nonsense upon stilts', but possibly 'a lot of noise, but nothing to say'.[18]

However, a closer reading of the subject would suggest that this area of law has developed in a significant way, but the outcomes are neither obvious nor dramatic. This is because the results are to be found in that intermediate 'derogation' zone where certain basic rights have been qualified. As has been noted, the major force of market liberalisation has encouraged (for the most part) large corporate actors to assert basic rights of economic freedom. But these claims, although dramatically framed in the language of fundamental human rights, have frequently been limited in the event by arguments based on a public-interest qualification. This general-interest qualification has often, in the market place context, been informed by the need to protect consumer and human health and safety interests, the very meat of protective ordoliberal regulatory control. In turn, such protective regulation, both in itself and in so far as it has contributed to the rebuttal of claims based on free-trading rights, has been increasingly informed and invigorated by a discourse of basic consumer rights, which by its nature infiltrates the steady but incremental process of standard setting, rather than the more opportunistic and haphazard process of litigation. The significant impact of basic rights discourse has therefore occurred more quietly, behind the scenes, rather than in the blaze of courtroom argument.

This conclusion – that the important site of argument is that of regulatory standard setting and its cousin, an almost regulatory judicial balancing of competing interests – may be linked to a number of other findings of the study, in particular what may be generally perceived as a certain scepticism regarding the assertion of basic (human) rights in the socio-economic, market place context. It will be recalled first of all that there is some doubt regarding the extent to which powerful corporate actors should be able to exploit the culture of basic rights protection, inspired mainly by the need to provide more effective legal protection for vulnerable human individuals.[19] Then, secondly, there have been some reservations concerning the protection of the range of socio-economic consumption interests through litigation based on claims to basic rights rather than via the techniques of protective regulation.[20] And, third, there is an element of doubt arising from the possible 'exhaustion' of the trumping value of basic rights argument used in litigation in this context.[21] But this is not to deny the value of rights rhetoric altogether, since less dramatically it would seem to inform both the positive process of standard setting and the more negative process of denying the force of expansive trade liberalisation rights claims.

---

18   Quote from Graham Parker, used by Jules Coleman (2001), *The Practice of Principle: In Defence of a Pragmatic Approach to Legal Theory* (Oxford: Oxford University Press), ix–x.

19   See Chapter 2 above.

20   See Chapter 3 above.

21   See Chapter 4 above.

In historical terms, the narrative of basic rights argument in the market place may therefore be usefully understood as part of the continuing exercise of balancing competing economic and other interests. Market liberalisation policies – first of all, principally in the European context, but more recently increasingly also at a global level – provided a boost for the idea of trading freedom and trading rights. Taken together then with the resources available to large corporate actors, it is not surprising that producers and suppliers seized the opportunity to exploit and develop the idea of basic trading rights. This in turn has encouraged the counter-assertion of competing consumption and 'life-interest' rights, either directly in response to producer and supplier claims in litigation, or through the standard-setting work of public regulatory bodies at both the national and supranational levels. In the market place context, it has been difficult to argue convincingly in favour of absolute protection, and inevitably the entitlement which has been gradually defined has been of a qualified nature – the important point is to understand the reasons for that qualification and how the basic rights argument is taken into account in the process of ethical weighting and responding to political priorities.

Models of Legal Process: Confronting Legal Fiction

In addition to these conclusions regarding the use of basic rights argument in the market place context, the study also leads to some wider reflections about legal categorisation and legal relations. In particular, it may be necessary to challenge more forcibly the 'horizontal fiction' which informs so much contemporary legal organisation. The horizontal fiction derives from a sense that there are in the world two main types of actor: the State, and all others. The relationship between the State and all others is 'vertical', and that as between virtually[22] all the others is 'horizontal', on the same level. Consequently, human individuals, corporate persons and a range of non-governmental organisations are seen as occupying the same plane, having a common identity and indeed a kind of equality with each other. This assumption informs much of the theory and the practice of law. Thus there is a common parlance which refers, often interchangeably, to 'natural and legal persons',[23] 'individuals' and 'private parties' as inhabiting the same kind of legal domain and having a common identity. It is also characteristic of much 'public law' theorising, which draws a cardinal ('vertical') distinction between State and non-State actors. It is furthermore an idea which informs much theorising about legal personality, which constructs 'legal' or 'corporate' personality by analogy with the human individual. An important consequence, for purposes of legal argument, is the idea that there

---

22 The main exception would be the intergovernmental organisation, which is itself composed of States. But certainly non-governmental organisations, like companies and other corporate actors, tend to be classified as 'private parties', or, at the international level, as 'non-State actors'.

23 As, for instance, under Article 230 of the EC Treaty, dealing with the judicial review of EC action – a classic instance of 'natural' (that is, human) and 'legal' (which usually means incorporated) persons being placed squarely alongside each other for purposes of standing to bring a legal claim.

should then be a 'level playing field' (or equality of opportunity) as between such horizontally located actors.

However, a socio-legal analysis of the range of actors at this 'horizontal' level suggests a real diversity of character and opportunity, which questions this very assumption of the horizontal. In particular, there may be convincing grounds for interrogating any assumed equality between such actors as transnational corporations and individual human consumers. It is evident that such actors differ from each other in three important respects. First, in terms of political, economic and legal power, the large corporation is manifestly privileged compared to the majority of human individuals, and it may be more appropriate to compare transnational companies to States in that kind of context. Secondly, some account should be taken of the fact of corporate identity, and in particular the fact that corporate actors, though rational, are inherently insensitive (and in that respect less vulnerable) by virtue of their non-human character. And third, corporate actors such as companies have a predominantly economic, profit-making role, which significantly determines character and behaviour, and is thus highly relevant in any process of normative assessment.

It may be that such an analysis already operates in a subliminal way, leading to the typical categorisation of economic rights as qualified rights. That is to say, without very often justifying their conclusions, courts and other bodies have tended to limit the scope of the claims made typically by well-endowed corporate actors in an economic and trading context, as demonstrated in a number of areas in the study above. That much can be reported as a practical outcome. But it is also worthwhile, as a contribution to the theory of the subject, to speculate further on the models for achieving such an outcome. Two particular models may be outlined, but it should be noted that both undermine the conventional wisdom of the horizontal, level playing field and the equality of arms.

The first model operates rather like admission to a vestibule. For instance, as under the European system, corporate actors are admitted into the house of basic rights protection: the door is opened with an apparent act of welcome. But frequently they proceed no further than the entrance hall, before being politely refused further entry. They have come into the domain of derogation and, after all, their basic right is qualified – it turns out that they did not hold a trump card. In a sense, this is something of a tease, combining a politic open-handedness with a hard-nosed decision making, a willingness to hear the case coupled with a resolve to grant sparingly. Such an approach gratifies an expansive concept of basic rights protection, but privately admits the danger of devaluing the currency of that system of protection. Under such a model the trump card would seem to be the public interest derogation.

A principal alternative model is perhaps more transparent in its motivation and method. This is the model of disarmament. The strategy here is to deny the right of engagement in the first place, for instance, by stipulating that (powerful) corporate actors do not qualify by definition for *human* rights protection. This may then shift the site of battle into the more political arena of lobbying, although then perhaps with the longer-term effect of recognising the need to *arm* the less-privileged individual human actor in that environment, for instance, with new legal rights of access, representation, information and participation. The final goal is still that of balancing competing interests, but via a more transparent process of arming and disarming, instead of the less obvious strategy of derogation.

As this study has shown, it is possible to identify both of these strategies – the vestibule of derogation, and the process of arming and disarming – in the contemporary field of market place rights contestation. The resort to one or the other may depend on context. What is important is to be able to recognise the actual flow and nature of argument in this area of legal activity. Perhaps the main conclusion to be drawn in this respect is that there is indeed now a great deal of talk about the basic rights of economic actors in the market place, but that the significant eventual impact of such discussion is in relation to the rather technical or even 'banal' balancing and weighting of interests and argument in the 'judicial everyday'[24] of derogation and in the 'sister domain' of standard setting.

---

24 Koskenniemi's phrase: Koskenniemi, 'Effect of Rights', note 3 above.

Select Bibliography

The works listed below comprise a selection from the literature which has informed this research and these are works which provide significant sources of information, discussion and argument. In addition – as will be evident from a perusal of the footnote references – there is also a large amount of information and argument which may be drawn upon from reported cases, the literature and reports of national and international agencies and also of a range of non-governmental organisations, and from reporting and feature articles in the press. While the provenance of some of this material should be kept in mind, in that some of it is based upon a particular position or policy adopted by such organisations, it should also be recognised that the information and argument contained in such sources has its own value and may contribute significantly to the development of the subject, and so form an important part of the subject-matter itself.

Aguirre, Daniel (2004) 'Multinational Corporations and the Realisation of Economic, Social and Cultural Rights', *California Western International Law Journal* 35, 53.

Alston, Philip (1984) 'Conjuring up New Human Rights: A Proposal for Quality Control', 78 (1984) *American Journal of International Law* 607.

—— (ed.) (1999) *The EU and Human Rights* (Oxford: Oxford University Press).

Bakan, Joel (2004) *The Corporation: the Pathological Pursuit of Profit and Power* (London: Constable & Robinson).

Barendt, Eric (2005) *Freedom of Speech* (Oxford: Oxford University Press, 2nd edn).

Baxi, Upendra (2005) *The Future of Human Rights* (Oxford: Oxford University Press, 2nd edn).

Bentham, Jeremy (1843, 2002) *Anarchical Fallacies*, reprinted in Schofield, Philip et al., *Rights, Representation, and Reform – Nonsense Upon Stilts and Other Writings on the French Revolution* (Oxford: Clarendon Press).

Berle, Adolf A. and Means, Gardiner C. (1932, 2005) *The Modern Corporation and Private Property* (Ardsley, NY: Transnational Publishers, 7th printing).

Bernauer, T. (2003) *Genes, Trade and Regulation: The Seeds of Conflict in Food Biotechnology* (Princeton, NJ: Princeton University Press).

Bottomley, Stephen and Kinley, David (eds) (2002) *Commercial Law and Human Rights* (Aldershot: Ashgate).

Bratton, William W. (1989) 'The New Economic Theory of the Firm: Critical Perspectives from History', 41 *Stanford Law Review* 1471.

Brewer, J. and Trentman, F. (eds) (2006) *Consuming Cultures, Global Perspectives: Historical Trajectories, Transnational Exchanges* (Oxford: Berg Publishers).

Clapham, Andrew (1990) 'A Human Rights Policy for the European Community', 10 *Yearbook of European Law* 309.

—— (1993) *Human Rights in the Private Sphere* (Oxford: Clarendon Press).

—— (2006) *Human Rights Obligations of Non-State Actors* (Oxford: Oxford University Press).

Commission of the European Communities (1999) *White Paper on Food Safety,* COM (1999), 719 final.

—— (2000) *Communication on the Precautionary Principle,* COM (2000), 1 final.

—— (2002) *Life Sciences and Biotechnology: A Strategy for Europe,* COM (2002), 27 final.

Coppel, Jason and O'Neill, Aidan (1992) 'The European Court of Justice: Taking Rights Seriously?' 29 (1992) *Common Market Law Review* 669.

Craig, Paul and de Búrca, Gráinne (2007) *EU Law: Text, Cases and Materials* (Oxford: Oxford University Press, 4th edn).

Cunneen, Chris (2002) 'Mandatory Sentencing and Human Rights', 13 (2002) *Current Issues in Criminal Justice* 322.

Department of Trade and Industry (1999) *White Paper: Modern Markets, Confident Consumers,* Cmnd 4410 (London: HMSO).

De Witte, Bruno (1999) 'The Past and Future Role of the European Court of Justice in the Protection of Human Rights', Ch. 27, in Alston, Philip (ed.), (1999) *The EU and Human Rights* (Oxford: Oxford University Press), 859.

Dignam, Alan J. and Allen, David (2000) *Company Law and the Human Rights Act 1998* (London: Butterworths).

Dine, Janet (2005) *Companies, International Trade and Human Rights* (Cambridge: Cambridge University Press).

Douglas Scott, Sionaidh (2002) *Constitutional Law of the European Union* (Harlow: Pearson, 2nd edn).

Dworkin, Ronald (1977) *Taking Rights Seriously* (London: Duckworth).

Emberland, Marius (2006) *The Human Rights of Companies: Exploring the Structure of ECHR Protection* (Oxford: Oxford University Press).

Faulks, Sir Neville (1975) *Report of the Committee on Defamation* Cmnd 5909 (London: HMSO).

Feldman, David (2002) *Civil Liberties and Human Rights in England and Wales* (Oxford: Oxford University Press, 2nd edn).

Franklin, Marc A., Anderson, David A., and Cate, Fred H. (2000) *Mass Media Law* (New York: Foundation Press).

French, M. and Phillips, J. (2000) *Cheated Not Poisoned: Food Regulation in the United Kingdom 1875–1938* (Manchester: Manchester University Press).

Frymas, Jedrzej George and Pegg, Scott (eds) (2003) *Transnational Corporations and Human Rights* (Basingstoke: Palgrave Macmillan).

Gearty, Conor and Tomkins, Adam (eds) (1996) *Understanding Human Rights* (London: Mansell).

GeneWatch UK and Greenpeace International (2005) *GM Contamination Report 2005: A review of cases of contamination, illegal planting and negative side-*

effects of genetically modified organisms <http://www.gmcontaminationregister. org>.

Gerber, David J. (1998) *Law and Competition in Twentieth Century Europe* (Oxford: Oxford University Press).

Gibney, M.J. (ed.) (2003) *Globalizing Rights* (Oxford: Oxford University Press).

Gourevitch, Alex (2004) 'Are Human Rights Liberal?' <http://www.columbia.edu/ cu/polisci/pdf-files/gourevitch.pdf>.

Grantham, Ross and Rickett, Charles (eds) (1998) *Corporate Personality in the Twentieth Century* (Oxford: Hart Publishing).

Grear, Anna (2007) 'Challenging Corporate 'Humanity': Legal Disembodiment, Embodiment and Human Rights', 7 *Human Rights Review* 511.

Greenwood, J. (2007) *Interest Representation in the European Union* (Basingstoke: Palgrave Macmillan, 2nd edn).

Günther, Klaus (1999) 'The Legacies of Injustice and Fear: A European Approach to Human Rights and their Effects on Political Culture', Chapter 4 in Alston (ed.) *The EU and Human Rights* (Oxford: Oxford University Press).

Harding, Christopher (1992) 'Who Goes to Court in Europe? An Analysis of Litigation Against the European Community', 17 (1992) *European Law Review* 105.

—— (2007) *Criminal Enterprise: Individuals, Organisations and Criminal Responsibility* (Cullompton: Willan Publishing).

—— and Joshua, Julian (2003) *Regulating Cartels in Europe: A Study of Legal Control of Corporate Delinquency* (Oxford: Oxford University Press).

—— and Gibbs, Alun (2005) 'Why Go to Court in Europe? An Analysis of Cartel Appeals 1995–2004', 30 (2005) *European Law Review* 349.

Henkin, Louis (1989) 'The Universality of the Concept of Human Rights', 506 *Annals of the American Academy of Political and Social Science* 10.

Hilton, M. (2003) *Consumerism in Twentieth-Century Britain* (Cambridge: Cambridge University Press).

Hindman, Elizabeth Blanks (2004) 'The Chickens Have Come Home to Roost: Individualism, Collectivism and Conflict in Commercial Speech Doctrine', 9 *Communication Law and Policy* 237.

Hoekman, Bernard M. and Kostecki, Michael M. (2001) *The Political Economy of the World Trading System* (Oxford: Oxford University Press, 2nd edn).

Holt, Tim and Phillips, Julie (1988) 'Bovine Spongiform Encephalopathy', *British Medical Journal*, 296:1581–2.

Hood, Roger (2002) *The Death Penalty: A Worldwide Perspective* (Oxford: Oxford University Press).

International Council on Human Rights (2002) *Beyond Voluntarism – Human rights and the developing international legal obligations of companies* (Versix).

Joseph, Sarah (2004) *Corporations and Transnational Human Rights Litigation* (Oxford: Hart Publishing).

Josling, T., Roberts, D. and Orden, D. (2003) *Food Regulation and Trade* (Washington, DC: Institute for International Economics).

Kelsen, Hans (1945) *General Theory of Law and State* (New York: Russell & Russell).

Kerr, Robert L. (2005) 'Subordinating the Economic to the Political: The Evolution of the Corporate Speech Doctrine', 10 *Communication Law and Policy* 63.

Korten, D. (2005) *When Corporations Rule the World* (London: Earthscan Publications).

Koskenniemi, Martii (1999) 'The Effect of Rights on Political Culture', in Alston, Philip (ed.), *The EU and Human Rights* (Oxford: Oxford University Press).

Lauterburg, D. (2003) *Food Law: Policy and Ethics* (London: Cavendish).

Lawson, R. and de Bloijs, M. (eds) (1994) *The Dynamics of the Protection of Human Rights in Europe* (The Hague: Kluwer).

Likosky, Michael (ed.) (2002) *Transnational Legal Processes: Globalisation and Power Disparities* (London: Butterworths).

Loftsed, R. and Frewer, L. (eds) (1998) *The Earthscan Reader on Risk and Modern Society* (London: Earthscan).

Loibl, Gerhard (2006) 'International Economic Law', Chapter 23 in: Evans, Malcolm D. (ed.), *International Law* (Oxford: Oxford University Press, 2nd edn).

MacMaoláin, C. (2007) *EU Food Law: Protecting Consumers and Health in a Common Market* (Oxford: Hart Publishing).

Makkai, T. and Braithwaite, J. (1995) 'In and Out of the Revolving Door: Making Sense of Regulatory Capture', 1 (1995) *Journal of Public Policy* 61.

McCormick, Neil (1982) *Legal Right and Social Democracy: Essays in Legal and Political Philosophy* (Oxford: Clarendon Press).

McManis, C. (ed.) (2007) *Biodiversity and the Law: Intellectual Property, Biotechnology and Traditional Knowledge* (London: Earthscan).

Mokhiber, Russell and Weissman, Robert (1999) *Corporate Predators* (Monroe, ME: Common Courage Press).

Morris, J. (ed.) (2000) *Rethinking Risk and the Precautionary Principle* (Oxford: Butterworth Heinemann).

Nicholson, Marlene Arnold (2000) 'McLibel: A Case Study in English Defamation Law', 18 *Wisconsin International Law Journal* 102.

Norberg-Hodge, H., Merrifield, T. and Gorelick, S. (2002) *Bringing the Food Economy Home: Local Alternatives to Global Agribusiness* (London: Zed Books).

Nottingham. S. (2002) *Genescapes: The Ecology of Genetic Engineering* (London: Zed Books).

O'Brien, Robert and Williams, Marc (2004) *Global Political Economy* (Basingstoke: Palgrave Macmillan).

Ohlin, Jens David (2005) 'Is the Concept of the Person Necessary for Human Rights?' *Columbia Law Review* 105, 209.

Okonta, Ike and Douglas, Oronto (2002) *Where Vultures Feast* (London: Verso).

Offer, Avner (2006) *The Challenge of Affluence: Self-Control and Well-Being in the United States and Britain Since 1950* (Oxford: Oxford University Press).

O'Riordan, Timothy and Cameron, James (eds) (1994) *Interpreting the Precautionary Principle* (London: Earthscan).

Pennington, H. (2003) *When Food Kills: BSE, E Coli and Disaster Science* (Oxford: Oxford University Press).

Petersmann, Ernst-Ulrich (2002) 'Constitutionalism and WTO law: From a state-centred approach to a human rights approach in international economic law', Chapter 2 in: Kennedy, Daniel L.M. and Southwick, James D. (eds), *The Political Economy of International Trade Law* (Cambridge: Cambridge University Press).

Philips Committee (2000) *The BSE Inquiry Report*, 16 volumes (Norwich: HMSO) <http://www.bseinquiry.gov.uk/pdf/index.htm>.

Radford, Mike (1996) 'Can Rights Extend to Animals?', in Gearty, Conor and Tomkins, Adam (eds) *Understanding Human Rights* (London: Mansell).

Ramsay, Iain (2007) *Consumer Law and Policy: Text and Materials on Regulating Consumer Markets* (Oxford: Hart Publishing).

Randall, Maya Hertig (2006) 'Commercial Speech under the European Convention on Human Rights: Subordinate or Equal?' 6 *Human Rights Law Review* 53.

Roshwald, Mordecai (1959) 'The Concept of Human Rights', 19 *Philosophy and Phenomenonological Research* 354.

Royal Society (2002) *Genetically Modified Plants for Food Use and Human Health – An Update,* Policy Document 4/02 (London: The Royal Society).

Salmon, Naomi (2002) 'A European Perspective on the Precautionary Principle, Food Safety and the Free Trade Imperative of the WTO', 27 (2002) *European Law Review* 138.

Sand, P (2000) 'The Precautionary Principle: A European Perspective', 6 (2000) *Journal of Human and Ecological Risk Assessment* 445.

Scott, Colin and Black, Julia (2000) *Cranston's Consumers and the Law* (London: Butterworths, 3rd edn).

Scott, Joanna (2007) *The WTO Agreement on Sanitary and Phytosanitary Measures: A Commentary* (Oxford: Oxford University Press).

Schabas, William A. (2002) *The Abolition of the Death Penalty in International Law* (Cambridge: Cambridge University Press, 3rd edn).

Shafir, Gershon (2004) 'Citizenship and Human Rights in an Era of Globalization', Chapter 2 in Brysk, Alison and Shafir, Gershon, *People Out Of Place: Globalization, Human Rights, and the Citizenship* (London: Routledge).

Shestack, Jerome J. (1998) 'The Philosophic Foundations of Human Rights', 20 *Human Rights Quarterly* 201.

Shiva, V. (2000) *Stolen Harvest: The Hijacking of the Global Food Supply* (London: Zed Books).

Slater, A., et al. (2003) *Plant Biotechnology: The Genetic Manipulation of Plants* (Oxford: Oxford University Press).

Slotboom, Marco M. (2006) 'Participation of NGOs before the WTO and EC Tribunals: which court is the better friend?' 5 (2006) *World Trade Review* 69.

Slovic, P. (ed.) (2000) *The Perception of Risk* (London: Earthscan).

Southwood, Sir Richard (1989) *Report of the Working Party on Bovine Spongiform Encephalopathy* (The Southwood Report) (London: HMSO).

Spielmann, Dean (1999) 'Human Rights Case Law in the Strasbourg and Luxembourg Courts: Conflicts, Inconsistencies and Complementarities', Chapter 23 in: Alston, Philip, *The EU and Human Rights* (Oxford: Oxford University Press) 757.

Steiner, Henry J. and Alston, Philip (2000) *International Human Rights in Context: Law Politics Morals* (Oxford: Oxford University Press, 2nd edn).

Stephens, Beth (2002) 'The Amorality of Profit: Transnational Corporations and Human Rights', 20 *Berkeley Journal of International Law* 45.

Stiglitz, Joseph (2002) *Globalization and its Discontents* (London: Penguin Books).

Stuyck, J (2000) 'European Consumer Law After the Treaty of Amsterdam: Consumer Policy in or Beyond the Internal Market?' 37 (2000) *Common Market Law Review* 367.

Toker, B (ed.) (2001) *Redesigning Life? The Worldwide Challenge to Genetic Engineering* (London: Zed Books).

Weatherill, Stephen (1997) *EC Consumer Law and Policy* (Harlow: Longman).

—— (2005) *EU Consumer Law and Policy* (Cheltenham: Edward Elgar).

Weiler, J.H.H. and Lockhart, N. (1995) '"Taking Rights Seriously" Seriously: The European Court and its Fundamental Rights Jurisprudence', 32 (1995) *Common Market Law Review* 51, and 579.

Weir, J.A. (1972) 'Local Authority v Critical Ratepayer – A Suit in Defamation', (1972A) *Cambridge Law Journal* 238.

Wheeler, Sally (2002) *Corporations and the Third Way* (Oxford: Hart Publishing).

Wilson, Scot (2002) 'Corporate Criticism on the Internet: the Fine Line between Anonymous Speech and Cybersmear', 29 *Pepperdine Law Review* 533.

Index